P9-DUV-725

DATE DUE

~~NOV 26 '99~~			
~~DE 18 99~~			
~~JE 1 '01~~			
NO 15 04			
~~FE 2 3 08~~			

DEMCO 38-296

Child Support and Child Well-Being

**IRWIN GARFINKEL
SARA S. McLANAHAN
PHILIP K. ROBINS**
Editors

Child Support and Child Well-Being

THE URBAN INSTITUTE PRESS
Washington, D.C.

Riverside Community College
FEB '99 Library
4800 Magnolia Avenue
Riverside, CA 92506

HV 741 .C4878 1994

Child support and child well
-being

2100 M Street, N.W.
Washington, D.C. 20037

Editorial Advisory Board

William Gorham   Demetra S. Nightingale
Craig G. Coelen   George E. Peterson
Adele V. Harrell   Felicity Skidmore
Marilyn Moon

Copyright © 1994. The Urban Institute. All rights reserved. Except for short quotes, no part of this book may be reproduced or utilized in any form or by any means, electronic or mechanical, including photocopying, recording, or by information storage or retrieval system, without written permission from The Urban Institute Press.

Library of Congress Cataloging in Publication Data

Child Support and Child Well-Being / Irwin Garfinkel, Sara S. McLanahan, Philip K. Robins, editors.

1. Child Support—United States.   2. Child Welfare—United States.   I. Garfinkel, Irwin.   II. McLanahan, Sara S.   III. Robins, Philip K.

HV741.C4878   1994   94-12552
362.7'1—dc20   CIP

ISBN 0-87766-626-1 (paper, alk. paper)
ISBN 0-87766-625-3 (cloth, alk. paper)

Printed in the United States of America.

Distributed by University Press of America

4720 Boston Way   3 Henrietta Street
Lanham, MD 20706   London WC2E 8LU ENGLAND

BOARD OF TRUSTEES
David O. Maxwell
  Chairman
Katharine Graham
  Vice Chairman
William Gorham
  President
Jeffrey S. Berg
Angela Glover Blackwell
Joan Toland Bok
James E. Burke
Marcia L. Carsey
Carol Thompson Cole
Richard B. Fisher
Joel L. Fleishman
George J.W. Goodman
Richard C. Green, Jr.
Fernando A. Guerra, M.D.
Reuben Mark
Ann McLaughlin
Robert S. McNamara
Charles L. Mee, Jr.
Robert C. Miller
Franklin D. Raines
Robert M. Solow

LIFE TRUSTEES
Warren E. Buffett
Joseph A. Califano, Jr.
William T. Coleman, Jr.
John M. Deutch
Anthony Downs
John H. Filer
Eugene G. Fubini
Aileen C. Hernandez
Carla A. Hills
Vernon E. Jordan, Jr.
Edward H. Levi
Bayless A. Manning
Stanley Marcus
Arjay Miller
J. Irwin Miller
Franklin D. Murphy
Lois D. Rice
Elliot L. Richardson
William D. Ruckelshaus
Herbert E. Scarf
Charles L. Schultze
William W. Scranton
Cyrus R. Vance
James Vorenberg
Mortimer B. Zuckerman

THE URBAN INSTITUTE is a nonprofit policy research and educational organization established in Washington, D.C., in 1968. Its staff investigates the social and economic problems confronting the nation and public and private means to alleviate them. The Institute disseminates significant findings of its research through the publications program of its Press. The goals of the Institute are to sharpen thinking about societal problems and efforts to solve them, improve government decisions and performance, and increase citizen awareness of important policy choices.

Through work that ranges from broad conceptual studies to administrative and technical assistance, Institute researchers contribute to the stock of knowledge available to guide decision making in the public interest.

Conclusions or opinions expressed in Institute publications are those of the authors and do not necessarily reflect the views of staff members, officers or trustees of the Institute, advisory groups, or any organizations that provide financial support to the Institute.

ACKNOWLEDGMENTS

The chapters in this book were originally commissioned for a conference on child support and child well-being at Airlie House, Virginia, December 5–7, 1991. Without the generous funding of the Ford Foundation, the Foundation for Child Development, and the Russell Sage Foundation, the conference, this volume, and much of our related research on child support could not have been undertaken. We are especially grateful to John Lanigan, former head of the Ford Foundation's urban poverty program, Barbara Blum, President, Foundation for Child Development, and Eric Wanner, President, Russell Sage Foundation for their enthusiastic support of our work. Finally, Sara McLanahan's research has been supported by grants from NICHD.

CONTENTS

Tables

Figures

About the Editors

About the Contributors

FOREWORD

Children who live in single-mother families are less successful as adults, on average, than children who live with both parents, at least in part because of lower family incomes and greater income instability. The greater difficulty these children have making it as adults has major implications for the development of human potential in this country. More than half of all U.S. children born during the late seventies and early eighties, and over three-quarters of black children, will live with a single parent before they reach adulthood.

In growing recognition that many absent fathers pay nothing toward the support of their children, and that every child deserves the support of two parents, the federal government has been taking increasing steps to see that child support awards are made, and to strengthen enforcement of child support obligations.

The Family Support Act of 1988 is the culmination of these efforts to date, greatly strengthening the states' hands in getting the courts to make adequate awards, imposing income withholding to ensure that those support awards are translated into payments, and strengthening procedures for establishing paternity at birth.

All this is expected to increase the amount and regularity of child support payments, which, in turn, is expected to increase children's well-being. But will these expectations be met and, if so, how large will the impacts be? The contributors to this volume address these and related questions on the basis of original research addressing the effects of different child support laws and practices and the relationship between child support payments and child well-being. Also addressed are the probable costs and benefits of a full child support assurance system. Such a system would combine universal award establishment and enforcement with a guaranteed benefit to ensure every child a certain minimum, irrespective of a particular absent parent's child support performance.

The editors of this book and their contributing authors are distinguished participants in the research and policy debate on the many complex issues surrounding single parenthood and child support and well-being. These issues have been central concerns of the Institute for the past 20 years. We are pleased to be publishing this newest contribution.

William Gorham
President

Chapter One

CHILD SUPPORT AND CHILD WELL-BEING: WHAT HAVE WE LEARNED?

Irwin Garfinkel, Sara S. McLanahan, and Philip K. Robins

Over the past 30 years the proportion of U.S. children living in single-parent families has increased dramatically. Whereas in 1960 about 8 percent of the nation's children were living with a single parent (usually their mother), by 1991 this figure had risen to 25 percent (U.S. Bureau of the Census [henceforth, Census Bureau] 1992). According to demographer Larry Bumpass (1984), more than half of all U.S. children born during the late seventies and early eighties will live with a single parent before reaching adulthood. The figures are even more striking for black Americans. Over half of all black children were living in a single-parent family in 1990, and the expectancy for this to occur over a lifetime was about 80 percent.

The transformation in children's living arrangements has been accompanied by a substantial increase in poverty and economic insecurity. Nearly half of mother-only families are living below the poverty line, and about 40 percent depend on welfare at some point during the year (Moffitt 1992).[1] Even nonpoor mother-only families are exposed to considerable economic insecurity. Most experience an income loss at the time the father moves out of the household, and many continue to experience income fluctuations long after the divorce (Bianchi and McArthur 1991; Duncan and Hoffman 1985; Holden and Smock 1991).

Increases in poverty and welfare dependence have long-term penalties for society, not only in terms of welfare costs but also in terms of children's future productivity. Children who live in single-mother families are less successful in adulthood than children who live with both parents, and at least part of their lower achievement is due to low income and income instability (McLanahan and Sandefur 1994).

One reason that children in mother-only families are insecure and poor is that most nonresident fathers pay little or no child support.[2] More than half of all children potentially eligible for child support receive nothing from their biological fathers (Census Bureau 1991).

Two decades ago, in response to this situation and the growing awareness of children's vulnerability, the U.S. Congress began taking action to strengthen child support enforcement.

In 1974, Congress enacted the landmark Child Support Act, which, by adding Title IV-D to the Social Security Act, created the federal Office of Child Support Enforcement; required all states to establish comparable offices at the state level (IV-D offices); and authorized federal funding to cover about three-quarters of the state's expenditures on child support enforcement. Federal funds were made available to all welfare cases and to nonwelfare cases for up to one year. In 1980, Congress extended federal support to all children eligible for child support, irrespective of income or of Aid to Families with Dependent Children (AFDC) status. In 1984, Congress enacted the Child Support Enforcement Amendments (PL 98-378), which required all states to establish numerical guidelines that the courts could use in determining child support obligations and to withhold child support from the wages of delinquent obligors.

The Family Support Act of 1988 (PL 100-485) went even further in strengthening child support enforcement. According to the new legislation, guidelines that states were required to adopt in 1984 are now presumptions from which judges can depart only if they provide a written justification for doing so. In addition, child support agencies must perform systematic reviews of awards every three years for AFDC cases, and for all non-AFDC cases handled by IV-D offices who request a review, unless it is not in the best interest of the child(ren). Instead of waiting for a delinquency before withholding child support obligations from wages and other sources of income, the 1988 legislation requires income withholding from the outset in all cases by 1994. The Family Support Act also created performance standards for the states with respect to paternity establishment, required states to obtain the Social Security numbers of both parents at birth, and authorized federal payment for 90 percent of the costs of blood tests used to establish paternity. Finally, in 1984 and 1988, respectively, Wisconsin and New York were given authority to use federal funds (which would otherwise have been devoted to AFDC) to pilot a government guarantee of a minimum child support benefit.

What effects will these profound changes in legislation have on child support payments and ultimately on child well-being? Stronger child support enforcement legislation and a government guarantee of a minimum child support benefit are expected to increase the amount and regularity of child support received by custodial parents. In turn, increases in the amount and regularity of payments are expected to increase children's well-being. But, how big will the effects be? And can we be sure they will be positive? Between the new legislation and increased child well-being there are many links in the chain.[3] To what extent are the new child support enforcement laws being implemented? How effective will the new laws and practices be in increasing child support payments? To what extent will increases in child support payments lead to increases in child well-being? This volume attempts to provide some preliminary answers to such questions.

Each of the remaining chapters in this book reports the results of original research on child support reform. The four chapters in Part One examine the effects of different child support laws and practices on various components of child support payments; the two chapters in Part Two report on estimates of the benefits and costs of different kinds of guaranteed minimum child support benefits; and the four chapters in Part Three investigate the relationship between child support payments and child well-being. The following sections of this chapter first provide a more detailed description of the transformation of the American child support system and then summarize the contributions of each succeeding chapter.

CHILD SUPPORT SYSTEM IN TRANSITION

Prior to 1974, child support in the United States was almost exclusively a state and local matter. State laws established the duty of nonresident parents to pay child support, but left all the details up to local courts. Judges had the authority to decide whether any child support should be paid, and if so, how much. They also had full authority over what action would be taken if nonresident parents failed to pay, jail being the most severe punishment. In short, the system was characterized by local judicial discretion.

The traditional child support system did not work well. In the late 1970s, only 6 of 10 mothers potentially eligible for child support had an award (Census Bureau 1981). Award rates varied widely, depending on the marital status of the mother. Whereas nearly 8 of 10 divorced mothers had an award, less than 1 in 10 unmarried mothers had one. The failure to establish paternity was a principal reason for the abysmal record of unmarried fathers.

Awards were low and were rarely updated to keep pace with inflation or increases in the nonresident parent's income. According to child support guidelines now used in most states, awards were between one-third and one-half of what they should have been (Garfinkel, Oellerich, and Robins 1991). They were inequitable, treating equals unequally (White and Stone 1976; Yee 1979) and imposing higher burdens, in percentage terms, on poor nonresident fathers than on nonpoor fathers (Garfinkel 1992). Finally, the system failed to collect all of what was owed. Of all custodial parents with awards, only about half received the full amount to which they were entitled, one quarter received less than what was owed, and one quarter received nothing (Census Bureau 1981).

One frequently heard explanation for the failure to pay child support was that nonresident fathers were too poor to pay. Although there are many poor fathers, they are a small part of the problem. According to the two most widely used child support guidelines, in 1983 nonresident fathers *should* have paid between $25 and $32 billion in child support, when in fact they *actually* paid only $7 billion and they *legally* owed only $9 billion (Garfinkel and Oellerich 1989; Haskins, Schwartz, and Akin 1985). If the private child support system were perfectly efficient—if all nonresident fathers were obligated to pay support in accordance with modern child support guidelines, and if all fathers paid the full amount owed—the poverty gap of children potentially eligible for child support would decline by 25 percent and welfare costs would decline by an equal amount. It is difficult to escape the judgment that a major part of the problem lies with the traditional child support enforcement system, which is run by the local judiciary in a highly discretionary manner (Garfinkel 1992).

As divorce, separation, and out-of-wedlock birthrates continued to rise during the 1970s and 1980s, AFDC caseloads and costs increased as well. And the shortcomings of the private child support enforcement system became increasingly apparent. Proposals for reform flourished (e.g., Cassetty 1978; Chambers 1979; Garfinkel and Melli 1982; Sawhill 1983) and Congress enacted stronger and stronger legislation. All of the reform proposals and legislation enacted to date involve replacing judicial discretion with bureaucratic regularity.

The most comprehensive proposal for reform—a new Child Support Assurance System (CSAS)—would replace the local judicial discretion of the traditional system with the bureaucratic regularity of our federal Social Security system. Under the new system, all nonresident parents would share their income with their children. The sharing rate is a proportion of the nonresident parent's gross income and is determined by legislation. The resulting child support obligation is withheld from the nonresident parent's earnings just as income and payroll taxes are withheld from earnings. The child receives either the full amount owed or a minimum benefit set by legislation and provided by the government, whichever is higher.

Like Survivors' Insurance, which is part of the current Social Security system, Child Support Assurance aids children of all income classes who suffer an income loss due to the absence of a parent. The cause of the absence differs, of course, from Survivors' Insurance, which compensates for the loss of income arising from widowhood. Child Support Assurance compensates for loss of income arising from divorce, separation, or nonmarriage. The percentage-of-income standard in conjunction with routine income withholding makes the bulk of the financing of Child Support Assurance similar to a proportional payroll tax, which is used to finance all of our social insurance programs. In the Child Support Assurance case, however, the "tax" applies only to individuals who are legally liable for child support. The assured-benefit component of Child Support Assurance makes the benefit structure of the system like all other social insurance programs, in that it provides greater benefits to low-income families than are justified on the basis of the family's contributions or taxes.

The guidelines and withholding provisions contained in the Family Support Act of 1988 are giant strides toward a Child Support Assurance System on the collection side. But the transition from judicial discretion to bureaucratic regularity has only begun. Despite the adoption of guidelines, the courts are still heavily involved in determining child support obligations. Few states have implemented universal routine withholding of child support obligations, and all states are a long way from universal establishment of paternity. Crossing state lines still remains an effective way to avoid a child support obligation. Moreover, neither the federal government nor any state has adopted an assured child support benefit. Although Wisconsin applied for and received a federal waiver to use federal AFDC funds to help finance an assured benefit, the initiative was stalled by a change in administration. New York State began piloting a restricted version of an assured benefit in 1989 that is limited to low-income families who qualify for AFDC.

Should the nation continue on its current path of reform? Should we adopt a full-fledged CSAS? Answers to these questions depend upon value judgments as well as factual information. To the extent that the research in this volume helps clarify the factual side of the issues, the debate will proceed more intelligently.

IMPLEMENTATION OF ENFORCEMENT REFORMS AND EFFECTS ON PAYMENTS

Despite a decade and a half of child support reform, some indicators suggest there has been little progress. In 1989, still only 6 of 10 eligible mothers had child support awards (Census Bureau 1991), and even worse, average awards and payments declined by 25 percent in real terms between 1978 and 1985. Do these trends indicate that the reforms were ineffectual or counterproductive?

Previous research suggests that the answer to this question is no. Like Alice in Wonderland, the U.S. child support system has had to go faster just to stay in place (Garfinkel 1992). For example, although there was an improvement in paternity establishment and award rates for children born out of wedlock during the 1980s—from 1 in 10 to nearly 3 in 10—there was also an increase in the proportion of children in this high-risk group. In 1978, unmarried mothers accounted for only 19 percent of mothers potentially eligible for child support; by 1989 they constituted about 30 percent of the eligible population (Census Bureau 1981, 1991). Thus, part of the decline in the real value of awards was due to a shift in the demographic composition of children potentially eligible for support (Beller and Graham 1991). Also important was the substantial increase in the earnings of divorced mothers and the stagnation in male wages during the past 20 years. Since most judges take the mother's as well as the father's earnings into account when setting child support awards, the relative increase in women's earnings led to a reduction in the value of the average awards (Robins 1992).

Existing research also leaves a number of questions unanswered. To what extent are the new laws and practices being implemented? What kinds of practical difficulties are being encountered? What policies or practices make a difference? Indeed, is there evidence that any of these reforms work? The chapters in Part One of this volume address these questions.

To effectively collect child support, a child support enforcement system must do well at every stage of the process: it must establish paternity and child support awards in virtually all cases, ensure that awards are adequate and updated on a regular basis, and collect what is owed. The following summary of findings in Part One is organized according to these stages of enforcement.

Award Rates and Paternity Establishment

Whereas Michigan establishes paternity for two-thirds of children born out of wedlock, in some other states the rate is below 10 percent (Nichols-Casebolt and Garfinkel 1991). What accounts for the enormous variation across jurisdictions in paternity establishment rates? To what extent are differences attributable to factors beyond the control of the state and local child support systems, and to what extent are differences attributable to factors that can be controlled and changed? Chapter 2, by Sonnenstein, Holcomb, and Seefeldt, sheds considerable light on these questions. The findings of these authors are derived from a multiple regression analysis of a national survey of paternity establishment rates and practices in 249 counties, covering 42 states and the District of Columbia.

According to Sonnenstein and colleagues, some of the differences in paternity establishment rates are clearly beyond the control of the child support system. For example, the authors find that the larger the county and the higher its unemployment rate, the more difficult it is to enforce support. Yet, many differences in paternity establishment rates are clearly related to differences in paternity enforcement practices. Counties that rely upon both a human services agency that provides multiple opportunities for voluntary consent and a legal agency to receive and prosecute contested cases as a last resort, as compared to counties that rely exclusively on either a human services or a legal agency—holding other factors constant— have higher paternity establishment rates of 24 to 37 percentage points. Similarly, the better-staffed and more highly funded counties have higher paternity establishment rates.

The effects of many other practices are also incredibly large. For example, counties that use stipulations to genetic test results in which fathers agree to accept the results of the test prior to its administration and counties that pay for blood or genetic tests used to establish paternity have rates that are, respectively, 20 and 14 percentage points greater than counties that do not. In addition, counties that systematically search criminal and education records to locate fathers, that use a computerized record-keeping system to manage their caseloads, and have child support located in the same agency at the local and state levels, as compared to counties that do not employ these practices, have paternity establishment rates that are, respectively, 7, 10, and 14 percentage points higher.

The magnitude of these effects is startling. Sonnenstein et al. appropriately caution readers about the reliability of their estimates. At the least, their results warrant further research to test the robustness of the findings.[4] For those with a more activist bent, the results provide a treasure trove of methods for increasing paternity establishment rates.

These findings are reinforced by Garfinkel and Robins in chapter 5. To assess the effects of a wide variety of child support laws and practices on child support payments, Garfinkel and Robins take advantage of the fact that the laws and practices mandated by the Child Support Enforcement Amendments of 1984 and the Family Support Act of 1988 had been adopted in one or more states prior to the federal legislation. They utilize the Current Population Survey— Child Support Supplement (CPS–CSS) for the years 1979, 1982, 1984, 1986, and 1988 to ascertain whether differences in state laws and practices are related to child support awards and payments as reported by custodial mothers in the CPS–CSS surveys. They find that states that publicize the availability of child support services have a government agency that receives, monitors, and disburses all child support payments; allow paternity to be established up to the age of 18 rather than limiting paternity establishment to the first few years of a child's life; and require child support payments to be withheld from income have child support award rates that are higher than states without these policies. In addition, award rates increase with increases in child support enforcement expenditures. As in the Sonnenstein et al. study, the estimated effects of these practices are large.

Unfortunately, neither the Sonnenstein et al. study nor the Garfinkel-Robins study is able to shed light on what may be the most promising recent development in paternity establishment: at-birth-in-hospital paternity establishment. Washington State and Virginia began their pioneering efforts with this practice after the data for these studies were collected.

Award Levels—Child Support Guidelines and Periodic Updating

Child support guidelines and periodic updating of child support awards are the two principal policies designed to increase child support award levels. To what extent have these policies been implemented? What have been their effects? Chapter 4, by Williams, tells us how far we have come from the old system and paints an optimistic picture of future possibilities. At the same time, it provides a disturbing portrait of how little has changed. This concern is reinforced by the Garfinkel-Robins finding that as of 1988 child support guidelines seem to have had no effect on child support collections.

Although guidelines have been adopted in all states and appear to be widely accepted, Williams notes serious contention over whether they are to be applied to all cases or only to contested cases. This is fundamental and surprising, in that we had thought the Family Support Act of 1988 required the guidelines to apply to all cases.

There is also strong disagreement about what kind of guideline is best. The percentage-of-income model, adopted by 15 states, differs in many fundamental respects from the income shares model, adopted by 31 states. In the former, child support obligations equal a flat percentage of the income of the nonresident parent, and the percentage depends only on the number of children owed support. In the latter, obligations depend also upon the income of the resident parent and child care and extraordinary medical care expenditures; and obligations decline as a percentage of the nonresident parent's income as income increases. Other issues are also under dispute. For example, whereas most states make no adjustment in support obligations in the event of remarriage and subsequent children of the nonresident parent, 10 states do.

Depending on one's point of view, differences in guidelines across states either appropriately reflect state differences in fundamental values with regard to child support obligations or create interstate inequities by treating those in similar circumstances differently. Such differences in a nation where nearly a third of child support cases are interstate cases clearly complicate enforcement (U.S. Commission on Interstate Enforcement 1992). Before a set of national guidelines can be enacted, the conflicting value judgments that underlie differences in state guidelines must be resolved.

Data about the degree to which state guidelines are followed are scant. For example, Wisconsin data on initial awards indicate deviations in more than a third of cases, whereas Delaware data on award modifications indicate deviations in only 13 percent and 19 percent of AFDC and non-AFDC cases, respectively.[5] But Delaware and Wisconsin pioneered numerical guidelines, and the judiciary in both states is undoubtedly more accustomed to them than the judiciary in other states. We suspect there is widespread deviation across the other states.

Williams identifies studies in five different states, all of which indicate that implementing child support guidelines has led to increases in child support award levels of from 5 percent to 35 percent. In addition, Williams notes that the downward trend in the real value of awards was reversed between 1985 and 1987, which is the time period when guidelines were being adopted. On the other hand, in their analyses of the effects of differences in state child support policies on award levels, Garfinkel and Robins find no significant effect of the guidelines. Although this finding could be due to the weakness of the guideline information in Garfinkel and Robins' data, if the effect were robust it should have been detected. Thus, we conclude that whereas guidelines are promising, questions about implementation and effectiveness remain unanswered.

With respect to periodic updating, Williams reviews the findings of five demonstration projects conducted in Oregon, Colorado, Delaware, Illinois, and Florida. The most striking finding is the very low rates of modification. Of all cases reviewed, only about 20 percent of the orders in AFDC cases were modified, and the proportion was about half that for non-AFDC cases.

Among the small proportion of awards that were modified, most were modified upward, resulting in a 60–144 percent overall upward increase in award levels. But it took approximately 200 days to complete the review and modification process. Despite the cumbersome and costly nature of the process, the data suggest that it is quite cost-effective and reduces welfare dependency by a small amount.

Taken together, these findings suggest to us that unless the Family Support Act updating provisions are strengthened, either legislatively or administratively, they are likely to lead to only a modest increase in updating. Williams recommends a number of changes in laws and practices that will reduce the costs of periodically reviewing and modifying child support awards. Even so, updating fixed-dollar orders is likely to remain burdensome and expensive. Thus, the feasibility and desirability of automatic updating that comes from making child support a simple proportion of the nonresident parent's income are worth investigating. Bartfeld and Garfinkel (1992), cited in Williams, suggest that payments increase substantially—by 50 percent within two to three years—if orders are percentage-based rather than fixed.[6]

Collection Rates—Withholding and Payment to Government Agency

Employer withholding of child support obligations has received more public attention than any other feature of the new child support system. Based on court record data from 30 child support offices in

11 states, Gordon, in chapter 3, finds that even though 90 percent of the sample had become delinquent at some point, withholding had been implemented in only about half of these cases. To some extent there are inherent limitations to withholding. Some obligors are self-employed, work for cash, have a temporary job, or don't work at all. Employment spells are also short, and it can take up to six months to locate the new employer.

As Gordon notes, her data overstate the inherent limits of withholding. Data on earnings are provided by the State Employment Security Agency (SESA). SESA earnings are lower than true earnings because neither out-of-state nor self-employed earnings are included. In view of the fact that estimates suggest that nearly one-third of all child support cases are interstate, the proportion of cases with no reported in-state earnings is almost certainly much too high an estimate of the cases in which withholding is impossible because of unemployment. Similarly, although both AFDC and non-AFDC cases are included in the sample, over half of the non-AFDC cases are former AFDC cases, which means that nearly 70 percent of the sample comprise current or former AFDC cases. Thus, this sample is limited to families at the bottom of the income distribution,[7] where unemployment, work in the underground economy, and frequent job changing are all more common.

It is even more difficult to gauge the inherent constraints placed on the system by frequent job changers. Although Gordon's data indicate a large proportion of short withholding spells—6 months or less in 33 percent of cases—Williams suggests that the problem of frequent job changers can be addressed by laws requiring employers to report new hires, similar to those pioneered in Washington and Alaska.

Most important, both Gordon and Williams identify a number of inefficiencies in the child support collection and disbursement system that are not inherent, but severely constrain implementation of withholding. These include the failure to automate, and even where there has been automation, the failure to adopt high-volume processing equipment typical of private-sector high-volume payment processing centers, and finally, the duplication and inefficiency arising from having two different agencies—child support enforcement offices and county clerk of courts—involved in receiving, monitoring, and disbursing child support payments. For example, of the 29 local child support offices Gordon surveyed, only 7 had fully automated record-keeping systems that could be used to track delinquencies, employment, and withholding. Eleven still relied totally on paper record-keeping and manual checking of individual files. In 16 of 29 child support offices, monitoring of child support payments was performed by another government agency—usually the county clerk of court office. Gordon and Williams both recommend automation of data processing and consolidation of the immediate withholding process into one agency.

One final note with regard to implementation. Although states are required to adopt immediate withholding in all new cases by 1994, they have not developed the administrative machinery to receive and disburse payments from employers. Since 1975, all states have required that child support payments due to children on welfare be paid to the state welfare department. In a few states, including Arizona, Iowa, Nebraska, North Dakota, Michigan, Pennsylvania, and Wisconsin, all private child support must be paid through a government agency, which monitors compliance and then forwards the payments to the custodial parent. To implement routine income withholding, all states will need to develop the administrative capacity to receive and disburse child support payments for the entire child support eligible population. At present, we are a long way from achieving this. As Williams notes, this calls into question the feasibility of implementing universal income withholding. Requiring employers to make direct payments to resident parents is not a workable long-run solution. He concludes, "As a first step, it is imperative that each state provide for a public entity for the collection and disbursement of income withholding. . . ."

Of all of the laws and practices measured, Garfinkel and Robins find that withholding laws have the strongest, most consistent effect on child support collections. Gordon, on the other hand, finds that withholding increases collections by only 8 percent (less than half the Garfinkel-Robins estimate), and the effect is not statistically significant. The Garfinkel-Robins estimate falls about halfway between the upper- and lower-bound effects estimated in previous research (Garfinkel and Klawitter 1990), whereas the Gordon estimate is consistent with the lower-bound. We suspect that the Gordon estimate is too low because it is based on a low-income sample, which excludes obligors most easily affected by withholding.

Garfinkel and Robins also find that requiring all payments to be made through a government agency, spending more on child support enforcement, publicizing the availability of enforcement services, and allowing paternity to be established up to age 18 all lead to higher collection rates. Except for the positive effect of the paternity variable—for which we have no explanation—the results appear plausible and suggest that some tools do work.

Medical Support

The 1984 Child Support Enforcement Amendments required child support enforcement agencies to petition for the inclusion of medical support in child support orders, to enforce the medical support orders, to collect information on the obligor's insurance coverage for cases in which the child is covered by Medicaid, and to forward that information to the Medicaid agency.

Gordon finds that implementation of the medical support provisions of the 1984 act were even more limited than implementation of withholding. She attributes the low level of enforcement to the lack of specificity in federal regulations and suggests that medical support orders might increase significantly if health insurance premiums were withheld in all cases with medical support orders at the same time that immediate wage withholding of child support orders occurs. Williams also presents some data from the updating projects that suggest a much greater potential for medical support enforcement.

An alternative possibility is that the potential gains from medical support enforcement may be smaller than the costs. However bleak the earnings potential of absent fathers, it is clear that the health insurance coverage picture is even bleaker. Thus, the proportion of current child support enforcement cases in which the nonresident father does not have health insurance coverage is certain to be quite large. We would not be surprised if the proportion were in the 75–80 percent range. Investigating whether coverage exists or not, however, is costly. Skepticism about the effectiveness of medical support provisions is reinforced by the Garfinkel-Robins finding that award rates and perhaps collection rates are lower in states with such provisions.

Of course, among the broader population of all children potentially eligible for child support, the proportion of nonresident fathers with private health insurance coverage is much higher. Even in these cases, we would not recommend extending child support enforcement to provide medical care coverage to the children. The best method of providing coverage to this population is via some form of universal national health insurance, toward which the nation now appears to be headed.

COSTS AND BENEFITS OF AN ASSURED BENEFIT

Previous research has developed microsimulation estimates of a new Child Support Assurance System (CSAS) (Garfinkel 1992; Garfinkel, Robins, Wong, and Meyer 1989). The estimates suggested that CSAS had the potential to achieve large reductions in poverty and welfare dependence for relatively small costs. For example, if child support award rates and collection rates improved by half the difference between the status quo and perfection, and if all child support awards were at the level of the Wisconsin percentage of income standard, a CSAS with a $2,000 benefit would lead to a 17 percent decrease in the poverty gap and a 20 percent decrease in AFDC caseloads, at a cost of only $0.1 billion.

The costs are small for two reasons. First, improvements in collections lead to savings in AFDC, which offset the extra costs of an assured benefit. Second, for the most part, men and women mate with individuals from backgrounds similar to their own, a phenomenon demographers call assortative mating. Thus, although wealthy custodial parents, in principle, would be eligible for an assured benefit, in practice few would receive a public subsidy because the fathers of their children would owe more than the assured benefit.

As was the case with child support enforcement, previous research on the potential benefits and costs of a CSAS leaves many questions unanswered. What are the costs and benefits of the assured benefit component alone? How much could be saved by limiting eligibility for the assured benefit to low-income families? How much more would it cost to extend eligibility to all families potentially eligible for support rather than limiting eligibility to those with legal entitlement to private child support? What have been the actual effects of New York State's limited version of an assured child support benefit? Part Two of this volume addresses these questions.

Microsimulation Estimates

As originally conceived, the CSAS encompasses all families, rich and poor alike, that are legally entitled to receive private child support. In principle, however, eligibility for an assured benefit may be limited to those legally entitled to private child support or to those with low incomes, or to both, or neither, and the assured benefit could be terminated upon remarriage. The effects of each of these variations are examined by Meyer, Garfinkel, Oellerich, and Robins in chapter 6.

The effects of restricting and liberalizing eligibility are examined in the context of varying levels of child support enforcement and three assured benefit levels. The data used are from the 1986 Current Population Survey—Child Support Supplement.

Several findings are especially noteworthy. First, consistent with previous research, an assured child support benefit would substantially reduce poverty and welfare dependence for a small cost. The extra costs of the assured benefit could easily be offset by savings in welfare that result from increased child support collections derived from the collection-side reforms of a Child Support Assurance System.

Second, as expected, both the benefits and costs of an assured benefit depend upon the restrictiveness of eligibility conditions. But the magnitudes of the effects are interesting. Compared to providing benefits to all families that are legally entitled to receive private child support, failing to restrict benefits to those with awards leads to very large increases in both benefits (reductions in poverty and welfare caseloads) and costs. Limiting benefits to those with low incomes or to those who do not remarry, however, leads to much smaller reductions in both benefits and costs.

Third, most of the benefits of an assured benefit accrue to families who are poor and near-poor (incomes between one and two times the poverty level), even when the benefit is not income-tested. For the highest assured benefit examined—$3,000 for the first child—the proportions range from 63 percent to 90 percent. As noted earlier, this natural targeting occurs because of assortative mating. Although we knew that assortative mating tended to improve the targeting of a non–income-tested assured child support benefit, the extreme degree of targeting was unexpected.

Fourth, and perhaps most striking, holding costs constant, a non–income-tested assured benefit achieves nearly as much or more reduction in poverty and welfare dependence as an income-tested assured benefit. To cite the most favorable example, under the perfect collection regime, the $3,000 income-tested benefit reduces poverty by 6 percent and welfare dependence by 13 percent, at a cost of $.9 billion, whereas the non–income-tested $2,000 assured benefit reduces poverty and dependence by as much or more—6 percent and 14 percent, respectively—at a smaller cost, $.6 billion.[8]

Effects of CAP and Generalizability to CSAS

The New York State Child Assistance Program (CAP) is like an assured child support benefit in that eligibility to participate depends upon legal entitlement to private child support. In other respects, however, CAP is more like welfare than a CSAS. To qualify for CAP, family income must be low enough to qualify for AFDC. Furthermore, CAP benefits are reduced by 10 cents for each dollar earned up to the poverty level, and by 66 cents for each dollar earned in excess of the poverty level. Finally, CAP benefits are accompanied by social services, which are more intensive than welfare provides. CAP also differs from welfare in other ways: there is no resource limit, there are no voucher payments for rent and utilities, Food Stamps are paid in cash, and there is a quarterly rather than a monthly reporting period.

CAP was implemented in seven New York counties. In four of these counties all families eligible for AFDC were eligible to participate in CAP. In three other counties, only a randomly selected group of families was eligible to participate in CAP. The former are referred to as saturation sites, and the latter as experimental sites.

Perhaps the most striking finding of the CAP evaluation is how small a proportion of eligible families received CAP benefits. One year after the program began, the average participation rate in the three experimental counties was only 6 percent. With such low participation, it is hard to imagine that CAP will have much effect. On the other hand, there is clear evidence from the saturation sites that these low participation rates underestimate the long-run effects of a true CAP program. Program participation rates in the saturation sites after 12 months were 10 percent, rather than 6 percent. Moreover, participation rates in saturation sites grew steadily over time, reaching an average of 14 percent by the end of 31 months. Despite the very low participation rates in experimental counties, CAP led to statistically significant increases in child support orders, employment, and total income.

One disturbing result is that although CAP increased the proportion of cases with orders, it had no effect on overall payments. Why? One possibility is that orders were secured from fathers with so little current ability to pay that the child support enforcement system in New York ordinarily does not pursue them. The orders may have been secured primarily to allow the mothers to participate in CAP with little additional effort on the part of child support enforcement to actually collect the support owed. Even so, payments may increase at a later period if the employment prospects of the fathers improve. Whether payments in CAP in fact increase over time should be monitored.

To what extent can the long-term results of CAP be generalized to CSAS? To the extent that CAP, like the assured benefit, is contingent upon eligibility for private child support and provides superior work incentives as compared to welfare, CAP can provide some evidence, first, on the effects on child support orders and payments of making entitlement to benefits conditional upon an order and, second, on the effects on work of providing better work incentives to welfare recipients with child support orders.

But the differences between CAP and an assured benefit in a full-fledged Child Support Assurance System are so great that it is difficult to generalize from CAP to CSAS. On the one hand, to the extent that services have a positive effect on work and on securing child support awards, the effects of CAP may overstate the effects of a CSAS without such services. On the other hand, whereas income is irrelevant in determining eligibility and benefits under CSAS, CAP benefits are income-tested and, as a consequence, do nothing to prevent poverty, and encourage work and remarriage much less than a full-fledged CSAS. This suggests that the effects of CAP on establishing child support awards and reducing welfare dependence will be smaller than the effects of a true CSAS. That participation rates in saturation counties are much higher than those in experimental counties and that the effects of CAP in experimental counties are growing over time also suggest that these short-run experimental effects understate the long-run effects of a true CSAS.

EFFECTS OF CHILD SUPPORT PAYMENTS ON CHILD WELL-BEING

The last four chapters in the book—Part Three—examine what is ultimately the most important child support question for citizens and policymakers: Will children be better off under a new child support system? A wide body of social science theory suggests that increasing the economic resources of custodial mothers will increase investments in children. If mothers have more income, children will live in better neighborhoods and attend better schools. If mothers are less insecure about financial matters, they will be able to spend more "quality time" with their children. Greater security will also allow mothers to be more selective in their choice of jobs and future mates, both of which should indirectly increase child well-being.

For all these reasons we expect children to be better off under the new child support system. There is also a growing body of empirical research linking parents' economic resources to children's well-being (Huston 1991) and reporting that children who live in non-intact families are less successful as adults than children who live in intact families, and that much of the difference is due to differences in income (McLanahan and Sandefur 1994). From the theory and empirical research, one might infer that increases in child support payments will increase child well-being in families where the parents live apart.

This link can only be inferred, because until recently there was no direct research on the effects of child support on child well-being. Moreover, some people fear that requiring fathers to pay more support will increase parental conflict, which, in turn, could reduce children's well-being (Furstenberg 1990). Fathers who pay child support have an interest in monitoring how their money is spent (Weiss and Willis 1985), which may lead to greater contact between the father and child and between the parents. This idea is supported by empirical studies that have found a positive association between paying child support and visiting the child (Furstenberg, Morgan, and Allison 1987; Seltzer, Schaeffer, and Charng 1989).[9] Greater contact, in turn, can increase parental conflict, which we know is bad for children (Emery 1982). Indeed, some people believe that the negative effects of parental conflict may be greater than the positive effects of economic security, which means that children could actually be worse off under the new child support system. These are serious concerns, suggesting that the nonmonetary consequences of stricter enforcement need to be monitored carefully as the country continues to reform its child support system.

The findings presented in Part Three represent a first step toward measuring the effects of child support on child well-being. They are reassuring insofar as they find no evidence that children whose fathers pay support are worse off than children whose fathers do not pay. On the contrary, chapters 8, 9, and 10, by McLanahan et al., Baydar and Brooks-Gunn, and Knox and Bain, respectively, find strong evidence that higher payments increase child well-being. These findings are particularly impressive, in that the researchers arrive at similar conclusions from very different starting points. Each of the chapters in Part Three is based on a different dataset, including two longitudinal surveys; each focuses on a somewhat different age group (although there is sufficient overlap to allow us to examine some groups with more than one dataset); and each looks at a different indicator of child well-being, although there is sufficient overlap to allow for replication. All of the researchers examine some aspect of children's school achievement.

McLanahan, Seltzer, Hanson, and Thomson, in Chapter 8, use the National Survey of Families and Households (NSFH), a nationally representative survey of approximately 13,000 families and households interviewed in 1987. They identify a sample of approximately 850 mother-child pairs in which the child is between the ages of 5 and 17 and is eligible for child support. Focusing on two measures of child well-being—*grade point average* (for high school students only) and *school problems* (for all school children)—McLanahan and colleagues find that child support has a positive effect on both groups of children.

Baydar and Brooks-Gunn, in chapter 9, use data from the Child Supplement of the National Longitudinal Survey of Youth (NLSY–CS) to study preschool and elementary school children. The NLSY is a survey of young adults who were first interviewed in 1979, when they were between the ages of 14 to 21, and who have been interviewed every year since 1979. In 1986, the children of the NLSY mothers were added to the original sample, and they have been assessed biannually since then. Because the mothers of the NLSY children were only 14 to 21 years old in 1979, this sample contains a disproportionate number of children born to young mothers.

Baydar and Brooks-Gunn's strategy for assessing the effects of child support on child well-being is to compare children whose fathers leave home with those whose fathers remain in the household, distinguishing between fathers who leave and pay support and fathers who leave and do not pay, and controlling for predisruption characteristics of parents and children. To make this design work, they limit their sample to children who were living with both parents in 1986 and who were between the ages of 3 and 5 in 1986. This yields 437 children, including only 63 children whose parents separated between 1986 and 1988. They find that family instability has a negative effect on the cognitive development of girls (but not boys), and that children whose fathers leave and pay child support are somewhat better off than children whose fathers leave and pay no support, although the difference is not statistically significant. Given the small sample size, we are inclined to give more weight to the sign of the coefficient being consistent with the other research than to the lack of statistical significance.

Knox and Bane, in chapter 10, use the Panel Study of Income Dynamics (PSID), a nationally representative survey of 5,000 American families followed annually since 1968. Their sample consists of 387 children who were between the ages of 2 and 8 in 1968 and who lived with a single mother for at least one year between the ages of 8 and 18. All of these children were at least 22 years old in 1987. The authors focus on two indicators of child well-being: whether or not the child graduated from high school by age 21 and whether he or she attended college by age 21. They find that child support payments have a strong, positive effect on both outcomes.

Graham, Beller, and Hernandez, in chapter 11, use data from the 1988 Current Population Survey (CPS) to construct a sample of approximately 1,100 mother-child pairs, in which the child is living at home, is between the ages of 16 and 20, and is potentially eligible for child support.[10] Graham and his colleagues focus on five measures of children's educational achievement, including years of schooling, dropping out of high school, grade retention, high school graduation, and college attendance. They find that child support has a strong positive effect on all of these outcomes except college attendance and high school graduation. The fact that their results for high school graduation and college attendance contradict those of Knox and Bane may be owed to the fact that the CPS data do not include children who have established independent households. As Graham et al. point out, if college attendance and home leaving are correlated with child support receipt, the CPS estimates could be biased. Since home leaving is more common among 19- and 20-year-olds, this is more of a problem for measures like college attendance or high school graduation (including getting a general equivalency diploma [GED]) than for indicators like dropping out of school and repeating a grade.

These studies not only indicate that child support payments are positively related to children's school achievement, but three of them (by McLanahan et al., Knox and Bane, and Graham et al.) show that child support dollars have a much larger effect on child well-being than ordinary dollars. Indeed, the papers suggest that $1 of child support is worth as much as $5 to $10 of other income. (Welfare income actually has a negative effect.) To emphasize the importance of this finding, Knox and Bane provide estimates of how much better children would do in school if the source of their mother's income changed, holding income level constant. They report that the likelihood of graduating from high school for a child who lives with a never-married mother who receives between 25 and 75 percent of her income from welfare would increase from slightly less than 76 percent to 95 percent if child support dollars were substituted for welfare dollars. This is an extraordinary improvement in school achievement.

The fact that child support dollars have a much stronger effect on child well-being than ordinary dollars suggests that the former may be measuring something other than child support per se. For example, fathers who have more education and higher incomes are more likely to pay child support than other fathers, and their children are more likely to do well in school. In addition, payments may be correlated with some other unmeasured family characteristic such as fathers' commitment to the child, mothers' determination to make the father pay, or parents' ability to cooperate in raising the child. Any one of these variables could cause both higher payments and higher levels of child well-being. The child support coefficient may be capturing the effects of these unmeasured variables as well as the effects of child support dollars.

The issue of whether the benefits associated with child support payments are due to the payments themselves or to something about the fathers who pay is important for policymakers. If child support dollars per se are making children better off, then strengthening the enforcement system will make children better off, as the example provided by Knox and Bane implies. If the benefits are related to characteristics of the fathers themselves, however, strengthening the current system will not necessarily make children better off. It will not, for example, give fathers more education, income, or commitment to their children.

All of the analysts confront the problem of unobserved differences in fathers' (or mothers') characteristics. Knox and Bane test the hypothesis that child support dollars are reflecting some unmeasured characteristic of the father by controlling for father's education and for whether a father paid any support at all. Neither variable is found to reduce the effect of child support payments on child well-being. Baydar and Brooks-Gunn use a lagged model that controls for children's cognitive development prior to family disruption. According to their reasoning, if unknown differences among fathers are affecting child well-being, this should be picked up in the predisruption measure of child well-being. Thus, controlling for predisruption well-being should control for unknown differences among fathers. As described earlier, they find a positive, but statistically insignificant, effect of child support.

The McLanahan et al. and Graham et al. chapters use statistical procedures to correct for the omitted variables bias. The statistical approaches have numerous problems, and the results based on these analyses are inconclusive. Graham et al.'s results suggest that unknown differences among fathers may account for some of the positive correlation between child support and child well-being, and

McLanahan et al.'s results suggest that unknown differences among fathers may be especially important in accounting for the positive effects of child support on children born outside marriage. At this point, based on all the evidence, we cannot say with certainty how much of the child support effect is due to unmeasured characteristics of the parents.

Part Three also addresses a number of other important questions about the consequences of child support. Three of the chapters provide information on the relationships among child support, father-child contact, and child well-being. Regarding the link between child support and father-child contact, McLanahan et al. find a positive relationship, whereas Baydar and Brooks-Gunn find a negative relationship. Both sets of results are statistically significant. Regarding the link between father-child contact and child well-being, both McLanahan et al. and Graham et al. find no relationship between the two variables. These findings are consistent with previous research, except for the finding by Baydar and Brooks-Gunn that child support and father-child contact are negatively related (Furstenberg, Morgan, and Allison 1987). This rather unusual finding may be due to the fact that the Baydar and Brooks-Gunn sample is limited to children whose fathers left home in the past two years. Some of these fathers may have left so recently that they have not started paying child support and yet are seeing the child frequently.

McLanahan et al. also provide some information on the relationship between child support and parental conflict. When they look at the relationship without adjusting for unknown differences among fathers who pay child support and fathers who don't, their findings suggest that payments do not increase parental conflict. When they adjust for unknown characteristics, however, they find that paying child support increases conflict among unmarried parents. This finding makes sense. Unmarried fathers are the least likely to pay child support, and those who pay are most likely to be selected on the basis of some unknown characteristic that is related to child well-being (e.g., commitment). This suggests that forcing unmarried fathers to pay child support may not have as positive an effect on child well-being as we might have hoped.

SUMMARY AND CONCLUSION

The American child support system is in the midst of a profound transformation. Local judicial discretion is being increasingly replaced by state and federal bureaucratic regularity. We may be on the verge of buttressing private child support with a publicly guaranteed minimum child support benefit. These vast changes constitute a natural experiment that will affect one-half of our children. This book provides a preliminary evaluation of this experiment.

The evidence presented in this volume indicates that many of the new child support enforcement policies increase child support payments. Although each policy has been successfully implemented in at least a few states, most states have yet to implement most of them. Nationwide implementation of these policies should substantially increase the amount and regularity of child support payments.

Although it appears that the newly emerging system will be more effective than the traditional child support system, enacting new laws may not be sufficient. Implementation should not be taken for granted. Despite the fact that for over a decade the federal government has offered to pay 90 percent of the costs to states of automating their child support record-keeping systems, most states have yet to automate. Most states lack the administrative capacity to receive, monitor, and disburse all child support payments and are therefore unlikely to be able to implement universal income withholding by 1994. Although child support guidelines have been enacted in all states, the degree to which they are being utilized is unclear. Demonstrations of periodic updating suggest that until we find a way of routinizing updating—by, for example, establishing child support orders as a percentage of income—in practice, the vast majority of cases will not be updated.

From a policy point of view, these shortcomings in implementation raise the question of whether Congress ought to establish a federal child support enforcement system rather than continue its nearly two-decade attempt to shape child support enforcement policy through federal mandates and incentives to the states. Unfortunately, both policy and research have only begun to address this question and the related but more narrow question of the potential for interstate enforcement under a state versus federal system. Thus, although we are not prepared to answer the federalism question, we are confident it will receive substantial attention in the next few years.

The simulations presented in this volume suggest that a publicly guaranteed minimum child support benefit for children legally entitled to private child support is a cost-effective method of reducing childhood poverty. Limiting benefits to poor families reduces costs by only a small amount because the benefits are effectively targeted due to assortative mating. In contrast, extending benefits to all children potentially eligible for support, including those without legal entitlement, would substantially increase reductions in poverty and dependence while also increasing costs.

The New York State CAP program provides some evidence of benefits from a highly income-tested operational variant of an assured benefit. But because it is so highly restricted, it is difficult to generalize from the CAP experience to the effects of a non–income-tested assured child support benefit.

In view of the promise of an assured benefit, it would be appropriate for the nation to test the real thing. As part of its plan to "end welfare as we know it," the Clinton Administration is considering some such test. It now appears that this test is more likely to take the form of limited state demonstrations than a real program.

Will increases in private and public child support translate into increases in child well-being? Although both theory and previous research suggest that increased income leads to increased well-being, the effects of child support per se have not been documented. Because we have not implemented an assured benefit even on an experimental basis, we still have no evidence on the effects of a publicly guaranteed minimum benefit.

The research presented in this book documents a strong positive association between higher child support payments and child well-being. The extent to which the relationship is causal or due to an unmeasured third variable—such as the absent parent's love for the child—remains ambiguous. Further research with better data and more sophisticated techniques is warranted. It is also worth noting that the evidence presented in this volume provides no grounds for believing that stricter child support enforcement will so increase conflict between parents that the overall effect will be to reduce child well-being.

In short, based on the preliminary evidence reported in this volume, we recommend continued efforts to strengthen private child support enforcement, implementation of an assured child support benefit, and further research on the effects of both on child support payments and child well-being.

Notes

1. For some children, poverty may predate exposure to single parenthood. Mary Jo Bane (1986) has estimated that this is true for about 25 percent of white children and

about 75 percent of black children. Bane's estimates are too high, however, because she does not take into account that family disruption and out-of-wedlock birth increase the poverty gap and reduce the likelihood of leaving poverty.

2. Other proximate causes are the mother's low earnings capacity, absence of economies of scale, and absence of publicly provided benefits such as free child care, health care, and children's allowances (Garfinkel and McLanahan 1986).

3. For example, increases in child support payments may change the labor supply and marital behavior of custodial parents. Each of these changes, in turn, is likely to affect child well-being. Garfinkel and McLanahan (1990) described most of the links in the chain and outlined a strategy for measuring these links. This volume is the first step in the evaluation process.

4. Some give no credence to non-experimental, correlational analyses. For a discussion of the issue, see Manski and Garfinkel (1992).

5. Williams (chapter 4, this volume) speculates that the difference might be attributable to the smaller number of factors considered by the Wisconsin percentage-of-income guideline. It seems plausible that judges, used to considering many factors and enjoying a great deal of discretion, are more likely to depart from guidelines the smaller the number of factors considered. But two cases is not a big sample size.

6. If, as Williams (chapter 4, this volume) cautions, percentage-expressed orders are inconsistent with the Bradley amendment—which requires treating child support arrears as judgments—this suggests that perhaps the Bradley amendment should be amended.

7. On the other hand, by limiting the sample to those with awards, the sample reflects the top part of the distribution of low-income families. Nationwide, only one-third of AFDC cases have child support awards.

8. The relative performance of the non-income-tested benefit increases with collection effectiveness.

9. Of course one cannot be sure about the direction of causality in these studies: fathers who have contact with their children may pay more support because they are informed about their children's needs. Or a third variable, such as "commitment to children" or "mothers' determination," may affect both payments and contact.

10. The sample misses children born to unmarried mothers who subsequently married.

References

Bane, Mary Jo. 1986. "Household Composition and Poverty." In *Fighting Poverty: What Works and What Doesn't*, edited by S. Danziger and D. Weinberg (209–31). Cambridge, Mass.: Harvard University Press.

Bartfeld, Judi, and Irwin Garfinkel. 1992. *Utilization and Effects on Payments of Percentage-Expressed Child Support Orders.* Special Report 55. Madison: Institute for Research on Poverty, University of Wisconsin-Madison, July.

Beller, Andrea A., and John T. Graham. 1991. "The Effect of Child Support

Enforcement on Child Support Payments." *Population Research and Policy Review* 10, 2: 91–116.

Bianchi, Suzanne, and Edith McArthur. 1991. "Family Disruption and Economic Hardship: The Short-Run Picture for Children." In *Household Economic Studies, Current Population Reports*, ser. P-70, no. 23. U.S. Bureau of the Census. Washington, D.C.: U.S. Government Printing Office, January.

Bumpass, Larry. 1984. "Children and Marital Disruption: A Replication and Update." *Demography* 21 (February): 71–82.

Cassetty, Judith. 1978. *Child Support and Public Policy: Securing Support from Absent Fathers*, Lexington, Mass.: D. C. Heath & Co. Census Bureau. See U.S. Bureau of the Census.

Chambers, David. 1979. *Making Fathers Pay: The Enforcement of Child Support*. Chicago: University of Chicago Press.

Duncan, Greg J., and Saul D. Hoffman. 1985. "A Reconsideration of the Consequences of Marital Dissolution." *Demography* 22 (December): 485–98.

Emery, Robert E. 1982. "Interparental Conflict and the Children of Discord and Divorce." *Psychological Bulletin* 92: 310–30.

Furstenberg, Frank F., Jr. 1990. "Supporting Fathers: Implications of the Family Support Act for Men." Paper presented at forum on the Family Support Act, Washington, D.C. Sponsored by the Foundation for Child Development.

Furstenberg, Frank F., Jr., S. Philip Morgan, and Paul D. Allison. 1987. "Paternal Participation and Children's Well-being." *American Sociological Review* 52: 695–701.

Garfinkel, Irwin. 1992. *Assuring Child Support: An Extension of Social Security*. New York: Russell Sage Foundation.

Garfinkel, Irwin, and Marieka M. Klawitter. 1990. "The Effect of Routine Income Withholding on Child Support Collections." *Journal of Policy Analysis and Management*, 9 (2, April): 155–77.

Garfinkel, Irwin, and Sara McLanahan. 1986. *Single Mothers and Their Children: A New American Dilemma?* Washington, D.C.: Urban Institute Press.

————. 1990. "The Effects of the Child Support Provisions of the Family Support Act of 1988 on Child Well-Being." *Population Research and Policy Review* 9 (3, September): 205–34.

Garfinkel, Irwin, and Marygold Melli. 1982. *Child Support: Weaknesses of the Old and Features of a Proposed New System*. Institute for Research on Poverty Special Report 32A. Madison: Institute for Research on Poverty, University of Wisconsin-Madison.

Garfinkel, Irwin, and Donald Oellerich. 1989. "Noncustodial Fathers' Ability to Pay Child Support." *Demography* 26 (2, May): 219–33.

Garfinkel, Irwin, Sara McLanahan, and Philip Robins, eds. 1992. *Child Support Assurance: Design Issues, Expected Impacts, and Political Bar-*

riers as Seen from Wisconsin. Washington, D.C.: Urban Institute Press.

Garfinkel, Irwin, Donald Oellerich, and Philip K. Robins. 1991. "Child Support Guidelines: Will They Make a Difference?" *Journal of Family Issues,* 12 (4, December): 404–29.

Garfinkel, Irwin, Philip K. Robins, Patrick Wong, and Dan Meyer. 1989. "The Wisconsin Child Support Assurance System: Estimated Effects on Participants." *Journal of Human Resources* (December): 1–31.

Haskins, Ronald, Schwartz, and John Akin. 1985. "How Much Child Support Can Absent Fathers Pay?" *Policy Studies Journal* 14: 201–22.

Holden, Karen C., and Pamela J. Smock. 1991. "The Economic Cost of Marital Dissolution: Why Do Women Bear a Disproportionate Cost?" *Annual Review of Sociology* 17: 51–78.

Huston, Aletha C., ed. 1991. *Children in Poverty.* Cambridge, England: Cambridge University Press.

Manski, Charles, and Irwin Garfinkel, eds. 1992. *Evaluating Welfare and Training Programs.* Cambridge, Mass.: Harvard University Press.

McLanahan, Sara, and Gary Sandefur. Forthcoming. *Growing Up with a Single Parent: What Hurts, What Helps.* Cambridge, Mass.: Harvard University Press.

Moffitt, Robert. 1992. "Incentive Effects of the U.S. Welfare System: A Review." *Journal of Economic Literature* 30: 1–61.

Nichols-Casebolt, Ann, and Garfinkel, Irwin. 1991. "Trends in Paternity Adjudications and Child Support Awards." *Social Science Quarterly* 72 (1, March): 83–97.

Robins, Philip K. 1992. "Why Child Support Award Levels Declined from 1978 to 1985." *Journal of Human Resources* 27, 2: 362–79.

Sawhill, Isabel V. 1983. "Developing Normative Standards for Child Support Payments." In *The Parental Child Support Obligation,* edited by Judith Cassetty. Lexington, Mass.: D. C. Heath & Co.

Seltzer, Judith, Nora Cate Schaeffer, and Hong Wen Charng. 1989. "Family Ties after Divorce: The Relationship between Visiting and Payment of Child Support." *Journal of Marriage and the Family* 51: 1013–31.

U.S. Bureau of the Census. 1981. *Child Support and Alimony: 1978, Current Population Reports,* ser. P-23, no. 112. Washington, D.C.: U.S. Government Printing Office.

————. 1991. *Child Support and Alimony, 1989. Current Population Reports,* ser. P-60, no. 173. Washington, D.C.: U.S. Government Printing Office.

————. 1992. *Household and Family Characteristics, 1991. Current Population Reports,* ser. P-20, no. 458. Washington, D.C.: U.S. Government Printing Office.

U.S. Commission on Interstate Child Support. 1992. *Supporting Our Children: A Blueprint for Reform.* U.S. Commission on Interstate Child Support's Report to Congress. Washington, D.C.: U.S. Government Printing Office.

Weiss, Yoram, and Robert Willis. 1985. "Children as Collective Goods and Divorce Settlements." *Journal of Labor Economics* 3: 268–92.

White, Kenneth R., and R. Thomas Stone, Jr. 1976. "A Study of Alimony and Child Support Rulings with Some Recommendations." *Family Law Quarterly* 10: 83.

Yee, Lucy Marsh. 1979. "What Really Happens in Child Support Cases: An Empirical Study of the Establishment and Enforcement of Child Support Awards in the Denver District Court." *Denver Law Quarterly* 57(1): 21–70.

Part One

THE EFFECTS OF CHILD SUPPORT ENFORCEMENT POLICIES ON CHILD SUPPORT PAYMENTS

PROMISING APPROACHES TO IMPROVING PATERNITY ESTABLISHMENT RATES AT THE LOCAL LEVEL

Freya L. Sonenstein, Pamela A. Holcomb, and Kristin S. Seefeldt

Paternity establishment in the United States is an area in child support enforcement that has been neglected in the past but has recently been gaining increased attention. This new emphasis stems from a substantial rise in the number of children that are so far ineligible for child support because paternity has not been established. The growth in this population of children is a result of the dramatic rise in births to unmarried women. In the face of this growth, it is now widely believed that improving the child support program's performance in paternity establishment is a key way to enhance child support transfers.

Paternity establishment is the legal process by which men assume the rights and responsibilities of parenthood for children they father outside of marriage. In 1990 a National Survey of Paternity Establishment Procedures in county child support agencies was conducted by the Urban Institute. This chapter uses information from that survey to describe how paternity establishment is organized and expedited. These data provide for the first time a nationally representative picture of how paternity establishment is working in localities across the country. Given the interest in improving program performance, the chapter also explores whether particular organizational approaches and practices are associated with higher rates of paternity establishment.

WHY IS PATERNITY ESTABLISHMENT IMPORTANT?

In 1991 childbearing among unmarried women in the United States reached record levels: the rate of 45.2 births per 1,000 unmarried women was 4 percent higher than in 1990, and 54 percent higher than in 1980. Because childbearing among married women has declined during this same period, nonmarital births comprise an increasing share of all births. In 1991 more than one-quarter of births (29.5 percent) were to nonmarried women (National Center for Health Statistics 1993).

Children born to unmarried mothers experience alarming rates of poverty. Poverty rates for families headed by mothers are high in general. In 1989 approximately two-fifths (42 percent) of such families fell below the official poverty line. But when the female head had never been married, more than one-half (53 percent) were likely to be poor (U.S. Bureau of the Census [henceforth, Census Bureau] 1991). As a result, female-headed families, especially those headed by young never-married mothers, are likely to require public financial assistance.

Increasingly the caseload of Aid to Families with Dependent Children (AFDC) is composed of nonmarital children. In fiscal year (FY) 1989 more than half (53 percent) of children on AFDC were eligible because their parents had "no marital ties." Ten years earlier, the statistic was 39 percent (U.S. Congress, House 1991). Families headed by young never-married mothers are also likely to remain on public assistance for long periods of time. Ellwood (1986) estimated that 40 percent of never-married women obtaining AFDC benefits before age 26 will spend 10 years or more on AFDC.

Although the reasons for poverty among never-married women with children are complex, one important contributing factor is the lack of child support from absent parents. The problem of nonsupport is directly linked to paternity establishment because child support cannot be ordered or enforced until paternity has been legally established. In 1989, only one-quarter (24 percent) of never-married mothers had child support orders. This rate was three times lower than the rate for ever-married mothers heading families (Census Bureau 1991). Even though the level of support obtained by never-married mothers is low, the evidence suggests that the proportion has tripled since 1979 (Nichols-Casebolt and Garfinkel 1991).

WHAT IS THE FEDERAL POLICY?

The history of the federal policy regarding paternity establishment reflects legislators' concern about the intimate connection between welfare dependency and the absence of fathers. The Child Support Enforcement (CSE) Program, authorized in 1975 under Title IV-D of the Social Security Act, was the federal government's first major effort to address the problem of nonsupport of children, especially children in AFDC families.[1] Even though the Title IV-D program was empowered in 1975 to establish paternities, a 1978 study found that although all states had statutory provisions for establishing paternity, only 13 states provided children undergoing this process with a legal status roughly equivalent to children born within marriages. In the remaining states the establishment of paternity neither constituted full legitimation nor provided inheritance rights (Hardy et al. 1979).

Major federal initiatives to strengthen child support services for both AFDC and non-AFDC families were passed in 1984 and 1988. Whereas the 1984 Child Support Enforcement Amendments primarily focused on improving approaches to setting and enforcing child support awards, the Family Support Act of 1988 (FSA—PL 100-485) contained several provisions aimed at improving the paternity establishment performance of child support agencies. These provisions included:

1. *Simplifying civil process and procedure.* The FSA explicitly *encouraged* states to adopt a simple civil process for establishing paternity in uncontested cases and a civil procedure for contested cases. This recommendation reinforces the trend to distance paternity establishment from its origins as a criminal proceeding. Civil processes and procedures are also thought to be less time-consuming and less expensive because they reduce reliance on overburdened courts.
2. *Expanding paternity establishment authority.* Any child under age 18 for whom paternity has not been established is eligible for paternity establishment services until a child's 18th birthday. Retroactive to 1984, any child for whom a paternity action was brought but whose suit was dismissed because of a statute of limitations of less than 18 years must be allowed to bring a new suit.
3. *Specifying performance standards.* In response to congressional frustration that states had not sufficiently emphasized paternity establishment, goals for establishing paternity were introduced. Beginning October 1, 1991, states were required to attain the following performance goals or risk triggering a penalty. The percentage for whom paternity is established must be: (1) at least 50 percent of all nonmarital children receiving IV-D child support services,[2] or (2) equal to or better than the national average of all

states, or (3) 6 percentage points higher than in FY 1988 (the base year) and increase 3 percentage points each subsequent year.

4. *Procedures for parentage testing.* The increased use and improved reliability of genetic testing has changed the character of the paternity establishment process. Scientific proof of paternity has, to a large extent, replaced often costly and protracted court trials. Under the FSA, states must adopt procedures that require all parties to submit to genetic testing upon the request of any party in a contested case. Federal reimbursement to states for laboratory testing costs was raised to 90 percent. Also, a provision was added allowing states to charge non-AFDC IV-D recipients a fee for performing genetic tests.

5. *Other provisions.* Other provisions included funding for states to implement automated tracking and monitoring systems, establishing specific time frames for processing cases, and requiring states to record parents' Social Security numbers when birth certificates are issued.

Congress continues to focus on improving program performance. The Budget Reconciliation Act of 1993 includes provisions requiring states to meet higher performance standards and to implement specific expedited processes. The new standard for measuring performance is a 75 percent paternity establishment rate. In addition, the new law requires states to have:

☐ A simple civil process for voluntarily acknowledging paternity and making the voluntary acknowledgment a rebuttable presumption of paternity for the purposes of seeking a child support award

☐ A hospital-based paternity program for voluntarily acknowledging paternity immediately before or after the birth of a nonmarital child, regardless of welfare status

☐ A rebuttable presumption of paternity when genetic test results meet a specified threshold

☐ Default paternity judgments when an alleged father has been notified of the allegation through service of process and has failed to respond

New legislation will soon be introduced that makes paternity establishment a prerequisite for the receipt of the full AFDC benefit. Moreover, the Clinton administration will undoubtedly address paternity establishment in its forthcoming welfare reform initiative.

EVIDENCE FROM PREVIOUS WORK

Little research has examined issues related to paternity establishment. Although demographic studies have addressed the causes and consequences of out-of-wedlock childbearing, especially among teenagers, these studies have not examined paternity establishment as one of the potential steps that can follow the birth of an out-of-wedlock child. Even simple descriptive data are not available regarding how many U.S. children born to unmarried parents have paternity established. Research has also not examined whether paternity establishment has any effect on the well-being of the child, although a number of analysts have suggested there would be economic, social, and psychological benefits (Nichols-Casebolt 1988; Wattenberg 1987). In the last five years, as Congress and program administrators have sought to increase the number of paternities established, a few studies have focused on developing indicators of program performance and identifying policies and practices that enhance performance.

Indicators of Program Performance

Since 1979 the Office of Child Support Enforcement has collected program statistics by state on the number of paternities established annually. Between fiscal years 1979 and 1990, about 2 million paternities were established. Each year the number has grown—from 111,000 in 1979 to 393,000 in 1990. Interpretation of these statistics, however, has been difficult because of the lack of a denominator allowing assessment of whether the proportion of paternities established relative to the pool of cases eligible for paternity establishment has improved over time or varies from state to state.

Several researchers (Nichols-Casebolt and Garfinkel 1991; Wattenberg 1984) have used the simple ratio of the number of paternities established to the number of nonmarital births in the same or the previous year. Using this statistic, the ratio of paternities in 1988 to births in 1988 was 31 percent nationwide compared to 19 percent in 1979. There is also considerable variation by state, from a low of 2 percent in Texas to a high of 115 percent in Vermont (U.S. Congress, House 1991). As Aron, Barnow, and McNaught (1989) have shown, these ratios are not perfect indicators of performance. Many children born out of wedlock are not candidates for paternity action because of adoption, death, and postbirth marriages; some paternities are established outside the child support system; and the pool of children eligible for action includes children born up to 18 years earlier and children born in different states.

An alternative approach to estimating paternity establishment rates has used survey data about never-married mothers with child support awards in the Current Population Survey to estimate the proportion of children with paternities established (Aron et al. 1989; Nichols-Casebolt and Garfinkel 1991). These authors have reasoned that never-married mothers must establish paternity to obtain a child support award. As noted earlier, the proportion of never-married mothers with orders has steadily risen to almost one-quarter in 1989. Again, these estimates are less than ideal because the survey does not include information about never-married mothers under the age of 18 or currently married mothers with children born out of wedlock. Information is only collected for a single child, and having a child support order is only a proximate measure of paternity status. Aron et al. (1989) dealt with this latter issue by developing upper- and lower-bound estimates. In a study that followed teenage mothers in Wisconsin after the birth of a nonmarital child, Danziger and Nichols-Casebolt (1989) found that after four years, less than 43 percent of the children had legally identified fathers and even fewer, 17.5 percent, had legal rights to financial support. The authors concluded that a large proportion of eligible cases fail to enter the paternity establishment/child support system, and those cases that do enter the system are primarily initiated through the public welfare system.

The new paternity performance goals mandated by the Family Support Act have made it possible, for the first time, to compare the number of paternities established through a state's child support program to the number of children in the program needing paternity established. States have had a fair amount of difficulty complying with these new data requirements. In 1988, the baseline year, the national average paternity establishment percentage was estimated as 45 percent (Maniha 1992).

Studies of Paternity Establishment Practices

In addition to constructing indicators of performance, another group of recent studies has used case study approaches to identify policies and practices related to exemplary performance in particular localities. These studies examine such issues as case flow; interorganizational and intraorganizational relations; management practices; and perspectives of clients, line workers, and administrators in selected

places (Adams, Landsbergen, and Hecht 1990; Monson and McLanahan 1990; Nichols-Casebolt 1990; U.S. Department of Health and
Human Services, Office of Child Support Enforcement 1989; U.S.
Department of Health and Human Services, Office of Inspector General 1990; Wattenberg 1984; Wattenberg, Brewer, and Resnik 1991;
Williams and Williams 1989). A couple of studies have focused on the
cost-effectiveness of paternity establishment in local sites (Williams
1988; Young 1984). Together these studies have demonstrated the
striking variety in the ways paternity establishment is organized and
carried out in localities across the country. They have also suggested
a number of promising strategies that should be explored more fully
in a larger national study.

DATA SOURCES

The earlier-mentioned National Survey of Paternity Establishment
Procedures was designed to collect nationally representative data to
complement the more focused local studies just described. Its major
objective was to obtain a nationwide picture of how paternity establishment is carried out by county child support agencies. In addition,
the association between specific practices and program performance
on paternity establishment rates was to be examined. This survey
collected information for 249 counties in 42 states and the District
of Columbia. The sample of counties was drawn as part of the cluster
sampling design used for the 1988 National Survey of Adolescent
Males, which conducted interviews with 1,880 young men about
their fertility behavior (Sonenstein, Pleck, and Ku 1989).[3] The sample
of counties is weighted when frequencies are reported, to make the
results representative of counties in the contiguous United States.[4]

The survey, which was conducted primarily in summer and fall
of 1990, used a combination of telephone interviews and mailed
questionnaires to gather information from program administrators at
the state and local levels. Semistructured telephone interviews were
conducted with state directors of CSE programs to determine how
paternity establishment was organized in each state, to arrange access
to local program administrators, and to obtain county/substate program statistics. Directors of county or substate child support programs
(or the person designated as the most knowledgeable about paternity
establishment) were also interviewed by telephone and then asked
to complete a close-ended mailed questionnaire.[5] The topics covered

included organizational relationships with the welfare agency, the court, county attorneys, and other relevant agencies in the county; staffing patterns; referral and intake procedures; techniques used to locate and notify fathers; case flow and case management; genetic testing; and perceived barriers, among others. The response rates on the survey were uniformly high and varied only slightly by the data collection method used. The completion rates were 100 percent for the state IV-D director's telephone survey, 98 percent for the local-level telephone surveys, and 87 percent for the local-level mail surveys.

Additional data about the demographic characteristics of the counties were added to the data file from the *County and City Data Book* (Census Bureau 1988). Nonmarital births in each county for 1988 were provided by the National Center for Health Statistics, U.S. Public Health Service.

FINDINGS: RATES OF PATERNITY ESTABLISHMENT

The National Survey of Paternity Establishment Procedures solicited information about the number of paternities established by the child support program for FY 1989, as well as the number of cases eligible for paternity actions. Two approaches were used to obtain information about eligible paternity cases. First, local respondents were asked, "How many paternity cases were active in your office in FY 1989?" In addition, the department in charge of state program statistics was asked to provide "the number of children in IV-D Cases Active in FY 1989 who were born out-of-wedlock" for the county or substate region covered by the local office. This latter terminology is the denominator used by the federal child support enforcement program to determine state paternity establishment performance rates.[6]

Missing information about the number of eligible paternity cases at the local level made it impossible to use caseload information as the denominator in calculating a paternity establishment rate. Less than half the sample (113 counties) provided information about their active paternity caseload. Only two-thirds (163 counties) provided the number of nonmarital children in IV-D cases. Using the available information, we computed an unweighted rate of .47 for counties providing information about paternities established and their active paternity caseload, and an unweighted rate of .41 for states providing information about paternities established and the numbers of non-marital children in IV-D cases.

Given the lack of uniform data across the counties, we decided to use the number of nonmarital births in 1988 in each county as the base for calculating standardized county paternity establishment rates. As noted earlier, state-level nonmarital births have been used as a base by other researchers, an approach that, despite some weaknesses, offers comparability and reliability across counties. Furthermore, it might be argued that the incidence of nonmarital births is the best base to use because it is not influenced by differences in program eligibility rules that could cause fluctuations in the indicator unrelated to performance. County data on nonmarital births for 1988, the most recent year available, were provided by the National Center for Health Statistics. A paternity rate was constructed for each county by dividing the number of paternities established in FY 1989 by the number of nonmarital births in the county in calendar year 1988.[7] The lowest rate was .04 and the highest was 3.25. Indeed, the rate was 1 or higher in 11 counties.[8] The weighted mean of the paternity rates for the sample was .49. This proportion is slightly higher than the national state average of .45, computed by the Office of Child Support Enforcement using eligible cases as the base for 1988.

METHODS USED TO IDENTIFY PROMISING PRACTICES

Having chosen a standardized indicator of county performance on paternity establishment, we were interested in examining the association between county paternity rates and the characteristics of counties and their paternity establishment programs. Our model assumed that the flow of cases through the paternity establishment process would be a function of the following classes of variables:[9]

1. The demographic and socioeconomic characteristics of the county;
2. The resources invested in child support services in terms of money and staff;
3. The overall organizational structure and process of paternity establishment;
4. The use of specific policies and procedures for intake, locating, adjudication, and management identified by the literature as characteristic of exemplary programs

Our analytic approach was essentially exploratory. We used ordinary least squares regression techniques to estimate models of paternity establishment. The paternity rate was regressed on measures of each of these classes of explanatory variables, using a method that sequentially entered groups of variables. At each stage, variables that failed to attain a significance level of .15 were eliminated.[10]

We began our analyses by regressing the paternity rate on measures of the demographic and socioeconomic characteristics of the counties thought to be associated with program performance. We hypothesized that paternity establishment would be more difficult, and that rates would therefore be lower, for populations that were more urbanized or densely populated, with higher unemployment and poverty rates, higher proportions of births to adolescent mothers, lower education levels, higher concentrations of blacks and Hispanics, and experiencing higher population growth. Measures of these variables were entered into the paternity rate model, and the number of predictor variables was reduced.[11] This set of variables essentially provides some controls for variations in paternity establishment rates that occur across counties because of differences in economic conditions, the demographic composition of the population, and the size of the community, which could potentially influence how easily fathers can be located.

In the second stage of the analysis, two sets of variables measuring the extent of resource investment in child support services were added to the model. We thought that paternity establishment rates would be higher in counties that spent more money on paternity relative to the need in the county and the size of the caseload. Unfortunately, because staff working on paternity cases also typically work on other types of child support cases, we were unable to isolate the costs associated with paternity cases alone. Consequently, our measures of resource investment represent funds spent on child support services as a whole.

The variables entered at this stage were the number of AFDC child support cases divided by the number of full-time-equivalent staff working on child support[12] and the total county child support budget for FY 1989 divided by the number of divorces in the county. The first measure assesses the average number of AFDC cases that each staff person carries. We only used AFDC cases, because there is substantial variation from place to place in the definitions used to count the non-AFDC caseload. We also broke this variable into quartiles, after an initial run using a squared term indicated the possibility of a nonlinear relationship. The second variable was constructed to measure the amount of funds spent on child support relative to the need for services in the county. The number of divorces in the county was chosen as the denominator to serve as a proximate measure of the need for child support services.[13]

At the third stage of the analyses, two sets of variables characterizing the organizational setting of paternity establishment and the manner in which voluntary consent was handled in the county were added to the regression equation. Our qualitative and quantitative analyses of the survey data had shown that these were two major dimensions defining how paternity establishment practices varied across counties (Holcomb, Seefeldt, and Sonenstein 1992). The first variable assesses the type of agency that handles paternity cases. The devolution of responsibility for paternity establishment from the state down to the local level can be extraordinarily complicated flowing through several agencies. At the local level, however, paternity establishment is usually located in one of three settings: a legal agency like a prosecuting attorney's office or court, a nonlegal agency like the human service department responsible for welfare,[14] or a shared situation in which cases with cooperative fathers are handled by the human service agency and contested cases are transferred to a legal agency. When paternity cases are handled totally by a human service agency, there are in-house attorneys to handle the legal work. The survey results showed that in one-fifth (21 percent) of counties, paternity establishment is located in a legal agency. In over two-fifths (42 percent) of the counties, it is in a nonlegal agency, and in over one-third (35 percent), contested cases are transferred from the nonlegal to the legal agency.

We expected that the type of agency interacting with the prospective father might influence the agency's success in obtaining paternities. Fathers dealing with a county attorney's office might be more responsive because the threat of court action might be more apparent to them. On the other hand, fathers interacting with a human service agency might be more cooperative because of the lower level of litigiousness, at least initially. The transfer approach might maximize both these advantages. In our initial analyses counties with the transfer approach had significantly better paternity establishment rates (Sonenstein, Holcomb, and Seefeldt 1992).

A second major distinction between counties' approaches to paternity establishment was how voluntary acknowledgment of paternity by the father was handled. There has been increasing reliance on voluntary consent by child support programs because it is believed to "expedite the resolution of cases, requires little or no court time, eliminates gathering sensitive details unnecessarily, avoids the adversarial nature of typical lawsuits, and minimizes embarrassment and inconvenience to the parties" (U.S. Department of Health and Human Services, Office of Child Support Enforcement 1989). Four prototypical approaches were found:

□ *A no-consent process*, in which all paternity cases are handled through the court and there are no opportunities to consent voluntarily outside of a court hearing;
□ *A one-time consent process*, in which alleged fathers are given a single opportunity to consent voluntarily, usually right after notification of the allegation;
□ *A multiconsent process*, in which alleged fathers are given at least two opportunities to consent, usually after notification and also after genetic testing; and
□ *A court-as-last-resort process*, in which alleged fathers have to respond to a notification by filing with the court their intention to consent to or contest the allegation. The court's role after the initial notification is generally limited to handling contested cases after genetic tests. Multiple opportunities for consent are available.

The majority of the counties have some opportunity for voluntary consent outside a court hearing. Only 20 percent of the counties do not have a consent process. The most common approach (37 percent) is the multiconsent process. In addition, 20 percent of counties have a one-time consent process and 16 percent have the court-as-last-resort process.[15] We expected that counties offering opportunities for consent outside of court would have higher rates of paternity establishment. In our initial analyses, counties with the multiconsent process had significantly better rates.

Given the preliminary evidence that the locus of the paternity establishment process and its opportunities for consent were associated with paternity performance, we examined whether particular combinations of organizational locus and consent opportunities were related to paternity rates. Combining these two dimensions created 13 potential categories, including a grouping of counties that were not classified on either process or locus.[16] We expected that counties with both the transfer approach to organizational locus and multiple opportunities for consent might have the best paternity rates, since both these characteristics were individually correlated with paternity rates in earlier analyses. After testing all the different combinations, three cross-categorizations that were significantly associated with paternity rates were retained in the subsequent analysis step. At the next stage, administrative practices identified in the literature as exemplary approaches to the paternity process were entered into the regression model, and variables having *t* statistics with a probability higher than .15 were eliminated. The practices tested included those associated with: (1) the intake of cases, (2) location of the alleged father, (3) adjudication and genetic testing, and (4) management of the agency. Each practice was thought to be associated with improved program performance. Table 2.1 presents the definitions and weighted distributions of all variables in the final reduced form of the model. Table 2.2 shows the regression results from the four stages of analysis. Table 2.3 provides the weighted distribution of the variables that were tested and eliminated from the models.

FINDINGS: CHARACTERISTICS ASSOCIATED WITH PATERNITY RATES

In the first step, model 1 shown in table 2.2, county paternity establishment rates are significantly associated with the demographic characteristics of the counties. The paternity rate is significantly and negatively associated with the county unemployment rate, the population growth rate (net population change), and an interaction term coupling population growth with residence in a northern county. The paternity rate is positively associated with rural and smaller urban counties—those with populations less than or equal to 200,000—in contrast to urban counties with more than 500,000 residents. It is also higher in counties with a higher proportion of families living below poverty. This finding is surprising, since we had hypothesized that higher proportions of the population below poverty would indicate a harder population for the child support program to work with. However, the poverty indicator may be associated with welfare participation rates. Since AFDC participants are required to cooperate with the Child Support Enforcement program, paternity rates may actually be higher in areas with higher levels of family poverty. In this first model, variation in these county demographic characteristics explains 11.5 percent of the variance in the paternity establishment rate.

The second model shown in table 2.2 shows the coefficients when

Table 2.1 WEIGHTED DISTRIBUTION OF VARIABLES IN MODELS

		Mean	Standard Deviation
Paternity rate	Paternities FY 1989/Nonmarital births, 1988	.499	.425
Unemployment rate	County unemployment rate, 1986	.106	.053
Families below poverty	Proportion, 1979	.140	.084
South	Census region: South [West and Midwest omitted]	.533	.500
North	Census region: North	.065	.248
North × population change	Interaction North × population change	.002	.011
Population change	Net change county population, 1980–86	.046	.118
Rural	Nonmetropolitan county	.783	.413
Urban, 200,000	Metropolitan, population ≤ 200,000	.143	.351
Urban, 500,000	Metropolitan, population 200,000 to 500,000	.048	.214
	[Metropolitan, population > 500,000 omitted]		
Cases/staff quartile 1	(AFDC cases/CSE staff)/100 ≤ 1.186	.275	.447
Cases/staff quartile 2	(AFDC cases/CSE staff)/100 = 1.187 to 2.231	.273	.447
Cases/staff quartile 3	(AFDC cases/CSE staff)/100 = 2.231 to 3.410	.189	.393
	[(AFDC cases/CSE staff)/100 > 3.410 omitted]		
CSE[a] budget/divorces	(CSE Budget FY 1989/divorces in county) × 1/1,000	5.785	16.731
Multiple consent/transferred	Multiple consent and contested cases transferred	.105	.308
Court as last resort/human service	Court as last resort in human service agency	.074	.262
Court as last resort/legal	Court as last resort in legal agency	.061	.240
Crime/school records	Criminal record files and school records Routinely used for location (number used)	1.003	.686
Default first notice	Defaults for failure to respond to first notice	.120	.326
State pays for test	State pays up front for genetic test	.121	.327
Stipulate to test results	Father agrees to accept test results	.125	.332
Quasi-judicial staff	Quasi-judicial staff used	.159	.366
Case tickler system	System alerts worker when case action required	.555	.498
Form generation	Computer system generates standard forms (0 = no, 1 = some, 2 = all or most forms)	.841	.857
Computer interface	Computer interface between IV-A and IV-D	.650	.478
Same CSE state/local	CSE agency is the same at state and local levels	.768	.423

a. CSE, child support enforcement.

Table 2.2 COUNTY CHARACTERISTICS AND PATERNITY PRACTICES ASSOCIATED WITH PATERNITY RATES
(ORDINARY LEAST SQUARES)

	Model 1		Model 2		Model 3		Model 4	
	Beta	t	Beta	t	Beta	t	Beta	t
Unemployment rate	-2.588	-3.096***	-2.345	-2.743***	-2.043	-2.544**	-1.307	-1.682*
Families below poverty	1.315	2.217**	1.067	1.754*	1.036	1.837*	0.714	1.282
North	-0.073	-1.018	-0.025	-0.344	0.050	0.726	0.120	1.819*
South	-0.138	-2.306**	-0.119	-1.993**	-0.073	-1.251	-0.055	-0.967
North × population change	-2.408	-1.825*	-3.128	-2.375**	-3.626	-2.964***	-2.807	-2.415***
Net population change	-0.502	-2.312**	-0.562	-2.528**	-0.596	-2.931***	-0.518	-2.684***
Rural	0.229	3.028***	0.191	2.514**	0.176	2.465**	0.142	1.998**
Urban, 200,000	0.301	4.894***	0.266	4.340***	0.231	4.044***	0.205	3.630***
Urban, 500,000	0.145	2.254**	0.130	2.042**	0.133	2.221**	0.136	2.372**
Cases/staff quartile 1			0.190	2.954***	0.162	2.710***	0.109	1.869*
Cases/staff quartile 2			0.129	1.963*	0.104	1.704*	0.014	0.227
Cases/staff quartile 3			0.126	1.977**	0.132	2.242**	0.103	1.852*
CSE budget/divorces			0.007	2.070**	0.007	2.211**	0.006	1.847*
Multiple consent/transferred					0.410	6.150***	0.372	5.807***
Court as last resort/human service					0.220	2.195**	0.131	1.333
Court as last resort/legal					0.132	1.672*	0.104	1.221
Crime/school records							0.069	2.511**
Default first notice							0.096	1.632
State pays for test							0.143	2.250**
Stipulate to test results							0.200	2.874***
Quasi-judicial staff							-0.148	-3.261***
Form generation							0.058	2.333**
Case tickler system							-0.073	-1.728*
Computer interface							-0.105	-2.187**
Same CSE state/local							0.142	2.481**
(Constant)	0.432	6.188	0.320	3.840	0.229	2.898	0.129	1.401
Adjusted R Square	.115		.139		.261		.359	

***p < .01
**p < .05
*p < .10

Table 2.3 WEIGHTED DISTRIBUTION OF VARIABLES TESTED AND NOT INCLUDED IN REDUCED MODELS

	Mean	Standard Deviation
County Demographic Characteristics		
Percentage of population hispanic	.021	.054
Percentage of population black	.056	.107
Percentage of population high school graduates	.566	.135
Per capita income	8244	1980
Percentage of births to mothers under age 20	.159	.060
Census region Midwest	.266	.443
Intake Practices		
Every non-AFDC mother is interviewed	.661	.474
Every AFDC mother is interviewed	.512	.501
IV-A collects primary information about father	.185	.389
Frequency cases referred for noncooperation are sanctioned	3.61	1.35
(1 = never, 2 = rarely, 3 = sometimes, 4 = often, 5 = frequently)		
Use of law enforcement agency to notify alleged father	.317	.466
Activity on AFDC referral before AFDC eligibility determined	.087	.283
Mother must attend hearing	.522	.501
Outreach efforts made by paternity establishment agency	.582	.494
Other agencies in community disseminate paternity information	.673	.470
Locate Practices		
Number of local sources (utility, tax, credit bureau)	1.45	1.12
Number of state/federal sources (wage, tax, department of motor vehicles, federal locator)	3.21	1.13
Adjudication Practices		
Father must make court appearance in voluntary consent	.159	.366
Court hearing required for genetic test	.393	.489
Father can request (stipulate to) a genetic test and avoid hearing	.323	.468
State pays for genetic test, requests reimbursement from father	.400	.491
Blood draws are conducted on-site	.235	.425

Legal and Court Characteristics

Level of attorney involvement in paternity process (0–3)	2.267	.654
On-site attorney supervised by outside agency	.076	.265
Judges dedicated to child support	.025	.157
Days per month court available for paternity cases	11.14	10.51
Commitment of court to paternity establishment	3.71	1.192
Judicial process	.754	.431
Quasi-judicial process	.204	.404
Administrative process	.045	.207
Defaults issued for failure to appear for genetic tests	.384	.487
Bench warrants are issued for failure to appear	.539	.500

Client Characteristics

Mothers who fail to show up for interviews (1 = <10%, 2 = 10%–24%, 3 = 25%–49%, 4 = 50%–75%, 5 = >75%)	2.19	1.23
Fathers who fail to appear for first appearance (1 = <10%, 2 = 10%–24%, 3 = 25%–49%, 4 = 50%–75%, 5 = >75%)	2.40	1.27
Proportion of CSE caseload AFDC	.849	.166

Management Practices

Automated system	.289	.454
Supervisors review case records for quality control	.801	.400
Court routinely reports status of cases	.367	.483
Cross-training IV-A and IV-D staff last six months	.308	.462
Agency commitment to paternity (1 = moderate, 2 = high, 3 = very high)	2.410	.856

variables assessing the resources invested in the county child support program are added to initial specifications. As expected, the paternity rate is higher in counties with lower average AFDC caseloads per child support worker and in counties allocating more funds to child support per each divorce in the county. Holding constant demographic differences between counties, those with the lowest staff AFDC caseloads—those in the first quartile—have the highest paternity rates. Counties in the second and third quartiles also have significantly higher rates than those with the highest average staff caseload—the omitted category in the equation. Child support programs with higher budgets relative to the number of divorces in the county also have higher paternity establishment rates. The coefficient indicates that increasing the dollars in the child support program by $1,000 per divorce in the county might be expected to be associated with a .7 point rise in the paternity rate, holding county demographics constant. The introduction of program investments into the equation does not diminish the independent influence of the county demographic variables. County demographics and program investments explain 13.9 percent of the variance in the dependent variable, a 2.4 percent increase over the model with just demographic variables.

In the third model in table 2.2, three combinations of organizational locus and voluntary consent are found to be significantly associated with paternity establishment rates. Counties with the highest rate of program performance offer multiple opportunities for consent and have adopted an organizational approach in which cooperative fathers are handled by the human service agency and contested cases are transferred to a legal agency such as a county prosecutor. Use of these combined approaches is associated with an astonishing 41 point rise in the paternity establishment rate. The second best approach appears to be one that combines the court-of-last-resort consent process with locating responsibility for paternity cases in the human service agency. In this approach multiple opportunities for consent are offered to the father, but his response to the initial contact must be filed in court. When this consent process is used by a human service agency, the paternity rate is 22 points higher. There is also the suggestion that the court-of-last-resort consent process used by a legal agency may also be effective. This combination is associated with a higher paternity establishment rate, $p \leq .10$, and the coefficient suggests a 13 point rise in the rate. When the combined organizational and consent approaches are added to the model, the variance explained by the model almost doubles, reaching .26. Moreover, the relationships of the demographic and program resource variables to the paternity establishment rates change very little.

The fourth column in table 2.2 shows the final reduced form of the model after the effects of exemplary intake, locate, genetic testing, court hearing, and management practices have been tested. One practice used to locate alleged fathers has a significant independent association with the paternity rate.[17] Counties using criminal record checks and school records show performance levels 7 percentage points higher for each type of record used. Two practices associated with genetic testing are also associated with higher performance levels. These are the use of stipulations to test results and the practice of states' paying for the genetic tests. These practices are fairly uncommon. Only 12 percent of the counties report using these approaches. The use of stipulations to test results appears to be particularly effective. In this practice, alleged fathers agree to testing and to not challenging the test results if a predetermined level of probability of paternity is indicated by the test. This approach is associated with a paternity rate 20 points higher than the rate for counties not using the practice ($p \leq .01$). When the state pays for genetic tests rather than asking fathers to pay for them, the paternity rate appears to be 14 points higher ($p < .05$).

Two practices thought to improve paternity establishment performance are associated with significant decreases in the paternity rates. The use of quasi-judicial staff to expedite case handling is negatively associated with paternity rates. In 16 percent of the counties, staff who can assume some of the functions of a judge are used presumably to expedite cases through the court. Surprisingly, counties using these staff have performance rates 15 points lower than other counties, holding other factors constant ($p < .01$). Similarly, paternity rates are lower when counties report that there is an automated computer interface between the child support and the AFDC program so that case status updates can be accessed by either agency. Two-thirds of the counties report the availability of this interface. When the effects of the other variables in the model are held constant, the interface is associated with a 10.5 point decline in the paternity rate ($p < .05$). There is also evidence that having a system to alert workers to take action on paternity cases may also be negatively associated with the paternity rate ($p < .10$) (see table 2.2).

Two management characteristics are associated with improved program performance. The more a county uses a computer system to generate standardized forms for paternity-related actions, the higher the paternity rate ($p < .05$).[18] Counties in which the child support program is located in the same agency at the state and county levels also appear to have higher paternity rates. The coefficient indicates that this practice might be associated with a 14 point increase in the rates, holding constant the effects of the other variables in the model (see table 2.2).

The introduction of these exemplary practices increases the variance explained by the model to .36. Their addition produces some interesting alterations in the coefficients of the demographic, program resources, and consent organization variables. The exemplary practices lead to a reduction in the size and significance of coefficients associating the county unemployment rate and the proportion of families below poverty with paternity performance. A similar pattern is observed for the program resources variables. After the introduction of the practice variables, both the staff caseload variables and the funds spent per divorce show a weakened association with paternity rates. These findings suggest that some of the exemplary practices in the model may compensate for the depressing effects that a difficult caseload and fewer staff and dollars can have on program performance.

The introduction of the practice variables also reduces the size and significance of the consent organization variables. The combined use of multiple consent and the transfer of cases remains strongly and significantly associated with the paternity rate, but the use of the court of last resort by either a human service agency or a legal agency becomes insignificant. This pattern suggests that some of the apparent effects of these forms of consent organization are the result of the influence of particular practices that are associated with the approaches. A further description of how particular practices tend to be used in conjunction with particular organization or consent approaches is available in an earlier report (Holcomb, Seefeldt, and Sonenstein 1992).

DISCUSSION

The National Survey of Paternity Establishment Procedures has uncovered a complicated but comprehensible array of organizational arrangements, voluntary consent processes, and administrative and management practices being used by child support programs throughout the country. Our multivariate analyses suggest that some of these approaches and practices are associated with enhanced paternity establishment performance. However, we caution readers that these findings from cross-sectional analyses are merely suggestive of possible avenues to follow in seeking improvements in program performance. We have observed associations between the presence of certain practices and paternity establishment rates, but we cannot establish the direction of causality between practice and performance because we have not observed what happens over time before and after a practice is implemented. Our analyses are also exploratory in the sense that we have attempted to identify specific policies and practices associated with program performance from a long list of candidate variables, and there are only 250 cases in the sample. The wide variation in paternity establishment policies and practices around the country made it difficult to winnow the list. Therefore, we used a regression approach that tested the introduction of variables sequentially. Although we ordered the sequence according to a logical framework, we caution that our results might have been different if the variable groupings had been shuffled or entered in a different order.[19]

Having pointed out these caveats, we think there is some evidence that the organizational and consent procedures used by counties are associated with different levels of paternity performance. Holding constant the effects of demographic and program resource differences between counties, the use of multiple consent with the transfer of contested cases from a human service to a legal agency appears superior to most other approaches to paternity. We can hypothesize that counties offering multiple consent opportunities to fathers but transferring contested cases to a legal agency have higher paternity establishment rates because they can tailor the system response to the father's level of cooperation. If he appears cooperative, he is dealt with administratively by the human service agency; if he appears noncooperative, he can be transferred to the county attorney's office. This approach therefore takes maximal advantage of the fact that there is a spectrum of father's responses to paternity allegations. Moreover, we suspect that systems with the transfer option may be more efficient in screening cases to identify the probable response of the alleged father, since noncooperative cases, the hardest cases, can be sent to another agency. Further research is needed to understand why this approach appears particularly effective.

For illustrative purposes, we have calculated the average adjusted paternity rates for counties using different approaches to organization and consent when the demographics, program resources, and exemplary practices used in the multivariate model are set at their means. The results are shown in table 2.4. The table also shows the unweighted frequencies of counties falling into each category. The 27 counties with multiple consent and the transfer of contested cases to a legal agency show an average paternity rate of 65 percent when other factors are held constant. In contrast, counties using the other approaches to consent and organization show adjusted rates between 22 percent and 45 percent. This table suggests the level of improvement that a county might obtain if it were to switch from one approach to another, holding constant the effects of demographics, program resources, and the use of exemplary practices. For example, a county with multiple opportunities for consent in a human service setting might double its paternity establishment rate on average by adopting the transfer approach. Counties currently providing a single opportunity for consent might attain paternity rates two to three times higher, if they adopt multiple opportunities for consent and a transfer approach for contested cases. Counties with no consent and locating paternity in a human service agency, a common pattern, might almost triple their paternity establishment rates. In general, paternity rates would also be expected to improve, but not quite so dramatically, if counties with paternity establishment located in a legal agency shift to the multiple consent/agency transfer approach. The expected improvement might vary from 44 percent to 88 percent.

Of course, most programs operate in an environment in which the effects of demographics, program resources, and the use of particular practices cannot be held constant. Indeed, each county's paternity establishment program is a unique blend of policies and practices that have emerged historically. Therefore, the paternity rates shown in table 2.4 that adjust for some of these differences are only illustrative. We cannot ascertain what types of difficulties counties would encounter if they tried to change their approaches to paternity. Moreover, although we tested numerous interactions of various exemplary practices with consent organizational approaches, the apparent effects of the multiple consent/agency transfer approach may be the result of the use of a composite of particular practices that we have not uncovered.[20]

Beyond the effect of multiple consent in a transfer setting, the other program practices appearing to have the strongest association with higher levels of paternity establishment are:

☐ Running routine checks on criminal and school records to locate fathers;

Table 2.4 ADJUSTED MEAN PATERNITY ESTABLISHMENT RATES BY PATERNITY ESTABLISHMENT ORGANIZATION TYPES AND CONSENT PROCESSES
(UNWEIGHTED N)

		Paternity Organization Types		
Consent Process Type	Legal Organizational Model	Human Services Organizational Model	Two-Agency Transfer Model	Not Categorized
No-consent process	.384 (9)	.229 (28)	.311 (15)	
One-time consent	.395 (10)	.308 (11)	.222 (32)	
Multiconsent process	.344 (18)	.298 (27)	.649 (27)	
Court as last resort	.450 (22)	.409 (11)	.254 (16)	
Not categorized				.338 (24)

Note: Data are adjusted for county characteristics, program investments, and exemplary paternity practices.

☐ Using stipulations to genetic test results so that fathers agree to accept the results of the test prior to its administration;
☐ Having the state pay for genetic tests, rather than seeking payment or reimbursement from the father;
☐ Using a computer system to generate standardized forms; and
☐ Maintaining the child support program in the same agency at the state and local levels.

Although these findings appear intuitively correct, we caution that the use of these practices may be markers for other characteristics of the program that have gone unmeasured. For example, criminal and school record checks may indicate a county that leaves no stone unturned in its location efforts.

Recent legislation requires states to implement some of these practices, but is silent on others. Under the new Budget Reconciliation Act of 1993, all states must implement simple civil procedures for voluntary acknowledgment and provide rebuttable presumption of paternity when genetic test results reach specified thresholds. These two changes will likely increase rates of paternity establishment in states lacking these practices as fathers are offered a single opportunity for voluntary acknowledgment prior to genetic testing and, for those not acknowledging, paternity is simply determined on the basis of genetic test results, obviating the need to offer a second opportunity for voluntary consent. However, the survey results also indicate that states may further improve their paternity establishment rates by paying attention to other aspects of the program like the organizational setting, office automation, locate procedures, and payment policies for genetic tests.

Some practices initially thought to lead to improved performance appear to be associated with lower levels of performance. These include using quasi-judicial staff, having a computer interface between the child support and AFDC programs, and having a system in place that alerts caseworkers when an action should be taken for each paternity case. These findings are particularly difficult to interpret.[21] One potential reason for some of these unanticipated findings could be that these practices may have been put in place because of problems with the caseload. In these instances, and probably in others as well, the use of these practices may be a response to poor performance and not vice versa. It is also possible that some practices identified in the literature as exemplary may actually make the paternity establishment process more cumbersome and less efficient.

There is considerable variation across counties in paternity establishment rates associated with demographic differences. These dissipate somewhat when program practices are factored in. However counties with large population size and high population growth, especially high population growth in the northern United States, show poorer performance on paternity establishment rates than counties without these characteristics. As Congress and the Family Support Administration implement performance standards, demographic differences may lead to differentials in states' ability to attain their requisite goals.

The performance of counties on paternity establishment appears to be positively associated with the investment of funds in the child support enforcement program. The rates of paternity establishment are higher in counties with higher child support enforcement program budgets relative to the number of divorces in the county. They are also higher when there are more child support staff relative to the size of the AFDC caseload. It is not surprising that more funds and staff are associated with higher performance. It is interesting, however, to note that the use of some exemplary practices appears to compensate for the effect of fewer program resources.

This cross-sectional picture of paternity establishment at the local level in 1990 provides a first look at the variation in practices and their potential effectiveness. The study uncovered a number of issues that need to be resolved as further research is pursued in this area. For instance, there is a clear need for longitudinal data on counties so that we can sort out the direction of some of the causal sequences— sequences that are only suggested by the correlations noted in this study. Another issue is the need for data about the paternity caseload. Less than half of the programs surveyed were able to provide information about the size of the active paternity caseload. Very few kept separate program statistics about paternity cases.

The growth of nonmarital children on AFDC and in the population in general suggests that more attention must be paid to tracking and serving this population by the Child Support Enforcement Program. An initial step is to determine how successful programs are in establishing paternity. But several critical policy questions remain even if information systems become more sophisticated. What happens after paternity is established? What proportion of these cases have child support awards? What are the levels of these awards? Do these fathers pay child support? Do they participate more extensively in their children's lives? Are children better off? These questions need answers as the Child Support Enforcement Program deals with the growing numbers of nonmarital children.

Notes

Funding for the project on which this chapter is based has been provided by grants from the Ford Foundation and the Assistant Secretary for Planning and Evaluation, U.S. Department of Health and Human Services. Portions of this chapter were also presented at the joint Institute for Research on Poverty—U.S. Department of Health and Human Services conference, "Paternity Establishment: A Public Policy Conference," in Washington, D.C., February 26–27, 1992. We would like to thank Allie Page Matthews, Deputy Director of the Family Support Administration, Office of Child Support Enforcement, and Stephanie Ventura, of the National Center for Health Statistics, for their assistance in obtaining the data analyzed here. Helpful comments on this chapter have been received from John Marcotte, Ann Nichols-Casebolt, Errol Rickets, Donald Oellerich, conference participants, and the editors. Opinions expressed here do not necessarily represent the views of the Urban Institute or the project's funders.

1. Although several provisions to improve the collection of support had been tried in the 1960s, most notably a 1967 change in the Social Security Act requiring welfare agencies to initiate paternity establishment for AFDC children born out of wedlock, none had been fully implemented.

2. The federal-state Child Support Enforcement Program, created in 1975, is known as the IV-D program because child support legislation is found in Title D, Part IV (of the Social Security Act), enacted in 1974.

3. A final objective of the study is to add the county paternity information as contextual data to the National Survey of Adolescent Males, to examine the association between county child support policies and practices and the fertility behavior of young men living in those counties.

4. The weight is the inverse of each county's probability of selection into the sampling frame. A poststratification adjustment was done to scale the weights to the known distributions of counties by population density, based on data in the 1988 County and City Data Book (Census Bureau 1988). The weights were set to average to 1.

5. In counties with more than one office conducting paternity establishment, a knowledgeable respondent in a single randomly chosen office was interviewed and surveyed.

6. States are required, however, to provide statewide, not county-level, statistics.

7. In places served by an office whose catchment area included more than one county, the ratio of paternities to births was calculated using the total nonmarital births in all the counties served by the office.

8. It is possible for a county to establish more paternities in one year than there were nonmarital births the previous year, because paternity may be established up to a child's 18th birthday. Also, not all paternities established in a county are for children born in that county.

9. In addition to the variables listed in the text, we attempted to obtain measures of

the demographic characteristics of each county's paternity caseload. These data were not available in most counties. As a result, the demographic characteristics of the counties must serve as controls for caseload characteristics.

10. The multivariate analyses were not weighted.

11. Several interaction terms were tested, and one term, North × *population change*, was retained.

12. Number of staff includes subcontracted staff.

13. We chose not to use the number of nonmarital births as a measure of need because this component had been used in the construction of the dependent variable, the paternity establishment rate.

14. Programs in Massachusetts, where child support is located in the Department of Revenue, were grouped in this category since the setting was not the court or a county attorney's office.

15. In 8 percent of the cases, the adjudication process did not fit easily into one of the categories.

16. Table 2.4 shows the unweighted frequency distribution of counties in each category.

17. The sets of locate practices were developed on the basis of a factor analysis of 18 variables identifying different sources of locate information that counties might use routinely to locate alleged fathers. Six factors explaining 61 percent of the variance emerged.

18. This variable distinguishes between counties without this capacity, those generating some of the forms, and those generating all or most of the forms.

19. Different sequential specifications were tested. The exemplary practice variables that are shown in the final models are the ones that were particularly robust in different specifications.

20. We did check whether counties using this approach concentrated in a particular state. This was not the case. Counties with this approach were located in 10 states.

21. Potential interactions of these characteristics with other program variables were examined, but no significant interactions were uncovered.

References

Adams, Charles F., Jr., David Landsbergen, and Daniel Hecht. 1990. "The Court-Agency Relationship in Paternity Establishment." Paper presented at the Association for Public Policy Analysis and Management Twelfth Annual Research Conference, San Francisco, October.

_____. 1991. "Interorganization Dependencies and Paternity Establishment." Paper presented at the Association for Public Policy Analysis and Management Thirteenth Annual Research Conference, Bethesda, Md.

Aron, Laudan Y., Burt S. Barnow, and William McNaught. 1989. "Paternity Establishment among Never-Married Mothers: Estimates from the

1986 Current Population Survey Alimony and Child Support Supplement." Washington, D.C.: Lewin/ICF.

Census Bureau. *See* U.S. Bureau of the Census.

Danziger, Sandra, and Ann Nichols-Casebolt. 1989. "Teen Parents and Child Support: Eligibility, Participation, and Payment." *Journal of Social Services Research.*

Ellwood, David T. 1986. "Targeting 'Would-be' Long-Term Recipients of AFDC." Princeton, N.J.: Mathematica Policy Research.

Hardy, Dorcas, P. Rank, M. Delker, E. Young, and D. Lawrence. 1979. "The Project to Determine the Legal and Social Benefits, Rights, and Remedies Accruing to Illegitimate Children upon Establishment of Paternity." Los Angeles: UCLA Center for Health Policy Research.

Holcomb, Pamela A., Kristin S. Seefeldt, and Freya L. Sonenstein. 1992. "Paternity Establishment in 1990: Organizational Structure, Voluntary Consent, and Administrative Practices." In *Paternity Establishment: Public Policy Conference,* edited by Daniel R. Meyer (57–81). Special Report Series. Madison: University of Wisconsin-Madison, Institute for Research on Poverty.

Maniha, John K. 1992. "New Data on State Performance in the Establishment of Paternity: Is It Valid and What Use Can Be Made of It?" In *Paternity Establishment: Public Policy Conference,* edited by Daniel R. Meyer (43–54). Special Report Series. Madison: University of Wisconsin-Madison, Institute for Research on Poverty.

Monson, Renee A., and Sara A. McLanahan. 1990. "A Father for Every Child: Dilemmas of Creating Gender Equality in a Stratified Society." Madison: University of Wisconsin-Madison.

National Center for Health Statistics. 1993. *Advance Report of Final Natality Statistics, 1991. Monthly Vital Statistics Report* 42 (3, suppl.). Hyattsville, Md.: U.S. Public Health Service.

Nichols-Casebolt, Ann. 1988. "Paternity Adjudication: In the Best Interests of the Out-of-Wedlock Child." *Child Welfare* 67: 245–54.

————. 1990. "Establishing Paternity: A Case Study of How the System Works and Implications for Improving Outcomes." Paper presented at the Association for Public Policy Analysis and Management Twelfth Annual Research Conference, San Francisco, October.

Nichols-Casebolt, Ann, and Irwin Garfinkel. 1991. "Trends in Paternity Adjudications and Child Support Awards." *Social Science Quarterly* 72, 1: 83–97.

Sonenstein, Freya L., Pamela A. Holcomb, and Kristin S. Seefeldt. 1992. "Paternity Establishment in 1990: Performance at the Local Level." Institute for Research on Poverty Special Report no. 56A. Madison, Wisconsin: University of Wisconsin-Madison, pp. 109–135.

Sonenstein, Freya L., Joseph H. Pleck, and Leighton C. Ku. 1989. "Sexual Activity and Contraceptive Use among Adolescent Males." *Family Planning Perspectives* 21 (4, July/August): 152–158.

U.S. Bureau of the Census. 1988. *County and City Data Book*. Washington, D.C.: U.S. Government Printing Office.

————. 1991. *Child Support and Alimony, 1989. Current Population Reports*, ser. P-60, no. 173. Washington, D.C.: U.S. Government Printing Office.

U.S. Congress. House. Committee on Ways and Means. 1991. *Background Material and Data on Programs within the Jurisdiction of the Committee on Ways and Means*. Washington, D.C.: U.S. Government Printing Office.

U.S. Department of Health and Human Services, Office of Child Support Enforcement. 1989. *A Guide to Initiating a Paternity Consent Process*. Washington, D.C.: Author.

————. 1990. *Fourteenth Annual Report to Congress for the Period Ending September, 1989*. Washington, D.C.: Author.

U.S. Department of Health and Human Services, Office of Inspector General. 1990. "Effective Paternity Establishment Practices." Dallas: Author.

Wattenberg, Esther. 1984. "The Project on Paternity Adjudication and Child Support Obligations of Teenage Parents." Minneapolis: University of Minnesota.

————. 1987. "Establishing Paternity for Nonmarital Children: Do Policy and Practice Discourage Adjudication?" *Public Welfare* 45 (3): 9–13, 48.

Wattenberg, Esther, Rose Brewer, and Michael Resnik. 1991. "A Study of Paternity Decisions: Perspectives from Young Mothers and Young Fathers." Minneapolis: Center for Urban and Regional Affairs, University of Minnesota.

Williams, R. G. 1988. "Summary of Child Support Research by Policy Studies, Inc. and Suggested Topics for Future Research." Discussion Paper prepared for the joint American Enterprise Institute/HHS-ASPE Conference on Child Support Enforcement. Washington, D.C. December 2.

Williams, Victoria Schwartz, and Robert G. Williams. 1989. "Identifying Daddy: The Role of the Courts in Establishing Paternity." *Judges Journal* 28 (3, Summer): 2–7, 40–42.

Young, Edward. 1984. "Costs and Benefits of Paternity Establishment." Pasadena, California: Center for Health and Social Services Research.

Chapter Three

IMPLEMENTATION OF THE INCOME WITHHOLDING AND MEDICAL SUPPORT PROVISIONS OF THE 1984 CHILD SUPPORT ENFORCEMENT AMENDMENTS

Anne R. Gordon

This chapter examines the implementation of provisions of the Child Support Enforcement (CSE) Amendments of 1984 pertaining to income withholding and medical support enforcement, based on a sample of CSE offices and cases.[1] *Income withholding* refers to the withholding of child support from noncustodial parents' paychecks (or other regular income sources); the 1984 Amendments required withholding for obligors in arrears. *Medical support* refers to health insurance coverage (and sometimes payment of medical expenses) for dependent children; the 1984 Amendments required CSE offices to petition for medical support if available at reasonable cost, and to collect data on medical coverage. Although the income withholding and medical support provisions of the 1984 Amendments strengthened the CSE system, they gave CSE agencies the difficult task of monitoring the employment and health coverage of obligors— many of whom change jobs and/or are unemployed frequently. Not surprisingly, administrative problems—insufficient automation; large caseloads; multiple agencies with child support responsibilities; and, in terms of medical support, weak enforcement tools— limited the implementation of these provisions.

The first section of this chapter describes the data and characteristics of the samples of CSE offices and cases. The second and third sections discuss the implementation of the income withholding and medical support provisions of the 1984 Amendments.[2] The fourth and final section presents policy conclusions.

DATA AND SAMPLE CHARACTERISTICS

The data for this study included a large sample of case records, as well as a survey of staff in the offices from which the case records sample was drawn. This section describes the data and characteristics of sample offices and cases.

Data Sources

Data were abstracted from case records for 1,906 child support cases with orders, distributed across 30 offices in 11 states.[3] State Employment Security Agency (SESA) records on the earnings of obligors in the case records sample were collected to supplement the case records data. In addition, staff surveys were completed by staff in 29 of the 30 offices in which case records were abstracted.

The case records sample is not nationally representative in a statistical sense, but it covers a wide range of geography and types of child support enforcement systems.[4] The sample was confined to cases with orders, because income withholding and medical support enforcement are largely relevant to cases with orders; however, this sample limitation implies that we cannot infer any indirect effects of these policies on the likelihood of obtaining an order. In addition, the effectiveness of these policies may change as the population of cases with orders changes.

The case abstractions were made between February and November 1990. SESA wage records data were collected, and most staff surveys were completed, in fall 1990. The data thus provide a snapshot of the child support enforcement system in 1990, about three years after the 1984 Amendments took effect, and just before the provisions of the Family Support Act of 1988 (FSA) began to take effect.[5]

Characteristics of Sample Offices

The 30 offices in the sample were drawn from 11 states, from all of the major census regions, and from urban, suburban, and rural areas. They ranged widely in size, staff levels, levels of automation, institutional structure, and legal environment. (The states and offices received assurances that their identities would not be revealed.)

The 29 offices that responded to the staff survey ranged from one that served just over 2,500 cases to one that served 360,000 cases. Their caseload per full-time-equivalent staff member ranged from 137 to 1,049, with an average caseload across offices of 464.[6] Caseload per staff member was highly correlated with office size (the correlation equaled .722). Levels of automation also varied greatly; we obtained lists of cases in formats ranging from handwritten lists to computer tapes. Some automated systems were statewide and some were office-specific; large offices tended to be more automated. Most offices had automated payment records, but few had comprehensive, on-line case management systems.

Most jurisdictions spread CSE functions across several agencies. In each locality, we identified the "lead agency" as the agency designated as the CSE agency by the state CSE office. This agency usually, but not always, carried out most CSE program activities, and was the state or county social services (welfare) agency in about two-thirds of the local offices (19 out of 29). In one state (4 offices) the lead CSE agency was the state attorney general's office, and in another state (4 offices) the CSE agency was an independent county agency. In one locality, the county attorney's office was the designated CSE agency, and in one locality an administrative office of the family court was the CSE agency.[7]

The lead agency typically delegated some CSE functions to other agencies through cooperative agreements that provided for the other agencies to be reimbursed for CSE activities by the lead agency. In 7 of the 29 offices in our sample, the CSE agency shared responsibilities with an administrative office of the court; often the court agency had prime responsibility for non-AFDC cases. Legal representation for obligees was delegated to another agency just over half the time (in 18 of 29 offices for paternity establishment, and in 17 offices for support order establishment)—typically the welfare agency delegated this function to the county attorney or prosecutor, but occasionally to the state attorney general. (In two offices, this function was delegated only for non-AFDC cases.) Collection of support payments was also frequently the responsibility of another agency (in 62 percent of offices); in all but one of these offices the function was lodged in the court clerk's office. In contrast, intake and location activities were almost always handled by the lead agency.

Courts typically hear child support and paternity matters for both CSE cases and private child support cases, but six sample offices had administrative processes for establishing support orders in nonpaternity cases. In most areas, court hearings were before quasi-judicial hearing officers rather than judges.

Characteristics of Sample Cases

Over half of the non-AFDC cases were formerly AFDC cases—of 1,201 non-AFDC cases in the sample, 609 were formerly on AFDC,

559 had never been on AFDC, and in 33 cases past AFDC status could not be determined. When examining the characteristics of cases formerly on AFDC and those never on AFDC separately, we found that obligees in cases formerly on AFDC tended to be more disadvantaged than those in cases never on AFDC, but less disadvantaged than those in cases currently on AFDC. Besides AFDC status itself, indicators of "disadvantage" available in our data are whether the obligee was ever married to the obligor, the amount of the order, the percentage of child support owed that was received in the past year, and the level of arrearages owed by the obligor (table 3.1).

In over half of the AFDC cases, and in nearly one-third of non-AFDC cases, the parents had never been married. In addition, most cases in the sample had only one child listed in the file (see table 3.1). In contrast, 1988 CPS data on child-support-eligible *families* with orders show fewer never-married custodial parents (29 percent in AFDC families and 7 percent in non-AFDC families) and fewer parents with only one child (27 percent in AFDC families and 37 percent in non-AFDC families) (Gordon et al. 1991, table 2.8). One reason for these discrepancies is that some *families* have multiple CSE *cases*. A woman with children from several fathers will have a case for each father. In addition, in some states, each child for whom paternity is established is counted as a separate case, even if there are several children with the same father.[8]

Our only information on the economic situation of the obligors in the sample is from SESA records of earnings subject to unemployment insurance (also known as "wage records data"). These data are made available to CSE agencies under federal law. As measured in the SESA data, obligor earnings were surprisingly low—median earnings were $3,535 per year and mean earnings were $8,553 per year (table 3.1). The data suggest that obligors in AFDC cases earned somewhat lower incomes on average than obligors in non-AFDC cases, and that obligors in cases formerly on AFDC earned lower incomes than obligors in cases never on AFDC.

Our estimates of noncustodial parents' average incomes from the SESA data are much lower than other estimates (Garfinkel and Oellerich 1989; Peterson and Nord 1987). One reason for this is that the other estimates were based on samples of noncustodial parents in general, not just those in the CSE system. The Survey of Absent Parents pilot study, the only study available that compared incomes of CSE and non-CSE noncustodial parents, found that noncustodial parents in the CSE system were much more likely to have low incomes (Sonenstein and Calhoun 1988).

A second reason our estimates are lower is that SESA wage records data understate earnings. The SESA databases do not include earnings in jobs not covered by unemployment insurance in the state of residence, such as self-employment, federal employment, "off-the-books" employment, and employment in a neighboring state.[9] Furthermore, state CSE staff, who provided MPR with these data, informed us that records maintained by some of the states in our sample are incomplete even for covered employment.[10] Earnings reported in the SESA data are thus not a reliable measure of obligor income; however, they do measure the income that the CSE system can most readily locate.

Child support orders were low on average (table 3.1). The median order was $125 per month for AFDC cases, $135 per month for formerly AFDC cases, and $210 per month for cases never on AFDC. These levels of child support are usually not enough to support a family, or to leave AFDC; for comparison, the average AFDC benefit maximum in the 11 sample states for a family with a mother and one child was $316 a month in 1990 (U.S. Congress, House 1990). Orders may have been low because guidelines were not used, because older orders were rarely updated, or because they truly reflected obligor ability to pay. However, a comparison of orders with obligor ability to pay as measured by SESA earnings shows that (1) orders did not match current ability to pay very closely, since those with higher SESA earnings owed much smaller percentages of their earnings than those with lower earnings, and (2) many obligors were required to pay lower proportions of their earnings than would be required under most guidelines. The median percentage of earnings owed as child support was 17 percent, which implies that half the obligors with earnings owed an even lower percentage. If obligor income were measured more completely, the median percentage of obligor income owed as child support would have been still lower.[11]

The median percentage of current child support that was received in the previous year was 69 percent (35 percent for AFDC cases and 89 percent for non-AFDC cases) (table 3.1). Twenty-eight percent of cases did not receive any support (36 percent of AFDC cases and 24 percent of non-AFDC cases), and 24 percent received over 100 percent of the amount due, because of payments on arrears or prepayments (20 percent of AFDC cases and 26 percent of non-AFDC cases).

Arrears were very high, despite the low awards. The median level of arrears was $1,845, and more than half the cases had arrears of 12 months of support payments or more (see table 3.1). The difference in arrears between AFDC and non-AFDC cases was small, with AFDC

Table 3.1 CHARACTERISTICS OF CHILD SUPPORT ENFORCEMENT CASES

	AFDC Cases	Non-AFDC Cases[a]			Total Cases
		Formerly AFDC	Never On AFDC	All Non-AFDC	
Number of Children in Case					
1	68%	74%	59%	67%	67%
2	22	20	33	26	25
3 or more	10	7	8	7	8
Marital Status of Parents					
Ever married	41%	51%	79%	64%	55%
Never married	52	43	15	29	38
Not determined	7	6	6	7	7
Annual Earnings of Obligors Reported in SESA Data[b]					
Zero[c]	33%	31%	36%	33%	33%
$1–$10,000	35	31	21	26	30
$10,001–$20,000	16	17	16	16	17
$20,001–$30,000	8	11	11	11	10
$30,001–$40,000	2	5	8	6	5
Over $40,000	[d]	1	3	2	1
Missing	6	5	6	6	6
Mean	$6,742	$8,941	$10,486	$9,617	$8,553
Median	$2,820	$4,912	$4,241	$4,610	$3,535
Median Monthly Amount of Child Support Owed	$125	$135	$210	$168	$150
Median Monthly Amount of Child Support Owed per Child	$100	$108	$150	$129	$113
Amount Due as Percentage of Obligor SESA Earnings[b]					
Percentage with zero earnings	33%	31%	36%	33%	33%
Median for cases with nonzero earnings	17	15	18	17	17

Median for cases with SESA earnings from:					
$1–$5,000	71	87	129	100	82
$5,001–$10,000	17	22	32	25	22
$10,001–$20,000	10	10	16	13	12
Over $20,000	8	8	10	9	9
Percentage of Current Child Support Received in Past Year					
None	36%	26%	21%	24%	28%
Over 100%[e]	20	25	27	26	24
Median	35	81	94	89	69
Arrears					
No arrearage	9%	15%	20%	17%	14%
Mean	$4,051	$3,958	$3,834	$3,974	$4,002
Median	$2,287	$1,624	$1,163	$1,430	$1,845
Arrears in Terms of Months of Support Owed[f]					
No arrearage	9%	15%	20%	17%	14%
Less than 1 month	6	11	13	12	9
1 to 11.99 months	22	19	23	20	21
12 months or more	60	52	41	47	52
Missing/not determined	3	4	3	4	4
Number of Cases	705	609	559	1,201	1,906

Sources: Weighted tabulations from Mathematica Policy Research (MPR) case record abstracts of 1,906 active CSE cases with orders, collected from February to November 1990, and SESA earnings records for the four most recent quarters available as of fall 1990.

a. The number of formerly AFDC and never on AFDC cases do not sum to the number of non-AFDC cases because we could not determine former AFDC status in 33 of the 1,201 cases.

b. SESA data include only earnings in jobs covered by Unemployment Insurance. Excluded jobs include self-employment, federal employment, "off-the-books" employment, and jobs in other states.

c. These cases had Social Security numbers in the SESA files but no earnings in the most recent four quarters. They include unemployed obligors and obligors who worked in jobs not covered by the SESA database.

d. Less than 0.5 percent.

e. This category includes cases with payments on arrears or prepayments.

f. When exact arrears were not available, abstractors coded them by the categories listed. For example, if there were no payments in the past year, the abstractor knew that the category "12 months or more" was appropriate. Thus, this variable is based on both exact and categorical data.

cases having higher arrears. The mean levels of arrears are much higher than the medians, owing to a small number of cases with very high arrears.[12]

These data confirm that the CSE caseload is a difficult caseload. Even in many non-AFDC cases, the custodial parent was previously on AFDC, and the noncustodial parent has a low income or income that is difficult to locate. Low orders highlight the importance of modifying orders to meet new state guidelines, as well as of enforcing current orders. High arrearages on current orders—and the fact that most cases have arrearages—indicate that more effort at enforcement is warranted, but also suggest that many obligors may not have the funds to cover the arrearage. The next section presents additional evidence that many obligors incur arrearages because they are unemployed or working irregularly.

INCOME WITHHOLDING

The 1984 Amendments required that states order employers to withhold child support from the earnings of obligors who accumulate one month or more of arrears in all CSE cases.[13] As a consequence, income withholding was widely used even before implementation of the Family Support Act's (FSA's) provisions concerning immediate withholding began in 1990; withholding collections comprised 44 percent of all CSE program collections in FY 1990 (U.S. Department of Health and Human Services, Office of Child Support Enforcement 1991a).

Based on the case records abstracts and the survey of local office procedures, CSE offices implemented the withholding provisions of the 1984 Amendments largely in accordance with federal law and regulations. The first group of subsections following discusses the extent of implementation of withholding under the 1984 Amendments and the barriers to greater use of withholding.

Immediate withholding of child support from earnings, without waiting for an arrearage to accrue, was permitted under the 1984 Amendments. The sample includes 11 offices in states with laws requiring the inclusion of immediate withholding in most child support orders prior to the passage of the FSA in 1988. In the other offices in the sample, immediate withholding was sometimes part of the support order in individual cases, but there was no legal requirement for inclusion of immediate withholding in most orders prior to 1990. We found that the use of withholding was greater in the offices with immediate withholding laws, but that collections were not significantly greater. The second group of subsections following analyzes the effects of immediate withholding laws.

Extent of Implementation

We examine here the implementation of withholding as a function of the available information on the obligor's employment in the case records and the SESA earnings data. We then describe the barriers to further implementation of withholding, based on data on office procedures from the staff survey.

AVAILABILITY OF EMPLOYMENT INFORMATION

To assess the availability of employment information, we analyzed (1) the case records and (2) the SESA wage records data. The case records indicate the employment information known to the CSE agency at the time of the abstraction.[14] The SESA data were available to the CSE agency with varying degrees of accessibility—sometimes the information was on-line and immediately available to caseworkers, whereas sometimes data had to be requested as part of a monthly or quarterly tape match. As a further complication, we collected SESA data several months after the case abstractions; thus, some of the SESA data we collected were not available to the CSE agency at the date of our case-record abstractions.[15]

In AFDC cases with arrears, the SESA records and the case files both reported employment for 29 percent of cases (see table 3.2).[16] For 16 percent of AFDC cases, the SESA records contained employment information but the case files did not; many of these cases are likely to be cases in which the CSE agency failed to learn about the obligor's employment.[17] For 20 percent of AFDC cases, the case file contained employment information but the SESA records did not; many of these obligors were probably working in jobs not covered by the SESA database.[18] For another 10 percent of the AFDC cases, the case file contained specific information that the obligor was not working, and there were no SESA earnings. For the remaining 26 percent of the AFDC cases, the case file did not specify whether the obligor was working, there were no SESA earnings, and it was thus not possible to determine from these sources whether the obligor was employed. The data for non-AFDC cases with arrears show similar patterns,

Table 3.2 AVAILABILITY OF EMPLOYMENT INFORMATION FOR CASES WITH
LEVEL OF ARREARS REQUIRED FOR WITHHOLDING
(CASES IN OFFICES NOT USING IMMEDIATE WITHHOLDING)

	AFDC Cases (%)	Non-AFDC Cases (%)
Any Evidence of Employment	64	71
Both wage records and case file contain evidence of employment	29	30
Wage records contain earnings, but case file does not contain evidence of employment	16	16
Case file contains evidence of employment, but wage records do not contain earnings	20	25
Case File Information Indicates Not Working	10	9
No Information on Employment	26	21
Number of Cases	441	673

Sources: Weighted tabulations from State Employment Security Agency (SESA) wage records and MPR case records abstracts of 1,906 active CSE cases with orders, abstracted from February to November 1990.
Note: Data are from the 18 offices not using immediate withholding in all new orders. We consider the case file to indicate that the obligor was employed if either the name of the employer was in the file and dated within the past 24 months or if the case had no arrears (for which employer information was not coded), unless there was specific information in the file that the obligor was no longer employed at the abstraction date. Still, in some cases, the obligor may have left the job by the time withholding was triggered. We consider the wage records to indicate the obligor was employed in cases where earnings for the obligor were found recorded in SESA records in at least one of the two quarters before the quarter in which the abstraction occurred. It is possible this information was not yet available on the abstraction date.

with a slightly larger proportion of obligors indicated as employed in one of the two sources (see table 3.2).

WITHHOLDING IMPLEMENTATION

For all cases with arrears exceeding one month of support, we examined whether withholding had been attempted (or was in place) in the past year, whether withholding had actually occurred in the past year, and whether withholding was ongoing as of the abstraction date (table 3.3).[19] We found that withholding attempts increased with the strength of the employment information available. When both the case files and the SESA records indicated the obligor was employed, withholding had been attempted (or was in place) in 71 percent of AFDC cases and 81 percent of non-AFDC cases with the triggering arrearage. In contrast, when the SESA data indicated employment, but the case files did not, withholding had been attempted in only 33 percent of AFDC cases and 26 percent of non-AFDC cases with arrears. (The attempts that did occur in this category most likely reflect cases with obligors employed earlier in the year who had since lost their jobs.) If the CSE agencies had monitored the SESA data more regularly, they probably could have attempted withholding in more of these cases.

For most cases in which withholding had been attempted, withholding was in place at some point during the year. However, considerably fewer cases had withholding still occurring at the abstraction date. For instance, withholding was in place at the time of the abstraction for only 45 percent of AFDC cases and 63 percent of non-AFDC cases with strong indicators of employment (table 3.3, top panel). The most common reason given in the case files for withholding not being implemented when it was attempted, or for withholding spells ending, was that the obligor had left the job.[20] Nonetheless, in many cases, there was no information in the case record on why withholding had not been implemented or had terminated.

DURATION OF WITHHOLDING

The results just cited suggest that both job turnover and unemployment limit the implementation of withholding. We examined these factors from another perspective by estimating the duration of withholding spells, and the duration of periods of time between withholding spells. The duration of these spells cannot be estimated accurately by directly tabulating the case records data, because many spells were in progress (or "censored") at the time of data collection, and the ultimate length of these spells would be understated by their length to date. To avoid such understatement, we estimated the distribution of durations using a statistical technique called the "product-limit" estimator, which properly uses data from censored spells (Kalbfleish and Prentice 1980).[21]

For each case, our data recorded the dates of the first withholding spell after 1985, and, for cases whose initial withholding spell had ended, of the first break in withholding.[22] Table 3.4 presents estimates of the distribution of the duration of the first withholding spell and of the first break in withholding derived using the product limit estimator. The estimated median length of the first withholding spell is 17 months—11 months for AFDC cases and 25 months for non-AFDC cases. Differences in spell durations for AFDC and non-AFDC

Table 3.3 WITHHOLDING OUTCOMES FOR CASES WITH REQUIRED ARREARS, BY EXTENT OF EMPLOYMENT INFORMATION
(CASES IN OFFICES NOT USING IMMEDIATE WITHHOLDING)

	AFDC Cases (%)	Non-AFDC Cases (%)
Cases for Which Both Wage Records and Case File Indicate Obligor Was Employed		
Cases for which withholding was attempted or in place in past year	71	81
Cases with withholding in past year	60	75
Cases with current withholding	45	63
Number of Cases	**128**	**206**
Cases with No Earnings in Wage Records for Which Case Files Indicate Obligor Was Employed		
Cases for which withholding was attempted or in place in past year	56	64
Cases with withholding in past year	52	61
Cases with current withholding	38	52
Number of Cases	**87**	**167**
Cases with Earnings in Wage Records but No Indication in Case File that Obligor Was Employed		
Cases for which withholding was attempted or in place in past year	33	26
Cases with withholding in past year	30	21
Cases with current withholding	11	8
Number of Cases	**69**	**103**
Cases for Which Neither Wage Records Nor Case File Indicate Obligor Was Employed		
Cases for which withholding was attempted or in place in past year	10	11
Cases with withholding in past year	5	7
Cases with current withholding	1	2
Number of Cases	**157**	**196**

continued

All Cases

Cases with withholding attempted or in place in past year	41	48
Cases with withholding in past year	34	44
Cases with current withholding	22	34
Number of Cases	**441**	**673**

Source: Weighted tabulations from MPR case records abstracts of 1,906 active CSE cases with orders, abstracted from February to November 1990.

Notes: Data are from the 18 offices not using immediate withholding in all new orders. We consider the case file to indicate that the obligor was employed if either the name of the employer was in the file and dated within the past 24 months or if the case had no arrears (for which employer information was not coded), unless there was specific information in the file that the obligor was no longer employed at the abstraction date. Still, in some cases, the obligor may have left the job by the time withholding was triggered. We consider the wage records to indicate the obligor was employed in cases where earnings for the obligor were found recorded in SESA records in at least one of the two quarters before the quarter in which the abstraction occurred. It is possible this information was not yet available on the abstraction date. Percentages given are of nonmissing data.

cases should be interpreted with caution, because AFDC cases with long withholding spells may have been more likely to go off AFDC. Most spells are either quite short or fairly long: 40 percent of spells for AFDC cases and 28 percent of spells for non-AFDC cases end within six months, whereas 37 percent of AFDC spells and 50 percent of non-AFDC spells last over two years. The time between the first and second withholding spells lasts a median of 10 months for AFDC cases and 8 months for non-AFDC cases. Long periods between withholding spells may reflect periods of unemployment and/or cases in which the office took a long time to reestablish withholding.

BARRIERS TO IMPLEMENTATION

The staff survey data suggest that procedures in many offices could be made more efficient by improvements in automation, by consolidation of the process in one agency or improved links between agencies, and by increased emphasis on rechecking the status of obligors who were not employed when withholding was initially triggered.

Although a few offices had fully automated systems for implementing withholding, most required that caseworkers or court clerks do at least some steps in the process by hand. For example, in 11 of the 29 offices surveyed, procedures for identifying an arrearage sufficient to trigger withholding were manual—caseworkers had to check payment records for each case, usually on a monthly basis. Another 11

Table 3.4 DURATION OF WITHHOLDING SPELLS AND PERIOD BETWEEN FIRST AND SECOND WITHHOLDING SPELLS

	AFDC Cases (%)	Non-AFDC Cases (%)	All Cases (%)
Estimated Duration of First Withholding Spell after January 1985			
1–6 months	40	28	32
7–12 months	15	12	13
13–24 months	8	10	9
More than 24 months	37	50	46
Median	11 months	25 months	17 months
(Number with first spell)	(322)	(592)	(913)
Percentage with First Spell That Was Still Ongoing at Time of Data Collection	38	53	48
Estimated Time between First and Second Spells after January 1985			
1–6 months	37	44	41
7–12 months	16	16	16
13–24 months	7	11	9
More than 24 months	41	29	34
Median	10 months	8 months	9 months
(Number with first spell ending)	(207)	(290)	(497)
Percentage with Period after First Spell Still Ongoing at Time of Data Collection	43%	35%	38%

Source: Weighted tabulations from MPR case records abstracts of 1,906 active CSE cases with orders, abstracted from February to November 1990.
Note: Only cases with at least one withholding spell are included in this table. Estimates were derived using product-limit estimator, a statistical technique that accounts for ongoing spells. No data were available on spells that began before January 1985.

offices used a combination of manual and automated procedures, usually involving manual checks of computerized payment records. Only 7 offices had this function fully automated.

There are two stages in the process of implementing income withholding in which the involvement of multiple agencies required additional coordination and may have caused delays. First, in more than half of the sampled offices (16 of 29), another agency (usually the court clerk's office) monitored arrearages and informed the CSE agency when the obligor reached the withholding trigger. Unless automated systems are linked and procedures are closely coordinated, the need for communication across agencies is likely to have caused delays. Second, 5 offices (of 18 not using immediate withholding) required a judge's signature on the withholding order, possibly in violation of federal regulations, which indicate that no court action should be required to initiate withholding. This additional step is likely to have slowed down implementation.

Finally, some offices did not fully exploit the SESA data, which is an important source of information on obligor employment status. Although all of the offices consulted SESA data, and the vast majority (93 percent) consulted SESA data within 30 days after the triggering arrearage was reached, a sizable minority (5 offices, or 17 percent) did not recheck the SESA data if no employment for the obligor was originally found there. Since some obligors are unemployed when they first run up arrears but later obtain jobs, rechecking the SESA data is important.

SUMMARY

The reasons that withholding was not occurring in cases with arrears fall into two categories: (1) the obligor was unemployed or had recently changed jobs, and (2) the CSE agency had not identified the obligor's employer, or had otherwise failed to take action, or had taken action slowly. In our data, it was not usually possible to distinguish which of the two factors was at work—for example, if there was no evidence of employment in the file or the SESA data, we could not determine if the obligor was unemployed or if the CSE agency failed to track down the obligor's employer. However, the two problems are intertwined; if most obligors were steadily employed for long periods, the process of implementing and monitoring withholding would be much more straightforward.

Effects of Immediate Withholding Laws

Because immediate withholding is being implemented nationwide under the Family Support Act of 1988, it is of interest to assess the effects of immediate withholding laws relative to withholding in response to delinquency. We examine here the effect of immediate withholding laws on the prevalence of withholding and on collections, using regression analysis to control for case characteristics and for state. We classify a case as subject to immediate withholding if the case is from a jurisdiction that required immediate withholding (by law at the time of the most recent order. However, many cases in nonimmediate withholding) jurisdictions had immediate withholding provisions included in their orders at the discretion of the judge or hearing officer or upon request of the parties.[23] Thus, our estimates of the effects of immediate withholding should be interpreted as the effects of having an immediate withholding *law* that applies to most cases, as compared with using immediate withholding in selected cases only. In some sites without immediate withholding laws, extensive use of immediate withholding orders probably reflects anticipation of the implementation of the FSA—which suggests we underestimate its impact.

We included all cases in the regressions, not just cases with arrears, since the availability of immediate withholding may affect the proportion of cases with arrears. The case characteristics controlled for in the regressions include demographic factors, case status measures, and measures of the obligor's ability to pay child support (see appendix table 3.A.1 for sample means). We report results obtained with ordinary least squares, since they are easiest to interpret, although they are not strictly appropriate given the limited nature of the dependent variables.[24]

In assessing the effects of the immediate withholding policies on the prevalence of withholding, we investigated three dependent variables: (1) whether withholding was in place or attempted in the past year; (2) whether withholding had occurred in the past year, and (3) whether withholding was occurring at the time of the abstraction. The regression results suggest that immediate withholding laws lead to a small but statistically significant increase in withholding, when other factors are held constant (table 3.5). The table shows only measure (2). The other two produced similar results. In particular, cases subject to immediate withholding have an 8.1 percentage point greater probability of having withholding in the previous year. (The mean of the dependent variables is 46.1 percent.)

Table 3.5 ESTIMATED COEFFICIENTS FROM REGRESSIONS PREDICTING
WITHHOLDING AND COLLECTION OUTCOMES

Independent Variables	Withholding during Past Year	Collections/ Amount Due	Months Paid/ Months Due
Immediate withholding	.0809**	.0497	.0410
	(.0391)	(.0470)	(.0299)
Mother's age	.000579	.00373	.00444**
	(.00266)	(.00320)	(.00208)
Father's age	−.00152	.00400	.00137
	(.00211)	(.00252)	(.00164)
Living with neither parent	−.0696	−.0690	−.0716
	(.0654)	(.0822)	(.0527)
Number of children	.0107	−.0403**	−.00411
	(.0143)	(.0174)	(.0113)
Ever married	−.00475	−.0219	.00314
	(.0267)	(.0323)	(.0209)
Years since support order	−.0177***	−.00413	−.0158***
	(.00395)	(.00476)	(.00310)
Order is original	−.0604**	−.0872***	−.0492**
	(.0246)	(.0301)	(.0194)
Interstate case	−.0266	.0518	−.00818
	(.0377)	(.0448)	(.0293)
Obligor earnings (in thousands)	.0126***	.0190***	.0159***
	(.00123)	(.00150)	(.000972)
Zero earnings indicator	−.162***	−.0803**	−.0574**
	(.0290)	(.0349)	(.0226)
AFDC case	−.0817***	−.123***	−.130***
	(.0282)	(.0338)	(.0219)
Former AFDC case	.0137	−.0458	−.0290
	(.0308)	(.0373)	(.0241)
Intercept	.492***	.458***	.314***
	(.0850)	(.103)	(.0669)
Number of cases	1,759	1,800	1,841
R^2	.238	.218	.337
Mean of outcome measure	.461	.618	.501

Notes: Standard errors of coefficients are in parentheses. State indicator variables were also included in these equations; the names of the sample states are confidential. Equations were estimated using ordinary least squares regression. The samples include all cases with nonmissing data on the dependent variable. For cases with missing data on independent variables, the sample mean for the missing variable was used.

*Significant at 10 percent level.
**Significant at 5 percent level.
***Significant at 1 percent level.

Two measures of collections were used as dependent variables: (1) the ratio of the amount of child support paid in the past year to the amount owed in the past year (the "pay-to-owe ratio") and (2) the ratio of months in which a payment was made during the past year to months in which a payment was owed (the "months-paid-to-months-owed" ratio). The pay-to-owe ratio may exceed 100 percent if obligors are paying off arrears—the mean for the full sample is approximately 62 percent (see table 3.5). The months-paid-to-months-owed ratio ranges from 0 to 100 percent; the mean for the full sample is approximately 50 percent. The latter variable picks up effects on the regularity of payments as well as the amount.

The regression results show no statistically significant effect of immediate withholding on either collection measure (see table 3.5). Immediate withholding is estimated to increase the pay-to-owe ratio by approximately 5 percentage points, and to increase the months-paid-to-months-owed ratio by 4 percentage points. In both cases, these increases would represent about 8 percent of the sample mean. However, neither estimated effect is significantly different from zero.

The major previous study of immediate withholding (Garfinkel and Klawitter 1990), using data from the evaluation of the Wisconsin Child Support Assurance System, estimated significant and somewhat larger immediate withholding impacts. Using the same dependent variables, but several different measures of immediate withholding, Garfinkel and Klawitter estimated that immediate withholding would increase collections by between 11 and 30 percent. Garfinkel and Klawitter's upper-bound estimate (a 30 percent increase in collections) is based on a measure of whether immediate withholding was ordered in specific cases. Estimates based on this measure tend to overstate the impacts of immediate withholding, because immediate withholding is more likely to be ordered in cases likely to pay anyway. Garfinkel and Klawitter also present a lower-bound estimate of an 11 percent increase in collections, which is based on comparing cases in offices that *usually* use immediate withholding with cases in offices that *sometimes* use immediate withholding. This lower-bound estimate is conceptually similar to our estimates. Furthermore, our estimates indicate that collections increase by 8 percent under immediate withholding, a figure close to the 11 percent lower bound of the Garfinkel and Klawitter estimates.[25]

In sum, our results suggest that immediate withholding laws have a small positive impact on the use of withholding, and possibly a small positive impact on collections. The small size of these estimated impacts is not surprising. As noted previously, immediate withholding was sometimes used in individual cases in states where it was not required by law, perhaps in anticipation of the FSA; it may also not have been fully implemented in states where it was required by law. Furthermore, fully 77 percent of the sample is subject to withholding in response to delinquency (see table 3.1). In addition, many cases accumulate arrears during periods of unemployment or job changes; withholding, whether immediate or not, is not possible (or is inevitably interrupted) during these periods.

MEDICAL SUPPORT ENFORCEMENT

The 1984 Amendments required CSE agencies to petition for the inclusion of medical support in orders, to enforce medical support orders, to collect information on obligor insurance coverage for cases in which the children are covered by Medicaid, and to forward that information to the Medicaid agency. The Mathematica Policy Research (MPR) evaluation found that agencies follow the regulations concerning petitioning for medical support in most but not all cases, and that medical support has been more frequently included in orders since the 1984 Amendments took effect. However, CSE agencies have largely failed to monitor obligor insurance coverage or to report the information (even when they have it) to the Medicaid agency.

Including Medical Support in Child Support Petitions and Orders

Our data suggest that the 1984 Amendments, in conjunction with state laws passed during the same period, have increased the use of petitions and orders for medical support. However, offices do not always petition for medical support when required to do so under federal regulations. The regulations require the CSE agency to petition for inclusion of any health coverage that is available to the absent parent at "reasonable cost" in all child support orders.[26] "Reasonable cost" coverage was defined as "employer-related" or "other group health insurance" (45 CFR 306.51[a][1]).[27]

Because our sample included cases with orders from both before and after the 1984 Amendments took effect, we assessed the impact of the amendments on the prevalence of petitions and orders for medical support by comparing cases with pre-1987 orders to cases with orders since 1987. We used the beginning of 1987 as the cutoff because that was the approximate date on which the 1984 Amendments were fully implemented nationwide. Inevitably, this pre-post comparison also captures the effects of changes in state child support laws that occurred around the same time.[28] However, we controlled for state, in order to capture state-specific policy changes. We also controlled for case characteristics, since cases with older orders may be systematically different from cases with newer orders in ways that affect the provisions of their orders.

There was a substantial increase between the two periods in the percentage of petitions that requested medical support. The percentage of petitions with requests for medical support increased by 13 percentage points, from 38 percent before 1987 to 51 percent after January 1, 1987, holding other factors constant. Case characteristics did not have significant effects on the use of petitions.

The percentage of cases with medical support orders also increased dramatically, from 46 percent of orders in 1986 or before, to 69 percent of orders after January 1, 1987—an impact of 22 percentage points. Interestingly, while obligor earnings (as measured in SESA wage records) had no effect on the likelihood of a medical support order, AFDC and former AFDC cases were significantly less likely to have medical support orders. One possible explanation is that obligors in AFDC or former AFDC cases were less likely to be in jobs offering health insurance, even after controlling for SESA earnings. Orders in ever-married cases were less likely to contain medical support, after controlling for other factors; perhaps these obligors had more resources to contest the medical support provision, or were more often providing medical support prior to the order (an order is not required if medical support is already being provided).

Despite the improvements shown in these data, even in the post-1986 period only 58 percent of AFDC cases and 54 percent of non-AFDC cases had petitions for medical support, although the 1984 Amendments required petitions for essentially all AFDC cases and all non-AFDC cases in which the custodial parent requested medical support. The staff surveys indicated that some offices did not bother to petition for medical support if coverage was not available to the noncustodial parent at that time, contrary to federal regulations; this situation could be easily remedied with increased attention to medical support.

Enforcing Medical Support Orders and Collecting Insurance Information

The 1984 Amendments and implementing regulations required the CSE agency to gather information about health insurance coverage

Table 3.6 PERCENTAGE OF CASES IN WHICH INSURANCE INFORMATION
WAS AVAILABLE IN CASE FILES

	AFDC Cases	Non-AFDC Cases	Total
All Cases	11%	15%	13%
	(625)	(1,032)	(1,657)
Cases with medical support orders	17	23	21
	(320)	(529)	(850)
Cases without medical support orders	3	7	6
	(305)	(503)	(808)
Employment Status (for Cases with Medical Support in the Order)			
Employed[a]	23%	27%	26%
	(155)	(362)	(516)
Not employed	8	20	14
	(52)	(55)	(107)
Not determined	13	10	12
	(114)	(113)	(226)

Source: Case-record data on 1,657 CSE cases with orders in which it was possible to determine whether a medical support order existed. Sample sizes for each cell are in parentheses.
a. This category includes those obligors who have no arrearages, for whom no employment information was collected.

available to the obligor in Medicaid cases and to provide this information to the Medicaid agency. In addition, the CSE agency is required
to inform the Medicaid agency when a new or modified child support
order for a Medicaid case includes medical support, and to periodically monitor the availability and provision of health insurance by
obligors with medical support orders. The regulations also state that
the agency is to "take steps to enforce" the medical support obligation; however, no specific steps are required (45 CFR 306.51). While
staff in most offices claimed they followed these regulations, the case
records data suggest that insurance information was rarely collected,
and even when collected, was not usually sent to the Medicaid
agency. When compliance is not regularly monitored, enforcement
must be lacking as well. Staff recognized that medical support
enforcement was a problem area, and offered many suggestions for
changes.
    Only a few case files contained any information on medical insur-
ance coverage, even among cases whose orders included medical
insurance (table 3.6). Overall, the files of 11 percent of AFDC cases

and 15 percent of non-AFDC cases contained insurance information.[29] Among cases with medical support orders, 17 percent of AFDC cases and 23 percent of non-AFDC cases had insurance information. These percentages were slightly higher (23 percent of AFDC cases and 27 percent of non-AFDC cases) for cases that had medical support orders and in which the obligor was known to be employed. Because our data reflect information on *available* insurance coverage, the dearth of information on insurance reflects both cases in which the CSE offices failed to obtain this information and cases in which obligors did not have access to health coverage. Although it is not possible to sort out the influence of these two factors fully, the lack of insurance information in most cases in which the obligor's employer was known suggests that CSE agency efforts to obtain this information were inadequate.

The case records also suggest that CSE agencies made little effort to transmit medical insurance information to the Medicaid agency, even when it was available. Only 20 percent of AFDC case files with insurance information (2 percent of AFDC case files in the sample) indicated that insurance information had been forwarded to the Medicaid agency. Although some insurance information may be transmitted to Medicaid agencies through automated systems and, thus, the transmission may not be captured in the files, 71 percent of the offices in the sample (21 offices) used paper forms to send this information, and it seems likely that copies of these forms would have been placed in the files.

The obstacles to obtaining medical insurance information most commonly cited by staff were: (1) lack of staff time to follow up on coverage issues (mentioned by 21 offices, or 72 percent), (2) not knowing the obligor's employer (mentioned by 19 offices, or 66 percent), and (3) noncompliance by the obligor with requests for proof of coverage (mentioned by 18 offices, or 62 percent). Seven offices (24 percent) mentioned that the obligor was not legally required to give proof of coverage.[30] Nine offices (31 percent) reported that employers were not required to provide medical insurance information.

Staff mentioned lack of time and lack of automated interface between the CSE agency and the Medicaid agency as the major barriers hampering transmission of insurance information to the Medicaid agency. As noted earlier, most offices use paper forms to send information to Medicaid; five offices sent the information through intermediaries such as the AFDC office, and none reported having direct on-line access to the Medicaid computer system. Nearly half the offices admitted that transmittal of insurance data between the offices took over 15 days; the case records data suggest that it rarely took place at all.

The case records did not contain sufficient data on insurance coverage to assess whether medical support orders were being complied with, or whether enforcement actions were taken when appropriate. When enforcement actions were pursued, most offices (23 of 29) began by a letter or telephone call to the obligor. When informal discussions were not sufficient, the most commonly used procedure was to file a contempt-of-court motion against the obligor (used by 20 of 29 offices).[31] Under the second most common method of enforcement, sometimes referred to as "medical withholding," state laws permit the CSE agency to issue a notice to the employer to withhold premiums from wages and secure insurance. Eleven offices in four states in our sample reported using medical withholding.[32]

In response to an open-ended question about problems that limit the effectiveness of the medical support enforcement program, staff again mentioned lack of time most often (in 13 offices). Seven offices complained they lacked sufficient enforcement authority. They wanted changes in state laws that would increase requirements for obligors, employers, and insurance companies to cooperate with the CSE agency and that would strengthen the enforcement powers of the CSE agency.[33] Five offices mentioned automation as an area in need of improvement; some specifically noted that their automated systems did not include medical support data. The lack of automation impedes the process of reviewing insurance information and sending it to Medicaid, and also makes it more difficult to assess how aggressively caseworkers pursue medical support issues. Three offices (13 percent) mentioned lack of coordination between agencies as a problem. The collection of medical insurance information in Medicaid cases is a shared responsibility of CSE agencies, AFDC agencies, and Medicaid Third Party Liability units. Furthermore, relevant CSE functions may be housed in several agencies, and it is not always clear which agency is responsible for medical support establishment and enforcement.

CONCLUSIONS

Our findings from studying the implementation of the income withholding and medical support enforcement provisions of the 1984

Child Support Enforcement Amendments suggest two lessons for implementation of the Family Support Act:

□ Implementation of the FSA provision requiring statewide automated systems is vitally important to improving the effectiveness of the CSE program, but will be very challenging.
□ Key factors that limit the effectiveness of withholding in response to delinquency—the difficulty of locating employment information, and the unemployment and/or frequent job changes of many obligors—will also limit immediate withholding.

In addition, these results suggest that medical support enforcement requires further attention from policymakers. One reason behind the difficulty of implementing the federal provisions concerning medical support enforcement is that federal policy provides little in the way of concrete tools for medical support enforcement. The rest of this section elaborates on these points.

Automation

Although enhanced federal matching funds have been available for the development of automated systems since the early 1980s (with the federal government paying 90 percent of development costs), states have been slow to take advantage of these funds. As of May 1991, only 7 states had federally approved automated systems, 2 were nearing approval, and 17 were in the development or implementation phases (*Federal Register*, vol. 56, no. 93, p. 22132).

Improvements in automated systems are crucial to effective child support enforcement. For example, to implement income withholding and to enforce medical support orders, CSE staff need to be able to monitor case status regularly, take routine processing steps (such as issuing notices) quickly, and communicate with other agencies efficiently. We found many offices performed these functions manually, which placed an enormous paperwork burden on staff. Even when automated systems existed, they were often not designed to perform routine case management functions (for example, many did not track medical support information), and/or were unable to communicate with the automated systems at other agencies.

The FSA recognized the crucial role of automated systems in implementing federal child support policy by requiring all states to have automated systems meeting federal standards by 1995, and added "teeth" by ending the enhanced funding in 1995. The draft regulations, published May 14, 1991, proposed stringent requirements for state automated systems, including automation of case tracking and issuing of routine notices, and automation of all aspects of the 1984 Amendments and the 1988 FSA (*Federal Register*, vol. 56, no. 93, pp. 22130–22145). Medical support information would have to be included in the automated system. The draft regulations also require the development of automated links between the CSE agency and the Medicaid, AFDC, and JOBS agencies.

Most states in our sample were some distance from implementing comprehensive automated systems at the time of our study. The diffusion of CSE responsibilities across offices will make instituting such systems more difficult. Incorporated in the regulations is a system of waivers that will allow some CSE functions to be performed manually or will permit separate (but interlinked) automated systems if the state can show this will not seriously hamper efficiency. Given the importance of automating CSE functions, it is critical that the federal Office of Child Support Enforcement (OCSE) monitor the issuance of waivers very carefully.

Barriers to Immediate Withholding

The results presented in this chapter suggest that factors limiting collections from withholding in response to delinquency will also limit the implementation of immediate income withholding. In particular:

☐ It is still necessary to delay or interrupt withholding if the obligor is unemployed when the child support order is made or later changes jobs—the situations in which arrears are most likely to accrue.
☐ Many obligors change jobs frequently, requiring extensive monitoring of employment information by the CSE agency.

The difficulty of tracking obligor income has not been sufficiently recognized. Our findings suggest that SESA reporting systems could be improved and local CSE agencies could make better use of these data. However, these data have inherent limitations. In 1992, former Congressman Thomas Downey (D-NY) and Congressman Henry Hyde (R-IL) proposed to have income withholding handled at the federal level by the Internal Revenue Service (IRS). They argued that nonsupport of children merits the use of the IRS's power and status to track income and enforce compliance among both employees and employers. This and other ideas to improve the process of tracking income merit careful consideration; it is important to ensure that concerns about privacy and due process are addressed.

Medical Support Enforcement

Current federal regulations require extensive monitoring by the CSE agency of the availability and provision of medical support, as well as enforcement of medical support obligations, but provide little in the way of tools with which to accomplish these goals. It seems likely that the vagueness of the federal mandates concerning medical support enforcement is partly responsible for the low level of implementation of these provisions. Contrasting the federal role in medical support enforcement with the federal role in collection of cash support, particularly the requirements for income withholding, is instructive, and suggests some possible policy directions.

Although the federal government has required states to pass laws making available a range of enforcement remedies for failure to pay cash support, federal law does not require that specific enforcement remedies be available to collect medical support. As we have seen, states differ considerably in the remedies available. Federal law and regulations required states to pass laws to make income withholding mandatory when arrears accrue (and later, under the FSA, immediately) and to require employers to cooperate. There is no corresponding requirement for mandatory enforcement of medical support through withholding and no requirement that employers or insurance providers cooperate with CSE agency requests for information on medical support. In fact, in some states insurance companies are prohibited from divulging coverage information.

One possible avenue to increased medical support enforcement suggested by these comparisons is a requirement for withholding of health insurance premiums in all cases with medical support orders, to be instituted at the same time as immediate withholding of cash support. Many states have moved in this direction in the past few years, in response to pressure from federal OCSE audits and the need to control Medicaid costs. An OCSE memorandum (U.S. Department of Health and Human Services, Office of Child Support Enforcement 1991b) described eight states with medical withholding provisions in their laws in 1991, but this list is not complete—for example, two states identified in our survey were not included. Medical withholding provisions range from requirements for medical withholding for all medical support orders (analogous to immediate withholding), to requirements for withholding if the obligor does not provide proof of coverage (analogous to withholding in response to delinquency), to permission for courts to order withholding of insurance premiums on a case-by-case basis. An evaluation of these state provisions would be useful.

The OCSE and the Health Care Financing Administration continue to conduct joint reviews of state medical support enforcement programs (see discussion in Gordon et al. 1991), and medical support has in recent years received attention in regular OCSE audits of state programs. The findings in the audits and program reviews have been highly consistent with the findings from MPR's study; many states have failed the medical support portion of the audit the first time around. However, OCSE staff report dramatic improvements when states are reaudited after a corrective action period.[34]

Although the recent changes in state laws and the growing success of federal audit activities are encouraging, medical support enforcement continues to need further attention from policymakers.

Notes

This chapter was originally prepared as a paper for the "Conference on Child Support and Child Well-being," Airlie House, Airlie, Va., December 5–7, 1991.

The chapter is based on work funded by the Office of Child Support Enforcement (OCSE) of the U.S. Department of Health and Human Services, under a contract with Mathematica Policy Research, Inc. (MPR). However, the views expressed are those of the author and do not necessarily reflect the views of the OCSE or of MPR.

I would like to thank James Ohls, Robert Harris, Sheila Kamerman, and this volume's editors for helpful comments, Dexter Chu for programming assistance, and Denise Dunn for word processing support. This paper is based on a larger report coauthored with James Ohls, Craig Thornton, Nancy Graham, Valarie Piper, Steven Rioux, Philip Robins, Robert Williams, and Victoria Williams.

1. As mentioned above, the results presented here are drawn from a larger study. Under contract to the federal Office of Child Support Enforcement, Mathematica Policy Research conducted a study of three of the topics covered by the 1984 Child Support Enforcement Amendments: income withholding, medical support enforcement, and services to non-AFDC cases (Gordon et al. 1991). The study focused on the implementation of the amendments, but also examined the impacts of provisions for which comparisons across states or across time periods were appropriate.

2. The MPR report (see note 1; Gordon et al. 1991) also considered specific procedures used by offices in enrolling and serving non-AFDC cases. Although these procedures are not discussed here, results concerning income withholding and medical support enforcement are presented for both AFDC and non-AFDC cases.

3. The number of offices per state ranged from one to four. Non-AFDC cases and cases with orders since 1987 were oversampled, but the tabulations were reweighted to account for the oversampling.

4. Chapter 2 of Gordon et al. (1991) compares the characteristics of the samples of offices and cases used in the MPR study to national characteristics.

5. The implementation of the 1984 Amendments was prolonged because most states had to change their laws to comply with them. These legal changes had essentially all occurred by the end of 1986. Actual implementation took still longer. A few provisions of the Family Support Act of 1988—most importantly the use of state guidelines as a rebuttable presumption in setting orders—took effect in October 1989. However, these provisions were not directly relevant to the MPR study.

6. Note that this ratio is calculated on the basis of all staff, not just line caseworkers, and includes staff that do CSE work in other agencies under cooperative agreements. The average caseload per caseworker (not available in our data) must be substantially higher.

7. Other lead agencies are used in states not included in our sample.

8. In a few states, the records on children in the case may be incomplete. In addition, there may not be an order for all of the children, or older children (over 18) may no longer be counted in the case.

9. There are few studies of the extent of the undercount. In studies of programs for unemployed workers in New Jersey and Pennsylvania, Paul Decker found wage records on earnings were roughly 10 percent less than self-reported earnings on average several quarters after filing for unemployment (Corson et al. 1991; Decker 1989). Decker also found evidence that self-employment and out-of-state employment accounted for much of the discrepancy. As part of the National Job Training Partnership Act (JTPA) Evaluation, Robert Kornfeld compared wage records data to interview data for JTPA applicants in 14 states (Bloom et al. 1993, Appendix E). He found earnings reported on the survey were 53 percent higher than wage records earnings for adult men, but was not able to determine to what extent the discrepancy reflected overreporting in the survey or underreporting in the wage records.

10. The extent of the problem is hard to assess. However, data from 3 of the 11 states appeared to have significant gaps, such as quarters in which no sample member was employed.

11. The high percentages owed by obligors with low SESA earnings may reflect an undercount of income, but may also indicate a true mismatch between very low current income due to unemployment and an obligation set when the obligor's income was much higher.

12. Ten percent of cases had arrears in excess of $10,000.

13. It must be possible to implement withholding without additional court action; this is usually accomplished by including language in the support order stating that withholding will occur if arrears accrue equal to one month of support. Obligors must be notified and given an opportunity to contest the withholding, although only on the grounds of a mistake about the arrearage or obligor identity. If no contest occurs, the employer must be notified to begin withholding, given instructions on how withholding is to be implemented, and notified of penalties for failing to cooperate. States were required to pass any laws needed to implement these provisions, on penalty of losing funding for their AFDC programs.

14. We coded the obligor as employed if the file had information less than two years old about an employer and there was no indication that the obligor had left the job.

15. In this analysis, we count only SESA earnings in the two calendar quarters prior to the quarter of the abstraction. However, because the SESA data are typically posted three to six months after the quarter ends, this restriction does not entirely eliminate the problem.

16. All figures in tables 3.2 and 3.3 refer to cases in the 18 offices not using immediate withholding for all new orders. Separate tabulations for cases in immediate withholding offices were reported in Gordon et al. (1991). Results concerning the role of employment information were very similar, but the overall levels of withholding implementation were higher in the immediate withholding offices.

17. In some cases, the relevant SESA data were not yet available to the CSE office as of the date of abstraction; however, if the obligor was employed, the CSE agency could potentially have learned of the obligor's employment from other sources. It is also possible that the obligor had left a job within the last two quarters, and not obtained another—in this case, the SESA earnings data would not reflect current unemployment.

18. Another possibility is that the case file information is dated; that is, the file may list an employer although the obligor had left the job over six months ago.

19. Abstractors coded a withholding attempt if the file included a withholding order to the employer or a request to the court for a withholding order. We included cases in which withholding was ongoing at the start of the year, along with attempts.

20. Attempts failed because the obligor had left the job in at least 45 percent of AFDC cases and 49 percent of non-AFDC cases with unsuccessful attempts. Terminations were due to job loss in at least 40 percent of AFDC cases and 55 percent of non-AFDC cases.

21. The product-limit estimator essentially estimates the probability of a withholding spell ending in a given period based on the percentage of spells *still active at the start of the period* that end during the period. The *overall* distribution of spell lengths is then estimated on the basis of the probabilities for specific periods. More formally, the product-limit estimator estimates the survivor function, $S(t)$, which is defined as the probability that a spell lasts at least to the end of period t. The probability of surviving to the end of period t is by definition equal to the probability of surviving to the end of period $t-1$, multiplied by the probability of surviving to the end of t, given survival to the end of $t-1$. The latter probability can be estimated by $(n_t - d_t)/n_t$, where n_t is the number of spells ongoing during period t, and d_t is the number of spells ending during period t. All spells censored before period t are omitted from both n_t and d_t. In symbols, $S(t) = S(t-1)(n_t - d_t)/n_t$. $S(t-1)$ may be defined similarly, and so forth, back to period 1. Thus,

$$S(t) = \prod_{j \leq t} (n_j - d_j)/n_j. \tag{3.1}$$

Because the conditional survival probability in each period is calculated by omitting spells censored before that period, the estimator avoids bias due to censoring. No assumptions about spell distributions are required.

22. Any break in withholding payments of one month or more was considered the end of a spell. To test the sensitivity of our results to that assumption, we recomputed the duration distribution of the first withholding spell, ignoring breaks that were only one month long. The median spell duration was unchanged for AFDC cases, but increased to 31 months for non-AFDC cases, and to 19 months for the combined sample.

23. We did not have the text of the order available in some cases and offices, so it was not possible to measure accurately the inclusion of immediate withholding

provisions in individual cases from the case records data. However, the available data suggested that immediate withholding provisions were included in most recent orders in some sites with no immediate withholding laws.

24. We obtained very similar results using probit and tobit estimation procedures.

25. Using CPS data on child support collections in 1987, Garfinkel and Robins, in chapter 5 in this volume, suggest that there were significant positive impacts of immediate withholding laws on collections.

26. In non-AFDC cases, the petition is to be made only with consent of the custodial parent.

27. In September 1988, the Department of Health and Human Services issued additional regulations that expanded the definition of "reasonable cost" to include "employment-related or other group health insurance regardless of service delivery mechanism," so as to clarify that the definition covers "fee for service, health maintenance organization, preferred provider organization, and other types of coverage under which medical services could be provided to the dependent child(ren) of the absent parent" (45 CFR 306.51 [a][2]).

28. For example, 26 offices responded in our staff survey that their state laws required that the ability of the obligor to provide medical support be considered in any child support proceeding. Seven offices reported that their state laws required that medical support be included in all orders with the limitation "if available at reasonable cost" or the equivalent. These provisions are in the spirit of the 1984 Amendments, and were often passed as part of legislation that implemented the amendments, but were not required by the amendments.

29. In determining whether a file contained insurance information, we counted any information on coverage, no matter how old. We included coverage held by the obligee as well as by the obligor. However, we did not include cases for which case files stated that the obligor did not have insurance available.

30. However, those offices in which obligors were legally required to provide this information were just as likely to list noncompliance by the obligor as a barrier, suggesting that legal requirements are not easily enforced.

31. Two offices noted they lacked the power under state law to use contempt citations to enforce medical support.

32. The case records do not provide direct evidence on the success of medical withholding. However, one office (in an immediate withholding jurisdiction) collected medical insurance information from the employer at the same time that it sent the employer the notice for immediate income withholding. The case files of this office were more likely than those in the other 29 offices to contain insurance information; insurance information was present for 42 percent of AFDC cases and 48 percent of non-AFDC cases in this office.

33. Recommended changes in state laws include legal requirements for obligors to provide coverage information, laws allowing medical withholding, laws requiring that employers or insurance companies provide IV-D staff with information on insurance coverage, and laws allowing noncompliant obligors to be held in contempt of court.

34. The most striking example was in Washington State, which received an efficiency rate of zero for medical support in the initial audit in 1987, but was rated at 98 percent in the follow-up audit in 1991. It is worth noting that the improvement in Washington involved not just administrative attention but improved state laws and a substantial increase in child support enforcement staff (U.S. Department of Health and Human Services, Office of Child Support Enforcement 1992).

APPENDIX 3.A

Appendix Table 3.A.1 MEANS AND STANDARD DEVIATIONS OF VARIABLES
USED IN REGRESSION ANALYSIS (UNWEIGHTED)

Variable	Mean	Standard Deviation
Mother's age	32.4	6.6
Father's age	35.5	7.5
Obligor is male	0.98	0.12
Child lives with neither parent	0.03	0.16
Number of children born before most recent order	1.5	0.79
Age of youngest child	9.3	4.5
Parents ever married	0.61	0.49
Time since most recent order (years)	4.2	3.2
Current order is first order	0.60	0.49
Interstate case	0.10	0.30
Earnings in four quarters (thousands)	9.0	11.4
No earnings in four quarters	0.35	0.48
Currently an AFDC case	0.46	0.50
Formerly an AFDC case (currently non-AFDC)	0.26	0.44
Immediate withholding case[a]	0.20	0.40
Post-1986 order[b]	0.54	0.50

a. Most recent order occurred when immediate withholding was required under state law.
b. Most recent order is dated after December 31, 1986.

References

Bloom, Howard S., Larry L. Orr, George Cave, Stephen H. Bell, and Fred Doolittle. 1993. *The National JTPA Study: Title IIA Impacts on Earnings and Employment at 18 Months.* Bethesda, Md.: Abt Associates, Inc.

Corson, Walter, Paul Decker, Shari Dunstan, and Stuart Kerachsky. 1991. "Pennsylvania Reemployment Demonstration: Final Report." Princeton, N.J.: Mathematica Policy Research.

Decker, Paul. 1989. Systematic Bias in Earnings Data Derived from Unemployment Insurance Records and Implications for Evaluating the Impact of Unemployment Insurance Policy on Earnings. Princeton, N.J.: Mathematica Policy Research.

Garfinkel, Irwin, and Marieka M. Klawitter. 1990. "The Effect of Routine Income Withholding of Child Support Collections." *Journal of Policy Analysis and Management* 9 (2, Spring): 155–77.

Garfinkel, Irwin, and Donald Oellerich. 1989. "Noncustodial Fathers' Ability to Pay Child Support." *Demography* 26 (2, May): 219–33.

Gordon, Anne R., James Ohls, and Craig Thornton. 1991. Income Withholding, Medical Support, and Services to Non-AFDC Cases after the Child Support Enforcement Amendments of 1984." Princeton, N.J.: Mathematica Policy Research, May.

Kalbfleish, John D., and Ross L. Prentice. 1980. *Statistical Analysis of Failure Time Data.* New York: John Wiley & Sons.

Peterson, James L., and C. Winquist Nord. 1987. "The Regular Receipt of Child Support: A Multi-Step Process." Report prepared for Office of Child Support Enforcement, U.S. Department of Health and Human Services. Washington, D.C.: Child Trends.

Sonenstein, Freya L., and Charles C. Calhoun. 1988. "Survey of Absent Parents: Pilot Results." Washington, D.C.: Urban Institute.

U.S. Congress. House. Committee on Ways and Means. 1990. *1990 Green Book: Background Material and Data on Programs within the Jurisdiction of the Committee on Ways and Means.* Washington, D.C.: U.S. Government Printing Office, June 5.

U.S. Department of Health and Human Services, Office of Child Support Enforcement. 1991a. *Fifteenth Annual Report to Congress.* Washington, D.C.: U.S. Government Printing Office.

————. 1991b. "Model Legislation and Incentives for Implementation of Medical Support Requirements." Information Memorandum OCSE-IM-91-1. Washington, D.C.: U.S. Department of Health and Human Services.

————. 1992. "Washington Medical Support Program Shines in Follow-up Audit." *Child Support Report* 14 (3, April).

Chapter Four

IMPLEMENTATION OF THE CHILD SUPPORT PROVISIONS OF THE FAMILY SUPPORT ACT: CHILD SUPPORT GUIDELINES, UPDATING OF AWARDS, AND ROUTINE INCOME WITHHOLDING

Robert G. Williams

The provisions of the Family Support Act of 1988 with the greatest potential impact on total child support collections were those focusing on the perceived inadequacy of child support award levels. Two issues were identified that contributed to this problem. The first was inadequacies in levels of original child support orders, compared with economic evidence on the costs of child-rearing, resulting from an absence of routinely applied child support guidelines. The second was the absence of a mechanism for periodic review and updating of child support orders despite courts' continuing legal jurisdiction over such decrees. The Family Support Act sought to rectify these deficiencies by mandating presumptive use of child support guidelines in each state and by phasing in a periodic review and updating process for Title IV-D (publicly enforced) child support orders. The issue of periodic review of non-IV-D orders was left for further study and possible future congressional action.

The federal government had already immeasurably strengthened child support enforcement with enactment of the Child Support Enforcement Amendments of 1984. The centerpiece of that legislation was arrearage-triggered income withholding for enforcement of child support orders, which each state was required to implement. This enforcement remedy was supplemented by others, such as property liens and credit bureau reporting. In 1988, the Family Support Act extended the use of income withholding by requiring states to implement immediate income withholding, initially for all IV-D child support orders, and subsequently for all child support orders, IV-D and non–IV-D.[1]

Clearly the intent of the immediate income withholding requirements was that the country would move toward a system in which child support obligations are routinely paid via payroll deductions, just like income taxes. Not specifically addressed by the act, however, was the potential impact of greatly expanded income withholding on child support collection and distribution systems. With the bulk of child support payments being made by employers, including some for non–IV-D cases, states may not be prepared to provide a public mechanism for receipting and disbursing all such payments, and for accommodating employers' needs for efficient handling of child support payments.

In child support, the federal government mandates, but the states execute. This chapter explores the implementation status of the Family Support Act provisions for child support guidelines. We also discuss implementation requirements for review and updating of child support orders and summarize evidence from a series of demonstration projects designed to evaluate these requirements. In addition, we discuss the immediate income withholding requirements and their potential administrative effects, focusing on the need for improvements in state collection/distribution systems for child support, and states' progress in making such improvements.

CHILD SUPPORT GUIDELINES

Family Support Act Requirements

The Family Support Act specified that states should accord rebuttable presumption status to child support guidelines, effective within a year of the law's enactment (that is, by October 13, 1989). With the language "any judicial or administrative proceeding", the act mandated application of child support guidelines to all child support cases, not just publicly enforced cases under the IV-D program. On its face, then, the act seems to require use of the guidelines for all child support cases. Left open for interpretation, however, is the question of whether the same language requires only that the guidelines be used in contested child support actions. The vast majority of child support orders are negotiated rather than being set in a court or administrative hearing. From the statutory language, it is unclear whether the guidelines must be applied to negotiated settlements as well as contested cases.

Also implied by the language that the guidelines must be applied to all cases is the notion that a state's guidelines must be in effect statewide. This requirement had a major impact on the states of California and Pennsylvania, both of which previously had county-based guidelines. California actually had a two-tier structure, with an "Agnos standard" used for lower- and lower-middle-income cases statewide, and county-option guidelines used in other cases or where the county guideline yielded higher results (see Williams 1990). Both states now have unitary, statewide guidelines.

After October 1987, all states were required to have child support guidelines, as specified by the Child Support Enforcement Amendments of 1984, but these guidelines did not have to be binding on judges and hearing officers. In mandating presumptive guidelines, the U.S. Congress only gave states a year to comply, knowing that legislation would be required in many states. Congress seemed to assume that states would simply make their advisory guidelines presumptive. However, for states needing to make major changes in their advisory guidelines, or—as was the case in some states—needing to scrap their advisory guidelines and start over, a 12-month implementation period was unusually short.

State Implementation of Guidelines

When the Family Support Act was enacted, approximately half of the states already had presumptive guidelines. As of May 1988, 19 states had guidelines with rebuttable presumption status for all child support cases, and another 9 states had guidelines with rebuttable presumption status for IV-D cases established under an administrative process (Munsterman and Henderson 1988: 3–4). By October 1989, all states had presumptive child support guidelines for IV-D and non–IV-D cases, except for a few stragglers such as Maryland and Wyoming, which complied soon thereafter. That states moved so quickly to implement this requirement is surprising in some respects. Congress had previously allowed at least two years for states to comply with other major new child support requirements, such as income withholding. And, indeed, there was some vocal resistance by state legislatures to succumbing to the dictates of the federal government in yet another area. Some states, such as Louisiana and New York, had to develop and legislate entirely new child support guidelines, but still did so within the one year allowed under the federal legislation.

In adopting guidelines, states have generally followed one of three models: (1) percentage of obligor income, (2) income shares, or the (3) Delaware Melson formula. The two exceptions are Massachusetts and the District of Columbia (D.C.), which basically use percentage-of-obligor-income approaches, but also incorporate limited income-sharing characteristics. We provide here a brief summary of these models, as well as of the Massachusetts and D.C. variants, and discuss implementation trends.[2]

PERCENTAGE-OF-OBLIGOR-INCOME MODEL

The simplest model determines child support based on a percentage of the obligor's income and number of children. The percentage can be based on either gross income or net (aftertax) income. Perhaps the most well-known guideline of this type is the Wisconsin Percentage of Income Standard, which sets child support based on the following proportions of *gross* income:

One child	17 percent
Two children	25 percent
Three children	29 percent
Four children	31 percent
Five or more children	34 percent

Unlike most other percentage-of-obligor-income models, the Wisconsin standard includes adjustments for shared and split custody arrangements, as well as for serial households (Wisc. Admin. Code HSS 80).

Minnesota has one of the more prominent examples of a percentage model based on *net* obligor income. Minnesota was the first state to legislatively establish presumptive child support guidelines, enacted in 1983. At net income levels above $1,001 per month, these guidelines set child support based on the following percentages of net obligor income:

One child	25 percent
Two children	30 percent
Three children	35 percent
Four children	39 percent
Five children	43 percent
Six children	47 percent
Seven children	50 percent

The child support percentages are lower for obligors with less income. For example, for those with net income of $401–500 per month, the percentage for one child is 14 percent. Minnesota sets a ceiling of $4,000 per month, above which child support is presumptively capped at the same amount as for income of $4,000. Like most other states with percentage models, Minnesota does not have special adjustments for child care, children's extraordinary medical expenses, shared or split custody, or additional dependents (Minn. Stat. §518.551.5).

INCOME SHARES MODEL

The income shares model was developed by the staff of the Child Support Guidelines Project, which was funded by the U.S. Office of Child Support Enforcement and administered by the National Center for State Courts. It utilizes several concepts from the earlier Washington (State) Uniform Child Support Guidelines, but diverges in basing its numerical parameters explicitly on a different and more recent body of economic analysis. The model is based on the concept that the child should receive the same proportion of parental income that he or she would have received if the parents lived together. A basic child support obligation is computed based on the combined income of the parents (replicating total income in an intact household). This basic obligation comes from a table derived from economic estimates of child-rearing expenditures, minus average amounts for health insurance, child care, and a child's extraordinary medical expenses. The basic child support obligation is divided between the parents in proportion to their relative incomes. Prorated shares of child care and extraordinary medical expenses are added to each parent's basic obligation. If one parent has custody, the amount calculated for that parent is presumed to be spent directly on the child. For the noncustodial parent, the calculated amount establishes the level of child support.

The income shares model has been specified in both net and gross income versions, which are designed to yield approximately equivalent results. In some states, the income shares model includes separate adjustments for shared physical custody, split custody, and additional dependents. A small number of states with this model also have adjustments for children's educational expenses and visitation-related transportation expenses.

DELAWARE MELSON FORMULA

Initially developed by Judge Elwood F. Melson, Jr., for use in his own courtroom, the Melson formula has been applied statewide in Delaware since 1979, under authority of the Family Court. It was the first presumptive child support standard to be used statewide, predating the Minnesota guidelines by 14 years.

The basic application of the Melson formula can be described as follows:

Step 1: Provide for each parent's minimal self-support needs. After determining net income for each parent, a self-support reserve ("primary support allowance") is subtracted from each parent's income. This reserve, currently $550 per month in Delaware, represents the minimum amount required for an adult to meet his or her own subsistence requirements.

Step 2: Provide for children's primary support needs. After determining the amount of each parent's income needed for self-support, remaining income is applied first to the primary support needs of the children, in proportion to the parents' relative incomes. Like the self-support reserve, the primary support amount represents the minimum amount required to maintain a child at a subsistence level. In Delaware, it is currently set at $220 per month for the first child, $165 per month for each of the second and third children, and $110 per month for each additional child. Actual costs of work-related child care and extraordinary medical expenses are added to the primary support needs of the children.

Step 3: Determine standard of living allowance (SOLA). To the extent that the parents have any remaining income available after meeting both the parents' and children's primary support needs, the parent(s) contribute(s) an additional percentage of income toward child support. The percentages currently used in Delaware for the standard of living allowance are: 18 percent for one child, 27 percent for two children, 35 percent for three children, 40 percent for four children, 45 percent for five children, and 50 percent for six or more children.

A total child support obligation for each parent is determined by adding the amounts calculated in steps 2 and 3. The custodial parent is assumed to spend his or her obligation directly on the child. The noncustodial parent's share is payable as child support. The Melson formula has an adjustment for equally shared joint physical custody and for additional dependents. As previously noted, it provides separately for child care and children's extraordinary medical expenses.

IMPLEMENTATION TRENDS

As states have developed their guidelines, the predominant model that they have chosen, especially during the past five years, has been the income shares model. Overall, 31 states have income shares guidelines, 15 have percentage-of-obligor-income models, 3 follow the Melson formula, and Massachusetts and D.C. have hybrid approaches. In classifying the status of guidelines, we began with the summary of the National Center for State Courts, published in 1990 (Munsterman et al. 1990). Since publication of this report, North Carolina has switched from a Wisconsin-type approach to an income shares model, and California has adopted a unitary income shares model to replace its two-tiered structure with a percentage-based statewide standard. In addition, as opposed to the National Center for State Courts' categorization, we classify Connecticut, New Hampshire, and New York as percentage models instead of income shares states. Although their worksheets appear to count custodial parent income, inclusion of such income has no mathematical effect on the support order calculation.[3] The status of guidelines is far from static since they are periodically reviewed and modified by the states—in many cases more frequently than the four-year interval mandated by the Family Support Act.

Of the 15 states with percentage-of-obligor-income guidelines, four states besides Wisconsin use gross income percentages: Georgia, Mississippi, Nevada, and New York. Of these, only New York follows the Wisconsin percentages, but its guideline has other features that differ considerably from the structure of the Wisconsin model. Ten states use percentages of net income: Alaska, Arkansas, Connecticut, Illinois, Minnesota, New Hampshire, North Dakota, Tennessee, Texas, and Wyoming. Of this group, few share the same percentages for determination of child support.

Of the 31 states with income shares guidelines, approximately 25 use the economic data developed under the Child Support Guidelines Project to compute their basic child support obligations (total child support excluding health insurance, work-related child care costs, and extraordinary medical expenses). These figures are, in turn, derived from Thomas Espenshade's *Investing in Children* (1984).[4] About 6 states have used other sources of economic data to derive the guidelines schedule.

Delaware, Hawaii, and West Virginia have adopted the Melson formula. Of the remaining jurisdictions, Massachusetts and D.C. use a hybrid approach, combining elements of the percentage and income shares models. The Massachusetts and D.C. guidelines are primarily based on percentages of obligor gross income. However, custodial parent income is counted in the calculation and reduces the child support amount—to the extent that gross custodial parent income exceeds $15,000 per year in Massachusetts or, in D.C., $16,500 per year if there is one child plus $2,000 per year for each additional child.

With the exception of the Delaware Melson formula, most of the earlier presumptive guidelines were percentage models (e.g., those of Illinois, Minnesota, and Wisconsin). Following development of the income shares model in 1985, a majority of states used that approach in developing their own guidelines. There are several reasons for this trend.[5] First, there was powerful sentiment that guidelines based on income of both parents would be perceived as more fair than guidelines based only on the obligor's income. Proponents of the percentage model argue that *both* parents are assumed to contribute to a child's upbringing in the same proportion as the obligor. Although this is a strong argument on the theoretical level, it is not convincing in practice. Without figuring custodial parent income overtly into the calculation, the noncustodial parent perceives that child support is based on noncustodial parent income alone.

Second, there was considerable appeal in having child support guidelines that are based directly on economic estimates of child-rearing expenditures. Although most states have understood that any single source of such data has weaknesses, they prefer that the guidelines be grounded in a credible body of research.

Third, many states perceived that application of the income shares model would be more equitable because it considers a broader range of variables. The most important of these are work-related child care expenses and children's extraordinary medical expenses, but the model also provides adjustments for shared and split custody, additional dependents, and other factors.

Fourth, percentage guidelines based on gross income were perceived to be unfair because they increase the proportion of aftertax income allocated to child support as income increases.

On the other hand, percentage guidelines have a considerable advantage over income shares (and Melson), in that they are simpler. This makes them easier to learn, easier to explain to the public, easier to automate, and less prone to erroneous calculations. Some IV-D agencies have found this to be a particularly compelling justification for adopting or keeping a percentage model. As guidelines are being used more often for modification of child support orders, as well as their establishment, simplicity of application becomes even more desirable.[6]

The Delaware Melson formula has substantial appeal based on its internal logic, its use of both parents' incomes, and its adjustments for a wide range of factors. That more states failed to adopt the Melson formula stems from the perception that it is the most complex of the three approaches, and that it gives results similar to income shares but is more difficult to apply. In 1990, Delaware made major changes to the Melson formula that reduced the number of variables considered, updated the economic parameters, and simplified the forms

(Del. Fam. Ct. Civil Rule 52[c]). The net effect has been a substantial streamlining of the formula, resulting in easier application.[7]

Evidence Concerning Impact of Guidelines

ACCEPTANCE AND USAGE

As yet, few empirical studies have directly assessed the level of acceptance and usage of child support guidelines. Anecdotally, however, based on my informal interviews with dozens of judges, attorneys, advocates, and child support administrators nationwide, the level of acceptance and usage of child support guidelines is high. Judges and hearing officers who frequently deviate from guidelines calculations seem to be exceptions. At least in contested hearings, judges and hearing officers appear to apply guidelines routinely and to allow the presumptive calculation to be rebutted only rarely. In fact, the most frequent complaint about judicial behavior with respect to child support guidelines is that judges and hearing officers follow the guidelines too rigidly, applying them in case after case in lockstep fashion even when deviations might be appropriate.

There was, of course, some initial judicial resistance to use of child support guidelines, but this resistance seems to have evaporated quickly. Guidelines are perceived to have a high degree of public acceptance, and they take judges "off the hook" by ascribing ordered child support amounts to impersonal legal authority. Many judges supported guidelines from the beginning as bringing needed structure to establishment of child support levels. Within the bar, guidelines have gained acceptance because they have provided a consistent framework for resolving an issue where previously there had been none. Guidelines provide a basis for settlement, or at worst, a starting point for negotiation and litigation. Complaints from attorneys tend to center not on the guidelines' existence but on their perceived rigidity, excessive simplicity (depending on the type of guideline), and inability to address high-income cases.

For the public, guidelines have brought benefits of perceived predictability and consistency of treatment. In public testimony in at least two states (Colorado and Minnesota), whereas few custodial parents have complained about the levels of support mandated by guidelines, noncustodial parents have strongly protested that the award levels mandated by guidelines are too high. Because of this noncustodial parent resistance, award levels resulting from the guidelines remain a volatile political issue, as are issues around credits for additional dependents, visitation, and shared custody. This political sentiment appears to have stimulated little organized resistance to guidelines themselves, but rather to their form and level.

As required, guidelines are routinely used by child support agencies in negotiating stipulations and formulating recommendations for orders. Typically, but not in all states, child support staff are not permitted to deviate from the guidelines, but must refer cases to a hearing if a deviation is sought.

There may be a relationship between the type of guideline and the extent of deviation. Because percentage guidelines take into account fewer factors, deviations may be more common than for income shares or Melson guidelines. In a Wisconsin study based on court data from 20 Wisconsin counties, guidelines were followed without deviation only in an estimated 64 percent of cases. The most common reasons cited for deviation were low obligor income; shared or split custody, or extensive visitation; and agreement of the parties. Deviations were also more common for paternity than divorce cases. Compliance with the percentage standard seemed to be increasing over time, however (Melli and Bartfeld 1991).

A much higher rate of compliance was reported in the Delaware Child Support Modification Project, where 83 percent of the modifications were consistent with the child support guidelines (Bishop 1992). Whereas deviations were recorded for only 13 percent of AFDC cases, they occurred in 19 percent of non-AFDC cases, where the non-AFDC obligee could agree to terms without agency approval. Several factors could be affecting this Delaware result. Since the IV-D agency was involved in all of these modifications, compliance with guidelines could be higher than in non–IV-D cases. On the other hand, since most cases are resolved in a mediation setting, Delaware might have a higher deviation rate than in other states where mediation is not mandatory in child support actions.

In addition, the lower deviation rate in Delaware may reflect Wisconsin's use of a simpler percentage model relative to other, more comprehensive, types of guidelines (e.g., income shares or Melson). For example, the incorporation of "self-support reserves" into income shares and Melson guidelines may reduce the incidence of deviations for low-income obligors. The frequency of deviations for shared custody and extensive visitation was somewhat puzzling in Wisconsin, since that state's standard has a formula adjustment for these situations. Guidelines with formula adjustments for nontraditional custody should be expected to have fewer deviations than guidelines without such adjustments.

States are required to evaluate the extent of, and reasons for, deviations from guidelines under new implementing regulations for the Family Support Act (45 CFR 302.56). This requirement applies to the reviews of child support guidelines that states must conduct at least every four years under the provisions of the act.

LEVELS AND CONSISTENCY OF ORDERS

There is limited and somewhat mixed evidence on the effects of child support guidelines on levels and consistency of child support orders. A pre/post study by the Center for Policy Research (1989) found that implementation of child support guidelines increased average child support awards by 5 percent in Colorado, 16 percent in Illinois, and 28 percent in Hawaii. It also found that the estimated increase in Illinois was questionable because it was associated with increases in employment and earnings. These increases are somewhat lower than might otherwise have been expected. This study also found that guidelines increased the level of uniformity of orders in some types of cases, but not in others. However, there appeared to be strong judicial and attorney support for guidelines in those states, based on survey data.

Pre/post studies of the impact of guidelines on the levels of awards have also been conducted by at least two states. In Vermont, a survey of child support orders in divorce cases estimated that guidelines increased awards by an average of 23.6 percent. The survey compared child support order levels immediately preceding implementation of child support guidelines with order levels following implementation (Vermont Agency of Human Services 1989). And in a pre-post comparison of state child support orders, the New Jersey Administrative Office of the Courts (1987) found that child support orders increased by 29.9 percent for one child and by 34.5 percent for two children for parents with combined net income of $0–$600 per week. These state-conducted studies provide estimated increases in child support orders that are generally higher than the estimates by the Center for Policy Research (1989). Anecdotally, there is also widespread belief among judicial and child support administrative officials that child support awards have significantly increased under child support guidelines in virtually all states.

An econometric study by Garfinkel, Oellerich, and Robins (1991) estimated a significant impact of guidelines on awards. Using Current

Population Survey data on child support, this study asserted that average child support awards would have increased 77–88 percent nationally if the 1985 awards had been set based on one of the three types of guidelines (income shares, Melson, or percentage). This result includes the impact of updating older awards to current levels, as well as of applying guidelines to new awards. However, the authors suggested that half or more of the estimated impact of guidelines on awards results from use of guidelines rather than an updating effect. Although any such finding assumes that guidelines would be universally applied, the study concluded that guidelines are likely to have had a much larger impact on levels of child support orders than were found in the previously cited Center for Policy Research study (1989).

Additional evidence that guidelines may have resulted in major increases in child support awards can be derived from the biannual Census Bureau studies of child support based on the Current Population Survey. From 1978 through 1985, the constant-dollar value of average child support awards declined steadily, from $3,680 to $2,877. However, by 1987, when many states had implemented child support guidelines, the value had increased to $3,293, and those gains were retained in 1989.[8] These results are only suggestive, especially since they pertain to the entire stock of orders in those years rather than only new ones, but it does seem reasonable to ascribe at least part of the post-1985 increase in the value of child support orders to the impact of child support guidelines.

Issues for Further Development of Guidelines

Although guidelines are widely accepted, numerous issues arise concerning their continued evolution. Most of these relate to the appropriateness of guidelines in specified situations, but others involve broader policy issues such as the adequacy of research data underlying the guidelines and the potential for national guidelines. The following is not intended to be an exhaustive review of such issues, but, rather, a brief description of several that arise most frequently and have the broadest ramifications.

QUALITY OF RESEARCH DATA ON CHILD-REARING EXPENDITURES

To one degree or another, all of the models for child support guidelines are linked to estimates of child-rearing expenditures. Although the income shares model is the only one that directly uses estimates of child-rearing expenditures in the child support calculation, the percentages used in various versions of the percentage model, and even the Melson formula parameters, are justified on the basis of economic research on child-rearing costs. However, there is no consensus among economists on the most valid theoretical model to use in deriving estimates of child-rearing expenditures. Moreover, use of alternative models yields widely divergent estimates of the percentages of parental income or consumption allocated to children.[9] Finally, whereas the U.S. Department of Health and Human Services funded at least six studies of child-rearing costs based on the 1972–73 Consumer Expenditure Survey, so far only one such study has been funded using Consumer Expenditure Survey data from the 1980s. More theoretical and applied research on this issue is needed to enhance the perceived validity of child support guidelines.

ADDITIONAL DEPENDENTS

Guidelines have been designed initially to address situations in which there is only one set of children. As guidelines have been applied in the real world, however, courts and child support agencies have frequently encountered more complex situations involving additional dependents of one or both parents. Apparently the incidence of multiple groups of children for a given set of parents is rather high. A recent American Bar Association monograph on the subject summarized relevant demographic research as follows: "An estimated 75 percent of divorced persons remarry, most within a few years of their divorce. . . . Data collected by the National Center for Health Statistics, for example, showed that . . . 88 percent [of remarried men] had or expected either new biological children, or stepchildren, or both" (Takas 1991: 2–3). The great majority of guidelines provide for a deduction from the payor's income for a preexisting child support obligation. A much more controversial issue is whether guidelines should provide credit for an obligor's subsequent children.

Traditionally courts have taken a "first families first" approach toward child support in which the needs of subsequent dependents are normally disregarded in computing child support obligations for earlier children. Under this philosophy, the obligor knows that obligations must be met for the existing children when deciding to have more dependents, so the addition of later-born dependents should not serve as grounds for reducing a support obligation to earlier ones. Contrary to the "first families first" approach is an "equal treatment" concept, which holds that children's interests should be given equal weight regardless of birth order or family group.[10]

State guidelines have generally followed predominant case law and have not given credit for additional dependents. However, more states are beginning to address this issue as there is growing concern about the consequences of failing to recognize the needs of additional dependents, particularly in modification situations. According to Takas (1991: 14–15), guidelines in 10 states plus the District of Columbia have adjustments that give credit for additional dependents. There are several mechanisms for providing credit, including prorating and imputing a child support order that is deducted from obligor income.

One approach used in Colorado and several other states attempts to strike a balance between the needs of earlier-born and later-born children. Colorado has an imputed child support order type of adjustment, but it can be applied only under the following conditions: (1) the adjustment cannot be used to reduce any preexisting child support order; (2) the adjustment can be used for initial orders when an obligor or obligee is directly supporting earlier-born dependents in his or her current household; and (3) the adjustment can be used to limit the amount of an upward modification or, in the case of additional dependents of an obligee, to increase the amount of an upward modification (C.R.S. §14-10-115).

The issue of additional dependents is emotion-laden and complex. It will arise even more frequently in the context of review and modification processes.

SHARED CUSTODY AND VISITATION

One issue that continues to perplex many states is the appropriate treatment of nontraditional custody situations, especially shared physical custody, but also split custody. These situations tend to arise with some frequency, but only some states address them through their guidelines. Designing a suitable adjustment for these situations raises complex issues, given an absence of data concerning the effects of nontraditional custody arrangements on allocation of child-rearing costs.

For shared physical custody, many states assume that some child-rearing costs are duplicated, and increase the shared child support allocation accordingly. Most states also define a time-sharing threshold that must be reached to qualify for the adjustment, usually based on a percentage of overnight physical custody exceeding 25, 30, or 35 percent. Most states with adjustments also base child support on a balancing of the parental income against parental time devoted to child custody. But designs of shared custody adjustments often result in compromises that cause parents to "game" visitation levels to reach or avoid the threshold, and disagreements remain about appropriate support levels in such situations. Split-custody adjustments involve some of the same considerations concerning duplicated costs, but are otherwise simpler to design.

As the full impact of child support guidelines is being felt, there is also growing pressure to build in credit for the noncustodial parent's visitation costs. Most states do not give credit for such costs (although a few specifically "assume" that routine visitation expenses have been considered), even though routinely ordered visitation may place the child with the noncustodial parent as much as 20 to 25 percent of the time. Until recently, California was one of the few states that automatically built in a credit for "normal" visitation, and actually increased the support obligation if there was no visitation. But that state recently eliminated this provision when it found that it caused child support orders in routine visitation situations to be well below those of most other states.[11]

From a national policy perspective, these issues are significant only in that many states are grappling with them as they carry out the periodic reviews of guidelines mandated by the Family Support Act. Most states relied heavily on federally sponsored research and technical assistance in their initial development of child support guidelines. Thus, there is a continuing demand by states for research and assistance in defining and analyzing options for commonly encountered issues. Limited but ongoing federal research in this area would be useful in helping states continue development of their guidelines so that they can be applied to a broader array of commonly encountered situations and achieve more equitable results.

SHOULD THERE BE A NATIONAL GUIDELINE?

Now that all states have child support guidelines, at least some support is being generated for adoption of a single national guideline, as in the Congressmen Thomas Downey and Henry Hyde proposal to federalize administration of child support enforcement. There are three primary reasons for the interest in a national guideline. First, there is concern over the variability in levels of child support from state to state. Second, interstate child support processing would be facilitated by a national guideline. Third, if a federally funded assured child support benefit were provided, as proposed by Downey-Hyde and others, a national guideline would ensure that actual awards were set at adequate levels relative to the assured benefit.

The advent of state child support guidelines has presumably reduced the variation in child support awards that previously existed. Since almost all states follow one of the three basic models, there is at least increased consistency among states with similar models. The three basic models still give divergent results in some situations, although their outcomes tend to be similar for "typical" cases in the low to moderate income range where there are common ratios of custodial to noncustodial parent income. Outside this fairly narrow band of incomes, the results tend to be more disparate, as when other common circumstances occur such as significant child care expenses or children's extraordinary medical expenses.

An obvious concern arising with a national guideline relates to the possible need to adjust for geographic economic differentials. However, it is interesting that there is no discernible geographic pattern in the use of existing guidelines models. As mentioned earlier, gross income percentages are used in New York, Georgia, Mississippi, and Nevada, as well as Wisconsin. Similarly, the income shares model is used, with only marginal adjustments, in a widely dispersed group of states, including Washington, Colorado, Missouri, Ohio, Vermont, New Jersey, South Carolina, Louisiana, and Arizona. States with the lowest guidelines tend to be those with one of the early percentage models, such as Illinois and Texas, or states where the legislature deliberately lowered established parameters, such as Arkansas and Hawaii. States with the highest guidelines are among the wealthier ones such as Connecticut and Massachusetts, but there is no obvious geographic pattern to the values of child support others yielded by guidelines for given levels of income. This lack of geographic specificity suggests that regional differences in economic conditions might not pose a significant obstacle to a national guideline.

Perhaps a more weighty obstacle to a national guideline, however, is the firm grounding of existing guidelines in the case law, legal traditions, and political environment of each state. Although the states have tended to use one of the national models as their basic framework, they have each made a multitude of adjustments. The states' guidelines have all emerged from a delicate balancing process in which the final form reflects how the state has traditionally dealt with low-income obligors, for example, or the legal provisions for shared custody, or whether there is a high incidence of private schooling, or whether there are significant concerns about additional dependents. Such considerations have affected, for example, whether states have incorporated some concept of a self-support reserve into their guidelines, whether there is a shared custody adjustment, whether there is a provision for children's educational expenses, and whether they have designed an additional dependents adjustment.

Promulgating a national guideline would require overriding 54 balancing acts as well as 54 sets of case law that have been accumulating already around the existing guidelines. Family law has traditionally been a state preserve. Although that preserve has been greatly eroded by the continuing stream of federal child support mandates (even affecting non–IV-D cases), a national guideline would go far beyond previous federal mandates in superseding what have previously been state prerogatives. Perhaps a national guideline makes most sense in the context of a federalized child support system. In the absence of such a revolutionary change, the justifications for a national guideline do not yet appear to be compelling.

REVIEW AND MODIFICATIONS

The Family Support Act of 1988 added requirements for child support agencies to perform systematic reviews of child support orders every three years, beginning in 1993. The review and adjustment process includes all AFDC cases unless the state determines that the review would not be in the best interests of the child. It also includes non-AFDC IV-D cases who request a review.

Prior to the Family Support Act, there had been little field experience with systematic review and modification procedures. However, anticipating the need to develop and test procedures for periodic review and modification of child support orders, the federal Office of Child Support Enforcement (OCSE) funded a two-year demonstration project in Oregon, beginning October 1, 1988. The Oregon Child Support Updating Project was later extended for a third year to gather additional information on the effects of modifications on obligor compliance and on welfare dependency. In addition, in accordance with the Family Support Act, the OCSE funded four demonstration projects in Colorado, Delaware, Florida, and Illinois, which began in August or September 1989 for two-year terms.

These five projects tested an array of review and modification procedures in diverse geographic, demographic, programmatic, and adjudicatory environments (see Williams et al. 1989; and Bishop et al. 1990). Following is a brief summary of some of the more important design characteristics of the five projects.

Types of cases. All of the projects tested review and modification procedures for both AFDC and non–AFDC IV-D cases.

Adjudicatory process. Oregon tested modifications using both administrative and judicial processes. Colorado used a judicial process, but also performed a limited test of an administratively based, expedited modification procedure that was legislatively authorized especially for the project counties. Delaware tested a court-based review and modification process that relied heavily on the Family Court's medication procedure. Florida and Illinois relied on traditional judicial processes.

Automated support. All states developed enhanced automated support for case selection and status tracking. In addition, Oregon, Delaware, and Illinois sought to test semiautomated reviews, in which the computer used available earnings information (from employment security files) to perform an initial guidelines calculation that was to be the basis for a proposed order. Oregon, Colorado, and Delaware also developed enhanced automated capability for guidelines calculation and document generation.

Geographic scope. Delaware tested review and modification procedures statewide. Oregon selected a statewide sample of orders to be modified administratively and a nine-county sample of orders to be modified judicially. Colorado operated the demonstration project in five Front Range counties and one western slope county. Florida conducted the demonstration in two counties. Illinois selected its largest sample from Cook County and also operated the project in one downstate judicial district.

Research design. Oregon conducted a pre-post evaluation with cases randomly selected and assigned to one of four treatment groups: (1) judicial orders, simulated guidelines calculation (semiautomated review); (2) administrative orders, simulated guidelines calculation; (3) judicial orders, no simulated calculation; and (4) administrative orders, no simulated guidelines calculation. Colorado implemented an experimental design with a single treatment group. Delaware implemented a pre-post design with four treatment groups: (1) mediation process, simulated guidelines calculation; (2) stipulation process (attempted settlement prior to court involvement); simulated guidelines calculation; (3) mediation process, no simulation; and (4) stipulation process, no simulation. Florida had a pre-post design

with a single treatment group. Illinois implemented an experimental
design, with a single treatment group featuring a semiautomated review.

Findings from the Demonstration Projects

LOW MODIFICATION RATE

One of the most significant findings from the demonstration projects
is the low modification rate of the cases selected for review. In the
Oregon demonstration, the rate of completed modifications was 22
percent for AFDC cases and 8 percent for non-AFDC cases (Price and
Venohr 1991: 7–9). For AFDC cases, the low completion rate resulted
mostly from a large proportion of cases unsuitable for modification:
either they were inappropriately selected (for example, the youngest
child verged on emancipation), the obligor (or obligee) could not
be located, the AFDC case was closed, or there was a good-cause
exemption. In a substantial proportion of cases, the agency did not
seek a modification following the review: in 18 percent of the cases,
no change was indicated, and in another 15 percent, a downward
modification was indicated, but the obligor did not authorize a modification and therefore the agency did not proceed.

In three of the four other states, modification rates for AFDC cases
with completed processing were comparable or slightly higher than
in Oregon: 17 percent in Colorado, 25 percent in Delaware, and 21
percent in Illinois. Reasons for noncompletion were similar to those
for Oregon. In Florida, the rate of modification for AFDC cases was
only 4 percent, but this rate seems to be an aberration resulting from
Florida's unique project design.

For non-AFDC cases Colorado and Delaware had only slightly
higher rates of modification than Oregon: 10 percent and 9 percent of
completed cases, respectively. Florida and Illinois had considerably
lower non-AFDC modification rates: 4 percent and 5 percent of completed cases, respectively. For non-AFDC cases, the much-lower completion rate came about primarily because few obligees requested a
review. In follow-up interviews with obligees, Oregon found there
were two reasons for obligees' unwillingness to request a review. If
the obligor was paying, the obligee was usually unwilling to "rock
the boat." If the obligor was not paying, the obligee saw no sense in
requesting a review (Price et al. 1991: 66–70). Similar findings came
from surveys of obligees in the other four states (Bishop 1992:
chap. 6). There was no evidence that enforcing the order through

income withholding affected the propensity of the obligee to make such a request (although cases under income withholding were more likely to be successfully modified if a review was initiated). However, obligees in Oregon were four times as likely to request a review if they had been given results from a preliminary calculation based on employment security data showing that the review was likely to result in an upward modification (Price and Venohr 1991: 29–32). This evidence suggests that the possibility of a downward modification may have been more of an inhibiting factor than suggested in the survey results, and that presenting obligees with a reliable predictor of ultimate results may constitute an important incentive for their participation in the process.

MODIFICATION OUTCOMES

Of orders modified in Oregon, 83 percent were upward and 17 percent downward. The net result was a 63 percent increase in levels of orders that were modified (Price and Venohr 1991: 15–16). There was also a large increase in orders for obligors to provide health insurance coverage. Ninety-six percent had such orders after modification, compared with 33 percent of AFDC orders and less than 30 percent of non-AFDC orders prior to modification (Price et al. 1991: 75–76).

Although the Colorado and Delaware demonstration projects had average increases in the same range as Oregon (67 percent and 60 percent, respectively), Florida and Illinois evidenced even larger increases in modified orders than in Oregon (97 percent and 144 percent, respectively). Smaller fractions of modifications were downward in the other four states than in Oregon: 13 percent in Delaware, 7 percent in Colorado, 1 percent in Illinois, and none in Florida (Bishop 1992: exhibits V-28, V-33). Florida and Illinois, and to a lesser extent Colorado, were more reluctant to initiate downward modifications than was Oregon. The low number of downward modifications in Florida and Illinois contributed to their larger average increases.

The increases recorded in Colorado, Delaware, Florida, and Illinois greatly exceeded the increases that would have occurred had the orders been subject instead to a consumer price index (CPI) adjustment. In Colorado, CPI adjustments would have increased the orders an average of 41 percent, compared with 67 percent actually measured; in Delaware, CPI adjustments would have resulted in an average increase of 27 percent, compared with an actual increase of 60 percent; in Florida, the average CPI increase of 36 percent was dramatically lower than the actual increase of 97 percent; and in Illinois, CPI adjustments would have yielded an average increase of 30 percent, compared with an increase through guidelines-based adjustments of 114 percent (Bishop 1992: 185–86). These results overstate the increases that would have been obtained from CPI adjustments, since there would normally be a provision (as in Minnesota) to limit the adjustments to actual earnings increases by obligors.

Congress rejected a CPI-type of adjustment because it would not be equitable for slower increases in obligor income, or in cases where obligor income decreased; because it would not increase awards fast enough if obligor income increased faster than the CPI; and because it would not adjust for changes in factors such as child care and children's extraordinary medical expenses, where addressed by the original guidelines. Evidence form the demonstrations seems to confirm that CPI adjustments are an imprecise method for updating orders. However, as used in Minnesota, CPI adjustments do seem to have the potential for moving most orders upward at the rate of inflation with much less effort than a full review, while still preserving rights of obligors to limit such adjustments if their earnings have not grown apace. Perhaps, then, it is appropriate to preserve CPI-based adjustments as one updating tool, while recognizing that periodic readjustment relative to guidelines may still be necessary to achieve equitable results for all parties.

PROCESSING TIME

The average number of days required to complete the review and modification process was much longer than expected: 200 days from case selection to disposition in Oregon, well over six months (Price and Venohr 1991: 16–18). The most significant contributing factors to this processing time were the inherent complexity of the process and the need to obtain service of process. But the notice requirements of the Family Support Act, particularly the challenge notice, appear to have contributed by introducing additional dead time into the process. Data from the other four projects show almost identical average results: 196 days from selection to modification (Bishop 1992: 165). Because of the time required to process modifications, none of the projects achieved steady-state operations within the two years allowed for the demonstrations.

OBLIGOR COMPLIANCE

There has been longstanding concern that periodic review and modifications would adversely affect obligor compliance. Data from all five projects suggest that this concern may have been exaggerated. Research from the Oregon project measured obligor compliance with child support orders during the 12 months following modification compared with obligor compliance during the 12 months prior to modification. For obligors whose child support orders were modified upward, compliance did indeed decrease: from 78 percent of child support due prior to modification to 68 percent afterward. Significantly, for obligors whose child support orders were modified downward, compliance *increased*: from 37 percent prior to modification to 48 percent afterward. Thus, overall compliance diminished from 70 percent to 64 percent. Compliance was related to the mode of modification. Compliance was virtually unaffected for obligors who consented to the changed order, it dropped most for those whose order was modified in a default hearing, and it dropped somewhat less for orders modified in an administrative or judicial hearing.

Data from the Oregon project reinforce other findings that wage withholding has limitations as an enforcement remedy. Oregon initiated wage withholding in only 58 percent of modified orders. Moreover, in only 55 percent of those cases was wage withholding still in effect a year after it was initiated (Price and Venohr 1991: 33–50).

Findings on compliance from the other four projects cover a shorter period because the projects lasted only two years. Compliance with orders was calculated for those relatively few cases with at least six months of payment data. For these cases, the average compliance rate across the four projects was unchanged: 65 percent before and after modification. The average compliance rate for AFDC cases rose slightly, from 59 percent to 62 percent, while average compliance rates for non-AFDC cases fell slightly, from 73 percent to 71 percent. Average compliance rates increased in Colorado and Delaware, and decreased in Florida and Illinois (Bishop 1992: 202–4).

PUBLIC DEPENDENCY

Research from the five projects suggests that there likely is a positive, although small, impact of review and modifications on reducing public dependency. In Colorado, Delaware, Florida, and Illinois, the amounts of modified AFDC orders exceeded the AFDC payment plus $50 in an average of 12 percent of modified orders; actual payments exceeded the AFDC payment plus $50 in an average of 5 percent of modified orders (Bishop 1992: 220–23). These figures do not reflect other sources of income. Evidence from these four states on AFDC exit and reentry rates is inconclusive because of the limited duration of project operations.

In Oregon, the exit rate from AFDC was 39 percent for cases where the child support order had been modified, within a year of the modification. In contrast, the exit rate from AFDC was only 22 percent for cases selected for review, but in which the order was not modified. Also of interest, the reactivation rate for former AFDC cases whose orders were modified was only 18 percent, compared with 36 percent for former AFDC cases whose orders were selected for review but not modified. Comparisons of exit and reactivation rates for Food Stamps and Medicaid recipients yielded similar findings. These comparisons must be interpreted with caution because of the absence of a control group, but they suggest that the review and modification process has the potential to make a meaningful contribution to self-sufficiency of AFDC recipients (Price and Venohr 1991: 51–61).

Additional data suggest that the addition of medical support orders in the review and modification process can significantly increase the availability of medical insurance for the affected children. In Oregon, 96 percent of orders had medical support provisions after modification, compared with 33 percent of AFDC orders and 30 percent of non-AFDC orders prior to modification. Unfortunately, not all of these medical support orders translate into actual medical coverage. However, the proportion of obligors carrying medical insurance for the children, as known by the Medicaid agency, increased from 9 percent to 43 percent 12 months after modification, an even more dramatic increase than the proportion with medical support provisions. In the other four states, cases with medical support provisions increased from 10–11 percent prior to modification, up to 42–69 percent after modification (Bishop 1992: 174–76). No evidence is available from those states on the proportion of cases actually carrying medical insurance.

COST-EFFECTIVENESS

The most complete demonstration project data on cost-effectiveness of review and modification come from Oregon. Based on two years of operation and actual obligor payment patterns for 12 months after modification, the estimated benefit-cost ratio in steady-state operations was 3.31 overall, 4.82 for Oregon, and 2.56 for the federal government. These data suggest that the process is quite cost-effective, even when measured narrowly on the basis of additional AFDC reimbursements gained, and ignoring (for inability to measure) any avoided costs or reductions in Medicaid and Food Stamp expenditures (Price and Venohr 1991: 63–71).[12]

The costs are higher than Oregon would have expected prior to implementing the project. The review and modification process is lengthy and labor-intensive. As already discussed, the modification rate is lower than expected, and it is more difficult than anticipated to obtain information from obligors and obligees. Nevertheless, the benefits are high, even when narrowly measured, and even though the project did not ever seem to reach steady-state because of the long processing pipeline. Paradoxically, the low request rate for reviews by non-AFDC obligees increased the cost-effectiveness of the review and modification procedure. Because there were so few non-AFDC reviews to perform, the project staff focused their efforts on AFDC cases, from which the direct governmental benefits are derived.

Review and Modification: Implementation Issues

Oregon has proceeded to implement a review and modification process statewide for IV-D cases, and Delaware is proceeding with statewide implementation at least for IV-D cases. I am not aware of any systematic survey of other states' progress with this requirement, but states seem to be proceeding slowly pending resolution of a regulatory issue concerning the deadline for completing AFDC reviews.

The most daunting issue for states is the increased resources required to perform the mandated review and modification process. Based on Delaware's experience in the demonstration project, the state has estimated that it will need a 13 percent increase in IV-D staff positions to meet Family Support Act requirements (Curley 1991). Using data from the demonstration projects, the Arizona Child Support Enforcement Administration has estimated that it will need an 11 percent increase in staff. On the other hand, discussions with Oregon officials suggest that resource demands in that state have declined as the agency has improved its position on the learning curve and continued to streamline the review and modification process. The impact on judicial time and other court resources in all states is less than might have been feared, because of the low modification completion rate. The apparent cost-effectiveness of the process will help justify acquiring additional resources needed for review and modification, but implementing the mandated version of the process will still be a challenge, particularly in view of the difficult fiscal situations of many states.

A continuing issue is the Family Support Act's requirement that states initiate downward, as well as upward, modifications—as indicated by application of the guidelines. After expressing initial resistance, Oregon staff became comfortable with this aspect of the process, finding that it improved their credibility with obligors and the courts. The increased compliance of obligors receiving downward modifications is also a positive result. But many states have statutes and procedures that establish a legal attorney-client relationship between public attorneys and IV-D obligees. Such states will have to make major adjustments in staff attitudes, as well as in statutes, procedures, and legal arrangements to implement this requirement successfully.

At least one state—Wisconsin—has a statute specifying that child support can be expressed as a percentage of income. This seems to offer the appealing prospect of a self-modifying order. Indeed, Bartfeld and Garfinkel (1992) estimated, using data from 21 counties, that obligations in Wisconsin would increase by about 23 percent over three years if fixed-dollar orders had been expressed in percentage terms. Because enforcement of percentage orders is more difficult, compliance rates were lower by more than 20 percent, apparently offsetting much of the increased obligation. But an econometric analysis corrected for differences in the types of orders (percentage-expressed orders seemed to be used more frequently for cases with low and variable income) yielded an estimate that percentage orders may result in payment increases of 51 percent. The percentage-expressed option is apparently used only infrequently in Wisconsin—for an estimated 17 percent of cases—because the unpredictability of the payment stream is upsetting to obligees, and because this order form poses complications for enforcement (Bartfeld and Garfinkel 1992).

An additional drawback of percentage orders is that they appear not to comply with the federal Bradley Amendment provisions (P.L. 99-509) requiring that, by operation of law, child support arrears must automatically accrue as judgments such that they can be afforded full faith and credit. For child support orders to comply with this provision, a corollary is that they must be expressed as a sum-certain so that, as unpaid installments accrue, there is no ambiguity concerning the amount of the arrearage. Percentage orders cannot be expressed as a sum-certain because the unpaid amount must be determined through further investigation. Hence, it appears under existing federal law that percentage orders are not an allowable mechanism for ongoing modification.

For routine modifications to become a reality beyond the AFDC population, it is apparent that a change in public expectations is required. The lack of interest in seeking a modification seems to reflect the common expectation, contrary to the legal theory of a court's continuing jurisdiction, that child support orders are more akin to fixed-rate mortgages than to obligations subject to ongoing readjustment. Perhaps the reaction evinced thus far will shift as parents become more used to the concept and have time to think about the need for modification in the intervening three years before another review. Alternatively, more public education may be needed, especially at the time the initial order is established, to instill an awareness of the child's and the parents' stake in an order that is periodically adjusted to maintain its fairness and equity. Certainly the initial experience raises a question as to how much effort the IV-D agencies should invest in encouraging non-AFDC obligees (and obligors) to request a review, or whether they should not make any special educational efforts and simply serve the presumedly small minority of such cases who are motivated to make the request.

The Family Support Act requires the secretary of the Department of Health and Human Services to "conduct and complete a study to determine the impact on child support awards and the courts of requiring each State to periodically review all child support orders in effect in the State" (§103[d]). As expressed in this statutory language, the issue is whether the federal government should mandate a periodic review and modification process for non–IV-D cases. Although such a requirement, if successfully implemented, could be expected to bring about major improvements in the adequacy and equity of non–IV-D child support orders, there seems no practical way to carry it out. It is clear from the demonstration projects that reviews and modification require substantial administrative effort. Locating parents, sending the proper notices, obtaining financial and other relevant information, calculating an accurate guidelines amount, and pursuing legal action are labor-intensive and time-consuming activities. They require proper organization and well-trained staff, with ample automated support, to perform efficiently and effectively. Courts are not administrative agencies. With the exception of those few states where the courts handle most IV-D functions, courts are not equipped to perform the types of duties required to conduct reviews and modifications, except for adjudicating the legal modification action.

Another problem is that the whereabouts of non–IV-D obligors and obligees are not known in most states, unless they are in a jurisdiction requiring payment through a public entity. Thus, in the great majority of states, there would be no way of identifying child support obligors and obligees over which the courts might still have jurisdiction. It might be feasible to require all non–IV-D cases coming before the court for enforcement action to be reviewed if the orders are more than three years old, but it would be awkward for the court to initiate such a procedure. It would also be possible to require all parties to new and modified orders to exchange information and appear before the court every three years for a review, but it is questionable whether all but a few courts would have the means to enforce such a requirement.

An administrative agency could perform the functions required for review and modification of child support in non–IV-D cases; this would be an appropriate executive branch function. The agency of choice for this responsibility, of course, would be the IV-D agency. If a IV-D agency would assume such a responsibility, then it would make sense for the cases to be converted to IV-D status so they could be monitored for enforcement purposes as well. This raises a much broader question: whether all child support cases should be publicly enforced through the IV-D program. Although some states are moving in that direction, there does not yet appear to be willingness at the federal level to cast the IV-D net so widely. Yet this appears to be the only practical mechanism for extending the review and modification requirements beyond the current target groups of AFDC and non–AFDC IV-D cases.

INCOME WITHHOLDING AND COLLECTION/
DISTRIBUTION SYSTEMS

Family Support Act Requirements for Immediate
Income Withholding

For child support agencies, immediate income withholding, as mandated by the Family Support Act, has an obvious advantage over arrearage-based withholding: agencies no longer have to wait until an arrearage occurs, then track down the obligor, give notice of impending withholding, locate an employer, and serve the income withholding order. Instead, they begin income withholding when the order is entered, at a time when the obligor's location is known, notice has been given, and better information is presumably available about the obligor's employer. Immediate income withholding thus saves considerable work for child support agencies, reduces time spans when the order cannot be enforced, and increases the probability of obtaining successful withholding. The only significant implementation issue is the incidence of good-cause exceptions. Here the attitude of judges and hearing officers is critical. In some jurisdictions, only a few such exceptions are granted in the absence of a written agreement between the parties. In other jurisdictions, judicial and administrative hearing officers are reported to be quite liberal, even excessively so, giving most obligors a first chance to comply in an arrangement that almost reverts to an arrearage-based withholding trigger.

Immediate income withholding is not a panacea for enforcement, however. First, many cases cannot be reached by income withholding because obligors are self-employed, work for cash, or work in temporary jobs. Second, many obligors have short employment spells. Once they leave a job, it can easily take agencies as long as six months to locate a new employer through the employment security wage files. In an evaluation of the Child Support Enforcement Amendments of 1984, Mathematica Policy Research found that 40 percent of the AFDC withholding spells in the sample ended within 6 months. The comparable figure for non-AFDC IV-D cases was 28 percent (Gordon et al. 1984: 20; see also chapter 3, by Gordon, in this volume).

Impact of Income Withholding on Requirements for Collection/Distribution Systems

Since enactment of the Child Support Enforcement Amendments of 1984, income withholding has become increasingly important as the primary enforcement remedy for child support. In federal fiscal year 1989, 41 percent of all IV-D child support collections were made by means of income withholding. In some states, over half of all collections were made via that mechanism. This represents a dramatic increase from the 23 percent reported in fiscal year 1986, the first year that the arrearage-based income withholding mandate took effect nationwide (U.S. Department of Health and Human Services, Office of Child Support Enforcement 1990: tables 3 and 24).

As a result of 1984–88 legislation, child support will increasingly be paid by employers through income withholding, and, particularly beginning by 1994, there will be an increasing amount of non–IV-D child support paid via income withholding. These outcomes have important implications for state collection and distribution systems for child support. First, as employers become more and more involved in child support transactions, there is a need to minimize the costs of handling these transactions and to expedite their payment to obligees. Second, as income withholding is used more often for non–IV-D cases, there is a critical need to ensure the availability of a public mechanism to collect and disburse those payments so that employers are not paying directly to individual obligees. Third, as child support collections continue to increase, and more come from employers, there is a need to utilize high-volume payment processing technologies to reduce program administrative costs. The remainder of this section discusses these issues, as well as efforts that have made to improve collection/distribution systems for child support, with special reference to income withholding.

Issues in IV-D Collections and Distribution

HIGH COST

In federal fiscal year 1989, states reported that they spent $246 million on the IV-D financial distribution process—more than 18 percent of total IV-D administrative expenditures. To place this figure in perspective, it is reported to be 59 percent more than they spent in establishing paternities, and more than half as much as they spent on the entire process of enforcing child support orders. Among the many factors contributing to this high cost are the infrequent use of advanced payment-processing technologies; the extreme complexity of the federally mandated payment distribution process, which allocates current support and arrearages between the obligee and AFDC reimbursement; duplicate payment handling by courts and IV-D agencies in many jurisdictions; and continuing lack of sufficient automation in most states for accounting and disbursement functions.

The function of receipting (recording and posting) child support is not significantly different than the receipting of credit card or utilities payments, yet only a few child support agencies avail themselves of high-volume payment-processing technologies used by commercial payment-processing centers. Typically child support payments are processed in small batches. In automated jurisdictions, payments may be entered into computer terminals (or personal computers) one payment at a time, and one payment per screen. In many county clerk's offices, payments are still manually receipted in ledger books.

In contrast, high-volume commercial payment-processing centers typically use remittance processing machines that scan encoded bills or coupons in conjunction with checks and perform numerous functions with a single pass, including recording payment; encoding, endorsing, and microfilming checks; and preparing bank deposit documents. Most facilities also use automatic letter-opening machines. Such equipment may cost from $75,000 to $100,000, or even more, but can typically process from 5,000 to 6,000 payment transactions per hour (Graham and Levy 1991).

States can lower their transaction costs by acquiring such technology, if justified by their volume, but some jurisdictions (e.g., Vermont; West Virginia; Wayne County, Mich.) are obtaining the same benefits by contracting with banks for lockbox services. Under this arrangement, payments are transmitted to lockboxes and processed by a commercial bank using high-volume receipting technology. This lowers the transaction cost for the agency, which receives a computer file of payment transactions.

Using a high-volume payment center, states may be able to use emerging electronic funds transfer (EFT) technologies to lower transaction costs further. This point is discussed more later in this section. In addition, if states are able to develop an up-to-date computer file of payment transactions, either through a central payment facility or through decentralized facilities with remote transaction entry to a central computer, they can use automated voice response technology to respond to payment status inquiries by obligees. This technology can improve service to the public by providing information on 800-number lines 24 hours a day, 7 days a week, and also achieve major savings in staff time by redirecting one of the largest sources of telephone calls to child support agencies (Graham and Levy 1991: 37–39).

Another factor contributing to high costs of the accounting and distribution function is the double handling of child support payments in many jurisdictions. In states where IV-D payments are collected by county court clerks and then forwarded to IV-D agencies, payments must be posted twice and accounted for in two locations. This duplicate handling raises costs. States such as Missouri and Nebraska are attempting to eliminate this functional redundancy by including clerk-of-court payment-processing functions in new integrated automated systems in their states (although Nebraska will establish a separate statewide automated system for court clerks that will interface with the statewide IV-D system).

With the current redundant structure, pending an automated solution, one study has estimated that it costs $8.36 per IV-D payment for collection and disbursement in Nebraska's dual clerk/IV-D agency system. In contrast, it costs an estimated $3 per IV-D payment for collection and disbursement in Iowa's central payment center operated by the IV-D agency. Iowa's estimated cost would be even lower if the center were handling the additional volume represented by non–IV-D payments. Although the payment and disbursement functions in the two states are not identical, these estimates suggest the potential for reducing collection/distribution costs through centralization and use of advanced payment-processing technologies (Levy et al. 1988; Starling et al. 1988).

An additional problem with using court clerks for child support collections is that some jurisdictions charge a payment-processing fee (referred to as "poundage" in Ohio). In Tennessee, the fee is 5 percent of child support, which is high enough to deter courts in many cases from ordering payment through the clerks.

A third factor contributing to high collection/distribution costs is the intricate set of rules on distributing child support collections. The complexity arises from the myriad decision rules for allocating arrearage payments between AFDC reimbursement and payments to the obligees. When overlaid with contingencies for multiple obligations on the part of a single noncustodial parent, and multiple orders for a single obligee—some of whom may have been on AFDC and some of whom may not—these rules constitute a logical structure of Aquinian proportions. It is beyond the scope of this chapter to describe the distribution regulations in depth. It may be worth considering whether it would be cost-effective to simplify distribution dramatically by simply counting child support collections as AFDC income in the month received.

A fourth factor contributing to high collection/distribution costs is the continuing lack of adequate automation for payments processing and accounting. This problem is being addressed by the mandated automation requirements of the Family Support Act (§123). Given the benefits of high-volume payment processing and the desirability of central state payment facilities for employers, as discussed later in this section, it would be advantageous to permit the 90 percent systems development funding to be used also for development of central payment registries, which would include non–IV-D cases. The marginal costs of extending development to non–IV-D cases would be low. Operational costs for non–IV-D payments processing would be a state responsibility and could be funded through modest transaction fees.

NEED FOR PUBLIC COLLECTION/DISBURSEMENT MECHANISM FOR ALL INCOME-WITHHOLDING PAYMENTS

Although I am not aware of any survey data concerning this issue, I believe there are numerous states in which income withholding can be ordered in private (non–IV-D) cases, with payment made directly from the employer to the obligee. This arrangement creates two difficulties for employers. First, employers must field direct inquiries from obligees concerning the status of child support payments. This might not only be uncomfortable for employers but, for large employers, could be very costly. Second, this arrangement raises the specter that employers might be hauled into court whenever there is a need to resolve a dispute about whether a payment was actually made. In a private-pay income-withholding situation, the employer is the only source of legally acceptable documentation for an obligor's child support payments. The obligor has no canceled checks and is likely to have only minimal or no documentation of the child support payment provided by the employer. Thus, the only legally acceptable way to prove payment in such a situation is to subpoena the employer to research the payment stream and appear in court to offer evidence.

Both of these difficulties place unacceptable demands on employers. Since the success of the income-withholding remedy for child support relies on employer cooperation, it is a serious matter to place the employer in the middle between the obligor and obligee. This is why a legislatively mandated Child Support Study Committee in Vermont recommended that the state establish a statewide child support payment registry through which all child support would be paid "except in cases where there is no wage withholding and the parties have agreed to direct payment (State of Vermont 1990: 12). In making the recommendation, which was enacted into law by the state legislature, the Study Committee was heavily influenced by the employer representative. One issue for consideration, then, is whether direct-pay income withholding should be prohibited. Since income withholding is a federally mandated remedy, the prohibition should perhaps be mandated federally as well.

NEED FOR EFFICIENT PAYMENT PROCESS FOR EMPLOYERS

As employers are faced with a growing number of income withholdings, it will be advantageous to minimize their transaction costs. The most important way to do this is to minimize the number of entities to which child support must be paid. Colorado has reduced the number of payment entities in the state from 63 counties to a single agency (albeit initially only for IV-D cases) when it inaugurated its central payment registry[13] Iowa channels all IV-D wage withholding payments through its IV-D Collection Services Center, even though county-court clerks handle non–IV-D direct payments. This centralized type of collections/distribution structure is most advantageous for large employers. It can greatly reduce the number of child support payment transactions they need to process, since all withholdings directed to a given source can be consolidated into a single payment.

In recent years, the Iowa-Nebraska Electronic Funds Transfer Project has pioneered in the development and testing of the use of EFT for handling employer payment of income withholding. The demonstration project was funded by the U.S. Office of Child Support Enforcement (OCSE). Through the project, Iowa and Nebraska have designed a format for enabling employers to make direct electronic deposits of child support to the Iowa Collections Services Center, and to selected county clerks in Nebraska. These electronic payments are generated as adjuncts to employers' payroll runs, essentially as a variation of direct deposit of the employee's pay. A national employer direct deposit format has been developed through a cooperative effort between OCSE and the National Automated Clearing House Association (NACHA). Payment of child support via EFT has the potential of lowering transaction costs for employers and IV-D agencies. It also has the potential for speeding up payments for employers, since they likely would forward EFT transactions at the time of payroll instead of waiting up to 10 days, as allowed by federal regulations (45 CFR 303.100 [d][ii]).

EMPLOYER REPORTING OF NEW HIRES

A serious weakness in the income-withholding process is the time required to identify employers when obligors have accrued arrearages for the first time or, more often, have changed jobs and not notified the child support agency. As discussed previously, employment spells are frequently short, especially for obligors in AFDC cases. The main tool available to IV-D agencies in locating an obligor's employer is the wage-reporting system operated in each state by the employment security agency. Employers report earnings for each employee to wage-reporting systems at the end of each calendar quarter. Because employers typically take more than a month to file reports (i.e., the 10th day of the second month after the end of the quarter), and because employment security agencies may take another month to enter, edit, and compile the reports, lags of five months or more can be encountered between the time an obligor becomes employed and the time this information is available to a IV-D agency. In that time, five months of potential payments are lost. Worse, the obligor may have changed jobs again.

Washington State and Alaska have enacted laws requiring employer reporting of new hires. In Washington, the requirement applies to large employers in certain industrial groups, which must report new hires or rehires within 35 days to the state child support office (Wash. Rev. Code §26.23.040). Washington reports that over 12,000 employers sent over 216,000 reports during the first 18 months of the program. Eight percent matched with open IV-D cases where the obligor was under order to pay support through the child support agency. Another 6 percent of the parents reported had IV-D cases, but a support order had not been established. In such cases, the reports would enable the agency to locate obligors and achieve legal service of process. The child support agency was able to take collection action on 43 percent of obligors who had support orders and who had paid nothing on their orders in the prior year. The agency reported that the benefit-cost ratio for the program was 22 to 1 (Welch 1992).

The Oregon Department of Justice proposed legislation for employer reporting in the 1991 session (Senate Bill 1204), which narrowly failed. That proposal would have applied to all employers, would have directed reports to the State Employment Security Agency (SESA), and would have required reports to be filed within five days of hiring. The Oregon approach has several advantages over the Washington statute. It would channel reports to the same agency (Employment Security) to which employers now report employment information. Employers would simply have to make those reports whenever employees are added, rather than quarterly. In addition, by making the SESA the repository for the new-hire information, the data could be made available for welfare fraud prevention and for employment security purposes as well as for child support.

CONCLUSIONS

By any reasonable standard, child support guidelines appear to be a successful social innovation. With respect to the relevant provisions of the Family Support Act, implementation is complete. When the Child Support Enforcement Amendments of 1984 were enacted, only a handful of states had presumptive guidelines, or even statewide advisory guidelines. Shortly after the implementation deadline of October 1989, however, all states had promulgated presumptive guidelines. No state fails to meet the basic requirement specified in the Family Support Act. The only compliance questions concern technical regulatory issues such as deviation criteria or income caps. Although there is no longer any serious debate about whether guidelines should be implemented, controversy remains regarding the levels of orders mandated by guidelines and the types of adjustments that should be included. Evidence on the impact of child support guidelines is limited and mixed, but guidelines seem to have generally raised child support orders. Moreover, there is a widely held perception that guidelines provide a rational structure for establishing levels of child support, and that orders have therefore become more consistent and more equitable.

Congress prescribed an extended implementation schedule for the review and modification provisions of the Family Support Act, recognizing that phasing-in was needed in view of the complexity of the requirements and the lack of extensive state experience. The act mandated that the federal government fund four demonstration projects to develop and test model procedures for review and modification. The OCSE had previously funded a project in Oregon with the same objectives. Pending the 1993 implementation deadline, states are moving only gradually to implement the review and adjustment requirements. Findings from the demonstration projects, although preliminary, indicate that the review and modification requirements will be administratively challenging but will yield beneficial results—at least for the limited proportion of cases that are ultimately modified. The findings also indicate, however, that the process is more time- and resource-consuming than may have been anticipated. These results do not suggest the need for any major policy changes in federal requirements for review and modification. Some fine-tuning may be useful concerning such issues as the need for access to courts for a review and modification based only on the age of the order, and the desirability of adjusting the specified notice requirements. But the basic requirements appear to be sound, and the phased-in approach to implementation appears well-justified by the experience gained in the demonstration projects.

The low request rate for reviews by non-AFDC IV-D parents is disappointing and demonstrates the need for a reshaping of public expectations if child support orders are to be kept current. For non–IV-D cases, there does not seem to be a practical court-based mechanism that could be implemented for identifying outstanding child support orders, sending the required notices, obtaining information from parents, performing a guidelines calculation, and initiating a legal modification action if appropriate.

The immediate income-withholding provisions of the Family Support Act have not been difficult to implement and will improve enforcement. But these requirements are not a child support enforcement panacea, because there are many cases where income withholding cannot be initially applied, and many others where the obligor changes jobs and child support agencies must go through the tedious and difficult process of reinstating the income withholding order. To ameliorate the problem of short spells of income withholding, a promising innovation is a requirement for employer reporting of newly hired and rehired personnel. Also, an issue that warrants continuing attention is the frequency with which good-cause exceptions to immediate income withholding are granted, and their impact on subsequent child support enforcement.

As remittance of child support by employers becomes the predominant form of payment, and as immediate income withholding is applied to non–IV-D cases after 1994, it is essential to reassess the adequacy of current mechanisms for collection and distribution of child support. As a first step, it is imperative that each state provide for a public entity for the collection and disbursement of income withholding; otherwise, employers will be placed in the intolerable situation of administering child support for private pay cases. More efficient methods of payment processing are also needed to reduce both the cost of income withholding for employers and the excessive overhead required for accounting and distribution in the IV-D program.

Overall, more attention to the program's basic operational structure with regard to payment processing is needed if the full potential of income withholding is to be realized. More efficient payment-processing can sustain employer cooperation, speed the disbursement of benefits, and reduce program operating costs. Special attention is required for income-withholding arrangements for non–IV-D cases. If the IV-D program continues to be limited to only a subset of child support cases, attention must be given to the role and funding base for public payment-processing structures to collect and disburse child support for non–IV-D child support cases.

Notes

This chapter is a revised version of a paper originally presented at the "Conference on Child Support and Child Well-being," Airlie House, Airlie, Va., Dec. 5–7, 1991.

1. Other important provisions included paternity establishment performance standards and enhanced federal funding for genetic testing, federally mandated performance standards for state child support agencies, and mandatory state implementation of automated child support systems.

2. For a more detailed description of these models, plus the income equalization approach, which has not been implemented by any state, see Williams (1987: II-65–96).

3. Garfinkel and Melli (1990) have pointed out that if the percentages used for income shares guidelines are constant at all income levels, then such guidelines become indistinguishable from percentage guidelines. Mathematically, this is correct, and we hold that a distinguishing feature of an income shares guideline is child support percentages that decline as income increases.

4. For an explanation of the derivation of the income shares schedule from Espenshade's study, see Williams (1987: II-67–80 and II-129–140).

5. This discussion is based primarily on my experience in providing technical assistance for development of child support guidelines in approximately 40 states.

6. The case for the percentage model is argued in Garfinkel and Melli (1992: 157–78).

7. Additional models for child support guidelines have been proposed beyond the three adopted by states to date. For a theoretical discussion of alternative approaches to child support guidelines, see Betson et al. (1992).

8. See, for example, *Child Support and Alimony: 1989*, Current Population Reports, Series P-60, No. 173, Washington, D.C.: U.S. Bureau of the Census, 1991.

9. A 1990 report released by the U.S. Department of Health and Human Services presented results from estimates of child-rearing expenditures using five theoretical models, based on data from the 1980–86 Consumer Expenditure Survey (Lewin/ICF 1990).

10. For a discussion of issues concerning treatment of additional dependents, see Williams (1987: II-51–55).

11. For an analysis of California guidelines before recent legislation, including an assessment of the impact of the visitation credit, see Williams (1990).

12. Steady-state benefits and costs were measured during the last six months of project operations. Modifications were still increasing at the end of that time period, so the project probably never reached steady state. Therefore, this estimate is probably conservative.

13. In an innovative step toward privatization, Colorado has contracted the development, implementation, and operation of its central payment registry to a private contractor.

References

Advisory Panel on Child Support Guidelines. 1987. Development of Guidelines for Child Support Orders, Part I. *Advisory Panel Recommen-*

dations. Report prepared for U.S. Office of Child Support Enforcement. Washington, D.C. Office of Child Support Enforcement: September.

Apao, William K. 1989. *In Support of Our Children: A Survey of Child Support Orders and Divorced Parents in Vermont.* Waterbury, Vermont: Vermont Agency of Human Services. July.

Bartfeld, Judi, and Irwin Garfinkel. 1991. *Utilization and Effects on Payments of Percentage-Expressed Child Support Orders.* Institute for Research on Poverty Special Report 55. Madison: Institute for Research on Poverty, University of Wisconsin-Madison, July.

Betson, David, et al. 1992. "Trade-Offs Implicit in Child Support Guidelines." *Journal of Policy Analysis and Management* 11 (1): 1–20.

Bishop, Sharon. 1992. *Evaluation of Child Support Review and Modification Demonstration Projects in Four States: Cross-Site Final Report.* Report prepared for Delaware Department of Health and Social Services. Fairfax, VA: Caliber Associates, May.

Bishop, Sharon, et al. 1990. *Evaluation of Child Support Review and Modification Demonstration Projects in Four States: Design Review Report.* Report prepared for Delaware Department of Health and Social Services. Fairfax, VA: Caliber Associates, March.

Center for Policy Research. 1989. *The Impact of Child Support Guidelines: An Empirical Assessment of Three Models.* Report prepared for State Justice Institute. Denver: The Center for Policy Research, October.

Curley, Richard. 1991. *Implementation Analysis of the Delaware Child Support Modification Project.* Report prepared for Delaware Department of Health and Social Services. Denver: Policy Studies, September.

Espenshade, Thomas. 1984. *Investing in Children.* Washington, D.C.: Urban Institute Press.

Garfinkel, Irwin, and Marygold Melli. 1990. "The Use of Normative Standards in Family Law Decisions: Developing Mathematical Standards for Child Support." *Family Law Quarterly* 24 (2, Summer): 157–78.

Gordon, Anne R., et al. 1991. *Income Withholding, Medical Support, and Services to Non-AFDC Cases after the Child Support Enforcement Amendments of 1984,* vol. 1. Report prepared for U.S. Office of Child Support Enforcement. Princeton, N.J.: Mathematica Policy Research, May.

Graham, Nancy L., and Mark A. Levy. 1991. *Implementing a Child Support Payment Center.* Report prepared for U.S. Office of Child Support Enforcement. Denver: Policy Studies, January.

Levy, Mark A., Nancy J. Starling, and Ernen M. Haby. 1988. *Analysis of the Iowa Collection Services Center: Process and Cost Analysis.* Report prepared for Iowa Department of Human Services. Denver: Policy Studies, September.

Lewin/ICF. 1990. *Estimates of Expenditures on Children and Child Support Guidelines*. Report prepared for U.S. Department of Health and Human Services. Washington, D.C.: Author, October.

Melli, Marygold, and Judi Bartfeld. 1991. "Use of the Wisconsin Percentage-of-Income Standard to Set Child Support: Experience in Twenty Counties, September 1987–December 1989. Photocopy, June.

Munsterman, Janice T., and Thomas A. Henderson. 1988. *Child Support Guidelines Summary*. Report prepared for U.S. Office of Child Support Enforcement. Arlington, VA: National Center for State Courts, May.

Munsterman, Janice, Claire B. Grimm, and Thomas A. Henderson. 1990. *A Summary of Child Support Guidelines*. Report prepared for U.S. Office of Child Support Enforcement. Arlington, VA: National Center for State Courts, February.

New Jersey Administrative Office of the Courts. 1987. *New Jersey Child Support Guidelines: First Year Evaluation*. Draft Report to Subcommittee on Child Support Guidelines. Trenton, NJ: New Jersey Administrative Office of The Courts, December.

Price, David A., and Jane C. Venohr. 1991. *Oregon Child Support Updating Project: Findings from the Third Year Research*. Report prepared for Oregon Department of Justice. Denver: Policy Studies, November.

Price, David A., Victoria S. Williams, and Robert G. Williams. 1991. *Oregon Child Support Updating Project: Final Report*. Report prepared for Oregon Department of Justice. Denver: Policy Studies, April.

Starling, N., et al. 1988. *Child Support Receipting and Disbursing in Nebraska: Process and Cost Analysis*. Report prepared for Nebraska Department of Social Services. Denver: Policy Studies, September.

State of Vermont. 1990. *Report of the Child Support Study Committee to the General Assembly*. Montpelier, VT: Author, January.

Takas, Marianne. 1991. *The Treatment of Multiple Family Cases under State Child Support Guidelines*. Report prepared for U.S. Office of Child Support Enforcement. Washington, D.C.: American Bar Association Center on Children and the law, July.

U.S. Congress. House. Committee on Ways and Means. 1992. *The Downey/ Hyde Child Support Enforcement and Assurance Proposal*. 102nd Cong. 2nd sess., May 12.

U.S. Department of Health and Human Services, Office of Child Support Enforcement. 1990. *Child Support Enforcement: Fourteenth Annual Report to Congress for the Period Ending September 30, 1989*. Washington, D.C.: U.S. Government Printing Office.

Welch, Carol. 1992. *Employer Reporting Program: Longitudinal Report, July 1990–January 1992*. Olympia, WA: Washington State Department of Social and Health Services, May.

Williams, Robert G. 1990. *Analysis of California's Child Support Guidelines*. Report prepared for California Judicial Council. Denver: Policy Studies.

————— . 1987. *Development of Guidelines for Child Support Orders: Part II, Final Report*. Report prepared for U.S. Office of Child Support Enforcement. Washington, D.C., September.

Williams, V., et al. 1989. *Design Report for the Oregon Child Support Updating Project*. Report prepared for Oregon Department of Justice. Denver: Policy Studies, June.

Chapter Five

THE RELATIONSHIP BETWEEN CHILD SUPPORT ENFORCEMENT TOOLS AND CHILD SUPPORT OUTCOMES

Irwin Garfinkel and Philip K. Robins

Since 1984, the child support enforcement system in the United States has undergone dramatic change. Two landmark pieces of federal legislation—the Child Support Enforcement Amendments of 1984 and the Family Support Act of 1988—have been enacted, giving states major responsibilities for improving their child support enforcement performance. Among numerous other provisions, the 1984 Amendments required states to develop nonbinding numerical guidelines for the establishment of child support awards and required that a system of wage withholding be instituted when child support obligations were not being met on a timely basis. The Family Support Act goes beyond the 1984 Amendments by making the guidelines presumptive (i.e., they must be followed unless a written justification is made that they are inappropriate) and by requiring that a system of universal and immediate wage withholding for all new child support cases be put in place by 1994.

Despite such sweeping reforms, there has been little formal evaluation of the potential impacts of these legislative changes. An exception is the study to evaluate the 1984 Amendments conducted by Mathematica Policy Research (Gordon et al. 1991); it focused mainly on the implementation of the provisions, with little attention devoted to their potential impacts on child support payment and award levels.

Although child support enforcement policies have been crystallized in these two pieces of legislation, the system has actually been evolving since the early 1970s. Indeed, numerous provisions in the 1984 and 1988 laws had already been implemented in many of the states. For example, as of the end of 1987, five states (Massachusetts, Minnesota, Ohio, Texas, and Wisconsin) had instituted a system of immediate withholding, and four other states (Arizona, Hawaii, Illinois, and Virginia) were about to pass similar legislation. As another example, many states (such as Delaware, Maine, and Virginia) had been using guidelines to set child support awards well before the 1984 Amendments required states to develop such guidelines.

Evaluating the impacts of child support enforcement policies is a complex undertaking and can be thought of as encompassing three interrelated steps. The first step consists of determining the degree to which various policies are being successfully implemented at the state level and identifying which state practices appear to be most successful in achieving the objectives of the legislation. The second step involves attempting to determine the impacts of such policies, once implemented, on major child support outcomes, such as child support payment and award levels. Assuming that such impacts exist and are positive, the third step is to determine how increased child support payments and awards further influence other aspects of individual behavior, such as parent-child interactions, parent-parent interactions, labor supply and welfare behavior of parents, and school performance and educational attainment of children. This chapter provides some evidence on the second of these steps—namely, the impacts of enforcement policies on four child support outcomes: the amount of child support collected in a given year, whether an award is obtained, the amount of an award, and the rate at which support is collected.

It is too early to definitively assess the impact of many provisions of the Family Support Act; the relevant data are simply not yet available. Instead, this chapter focuses mainly on one key provision of the act—immediate wage withholding—plus some of the major provisions of the 1984 Child Support Enforcement Amendments (pertaining to withholding under delinquency, guidelines, medical support, paternity, fees for non-AFDC families, and publicizing child support services).[1] In addition, two other factors are investigated: whether child support outcomes are systematically related to the amount of money states spend on administering their child support enforcement programs, and whether state laws provide for payment of child support to an agency (administrative agency, clerk of the court, etc.), rather than directly to the obligee.

The methodological approach taken here is to exploit state and time variation in the implementation of these child support enforcement policies to determine their impacts on child support payments and award levels spanning the years 1978 through 1987.[2] The data used to conduct the analysis are the household survey data collected in a Child Support Supplement to the April Current Population Survey that has been merged by the U.S. Bureau of the Census with the economic and demographic data in the March Current Population

Survey (the merged March–April survey is hereafter referred to as the CSS–CPS).[3]

This chapter's analysis is largely exploratory. A relatively large number of policies are examined and very crude statistical methods are utilized to determine which seem to be having the most impact. Future research will develop more sophisticated methods of evaluating these policies and will use later versions of the CSS–CPS to determine longer-run effects.

Despite the crudeness of the analysis, a remarkably consistent and sensible pattern seems to emerge. In particular, several policy variables appear to exert a statistically significant effect on the various outcomes examined, and the signs of the effects are for the most part in the expected direction. Specifically, our results imply that provisions for wage withholding (particularly immediate wage withholding), paying child support through an agency, regularly publicizing the availability of child support enforcement services, charging non-AFDC families a fee for applying for child support enforcement services, permitting paternity establishment at any time during the child's minority, and administrative spending by the state child support enforcement programs are all significantly related to the child support outcomes examined. With the exception of the non-AFDC fees variable, all of the estimated effects are positive, suggesting that these policies have led to an improvement in the child support situation of American families. The negative effect of charging fees for non-AFDC families is consistent with economic theory and suggests price responsiveness on the part of families needing enforcement services.

The positive effects estimated in this paper adjust for the effects of family economic and demographic characteristics and time. The positive effects are estimated despite the fact that the raw data on child support award and payment levels have exhibited a sizable downward trend over time.[4] Thus, taking advantage of state variation in policy implementation appears to be a fruitful approach to estimating the impacts of child support legislative policies, even when trends over time are negative. Interestingly, the positive policy effects estimated here are not generally sensitive to whether or not the data are adjusted for time trends.

Our methodology has a potential drawback: it could produce estimated effects that are spurious and possibly due to reverse causation. In other words, the states may have enacted a given policy in response to their child support performance, rather than to the policy directly influencing child support performance. To explore whether this source of bias might be present, we performed a specification test for the policy that seemed to be exerting the largest impact—immediate withholding.[5] The hypothesis of reverse causation was rejected by the data, suggesting a real impact of immediate withholding on the child support outcomes examined.

The remainder of this chapter is organized as follows. The second section discusses the child support policies analyzed. The third section outlines the methodology for estimating the impacts of those policies, along with the data used to estimate the impacts. The fourth section presents the empirical results. The final section summarizes the results and includes suggestions for future research.

CHILD SUPPORT POLICIES

The 1984 Child Support Enforcement Amendments were far-reaching, putting into place a large number of policies aimed at improving the efficiency of the child support enforcement system. As mentioned, many of those policies had already been implemented by a number of states, and many were refined further by the 1988 Family Support Act.

No central data source exists that documents how states have been implementing the various provisions mandated by the 1984 legislation. As part of their contracts with the federal Office of Child Support Enforcement (OCSE) to evaluate the 1984 Amendments, Mathematica Policy Research (MPR) and Policy Studies compiled information on the status of the implementation as of the end of 1987. This information is useful because the survey data we analyze cover the years 1978 through 1987. The data on implementation status were derived from the OCSE *Legislative Tracking System's Accomplishment Reports* (1987) and information compiled by Policy Studies. These data may be highly unreliable, but are the only currently available data describing the implementation status at that time.

In total, 23 policies are described in the data compiled by MPR and Policy Studies.[6] All but a few of the policies were mandated by the 1984 Child Support Enforcement Amendments. Most were in force as of December 1987, but more often than not had been in effect for only a short time, although several states had implemented some of the policies prior to the 1984 Amendments. Nevertheless, it is important to emphasize that any impacts estimated for these policies *as of the end of 1987* are likely to represent short-run impacts, and can probably be interpreted as lower-bound estimates of the longer-run impacts of these policies (when fully implemented in all of the states).

Of the original 23 policies, those related to wage withholding under delinquency, immediate wage withholding, medical provisions, guidelines, paternity, fees for non-AFDC families, and publicizing child support enforcement services were selected for the final analysis. The implementation dates for these policies by state are presented in appendix table 5.A.1.

In addition to the policy variables related to the 1984 Child Support Enforcement Amendments and the 1988 Family Support Act, we constructed two additional policy variables for the final analysis that we felt had the potential to exert statistically significant impacts on child support. These variables were the amount states spend per potentially eligible family on administering their child support enforcement programs and the method they use to funnel payments from obligor to obligee. These additional policy variables are also presented in appendix table 5.A.1. The next section describes the methodology for examining the impact of these policies on various child support outcomes.

METHODOLOGY FOR ESTIMATING IMPACTS OF CHILD SUPPORT POLICIES

To examine the relationship between the child support policies and child support outcomes, we specified a multivariate regression model. The model uses the individual mother as the unit of observation and takes advantage of state and time variation in implementing these policies as a means of identifying their influence on various child support outcomes.

Outcomes Analyzed

Four child support outcome measures were analyzed—whether or not a child support award existed, child support award levels, the ratio of payments received to payments owed (the collection rate), and the total amount in child support payments received by the mother. Child support payments are the product of the award rate, the award level, and the collection rate. To be effective, child support enforcement must secure awards in most cases, ensure that the awards are adequate and updated, and collect most of what is owed. In addition, specific policies directly affect different components of total child support payments. For example, guidelines directly affect award levels, and wage withholding directly affects collection rates, but both may indirectly affect award rates by making an award more valuable to custodial parents. Therefore, it is useful to examine the effects of the policy variables on each of the three components of aggregate child support payments.

Each outcome was first analyzed using the entire sample of mothers potentially eligible for child support. This was done to avoid potential problems of selectivity bias. Thus, in the initial analysis of award levels and the collection rate, mothers without awards were included in the sample. Then, award levels and collection rates were analyzed using only the sample of mothers with child support awards and correcting for selectivity biases associated with such a restricted sample.

Data

The data used to estimate the impacts of child support policies were drawn from the Child Support Supplement to the Current Population Survey (CSS–CPS) for the years 1979, 1982, 1984, 1986, and 1988. The CSS–CPS is the most comprehensive data available at the national level on child support outcomes. The strengths and weaknesses of this dataset for analyzing child support issues have been well documented in earlier studies (see Robins, 1987, 1992, and the references therein) and are not reviewed here.

The CSS–CPS consists of a sample of mothers with children from an absent parent. The 1988 sample covers their child support situation during the year 1987, the 1986 sample covers their child support situation during the year 1985, and so on. The sample analyzed in this paper includes women 18 years of age and older (the 1988 CSS–CPS also contains a small number of mothers between the ages of 14 and 17, but they were excluded from this study). The sample size is 19,220 (3,325 in 1978, 3,979 in 1981, 4,017 in 1983, 3,882 in 1985, and 4,017 in 1987).

The CSS–CPS also contains economic and demographic information about the family. All models estimated in this paper include the following control variables: dummy variables for region of the country (Northeast, North Central, West, and South), years of education, race (black and other), marital status (divorced, [re]married, separated, and never-married), number of children, age, years since

Table 5.1 DEFINITIONS AND MEANS OF OUTCOME AND CONTROL
          VARIABLES
          (POOLED 1979, 1982, 1984, AND 1988 CSS–CPS; N = 19,220)

	Definition	Sample Mean
Outcome Variables		
CHDSPREC	Amount of child support received	$976.4[a]
DUE	1 if due child support	.501
CHDSPDUE	Amount of child support due	$1,475.8[a]
COLLRATE	Collection rate (amount received/amount due)	.313
Control Variables		
NE	1 if resides in Northeast region	.197
NC	1 if resides in North Central region	.239
WEST	1 if resides in West region	.232
SOUTH	1 if resides in South region	.332
BLACK	1 if black	.240
NONBLACK	1 if not black	.76
EDUCATION	Years of education	11.940
DIVORCED	1 if divorced	.349
MARRIED	1 if (re)married	.157
SEPARATED	1 if separated	.157
UNMAR	1 if never-married	.227
KIDS	Number of children	1.717
AGE	Age	33.622
PARMAR	1 if married part of survey year	.136
YEARSDIV	Years since marital disruption (if married)	4.521
Y2	1 if survey year is 1981	.172
Y3	1 if survey year is 1983	.173
Y4	1 if survey year is 1985	.167
Y5	1 if survey year is 1987	.173

Source: Child Support Supplement–Current Population Survey (see text for explanation).
Note: Horizontal lines were inserted in table for ease of reading.
a. In 1987 dollars, adjusted using the consumer price index (CPI). The deflators used
are .5739 for 1978, .8002 for 1981, .8769 for 1983, and .9474 for 1985.

the marital dissolution if the mother was previously married, and a
dummy variable indicating whether the dissolution occurred during
1987. All variables refer to the mother—the CSS–CPS does not contain data on the father. The means of the outcome measures and the
control variables are presented in table 5.1.

Construction of Policy Variables

The data in the Appendix tables were used to construct 16 policy
variables that are hypothesized to influence the four child support

Table 5.2 DEFINITIONS AND MEANS OF CHILD SUPPORT POLICY VARIABLES
(N = 19,220)

Policy Variable	Definition	Sample Mean
DWITHDEL	Withholding under delinquency or withholding	.264
TWITHDEL	provision in child support order and court action not required to initiate withholding	6.201
DIMMWITH	Immediate wage withholding	.0343
TIMMWITH		.578
DMEDICAL	Provision for including medical support as part	.316
TMEDICAL	of an order if medical coverage is available to absent parent	8.480
DGUIDE	Guidelines for child support awards	.242
TGUIDE		8.720
DPATERN	Statute permitting paternity to be established	.592
TPATERN	until child's 18th birthday	30.542
DNAFDCFEE	Application fee for non-AFDC cases	.393
TNAFDCFEE		8.906
DSERVPUB	Provision for regularly publicizing availability of	.391
TSERVPUB	child support enforcement services	6.692
DMANDPAY	Provision for payment of child support to an agency	.141
CSEEXP	Administrative expenditures for Child Support Enforcement Program per female-headed family with children in the state	$152.5

Sources: For means of binary and time variables, Mathematica Policy Research and Policy Studies. For CSEEXP variable, see appendix 5.A, "Additional Notes to Table 5.A.1."
Notes: "D" before the variable name indicates that the variable is measured as a binary (0,1) variable denoting whether the policy had been implemented in the state as of December 1987. "T" before the variable name indicates that the variable is measured as months (as of December 1987) since the policy was implemented in the state. CSEEXP is measured in 1987 dollars, adjusted using the consumer price index. See appendix 5.A, "Additional Notes to Table 5.A.1," for further details on the definitions and sources of the policy variables.

outcomes. The definitions of the policy variables used in the empirical analysis are given in table 5.2. These are variables for provisions related to wage withholding under delinquency (WITHDEL), immediate wage withholding (IMMWITH), medical support (MEDICAL), numerical guidelines (GUIDE), paternity (PATERN), fees for non-AFDC families (NAFDCFEE), publicizing child support enforcement services (SERVPUB), requiring payment of child support to an agency (MANDPAY), and administrative expenditures by the state child support enforcement program (CSEEXP). For all but two of the policies (MANDPAY and CSEEXP), two separate variables were defined—a binary 1,0 variable indicating whether the state had adopted the policy prior to or during the relevant survey year and a variable measuring months elapsed between the date of implementation of the policy and the end of the survey period (December 1987). For MANDPAY only a binary variable could be constructed because we did not have information on the date of implementation. CSEEXP is defined as real (1987 dollars) administrative expenditures per female-headed family in the state.

All policies were allowed to affect all outcomes. This was done for methodological and practical reasons. In some cases, the policies were only expected to affect child support awards (MEDICAL, GUIDE, and perhaps PATERN), but because in the initial analysis all the observations were used (including the zeros), child support payments are the product of the probability of having an award, the amount of the award conditional on having an award, and the collection rate conditional on having an award. Thus, payments could be potentially related to policy variables that are only expected to affect awards. For award levels, it is theoretically possible that all of the policy variables could exert an impact.[7]

Econometric Model

The econometric model was specified as follows:

$$C_j = a_0 + a_{1j}X + a_{2j}P_i + e_j, \tag{5.1}$$

where C_j = the jth child support outcome, X = the control variables, and P = the policy variables for the jth outcome.

Because of the high degree of multicollinearity between the binary and the time policy variables, as well as between each of these and the binary variables for the survey year, six different specifications of the econometric model were estimated. The first specification included only the binary policy variables; the second included the binary policy variables and the binary variables for the survey year; the third included the time policy variables only; the fourth included the time policy variables and the binary variables for the survey year; the fifth included the binary and time policy variables only; and the sixth included the binary and time policy variables and the binary variables for the survey year. The control variables and the CSEEXP policy variable were included in each specification.[8]

To determine the relative importance of each policy measure, all the policy variables were entered into each equation and then removed systematically. This procedure is sometimes called "backward elimination." Specifically, policy variables were removed one at a time with the least significant policy variable removed first (i.e., the one that had the lowest partial correlation with the dependent variable). A final "best" equation was selected when all of the remaining policy variables were significant at the 15 percent level or lower.[9]

RESULTS

Full Sample for All Outcomes

The results of the backward elimination analyses for each of the four child support outcomes are presented in tables 5.3 through 5.6. Table 5.3 gives the results for the amount of child support received, table 5.4 for whether child support is due, table 5.5 for the amount of child support due, and table 5.6 for the collection rate (amount received/amount due).[10]

For the amount of child support received (table 5.3), several policy variables are statistically significant as one reads across the columns of the various model specifications. Only two variables, however, IMMWITH and NAFDCFEE, are statistically significant in all specifications (in either the dummy or time form). The estimated coefficients for IMMWITH are all positive, indicating that this policy is associated with higher child support payments. The estimated coefficients for NAFDCFEE are all negative, indicating that this policy is associated with lower child support payments. The negative coefficients for NAFDCFEE are consistent with economic theory and suggest that families are price sensitive when applying for child support enforcement services.[11]

A few other variables are also statistically significant in various specifications for the payments outcome. In four of the specifications, the results imply that the more states spend on administering their child support enforcement programs, the more parents collect in child support (the effect for CSEEXP). For every dollar spent per female-headed family, approximately 52 cents more in child support is collected, implying that the expenditures are not cost-effective.[12] Evaluated at the means, this effect implies an elasticity of .08, which is not very large.[13]

Table 5.3 BACKWARD ELIMINATION RESULTS FOR AMOUNT OF CHILD SUPPORT RECEIVED

Policy Variable	Model Specification					
	Dummy Only	Dummy and Year	Time Only	Time and Year	Time and Dummy	Time, Dummy, and Year
DWITHDEL	—	—	—	—	—	—
TWITHDEL	—	—	—	—	—	—
DIMMWITH	283.2[a] (89.60)	211.3[b] (92.41)	—	—	243.6[a] (90.80)	197.4[b] (92.73)
TIMMWITH	—	—	9.44[b] (4.75)	8.22[c] (4.91)	—	—
DMEDICAL	—	—	—	—	—	—
TMEDICAL	—	—	—	—	—	—
DGUIDE	—	—	—	—	—	—
TGUIDE	—	—	—	—	—	—
DPATERN	—	73.10[c] (43.79)	—	—	—	82.09[b] (43.99)
TPATERN	—	—	—	0.71[d] (0.47)	—	—
DNAFDCFEE	−70.68[b] (34.22)	−96.22[d] (62.81)	—	—	−156.3[a] (45.78)	—
TNAFDCFEE	—	—	−2.52[b] (1.13)	−2.30[c] (1.26)	—	−1.98[b] (1.21)

(continued)

Table 5.3 BACKWARD ELIMINATION RESULTS FOR AMOUNT OF CHILD SUPPORT RECEIVED (continued)

Policy Variable	Model Specification					
	Dummy Only	Dummy and Year	Time Only	Time and Year	Time and Dummy	Time, Dummy, and Year
DSERVPUB	—	—	—	—	—	—
TSERVPUB	—	—	4.04^b (1.75)	—	6.00^a (1.93)	—
DMANDPAY	—	—	—	—	—	—
CSEEXP	$.467^d$ (.289)	$.599^c$ (.312)	—	$.563^c$ (.320)	—	$.515^d$ (.317)

Source: Authors' calculations based on Child Support Supplement–Current Population Survey. See also appendix 5.A, "Additional Notes to Table 5.A.1."

Notes: "D" before the variable name indicates that the variable is measured as a binary (0,1) variable denoting whether the policy had been implemented in the state as of December 1987. "T" before the variable name indicates that the variable is measured as months (as of December 1987) since the policy was implemented in the state. Variables are removed in the order of statistical significance, with the least significant being removed first. The criterion used to select the final equation is that all variables remaining in the equation be significant at the 15 percent level or lower. The signs and level of statistical significance are reported for the included variables.

a. Significant at 1 percent level.
b. Significant at 5 percent level.
c. Significant at 10 percent level.
d. Significant at 15 percent level.

Table 5.4 BACKWARD ELIMINATION RESULTS FOR WHETHER CHILD SUPPORT IS DUE

Policy Variable	Model Specification					
	Dummy Only	Dummy and Year	Time Only	Time and Year	Time and Dummy	Time, Dummy, and Year
DWITHDEL	—	—	—	—	—	—
TWITHDEL	—	—	.000791[a] (.000258)	.000792[a] (.000275)	.000583[b] (.000272)	.000637[b] (.000283)
DIMMWITH	.0447[b] (.0179)	.0319[b] (.0185)	—	—	.0292[d] (.0188)	.0291[d] (.0190)
TIMMWITH	—	—	—	—	—	—
DMEDICAL	—	—	—	—	—	—
TMEDICAL	—	—	-.000385[b] (.000184)	-.00040[b] (.00019)	-.000349[b] (.000180)	-.000338[c] (.000182)
DGUIDE	—	—	—	—	—	—
TGUIDE	—	—	—	—	—	—
DPATERN	.0135[d] (.00827)	.0195[b] (.00878)	—	—	.0142[c] (.00839)	.0206[b] (.00886)
TPATERN	—	—	.00014[d] (.000091)	.00016[c] (.000093)	—	—
DNAFDCFEE	—	—	—	—	-.0226[c] (.0127)	-.0197[d] (.0131)
TNAFDCFEE	—	—	—	—	—	—

(continued)

Table 5.4 BACKWARD ELIMINATION RESULTS FOR WHETHER CHILD SUPPORT IS DUE (continued)

			Model Specification			
Policy Variable	Dummy Only	Dummy and Year	Time Only	Time and Year	Time and Dummy	Time, Dummy, and Year
DSERVPUB	.0358[a] (.00835)	.0375[b] (.0179)	—	—	.0327[a] (.0133)	.0407[b] (.0191)
TSERVPUB	—	—	.00019[a] (.00034)	.00185[b] (.00085)	.00146[a] (.000426)	.00168[c] (.000868)
DMANDPAY	.0282[a] (.0101)	.0279[a] (.0101)	.0263[a] (.0102)	.0268[a] (.0102)	.0309[a] (.010)	.0310[a] (.010)
CSEEXP	.000097[d] (.0000617)	—	—	—	—	—

Source: Authors' calculations based on Child Support Supplement–Current Population Survey. See also appendix 5.A, "Additional Notes to Table 5.A.1."

Notes: "D" before the variable name indicates that the variable is measured as a binary (0,1) variable denoting whether the policy had been implemented in the state as of December 1987. "T" before the variable name indicates that the variable is measured as months (as of December 1987) since the policy was implemented in the state. Variables are removed in the order of statistical significance, with the least significant being removed first. The criterion used to select the final equation is that all variables remaining in the equation be significant at the 15 percent level or lower. The signs and level of statistical significance are reported for the included variables.

a. Significant at 1 percent level.
b. Significant at 5 percent level.
c. Significant at 10 percent level.
d. Significant at 15 percent level.

Table 5.5 BACKWARD ELIMINATION RESULTS FOR AMOUNT OF CHILD SUPPORT DUE

Policy Variable	Model Specification					
	Dummy Only	Dummy and Year	Time Only	Time and Year	Time and Dummy	Time, Dummy, and Year
DWITHDEL	—	—	—	—	—	—
TWITHDEL	—	—	—	—	—	—
DIMMWITH	267.71[b] (108.6)	—	—	—	197.3[c] (110.3)	—
TIMMWITH	—	—	—	—	—	—
DMEDICAL	—	—	—	—	—	—
TMEDICAL	—	—	—	—	—	—
DGUIDE	—	—	—	—	—	—
TGUIDE	—	—	—	—	—	—
DPATERN	—	—	—	—	—	—
TPATERN	—	—	.942[c] (.561)	1.55[a] (.566)	—	1.55[a] (.566)
DNAFDCFEE	−82.60[b] (40.58)	−162.6[b] (75.05)	—	—	−220.7[a] (55.40)	—
TNAFDCFEE	—	—	−4.11[a] (1.47)	−3.74[a] (1.47)	—	−3.74[a] (1.47)
DSERVPUB	—	—	—	—	—	—

(continued)

Table 5.5 BACKWARD ELIMINATION RESULTS FOR AMOUNT OF CHILD SUPPORT DUE (continued)

Policy Variable	Model Specification					
	Dummy Only	Dummy and Year	Time Only	Time and Year	Time and Dummy	Time, Dummy, and Year
TSERVPUB	—	—	6.64[a] (2.25)	—	8.57[a] (2.34)	—
DMANDPAY	150.4[a] (59.40)	141.4[b] (59.11)	157.0[a] (61.03)	132.9[b] (59.25)	154.1[a] (59.39)	132.9[b] (59.25)
CSEEXP	—	—	−.664[c] (.386)	—	—	—

Source: Authors' calculations based on Child Support Supplement–Current Population Survey. See also appendix 5.A, "Additional Notes to Table 5.A.1."

Notes: "D" before the variable name indicates that the variable is measured as a binary (0,1) variable denoting whether the policy had been implemented in the state as of December 1987. "T" before the variable name indicates that the variable is measured as months (as of December 1987) since the policy was implemented in the state. Variables are removed in the order of statistical significance, with the least significant being removed first. The criterion used to select the final equation is that all variables remaining in the equation be significant at the 15 percent level or lower. The signs and level of statistical significance are reported for the included variables.

a. Significant at 1 percent level.
b. Significant at 5 percent level.
c. Significant at 10 percent level.
d. Significant at 15 percent level.

Table 5.6 BACKWARD ELIMINATION RESULTS FOR CHILD SUPPORT COLLECTION RATE
(AMOUNT RECEIVED/AMOUNT DUE)

Policy Variable	Model Specification					
	Dummy Only	Dummy and Year	Time Only	Time and Year	Time and Dummy	Time, Dummy, and Year
DWITHDEL	—	−.0239[b] (.0116)	—	—	−.0306[b] (.0126)	−.0328[b] (.0136)
TWITHDEL	—	—	—	—	.000644[c] (.000372)	.000745[b] (.000378)
DIMMWITH	.0527[a] (.0206)	.0517[b] (.0217)	—	—	.0484[b] (.0219)	.0524[b] (.0222)
TIMMWITH	—	—	.00174[d] (.00110)	.00202[2] (.00113)	—	—
DMEDICAL	—	—	—	—	−.0198[c] (.0117)	−.0244[c] (.0130)
TMEDICAL	—	—	—	—	—	—
DGUIDE	—	—	—	—	—	—
TGUIDE	—	—	—	—	—	—
DPATERN	.0250[a] (.00816)	.0251[a] (.0102)	—	—	.0292[a] (.00959)	.0272[a] (.0103)
TPATERN	—	—	—	—	—	—
DNAFDCFEE	—	—	—	—	−.0198[c] (.0117)	—

(continued)

Table 5.6 BACKWARD ELIMINATION RESULTS FOR CHILD SUPPORT COLLECTION RATE (continued)
(AMOUNT RECEIVED/AMOUNT DUE)

			Model Specification			
Policy Variable	Dummy Only	Dummy and Year	Time Only	Time and Year	Time and Dummy	Time, Dummy, and Year
TNAFDCFEE	—	—	—	—	—	—
DSERVPUB	—	—	—	—	—	—
TSERVPUB	—	—	$.00110^a$ (.00035)	$.0197^b$ (.000981)	$.00142^a$ (.000460)	$.00207^b$ (.00100)
DMANDPAY	$.0235^b$ (.0118)	$.0269^b$ (.0119)	$.0192^c$ (.0116)	$.0195^c$ (.0117)	$.0284^b$ (.0119)	$.0284^b$ (.0119)
CSEEXP	$.000118^c$ (.000070)	$.000128^c$ (.000074)	$.000120^c$ (.00072)	$.000126^c$ (.000074)	—	—

Source: Authors' calculations based on Child Support Supplement–Current Population Survey. See also appendix 5.A, "Additional Notes to Table 5.A.1."

Notes: "D" before the variable name indicates that the variable is measured as a binary (0,1) variable denoting whether the policy had been implemented in the state as of December 1987. "T" before the variable name indicates that the variable is measured as months (as of December 1987) since the policy was implemented in the state. Variables are removed in the order of statistical significance, with the least significant being removed first. The criterion used to select the final equation is that all variables remaining in the equation be significant at the 15 percent level or lower. The signs and level of statistical significance are reported for the included variables.

a. Significant at 1 percent level.
b. Significant at 5 percent level.
c. Significant at 10 percent level.
d. Significant at 15 percent level.

In three of the specifications, PATERN is significantly positive, suggesting that in states where paternity can be established up until age 18, child support collections are higher. In two of the specifications, SERVPUB is statistically significant, implying that in states that are required to regularly publicize child support enforcement services, child support payments are higher.

As displayed in table 5.4, all policy variables but one (GUIDE) are significantly related to the probability of having a child support award. Three variables—PATERN, SERVPUB, and MANDPAY— are statistically significant in every specification. Thus, allowing paternity to be established until age 18, publicizing the availability of child support enforcement services, and requiring payment of child support through an agency all increase the probability of having an award. Furthermore, the effect of publicizing services seems to intensify over time, as evidenced by the results in the last column where the coefficient of both the binary variable and the time variable (DSERVPUB and TSERVPUB) are significantly positive.

The effect of MEDICAL on the probability of having an award is negative, suggesting that awards are *less* likely to be given when there is a provision for including medical support as part of a child support order. In addition, CSEEXP is estimated to positively affect the probability of having an award.

Several variables appear to influence award levels (table 5.5). Many of them are the same ones that influence payment levels (IMMWITH, NAFDCFEE, PATERN, SERVPUB, and DMANDPAY), but there is one important difference. Although only significant in one of the specifications, CSEEXP is estimated to have a *negative* effect on award levels (as opposed to a positive effect on payment levels).[14] Thus, it appears that to the extent that administrative expenditures facilitate getting an award, such awards are, on average, much lower than awards obtained through other means.

The final set of estimates is for the collection rate (table 5.6). Once again, all of the policy variables are statistically significant except GUIDE. In the specification with the binary and time variables included, the results for withholding under delinquency imply that initially the collection rate falls and then rises as the system evolves. For the last specification (column 7), the results imply that after about 3.5 years (.0328/.000745) subsequent to implementing the system, the effect of withholding under delinquency on the collection rate is positive.

Disentangling the Policy Effects on Child Support Collections

The results presented in tables 5.3 through 5.6 were estimated using all sample observations ($N = 19,220$). Therefore, they combine the effects of the policy variables on both the conditional and the unconditional values of the outcome variables. For example, the results in table 5.3 for the amount of child support collections combine the effects of the policy variables on whether there is an award, the amount of the award, and the collection rate, the latter two conditional on having an award.[15] In this section, we use sample selection techniques to attempt to disentangle the effects of the policy variables on these components of child support collections. In addition, we reestimate the probability of having an award using a probit model rather than an ordinary least squares (OLS) model.

The basic relationship defining the components of child support collections may be written as follows:

$$E(\text{Collections}) = P(\text{Award}) \times E(\text{Amount of Award}|\text{Award}) \\ \times E(\text{Collection Rate}|\text{Award}) \qquad (5.2)$$

The same variables that were significant using the backward elimination procedures on the unconditional outcome (tables 5.4–5.6) are included in each component's equation. The probability of having an award is estimated over the entire sample ($N = 19,220$) using a probit model; the amount of the award conditional on having an award is estimated using a probit-OLS model with sample selection (first-stage probit, second-stage OLS on the selected sample of 9,652 persons with an award); and the collection rate conditional on having an award is estimated using a probit-tobit sample selection model (first-stage probit, second-stage tobit on the selected sample of 9,652 persons with an award).

The results for the various components are presented in tables 5.7, 5.8, and 5.9. Qualitatively, the results are quite similar to those in tables 5.4–5.6, but the coefficients in the conditional regressions are substantially larger than those in the unconditional regressions— usually about twice the size. Several other findings are worth noting.

First, requiring payments to be made through a public agency significantly increases all three components of child support collections. That this variable is not significantly related to aggregate payments, however, is something of a mystery and may reflect a weakness of the backward elimination technique.

Second, publicizing IV-D services seems to influence the probability of having an award; there is also some evidence that it affects the

Table 5.7 PROBIT RESULTS FOR WHETHER CHILD SUPPORT IS DUE

Policy Variable	Model Specification					
	Dummy Only	Dummy and Year	Time Only	Time and Year	Time and Dummy	Time, Dummy, and Year
DWITHDEL	—	—	—	—	—	—
TWITHDEL	—	—	.0027[a] (.00083)	.0027[a] (.00088)	.0020[b] (.0008)	.0022[b] (.0009)
DIMMWITH	.14[b] (.057)	.097[c] (.058)	—	—	.086 (.060)	.087 (.061)
TIMMWITH	—	—	—	—	—	—
DMEDICAL	—	—	—	—	—	—
TMEDICAL	—	—	-.0012[b] (.00058)	-.0012[b] (.00058)	-.0011[c] (.00057)	-.0011[c] (.00057)
DGUIDE	—	—	—	—	—	—
TGUIDE	—	—	—	—	—	—
DPATERN	.039[d] (.026)	.056[b] (.028)	—	—	.041[d] (.026)	.060[b] (.028)
TPATERN	—	—	.00038 (.00029)	.00043 (.00029)	—	—
DNAFDCFEE	—	—	—	—	-.067[c] (.040)	-.059[d] (.041)
TNAFDCFEE	—	—	—	—	—	—

(continued)

Table 5.7 PROBIT RESULTS FOR WHETHER CHILD SUPPORT IS DUE (continued)

			Model Specification			
Policy Variable	Dummy Only	Dummy and Year	Time Only	Time and Year	Time and Dummy	Time, Dummy, and Year
DSERVPUB	.12[a]	.12[b]	—	—	.11[b]	.13[b]
	(.026)	(.056)			(.042)	(.060)
TSERVPUB	—	—	.0061[a]	.0060[b]	.0045[a]	.0055[b]
			(.0011)	(.0027)	(.0013)	(.0027)
DMANDPAY	.089[a]	.088[a]	.084[a]	.086[a]	.097[a]	.097[a]
	(.032)	(.032)	(.032)	(.033)	(.033)	(.033)
CSEEXP	.00032[c]	.00035[c]	—	—	—	—
	(.00019)	(.0002)				

Source: Authors' calculations based on Child Support Supplement–Current Population Survey. See also appendix 5.A, "Additional Notes to Table 5.A.1."

Notes: "D" before the variable name indicates that the variable is measured as a binary (0,1) variable denoting whether the policy had been implemented in the state as of December 1987. "T" before the variable name indicates that the variable is measured as months (as of December 1987) since the policy was implemented in the state.

a. Significant at 1 percent level.
b. Significant at 5 percent level.
c. Significant at 10 percent level.
d. Significant at 15 percent level.

Table 5.8 OLS SAMPLE SELECTION RESULTS FOR AMOUNT OF CHILD SUPPORT DUE, CONDITIONAL ON HAVING AN AWARD

Policy Variable	Model Specification					
	Dummy Only	Dummy and Year	Time Only	Time and Year	Time and Dummy	Time, Dummy, and Year
DWITHDEL	—	—	—	—	—	—
TWITHDEL	—	—	—	—	—	—
DIMMWITH	272.42[d] (185.7)	—	—	—	278.6 (196.4)	—
TIMMWITH	—	—	—	—	—	—
DMEDICAL	—	—	—	—	—	—
TMEDICAL	—	—	—	—	—	—
DGUIDE	—	—	—	—	—	—
TGUIDE	—	—	—	—	—	—
DPATERN	—	—	—	—	—	—
TPATERN	—	—	1.11 (1.028)	2.28[b] (1.11)	—	2.82[b] (1.11)
DNAFDCFEE	−266.43[a] (83.51)	−312.51[b] (142.3)	—	—	−409.5[a] (101.5)	—
TNAFDCFEE	—	—	−7.39[a] (2.663)	−7.18[b] (2.847)	—	−7.18[b] (2.85)
DSERVPUB	—	—	—	—	—	—

(continued)

Table 5.8 OLS SAMPLE SELECTION RESULTS FOR AMOUNT OF CHILD SUPPORT DUE, CONDITIONAL ON HAVING AN AWARD (continued)

Policy Variable	Model Specification					
	Dummy Only	Dummy and Year	Time Only	Time and Year	Time and Dummy	Time, Dummy, and Year
TSERVPUB	—	—	10.866[b] (4.984)	—	14.15[a] (4.96)	—
DMANDPAY	185.15[c] (107.4)	276.09[b] (119.9)	259.41[b] (115.7)	274.52[b] (122.6)	258.7[b] (115.6)	274.5[b] (122.6)
CSEEXP	—	—	−.92 (.71)	—	—	—

Source: Authors' calculations based on Child Support Supplement–Current Population Survey. See also appendix 5.A, "Additional Notes to Table 5.A.1."

Notes: "D" before the variable name indicates that the variable is measured as a binary (0,1) variable denoting whether the policy had been implemented in the state as of December 1987. "T" before the variable name indicates that the variable is measured as months (as of December 1987) since the policy was implemented in the state.

a. Significant at 1 percent level.
b. Significant at 5 percent level.
c. Significant at 10 percent level.
d. Significant at 15 percent level.

Table 5.9 TOBIT SAMPLE SELECTION RESULTS FOR COLLECTION RATE CONDITIONAL ON HAVING AN AWARD

Policy Variable	Model Specification					
	Dummy Only	Dummy and Year	Time Only	Time and Year	Time and Dummy	Time, Dummy, and Year
DWITHDEL	—	-.049[c] (.029)	—	—	-.057[c] (.033)	-.062[c] (.035)
TWITHDEL	—	—	—	—	.0011[b] (.00095)	.0014[b] (.00096)
DIMMWITH	.10[b] (.051)	.10[c] (.054)	—	—	.10[c] (.056)	.11[c] (.057)
TIMMWITH	—	—	.0036 (.0028)	.0043 (.0029)	—	—
DMEDICAL	—	—	—	—	-.053[d] (.033)	-.060[c] (.032)
TMEDICAL	—	—	—	—	—	—
DGUIDE	—	—	—	—	—	—
TGUIDE	—	—	—	—	—	—
DPATERN	.058[a] (.020)	.058[b] (.023)	—	—	.076[a] (.023)	.068[a] (.024)
TPATERN	—	—	—	—	—	—
DNAFDCFEE	—	—	—	—	-.0024 (.030)	—

(continued)

Table 5.9 TOBIT SAMPLE SELECTION RESULTS FOR COLLECTION RATE CONDITIONAL ON HAVING AN AWARD (continued)

			Model Specification			
Policy Variable	Dummy Only	Dummy and Year	Time Only	Time and Year	Time and Dummy	Time, Dummy, and Year
TNAFDCFEE	—	—	—	—	—	—
DSERVPUB	—	—	—	—	—	—
TSERVPUB	—	—	.0021[b] (.00084)	.0039[b] (.0019)	.0032[a] (.0012)	.0048[b] (.0021)
DMANDPAY	.051[c] (.027)	.058[b] (.028)	.038 (.027)	.040[d] (.027)	.070[b] (.028)	.069[b] (.029)
CSEEXP	.00031[c] (.00017)	.00031[c] (.00018)	.00034[c] (.00018)	.00033[c] (.00018)	—	—

Source: Authors' calculations based on Child Support Supplement–Current Population Survey. See also appendix 5.A, "Additional Notes to Table 5.A.1."

Notes: "D" before the variable name indicates that the variable is measured as a binary (0,1) variable denoting whether the policy had been implemented in the state as of December 1987. "T" before the variable name indicates that the variable is measured as months (as of December 1987) since the policy was implemented in the state.

a. Significant at 1 percent level.
b. Significant at 5 percent level.
c. Significant at 10 percent level.
d. Significant at 15 percent level.

collection rate and, to a lesser extent, award levels for those with an award. Earlier it was seen (table 5.3) that publicizing IV-D services only has a significant effect on aggregate collections in two specifications of the model.

Third, withholding appears to be influencing aggregate collections by increasing both the probability of having an award and the collection rate for those with awards, although the positive effect of withholding under delinquency on the conditional collection rate only occurs four to five months after implementation (similar to its effect on the unconditional collection rate in table 5.6). The effect of withholding on the award rate is probably an indirect one, reflecting the potential collection value of having an award.

Fourth, the negative effect on collections of charging a fee for non-AFDC cases appears to act primarily by reducing the probability of having an award, as well as the level of the award for those with an award, rather than by reducing the collection rate.

Fifth, IV-D expenditures appear to be influencing aggregate collections primarily by increasing the collection rate. In results not shown, IV-D expenditures exert their largest influence on the amount of collections for those already receiving child support, and have no effect on the probability of receiving collections. That IV-D expenditures seem to be operating mainly through collections may partially reflect an emphasis on pure enforcement activities. In recent years, much of the IV-D program has been directed toward increasing collection rates for those who have an award and who are delinquent in their payments. Only recently (since the 1988 Family Support Act) have policymakers begun to recognize that the greatest gains in child support enforcement in the future can be made by increasing the number and amount of awards. As later CPS data become available, it will be of great interest to determine whether IV-D expenditures exert a stronger influence on the number and amount of child support awards.

Sixth, although provisions for including medical support in a child support order seem to have no significant effect on aggregate collections, they do appear to slightly reduce the probability of having an award.

Finally, it is surprising that paternity provisions influence all three components of collections. They increase the probability of having an award, they increase the amount of the award—given that there is an award—and they increase the collection rate. It is unclear why paternity provisions would affect award levels or collection rates, once an award has already been established. It seems likely that states with laws allowing paternity to be established up to age 18 also have other policies not measured here that lead to higher award levels and collection rates.

Specification Tests for Effects of Immediate Wage Withholding

The multivariate analysis just presented reveals statistically significant impacts of a variety of different policies. Generally, immediate wage withholding has the largest and most consistent impact of all the policy variables considered, although other policy variables are also often significant. The impact of most of the policy variables is quite robust with regard to model specification. In addition, the significance of the variables is generally insensitive to which other policy variables are included in the equations.

Nonetheless, two qualifications are in order. First, as already noted, it is possible that some of our policy variables are correlated with other unmeasured policies or factors that are affecting child support payments. Second, it is possible that the policy impacts are reflecting reverse causality. That is, it may be that states with better (or worse, in the case of NAFDCFEE) child support performance records were the ones that passed these policies in the first place.

Although it is not possible to determine the importance of the first qualification, it is possible to test for the second qualification (reverse causation). Because immediate wage withholding has the largest and most consistent impacts on the child support outcomes we examined, we utilized this variable to test for reverse causality.[16] This was done by assuming the counterfactual and then reestimating the multivariate model. Specifically, we tested for an effect for immediate withholding using earlier CSS–CPS data *before immediate withholding was implemented*, thus enabling a comparison of child support outcomes in states with and without immediate wage withholding prior to the implementation of immediate wage withholding. If reverse causality were present, spurious impacts of immediate withholding would exist in the years prior to the implementation of immediate withholding in the relevant states as well as in the years subsequent to the implementation of immediate wage withholding.

The earlier CSS–CPSs (1979, 1982, 1984, and 1986) were used to conduct the specification tests.[17] The results of the tests are presented in table 5.10. The tests reveal that for every outcome, the differences that existed in 1987 did *not* exist in earlier years (not a single coefficient is statistically significant in the years prior to 1987). In fact, in some earlier years, the states with immediate withholding fared *worse*

Table 5.10 SPECIFICATION TESTS FOR EFFECTS OF IMMEDIATE WAGE WITHHOLDING ON CHILD SUPPORT OUTCOMES

Outcome	Year					
	1978	1981	1983	1985	1987	
Amount of Child Support Received						
Effect	−193.2	68.3	79.4	100.0	219.5**	
(Standard error)	(129.8)	(97.7)	(112.3)	(74.6)	(104.8)	
Sample mean	$1,136.5	$942.5	$922.0	$893.7	$1,010.5	
Whether Child Support Is Due						
Effect	.007	.033	−.014	.007	.027	
(Standard error)	(.022)	(.021)	(.021)	(.020)	(.020)	
Sample mean	.497	.494	.477	.407	.530	
Amount of Child Support Due						
Effect	−56.3	159.6	−21.8	83.7	204.1*	
(Standard error)	(153.6)	(152.6)	(120.3)	(81.1)	(117.2)	
Sample mean	$1,738.8	$1,494.3	$1,337.2	$1,345.0	$1,502.6	
Collection Rate						
Effect	.002	−.016	.016	−.015	.037**	
(Standard error)	(.023)	(.022)	(.030)	(.025)	(.019)	
Sample mean	.303	.305	.307	.318	.332	
Sample Size	3,406	4,034	4,073	3,936	4,075	

Source: Authors' calculations based on Child Support Supplement–Current Population Survey. See also appendix 5.A, "Additional Notes to Table 5.A.1."

Notes: Standard errors in parentheses. Effects are adjusted for economic and demographic characteristics of custodial mothers and their families. Effects are measured over all custodial mothers identified in the CSS-CPS.

*Significant at 10 percent level.
**Significant at 5 percent level.

(negative coefficients, although not statistically significant) than the states without immediate withholding. Thus, there is a good chance that the differences estimated as of 1987 are not due to reverse causality.[18]

As indicated earlier, the CSS–CPS indicates a general downward trend in child support payments and award levels between 1978 and 1985 and a slight upward trend between 1985 and 1987. This trend remains after adjusting for the effects of the control variables (see the negative coefficients on the survey year dummies in appendix table 5.A.2). Despite the strong downward trend in the data, our results indicate positive effects for most of the policies, and these positive effects appear to increase over time. What is interesting is that these positive effects of the policy variables are generally *insensitive* to whether or not the estimated equation includes the year dummies. This robustness with respect to model specification also adds credibility to our findings.

CONCLUSIONS

This chapter has used Current Population Survey data to investigate whether any of the child support policies implemented in recent years in the United States are significantly related to key child support outcomes. Our preliminary analysis produces interesting results that offer considerable encouragement for future studies along the lines adopted here. Of the large number of policies evaluated, a sizable number appear to be exerting significant effects in the expected direction. Those exerting positive effects on child support payments and award levels include wage withholding (both immediate as well as in response to delinquency), publicizing the availability of child support enforcement services, allowing paternity to be established until a child's 18th birthday, requiring payment of child support through a third party, and, with one exception, administrative expenditures by state child support enforcement programs. Those exerting negative effects include charging fees for non-AFDC families and requiring that medical support be included in a child support order. Noticeably insignificant in every specification for every outcome are variables denoting whether numerical guidelines have been implemented. It is probably too early to determine whether the guidelines are having an effect in most of the states. Future work needs to focus more on evaluating the impacts of the guidelines.

An analysis of how the policies influence the various components of child support collections reveals that many of the policies are affecting only certain components of aggregate child support collections. Perhaps the most interesting finding is that IV-D expenditures appear to be primarily influencing collection rates through increasing payments for persons already receiving child support. IV-D expenditures have not generally been exerting a significant influence on the probability either of obtaining an award or of receiving child support given that an award exists (the latter result is not shown in this chapter). With the passage of the Family Support Act in 1988, the IV-D program appears to be moving toward focusing on establishing and maintaining child support awards, in addition to collecting child support for those with an award. As later CPS data become available, it will be interesting to update the analysis performed here to determine whether this new emphasis of the IV-D program will affect the influence of IV-D expenditures on the various components of aggregate child support collections.

Although these results are, for the most part, quite plausible, a few anomalies suggest that the findings presented here should be viewed as preliminary. Future research should incorporate additional years of data and should seek to develop better measures of state policies.

Notes

We wish to thank Mary Jo Bane, Andrea Beller, Andrew Cherlin, Frank Furstenberg, Sara McLanahan, Linda Melgren, Kristin Moore, Donald Oellerich, Isabel Sawhill, and Judith Seltzer for helpful suggestions during the early stages of this research and/or helpful comments on an earlier version of this chapter, and Paul Fronstin for excellent research assistance. A special debt of gratitude is owed to Elizabeth Phillips, who spent many painstaking hours compiling the data on the child support policies analyzed in this chapter. The data on policies were generously provided to us by Mathematica Policy Research and Policy Studies, Inc., as part of their contracts with the Office of Child Support Enforcement to evaluate the 1984 Child Support Enforcement Amendments. All opinions and conclusions presented in this chapter are those of the authors and do not necessarily reflect the opinions or views of the sponsoring organizations.

1. Numerous other provisions were examined during the exploratory stages of this research, but were excluded from the final set considered because they were mostly minor provisions that never exerted a statistically significant impact on any of the outcomes examined. The excluded provisions related to expedited processes, state and federal tax refund offsets, liens, securities or bonds, consumer credit, retroactive arrears, fees for late payments, continuation of services, enforcement for foster care, incentive payments, and extension of Medicaid eligibility. Implementation dates for these provisions are presented in an appendix available from the authors.

2. Two earlier studies using a similar approach to evaluate child support policies are Dickinson and Robins (1983) and Beller and Graham (1991).

3. The analysis utilizes data from the first five rounds of the CSS–CPS, administered in March–April 1979, 1982, 1984, 1986, and 1988, and covering the calendar years 1978, 1981, 1983, 1985, and 1987. The sixth round of the CSS–CPS, administered in March–April 1990 and covering the year 1989, was not available when this study was initially undertaken.

4. See Robins (1992) for details on this downward trend in child support.

5. The test we performed is similar to one performed by Beller and Graham (1991).

6. A detailed description of these policies is available from the authors.

7. One might argue that wage withholding is likely to exert an impact only on child support payments and not award levels. However, it is possible that the existence of wage withholding could induce a mother to seek an award. Since the award level (in the analysis of the full sample of mothers, including those without awards) is the product of the probability of having an award and the level of the award given that there is one, withholding could also affect the award level.

8. As appendix table 5.A.1 indicates, the value of CSEEXP in Alaska is more than double the value in almost every other state. Our exploratory analyses indicated that the results for this variable were quite sensitive to whether or not Alaska was included in the sample. Therefore, we excluded the 304 observations in Alaska from the final sample. This is equivalent to including the Alaska observations and allowing the coefficients to differ from those for the other states. Including Alaska and allowing it to have a separate additive impact yielded similar, but slightly less significant, impacts.

9. Because the policy variables are correlated with one another, this procedure does not guarantee that another "best" specification would result if the variables were removed in a different order. Thus, it is not an exact method for determining the "best" specification. However, it is a reasonable approach to sorting out the effects of a large number of correlated variables. Other methods, such as factor analysis, could be used, but factor analysis also has limitations. We estimated several factor models on the larger set of policy variables, but this exercise was generally uninformative.

10. The estimated effects of the control variables (including the year dummies) are presented in appendix table 5.A.2, for the broadest specification tested. Although not the focus of this chapter, the coefficients of the control variables are sensible and often statistically significant. The control variables indicate that child support payments and awards are lower for blacks; increase with education; are higher for divorced, (re)married, and separated mothers relative to never-married mothers; increase with the number of children in the family; increase with the age of the mother; are lower for mothers who suffered a marital disruption during the survey year (shown by the coefficient on PARMAR); and decline over time since the disruption. The coefficients also indicate that there was a general downward trend in child support award and payment amounts from 1978 to 1985 and than a slight turn upward in 1987, but not enough to return to 1978 levels (see Robins 1992, for more details on the downward trend in award amounts from 1978 to 1985).

11. The negative price sensitivity implies that the child support enforcement services lead to higher child support payments for those that use them.

12. This effect, however, holds the policy variables constant and implies that given the existence of the policies in the equation, additional expenditures are not cost-effective.

13. The elasticity (.08) is calculated as the coefficient (.515) times the ratio of the average per capita expenditures ($152.50) to the average amount of child support received ($976.40).

14. In several of the other specifications, the coefficient of CSEEXP was also negative and very close to being statistically significant.

15. This is not the only way to break down total collections into several components. Another way is to break down total collections into the probability of having an award, the amount of the award given that there is an award, and the collection rate given that there is an award.

16. It is possible that some of the *measured* policies interact with immediate wage withholding (rather than being simply additive, as we have specified). This possibility is testable, but later CSS–CPS data are really needed to perform tests of interactions in a rigorous fashion.

17. Only Texas had instituted a system of immediate wage withholding prior to 1986, and their system was only in place for three months in 1985. Thus, we would expect no impacts in 1978, 1981, and 1983, and very small impacts in 1985.

18. Note that the coefficients in table 5.10 are not directly comparable to the coefficients in tables 5.3–5.9 because the data are not pooled over time and a slightly different specification is used.

Appendix Table 5.A.1 IMPLEMENTATION DATES FOR POLICY VARIABLES AND AVERAGE CSE EXPENDITURES, BY STATE

State	WITHDEL	IMMWITH	MEDICAL	GUIDE	PATERN	NAFDCFEE	SERVPUB	MANDPAY	CSEEXP
AL	5/84	—	10/85	9/85	5/84	9/85	9/85	—	107.57
AK	—	—	3/86	5/86	11/85	11/85	11/85	—	515.12
AZ	8/85	—	8/73	8/73	8/71	10/85	5/86	Yes	112.69
AR	11/85	—	8/85	8/85	8/85	8/85	10/85	—	100.85
CA	—	—	3/87	7/85	5.75	2/86	11/85	—	228.81
CO	10/85	—	10/86	7/86	10/85	12/83	10/85	—	138.20
CT	10/85	—	7/82	—	10/85	4/86	10/85	—	186.52
DE	—	—	10/85	11/77	5/83	9/85	10/85	—	154.81
DC	4/87	—	10/85	—	8/84	10/85	10/85	—	216.88
FL	12/86	—	9/85	—	11/85	9/85	10/85	—	98.56
GA	—	—	12/85	12/85	10/75	9/85	8/85	—	58.44
HI	9/86	—	7/87	10/86	1/83	10/85	9/85	—	216.88
ID	6/86	—	10/85	—	10/85	7/86	7/86	—	143.36
IL	1/86	—	1/84	2/85	7/85	10/86	10/85	—	79.64
IN	—	—	5/84	—	9/80	6/85	3/85	—	70.48
IA	3/86	—	12/84	11/84	10/85	12/84	10/85	Yes	142.34
KS	—	—	7/85	—	7/85	6/85	10/85	—	129.54
KY	—	—	11/84	—	10/86	10/85	11/85	—	114.44
LA	12/85	—	5/86	—	10/81	3/86	11/85	—	120.84
ME	9/86	—	9/86	12/75	12/68	12/76	10/85	—	149.49
MD	—	—	10/85	—	7/85	1/84	10/85	—	176.67
MA	7/83	7/86	6/86	—	12/82	6/86	6/86	—	192.84
MI	7/83	8/87	5/86	5.87	6/86	10/85	10/85	Yes	186.65
MN	7/81	—	7/83	9/83	8/80	10/85	10/85	—	273.95
MS	10/85	—	10/85	—	12/81	10/85	10/86	—	52.02

MO	7/86	—	3/85	—	8/81	10/85	10/85	—	104.90
MT	10/85	—	10/86	10/85	6/87	12/80	10/85	—	103.37
NE	3/86	—	7/84	—	3/86	10/85	9/85	Yes	155.89
NV	—	—	8/86	10/86	8/81	10/85	10/85	—	187.75
NH	6/82	—	10/84	10/85	10/85	7/82	10/85	—	117.78
NJ	10/85	—	—	11/85	10/84	3/86	12/85	—	239.36
NM	11/85	—	1/85	10/85	10/85	10/85	11/85	—	109.18
NY	11/85	—	—	—	11/85	12/85	8/85	—	200.21
NC	—	—	5/85	9/86	9/85	9/85	12/83	Yes	103.83
ND	—	—	10/85	2/84	7/78	10/85	10/84	—	176.45
OH	6/87	12/86	10/84	—	6/82	10/85	7/85	—	98.85
OK	1/86	—	10/86	—	1/86	1/86	1/86	—	104.15
OR	10/85	—	10/85	4/86	10/83	10/85	10/85	Yes	228.44
PA	1/86	—	1/86	1/86	1/86	10/85	10/85	Yes	202.72
RI	7/84	—	6/77	—	5/79	12/76	10/85	—	108.97
SC	9/85	—	10/84	3/80	8/85	10/85	10/85	—	66.32
SD	9/86	—	11/85	12/85	9/86	10/84	4/85	—	143.43
TN	10/85	—	10/85	—	5.84	10/85	10/85	—	73.12
TX	3/87	9/85	3/87	2/87	9/83	10/85	10/85	—	60.10
UT	7/84	—	3/86	3/84	12/76	10/85	10/83	—	315.07
VT	—	—	3/86	9/87	3/83	6/80	1/86	—	133.16
VA	—	—	10/85	7/77	10/75	10/85	10/85	—	95.60
WA	10/85	—	11/85	3/86	2.76	10/85	12/85	—	215.01
WV	4/87	—	3/87	—	8/86	9/85	11/85	—	105.17
WI	2/78	8/87	7/82	2/82	7/81	10/85	10/85	Yes	216.45
WY	—	—	10/85	10/85	7/78	10/84	10/85	—	77.78

Notes: Implementation dates are as of December 1987 and CSE expenditures are average administrative expenditures per female-headed family over the sample period (1978, 1981, 1983, 1985, 1987), in constant 1987 dollars. Horizontal rules were inserted in table for ease of reading.

(continued)

Additional Notes to Table 5.A.1.

All dates in table 5.A.1 refer to implementation dates, as indicated on the Office of Child Support Enforcement *Legislative Tracking System's Accomplishment Report* (henceforth, OCSE LTS) for each state, as of December 1987. Sometimes, however, the date may in fact refer to the date that the procedure was approved by the OCSE (thus, the state could, perhaps, have been operating a similar procedure before).

WITHDEL

Withholding under Delinquency: For cases in which a support order is or has been issued or modified in the state, and is being enforced under the state plan, states must have a law whereby an absent parent becomes subject to mandatory wage withholding when unmade payments are at least equal to support payable for one month, when the absent parent requests such withholding, or at an earlier date if the state feels it is in the best interests of the parties involved. Source: OCSE LTS (1987).

Withholding Provision in Order: States are required to have legal procedures requiring that all child support orders that are issued or modified will include a provision for withholding from wages in order to assure that withholding as a means of collecting child support is available if arrearages occur without the necessity of filing an application. Source: OCSE LTS (1987).

Court Action Required for Withholding: In some states court action is required to initiate withholding. This does not include the original support order or court involvement should the obligor contest withholding. Source: Policy Studies. Note: If "clerk of court" was required, this was not taken to mean court action was required.

IMMWITH

Immediate Withholding: A few states had immediate withholding in 1987; not every child support order in those states was subject to the provision, however. Four states (Arizona, Hawaii, Illinois, and Virginia) passed immediate withholding legislation after 1987. Source: Mathematica Policy Research final report on evaluation of the 1984 Child Support Enforcement Amendments (Gordon et al. 1991).

MEDICAL

Medical Support in Orders: State agencies are required to petition for inclusion of medical support as part of any child support order whenever health care coverage is available to the absent parent at a reasonable cost. Source: OCSE LTS (1987).

GUIDE

Child Support Guideline: Each state must establish guidelines for child support award amounts, and make them available to all judges or other appropriate officials. The guidelines are not necessarily binding. Source: OCSE LTS (1987).

PATERN
Paternity Statute: States were required to have a law permitting the establishment of paternity until the child's 18th birthday. Source: OCSE LTS (1987).

NAFDCFEE
Non-AFDC Application Fee: The federal government required that states impose an application fee for furnishing child support services to non-AFDC cases. The state may set it at any amount it wants, not exceeding $25, and may collect from the individual applying, the absent parent, or may pay it out of state funds (though if they do this, it cannot count as an administrative cost to be reimbursed by the federal government.) Source: OCSE LTS (1987).

SERVPUB
Services Publicized: The state must regularly and frequently publicize, through public service announcements, the availability of child support enforcement services, including any fee and the phone number and address for more information. Source: OCSE LTS (1987).

MANDPAY
Mandatory to Pay Agency: This policy was not part of the 1984 Child Support Enforcement Amendments or the 1988 Family Support Act. In some states, payments must be made directly to an agency (administrative agency, clerk of court, etc.) as opposed to, for instance, the obligee. The states that had such a requirement by July 1984 are listed in table 5A.1 (Source: Melli 1989: table 10, pp. 37–39). Only those states listed in the Melli table under "Mandatory to pay agency" purely, or not qualified by footnotes "h" (either friend of court or clerk of court) or "k" (in nonwelfare cases, the payments may be to either agency or clerk of court; under special provision, payment may be deposited to bank account with receipt sent to clerk) were included.

CSEEXP
Administrative Expenditures per Female-Headed Family for Child Support Enforcement Program (in 1987 dollars): This variable is constructed by dividing reported administrative expenditures for the Child Support Enforcement Program by the number of female householder families with children and is adjusted using the consumer price index. The source for the administrative expenditure date is U.S. Department of Health and Human Services, Office of Child Support Enforcement, *Annual Report to Congress*, various issues. The source for the number of female householder families with children for 1980 is U.S. Bureau of the Census (1983). For the other years, the number of female householders with children was adjusted by nationwide percentage changes in the number of female-headed families with children. The percentage adjustments were -7.6 percent for 1978, 3.47 percent for 1981, 5.01 percent for 1983, 10.3 percent for 1985, and 15.65 percent for 1987. The source of these nationwide changes is U.S. Bureau of the Census, *Statistical Abstract of the United States*, various issues.

Appendix Table 5.A.2 COEFFICIENTS FOR CONTROL VARIABLES
(STANDARD ERRORS IN PARENTHESES)

Control Variable	Outcome Variable			
	CHDSPREC	DUE	CHDSPDUE	COLLRATE
CONSTANT	−2082.8[a] (113.6)	−.0271 (.022)	−2080.2[a] (135.2)	−.218[a] (.026)
NE	82.53 (55.94)	.00706 (.0094)	187.4[a] (57.18)	.00954 (.0111)
NC	−27.23 (44.27)	.00325 (.00930)	44.15 (55.50)	−.0215[b] (.0108)
WEST	−259.3[a] (55.10)	−.0159[c] (.00940)	−152.2[a] (60.01)	−.0537[a] (.0109)
BLACK	−629.9[a] (43.18)	−.125[a] (.00858)	−625.0[a] (52.15)	−.121[a] (.00995)
EDUCATION	148.60[a] (6.82)	.0204[a] (.00136)	161.9[a] (8.24)	.0241[a] (.00158)
MARRIED	950.6[a] (62.90)	.525[a] (.0125)	1772.6[a] (75.96)	.288[a] (.0145)
SEPARATED	707.8[a] (62.89)	.282[a] (.0125)	1195.0[a] (76.03)	.163[a] (.0145)
DIVORCED	1243.6[a] (56.66)	.594[a] (.0113)	2024.8[a] (68.45)	.354[a] (.0131)
KIDS	306.9[a] (17.47)	.0280[a] (.00347)	411.5[a] (21.11)	.0175[a] (.00404)
AGE	20.14[a] (2.02)	−.00208[a] (.000401)	14.13[a] (2.44)	.00231[a] (.000466)
PARMAR	−370.1[a] (56.06)	−.0805[a] (.0112)	−701.8[a] (67.77)	−.0137 (.0130)
YEARSDIV	−78.01[a] (4.94)	−.0118[a] (.000982)	−100.3[a] (5.97)	−.0126[a] (.00114)
Y2	−250.5[a] (51.63)	−.0121 (.0103)	−288.7[a] (62.07)	−.0106 (.0119)
Y3	−298.6[a] (53.75)	−.0299[a] (.0105)	−455.6[a] (62.77)	−.01008 (.0122)
Y4	−342.6[a] (61.33)	−.0292[d] (.0203)	−419.2[a] (64.64)	.00356 (.0163)
Y5	−184.4[b] (76.44)	−.0382 (.0319)	−145.7[a] (77.05)	−.0221 (.0349)

Notes: Results are for the specification given in the last column of tables 5.3 to 5.7. SOUTH, UNMAR, and NONBLACK are the omitted categories.
a. Significant at 1 percent level.
b. Significant at 5 percent level.
c. Significant at 10 percent level.
d. Significant at 15 percent level.

References

Beller, Andrea H., and John W. Graham. 1991. "The Effect of Child Support Enforcement on Child Support Payments." *Population Research and Policy Review* 10 (1, January): 91–116.

Dickinson, Katherine P., and Philip K. Robins. 1983. "Child Support and Welfare: An Analysis of the Issues." Report submitted to U.S. Department of Health and Human Services, January. Photocopy.

Economic Report of the President. 1991. Washington, D.C.: U.S. Government Printing Office, February.

Gordon, Anne R., et al. 1991. *Income Withholding, Medical Support, and Services to Non-AFDC Cases after the Child Support Enforcement Amendments of 1984*. Final report submitted to U.S. Office of Child Support Enforcement. Princeton, N.J.: Mathematica Policy Research, May.

Melli, Marygold S. 1989. *Child Support: A Survey of the Guidelines*. Institute for Research on Poverty Special Report 33. Madison: University of Wisconsin-Madison.

Munsterman, Janice T., and Thomas A. Henderson. 1988. *Child Support Guidelines Summary*. Report prepared for U.S. Office of Child Support Enforcement. Arlington, Va.: National Center for State Courts, May.

OCSE LTS. See U.S. Department of Health and Human Services, Office of Child Support Enforcement. *Legislative Tracking System's Accomplishment Reports*.

Robins, Philip K. 1987. "An Analysis of Trends in Child Support and AFDC from 1978 to 1983." Institute for Research on Poverty Discussion Paper 842-87. Madison: Institute for Research on Poverty, University of Wisconsin-Madison, October.

_____. 1992. "Why Did Child Support Award Levels Decline from 1978 to 1985?" *Journal of Human Resources* 27 (2, Spring): 362–79.

U.S. Bureau of the Census. 1983. *1980 Census of Population* 1 (chap. D, Pt. 1–52). Washington, D.C.: U.S. Government Printing Office, September.

_____. Various years. *Statistical Abstract of the United States*. Washington, D.C.: U.S. Government Printing Office.

U.S. Department of Health and Human Services, Office of Child Support Enforcement. 1987. *Legislative Tracking System's Accomplishment Reports*. December 4. Photocopy.

_____. Various years. *Annual Report to Congress*. Washington, D.C.: U.S. Government Printing Office.

Part Two

THE COSTS AND BENEFITS OF AN ASSURED CHILD SUPPORT BENEFIT

Chapter Six

WHO SHOULD BE ELIGIBLE FOR AN ASSURED CHILD SUPPORT BENEFIT?

Daniel R. Meyer, Irwin Garfinkel, Donald T. Oellerich, and Philip K. Robins

Concern about the well-being of children living in single-parent families, particularly female-headed families, has grown substantially in the last 20 years for a variety of reasons. First, the proportion of children living in female-headed families has dramatically increased (Garfinkel and McLanahan 1986). Second, female-headed families with children are the poorest of all major demographic groups (Garfinkel and McLanahan 1986). Third, there is growing evidence that the children in female-headed families are worse off with respect to a number of factors than the children of two-parent families (Featherman and Hauser 1978; Hill, Augustiniak, and Ponza 1985; McLanahan 1988).

The growth, poverty, and adverse impacts on children of female-headed families have all contributed to a heightened interest by public policymakers in examining the public policies that affect this group. Since the mid-1970s the child support system has received increased attention, and many have advocated drastic change. In 1982, Garfinkel and Melli proposed a Child Support Assurance System (CSAS), which included three reforms: (a) a uniform standard for establishing child support obligations; (b) immediate withholding of the child support obligation from the income of the noncustodial parent; and, (c) an assured or minimum-guaranteed child support benefit for each family. The first two reforms were incorporated into the Family Support Act of 1988 and are currently being implemented nationwide. Although an assured benefit has not been implemented, it is receiving increased national attention (see, for example, the report of the National Commission on Children 1991).

In previous research we have estimated some of the costs and effects of an assured benefit plan in the context of the Child Support Assurance System. This chapter reviews these results and then focuses specifically on the costs and benefits of several assured benefit plans that vary in both generosity and eligibility rules. We begin with a brief discussion of the policy decisions involved, followed by a synopsis of prior research; we then discuss our data and methodology; we summarize the costs and benefits of a basic assured benefit plan; and we conclude with a discussion of the effects of different levels of assured benefits and various eligibility rules.

DESIGN OF AN ASSURED BENEFIT PLAN

Garfinkel and Melli's (1982) assured benefit proposal was one part of a series of proposed reforms, the philosophy behind which was that all parents should be required to share their income with their children. The assured benefit, then, was not proposed as a substitute for private support, but as a backup for private support. All eligible families would be able to count on receiving at least a minimum level of child support each month. This would protect them against the insecurity that comes from irregular or late child support payments. In addition, some custodial-parent families (probably the poorest) would receive a supplement because the level of support obtained from the nonresident parent would be inadequate to meet the basic needs of the child(ren). Thus, an assured benefit would provide income support to the families of children with poor noncustodial parents as well as ensure the regularity of child support income for other families.

A number of design options fit within this basic idea of an assured child support benefit.[1] These options require decisions regarding two closely related areas: who would be eligible for the benefit and the level of the assured benefit. The debate regarding eligibility focuses on whether such a benefit should be available to all custodial families without regard to award, income, and/or marital status or whether it should be restricted to some subgroup of custodial families. Decisions on rules relating to eligibility will likely center around the following major issues:

☐ Should the assured benefit be restricted only to those with awards?
☐ Should the assured benefit be available only to single parents?
☐ Should the assured benefit be restricted only to those with low income?
☐ Should the assured benefit be available only to recipients of Aid to Families with Dependent Children (AFDC)?

Other key decisions include the level of the assured benefit, whether the benefit is taxable, and whether any additional services will be provided to recipients. The interaction of the assured benefit with current programs will also require some decisions, including:

☐ How is the assured benefit treated by the AFDC program—as unearned income (making it taxed at 100 percent, and thus there is no financial advantage to receiving both AFDC and the assured benefit); as a new category of income (perhaps taxed at 50 percent, as proposed by the National Commission on Children [1991]); or as the child support disregard (AFDC recipients could keep the first $50 per month only)? Would an assured benefit replace the child support disregard?

☐ How is the assured benefit treated in other means-tested programs? For example, does it count as income in the Food Stamp Program, in subsidized housing, or in the determination of eligibility for the Earned Income Tax Credit?

In addition, decisions would be needed regarding the administration of the assured benefit. This includes, but is not limited to, such issues as the relative roles of different levels of government, and the appropriate administrative agency. Administrative agency possibilities include the state child support agency, the state agency that distributes welfare benefits, a division of the family courts in each state, the state tax agency, the Social Security Administration, and the Internal Revenue Service, among others.

Although this chapter focuses on eligibility issues, we also touch upon two other issues: first, taxation, since it is closely connected to the issue of whether the assured benefit should be available only to those with low income or to all income levels; and second, the level of the assured benefit. The other questions, although important, are not the focus of this chapter.

Should the Assured Benefit Be Available Only to Those with Awards?

The critical argument against limiting eligibility to those with child support awards is that it keeps some vulnerable children from receiving a potentially important benefit through no fault of their own. Even if their custodial parent has done all that is expected in cooperating with the child support system, but for some reason an award has not been established, should the family be penalized? One alternative would be to require cooperation with the child support agency, rather than the existence of an award as one eligibility criterion for an assured benefit, similar to the AFDC program. Or an award could be required, but those who can demonstrate "good cause" could be exempted.

Garfinkel (1992) has argued that limiting eligibility to those legally entitled to receive private child support is "essential to creating and preserving the system's integrity." He argues that limiting eligibility underscores the responsibility of parents to provide for their own children and limits the government's role to enforcing that private responsibility and providing public support only when private efforts are inadequate. The social contract is clear: in return for custodial parents doing what they can about securing support for their children, society agrees to supplement that support when it is insufficient. Providing the benefit only to those with awards differentiates it from current welfare programs and thus can help make the benefit less stigmatizing. Limiting eligibility to those with awards may also add new incentives for the custodial parent to pursue paternity establishment and to gain awards. A final argument is that a benefit with limited eligibility may cost less than a benefit available to all.

Given the controversial nature of this issue, later in this chapter we present estimates of the costs and benefits of an assured benefit plan restricted to those with current awards versus a plan that is available to all custodial families, regardless of award status.

Should the Assured Benefit Be Available Only to Single Parents?

The argument for limiting eligibility only to single parents is that remarried custodial parents have access to the resources of the new spouse and need less public support. Thus this limitation, like the others, reduces costs and targets more of the benefits to the poor.

One argument against this limitation is that many remarried custodial families are near poverty, and thus may need assistance. Second, limiting benefits to single parents may discourage remarriage, when remarriage may eventually increase economic security. Another reason is that private child support obligations do not terminate upon remarriage of the custodial parent, in part because stepparents have no legal obligation to support children that are not theirs. Since the assured benefit is closely tied to the private child support obligation, it can be argued that it should be treated similarly and not stop at remarriage.

The primary advantage of limiting eligibility for the assured benefit to single parents is cost. Consequently, later in this chapter we present estimates of potential costs and effects of assured benefit plans that are both restricted to single parents and unrestricted by current marital status.

Should the Assured Benefit Be Income Tested?

The main reason for limiting eligibility for the assured benefit to those with low incomes is a pragmatic one: cost. When public resources are limited, targeting those resources on the most needy is appealing. Providing benefits to all custodial families would be more expensive than limiting eligibility to the poor, but the magnitude of these additional costs is unclear. A second reason for limiting eligibility to low-income families is that an assured benefit that is available to all would lead to some wealthy custodial families receiving a public benefit.[2] It could be argued that the public should not be supporting a high-income custodial family, just because a noncustodial parent has not paid in a particular month.

On the other hand, other universal programs support high-income families without public outcry. For instance, very few consider it an outrage that wealthy individuals receive Social Security or attend public schools. Similarly, unemployment insurance is available to all regardless of income and is primarily seen as an important buffer against insecurity for all individuals, not just those who have low incomes.

One key reason not to income test the benefit is that limiting eligibility may discourage work. Income-tested programs must reduce benefits as the income of the recipient increases. This reduction in benefits is equivalent to an extra tax placed on income. An advantage of a non–income-tested benefit is that it may supplement earnings, rather than replace them. However, the overall effect of a non–income-tested benefit compared to an income-tested benefit is ambiguous because the income effect could discourage work.[3]

A second important reason for not limiting eligibility is that the assured benefit could then *prevent* poverty. A variety of recent empirical studies have all shown that children experience a substantial decline in their economic situation when their parents separate (Lewin/ICF 1990). An assured benefit available to all may help to cushion this fall for the near-poor and may prevent others from slipping into poverty.

A third argument against limiting the benefit is that it segregates the poor, and this may stigmatize them. In contrast, a non-income-tested program integrates the poor into the social mainstream, and receiving benefits may be less likely to be seen as an indication of moral failure.

Fourth, income-tested programs require larger administrative costs per recipient. A bureaucracy must be developed that checks income to determine eligibility, monitors income over time, and adjusts benefits based on income. In contrast, a non–income-tested program would not have to check income at application or over time, and would not have to vary the amount of the benefit each month.

Finally, political support would be higher if benefits were available to all, not just to the poor. Again, because cost savings are the primary reason for limiting eligibility to the poor, this chapter presents the costs and effects of both an income-tested and a non–income-tested assured benefit.

Should the Assured Benefit Be Available Only to AFDC Recipients?

As with the income-tested argument, the arguments for limiting the benefit to AFDC recipients are that it would cost less and target benefits on the most needy. In addition, it targets the needy without requiring a new and potentially large bureaucracy that determines eligibility.

However, this limitation makes the benefit available only to former welfare recipients. One hope for the assured benefit is that it might prevent welfare recipiency, yet this limitation would keep this key benefit from occurring. In fact, the limitation might actually encourage welfare recipiency, at least temporarily, in addition to not being able to prevent it. This type of assured benefit would be inequitable in that it sets up two different income conditions: individuals must be very poor first (to be eligible for AFDC), but once on AFDC they can have substantial incomes and be eligible for the assured benefit. In addition, this limitation changes the way the assured benefit would be viewed: it would be seen as an adjunct to the current welfare system rather than as an alternative, and this difference means that recipients may be stigmatized and continue to be separated from the mainstream instead of being integrated into it. The effects of restricting the assured benefit to AFDC-eligible families would be similar to those of the income-testing plan. We currently lack the model necessary to produce these estimates, but we plan to incorporate this eligibility plan in our future work.

Should the Assured Benefit Be Subject to Income Taxes?

The issues involved in the taxation of an assured benefit are closely related to the income-testing arguments. Means-tested transfers have not been subject to income tax in this country; as a result, if the assured benefit is limited to the poor, there is little justification for subjecting the public portion of the benefit to the income tax. Although originally no government transfers were taxed, there has been some recent movement toward taxing universal benefits (unemployment compensation, part of Social Security benefits, etc.). The rationale for taxing benefits is that the tax code already exempts poor individuals from paying taxes; presumably if recipients are not poor, this income should be subject to income taxation. Making the public portion of the assured benefit taxable also reduces the cost of the program and targets more of the benefits on the poor, without limiting benefits only to the poor. In general, then, the most economical options for an assured benefit are either a benefit available only to the poor that is not taxed through the income tax system or a benefit available to all, in which the public portion of the benefit is subject to income tax. This chapter presents estimates of the effects of both types of assured benefit plans.

In summary, this chapter focuses on eligibility decisions, rather than on all possible permutations of the assured benefit concept. We focus on eligibility because relative costs are important features in the discussion, and the simulation framework used here is most adaptable to determining effects of alternative eligibility criteria. In addition to simulating the costs and benefits of an assured benefit plan that would provide an assured benefit to all families (i.e., those with and without awards), we present information on three eligibility limitations: restricting the benefit to (a) families with awards, (b) those who have low incomes, and (c) single-parent families.

THEORY AND PREVIOUS RESEARCH

Predictions about the effects of the various components of a child support assurance system can be made: the uniform standard should increase the dollar amounts of awards (Garfinkel, Oellerich, and Robins 1991; Williams, chapter 4, in this volume); immediate withholding should increase child support collections (Garfinkel and Klawitter 1990); and poverty among custodial-parent families should decrease through increased private child support and the assured benefit. The CSAS should also increase the number of families with child support awards, primarily because having an award will become more worthwhile economically.

The CSAS should also decrease AFDC recipiency. The traditional model of the welfare-recipiency decision has come from microeconomics and is an extension of the static theory of labor supply, which holds that individuals consider the trade-offs between income and leisure from all possible hours of work. Individuals then select the amount of work and whether they will receive welfare based on the option that maximizes their utility, budget, and time constraints. AFDC recipiency could be decreased by the CSAS for three reasons. First, for some women, the combination of private child support, the minimum benefit, and unearned income may provide more income than welfare, and thus they will choose to leave welfare. In fact, the minimum benefit alone may be greater than the AFDC maximum in some states, and women residing in those states may choose to leave AFDC. Second, the minimum benefit may provide enough support so that when it is combined with earnings, a woman is able to leave AFDC. The third possibility affects preferences rather than the budget constraint; eventually there may be a change in community values that has a feedback effect: dependence on child support rather than AFDC may become the norm for single parents, and this may further decrease welfare recipiency (Garfinkel, Manski, and Michalopoulos 1992).

The static theory of labor supply also provides predictions about the effect of the CSAS on labor supply. In the absence of welfare, any increase in unearned income (whether an increase in private child support or an assured benefit) will decrease labor supply, partly because individuals could achieve the same total income as before while working fewer hours. So nonrecipients of AFDC would be expected to decrease their labor supply if they receive additional child support or an assured benefit. But AFDC recipients may increase their labor supply if the new combination of the assured benefit, private child support, and earnings is more attractive than staying on AFDC. The aggregate effect on labor supply, therefore, is ambiguous.

Although theory provides clear hypotheses about the direction of most of the effects of the CSAS (increased number of awards, increased award levels, increased collections, increased incomes for custodial families, decreased welfare recipiency, and decreased labor supply for nonwelfare custodial families), the magnitude of these effects is not clear, nor are there any a priori predictions about overall labor supply or program costs.

Some previous research has been completed on the possible effects of various configurations of a CSAS. A simulation of the effects of a CSAS available only to low-income families in Wisconsin found that if there were a "medium" increase in awards and collections, an assured benefit of $3,000 may save money ($20 million), because increased collections from the noncustodial parents of AFDC recipients would offset part of the costs of AFDC (Garfinkel, Robins, Wong, and Meyer 1990). Welfare recipiency was predicted to decrease by 3 percent, the poverty gap for custodial families was predicted to decrease by 16 percent, and the labor supply of custodial families was predicted to decrease by 2 percent.[4]

Robert Lerman (1989) tested a simulation model that examines four different national child support systems: (a) the Wisconsin CSAS with an assured benefit, restricted to those with awards, of $3,000 a year for the first child and a surtax on custodial-parent income; (b) a lower assured benefit of $1,080 a year, restricted to those with awards; (c) a low assured benefit ($1,080) available to all custodial mothers, not just to those with awards; and (d) a low assured-benefit plan ($1,080) available to all that also includes a tax credit of $1,080 a year for a family of three that would replace the $2,000 personal exemption for children. Lerman did not simulate increases in the percentage with awards or the percentage collected, and did not allow a labor supply response. He reported that the four plans are estimated, first, to cost from $1.1 billion (Wisconsin plan) to $3.6 billion (low assured benefit available to all); second, to reduce the poverty gap by 2 percent to 45 percent (low assured benefit available to all with the change in the tax credit); and third, to reduce AFDC caseloads by about 4 percent (low benefit restricted to those with awards), 12 percent (Wisconsin plan), or 30 percent (low assured benefit with tax credit).

Although they do not simulate an assured benefit, Oellerich, Garfinkel, and Robins (1991) provided simulation estimates of the effects of the collection-side reforms of a national CSAS. They found that implementing the Wisconsin child support guidelines without changing award or collection rates would decrease AFDC caseloads by 2.7 percent, decrease the poverty gap by 6.8 percent, and increase custodial income by 8.9 percent.

Robins (1986) also examined the effects of increased child support collections on AFDC participation and poverty. He concluded that the full enforcement of the child support obligations that existed in 1981 would have little effect on AFDC participation and would decrease the poverty rate of custodial families by only 3 percentage points over the child support system in effect in 1981.

The previous studies have several limitations, including the lack of labor supply response (Lerman 1989; Oellerich, Garfinkel, and Robins 1991; and Robins 1986), the lack of modeling other effects of the Family Support Act (Lerman 1989; Robins 1986), and the potential lack of generalizability of the Wisconsin results to a national assured benefit (in Garfinkel, Robins, Wong, and Meyer 1990). We have therefore recently developed estimates of a national assured benefit, summarized later in this chapter, and present information on the relative effects of several different eligibility options.

SIMULATING THE EFFECTS OF A NATIONAL CHILD SUPPORT ASSURANCE SYSTEM

Data

To perform the microsimulation, a data source is needed that provides information on all those who will be eligible for the CSAS. The 1986 Current Population Survey—Child Support Supplement (CPS–CSS), although not perfect,[5] is a national dataset that provides complete and relatively current information available on most of those eligible for the CSAS. It includes demographic information on custodial parents (age, race, education, etc.); their children (number, age of the youngest, etc.); income and labor force information (annual earnings, the amounts of welfare reported, the number of weeks worked in 1985, and the number of hours per week usually worked); and information on the existence and amount of a child support award, and the amount received. All women aged 18 and over who are eligible for child support (including remarried women) are included, for a total of 3,631 cases. Missing from the sample are the male custodial parents.

Model

The simulation analysis requires estimating the amount of private child support each woman may receive, estimating the amount of AFDC received (because recipiency is underreported in the CPS), estimating a labor supply and welfare-recipiency response to the

CSAS, and identifying the features of each CSAS and assured benefit plan tested.

ESTIMATING THE AMOUNT OF PRIVATE CHILD SUPPORT

Estimates of the amount of private child support each woman may receive depend on the existence of an award, the level of that award, and the percentage of the award collected. Because of legislation already enacted that improves the establishment of paternity and makes having an award more worthwhile, it is likely that the percentage of cases with awards will increase in the future. Therefore, we included in our simulations an increase in the percentage of families with a child support award.[6]

To determine the level of an award, we needed to know the income of the noncustodial parent. Unfortunately, the CPS–CSS does not report the incomes of noncustodial parents, so to estimate noncustodial income we used procedures developed by Oellerich (1984) that base estimates of noncustodial parent income on the race, education, age, region, marital status, and AFDC use of the custodial parent. These procedures estimated the mean annual income of noncustodial parents as $20,379 in 1985 dollars.[7] The income of the noncustodial parent and the number of children were then used to determine the award amount using the Wisconsin percentage-of-income standard. The percentage of the award collected was then estimated based on a variety of custodial parents' demographic characteristics. Again, because of recent legislation requiring the use of wage withholding, we believe that compliance with awards is likely to increase, and we included an increase in our simulations.

ESTIMATING AFDC RECIPIENCY

A second series of intermediate steps was required to estimate the amount of AFDC received, because AFDC is significantly underreported in the CPS–CSS (U.S. Bureau of the Census 1990), as in most self-reported surveys. Our basic approach was to ignore the amount of AFDC reported and to use the maximum amount of AFDC available for each family (based on state of residence and family size) and an estimated tax rate on earnings (based on Fraker, Moffitt, and Wolf 1985) to determine if each family was income-eligible.[8] An AFDC benefit was then imputed to each recipient based on the maximum and the estimated tax rate. This approach yielded 2.7 million AFDC families and total AFDC payments of $10 billion, figures somewhat lower than those given in the administrative records, because all AFDC recipients are not in the CPS–CSS.[9]

ESTIMATING LABOR SUPPLY AND RECIPIENCY RESPONSES TO THE CSAS

The third part of the simulation model predicts welfare recipiency and labor force behavior after the CSAS is implemented. The static theory of labor supply (mentioned previously) suggests that women choose the number of hours they will work and that they choose to receive AFDC, the assured benefit, or neither, based on the alternative that provides the highest utility. The labor supply response model used in this chapter is based on the general theoretical approach developed by Burtless and Hausman (1978). It specifies a budget constraint, calculates utility on each segment of the budget constraint, and then assumes that custodial parents select the number of hours that provides the highest utility. The form of the utility function that we used to derive the estimates of the effects of the CSAS was an augmented Stone-Geary direct utility function used by Garfinkel, Robins, Wong, and Meyer (1990) and is given as follows:

$$U(C, H) = (1 - \beta) \ln(\frac{C}{m} - \delta) + \beta \ln(\alpha - \frac{H}{r}), \quad (6.1)$$

where C = annual consumption of market goods,
           H = annual hours of work,
           β = marginal propensity to consume leisure
               $(1 - \beta$ = marginal propensity to consume
               market goods),
           δ = subsistence consumption,
           α = total time available for work, and
     m, r = indexes that normalize C and H in accordance with
               the size and composition of the household.

To directly estimate the parameters of this utility function was beyond the scope of this chapter. Therefore, we drew upon results from the existing labor supply literature. For our baseline estimates of the effects of our proposed CSAS, we used the results obtained by Johnson and Pencavel (1984) in their analysis of the labor supply response to the Seattle and Denver Income Maintenance Experiments (SIME-DIME). In particular, we assumed β = .128, δ = -2,776, α = 2,151, m = 1 - .401 ln(1 + K) (K being the number of children in the family under the age of 18), and r = 1 - .071P (P being 1 if there are preschool-age children in the family, 0 otherwise). Hence, the total income elasticity estimated in the Johnson-Pencavel study was $-.128$ and the uncompensated wage elasticity was $.303$ (from $.128 (n + 2,776m)/wH = .303$), evaluated at the means of our analysis sample.[10]

The preceding utility function was used to estimate the effects of the CSAS. Using existing data, a family's preprogram labor supply, welfare position, and an error term that could represent taste for work were defined.[11] We then calculated a net wage and an amount of unearned income on each budget segment. Net wages were determined by adjusting gross wages for income taxes, payroll taxes, and implicit taxes on earnings for AFDC recipients.[12]

Given current net wages, current unearned income, changes in private child support, and the amount of the assured benefit, we estimated optimal hours and utility on each budget segment. The segment with the highest utility level then determined the woman's postprogram labor supply and program participation status.

In summary, the model simulates the amount of child support women would receive and their AFDC program participation and labor supply responses to the implementation of the CSAS. By aggregating these individual responses, we can estimate the total costs, decreases in AFDC recipiency, effects on poverty and income, and effects on labor supply. The costs included in this model are the direct (nonadministrative) cost of the assured benefits paid to custodial parents and any decreased tax revenue that results from higher income custodial parents who work less in response to increased child support. These costs are offset by taxing the public portion of the assured benefit, by savings in the AFDC program that result when women no longer receive AFDC, and by savings in the AFDC program that result from increased collections from noncustodial parents even when the custodial parent remains on AFDC. Administrative costs have not been estimated.

Although the simulation provides some interesting information about the magnitude of some of the costs and benefits of our CSAS, a few words of caution are in order. To conduct the simulations, a number of simplifications had to be made. First, Food Stamps and Medicaid were ignored, resulting in an overestimate of the number of women who will leave AFDC. (However, recent legislation that eventually makes Medicaid available to all poor children mitigates this error.) On the other hand, the Earned Income Tax Credit is also ignored, which may lead to an underestimate of the number of women who would leave AFDC. In addition, potential "macro" or "community" effects of changing norms are ignored. We have also not included the effects of the CSAS on noncustodial parents: for example, an increase in child support obligations may (depending upon the precise guideline used) increase or decrease the labor supply of noncustodial parents, may increase or decrease noncompliance with child support awards, and may move some noncustodial parents and their families into poverty. An assured benefit will decrease the incentive for noncustodial parents to pay child support, since their children would receive benefits regardless of whether payments were made, although this may be mitigated by the universal use of wage withholding. Estimating the effects of the CSAS on noncustodial parents is beyond the scope of this research. Finally, we have not accounted for the absence of custodial fathers in the CPS–CSS, a group that may receive a substantial portion of assured benefit funds.[13]

IDENTIFYING THE FEATURES OF THE CSAS

The three elements of the CSAS (guidelines for awards, immediate income withholding, and an assured benefit) could take a variety of forms. The particular CSAS that we tested has the following features:

1. Child support awards are initially set and updated using Wisconsin's percentage-of-income standard. Award levels are based only on the number of children and on the income of the noncustodial parent. For one child, the award is 17 percent of the first $75,000 of noncustodial income; for two children it is 25 percent, then 29 percent, 31 percent, and 34 percent for three, four, and five or more children, respectively. Variants of percentage-of-income standards are currently used by 16 states and the District of Columbia (Lewin/ICF 1990).[14]
2. Three potential levels of assured benefits, with the first child entitling the custodial parent to either $1,000, $2,000, or $3,000 annually, are presented. In each plan the benefit increases by $1,000 for the second child, $1,000 for the third, $500 for the fourth, and $500 for the fifth.[15]

The assured benefit plans reflect the following eligibility rules:

1. For our baseline simulations the availability of the assured benefit is restricted to only those custodial families with a current child support award. The public portion of the child support transfer (assured benefit) is subject to the federal income tax.

2. The next two simulations continue to restrict the assured benefit to those with awards and add the additional restrictions of, respectively, (a) single-parent families only (again, the public portion of the child support transfer is subject to the federal income tax) and (b) low-income families.[16]
3. Our last group of simulations provides an assured benefit to all custodial families regardless of their award, income, and marital status. The public portion of the income transfer is subject to the federal income tax.

In all simulations, we assume that the AFDC program would tax the assured benefit at a rate of 100 percent. As a result, there would be no financial advantage to a custodial parent if he or she received both AFDC and the assured benefit.

RESULTS AND DISCUSSION

We examined the effects of an assured benefit under four different CSAS scenarios. The first scenario describes the child support situation in 1985. In the second scenario there is no change in the percentage of cases with awards or the percentage of child support collected, but all awards are set according to the Wisconsin child support guidelines. In the third scenario, awards are set according to the Wisconsin standard, collection rates are increased by half the distance between the 1985 percentage and 100 percent, and 40 percent of those who do not have an award in 1985 are assumed to receive one—a "medium improvement" scenario. In the fourth scenario, all cases are given awards, all awards are set according to the Wisconsin standard, and all award amounts are collected. We believe some increases in awards and collections will occur because the provisions of the Child Support Enforcement Amendments of 1984 and the Family Support Act of 1988 are intended to generate increases in child support obligations and improvements in collections. The second scenario, in which all awards are based on the Wisconsin standard, could be implemented fairly easily by making updated child support awards a condition of eligibility for an assured benefit and by updating all the child support awards of AFDC recipients. The medium improvement can be interpreted as a level of improvement that could be expected from a CSAS in perhaps 15 to 20 years. The perfect system is the upper bound and could at best be approached, but never fully achieved, in the long run.

Within each CSAS scenario we estimated the effects of the four assured benefit plans with the following eligibility options: (a) benefits restricted to all families with a current award; (b) benefits restricted to low-income families with current awards; (c) benefits restricted to single-parent families with current awards; and (d) benefits available to all custodial families, that is, regardless of current income, marital, and award statuses. The particular income-tested plan we simulated was modeled after a Wisconsin proposal that would restrict the benefit to custodial families with incomes below an income cutoff of $2,000 less than the median income. The tax on the custodial parents' earnings was set at a rate equal to the noncustodial parents' tax rate for the number of eligible children (i.e., 17 percent for one child and 25 percent, 29 percent, 31 percent, and 34 percent for two, three, four, and five or more children, respectively). In all non–income-tested options the assured benefit was regarded as taxable income subject to federal income tax.

Our basic results, restricted to those with a current award, are summarized in table 6.1. Providing an assured benefit of $3,000 to those with awards regardless of current marital status or income level could cost $4.2 billion if the rest of the child support system remains as it was in 1985 (scenario one in the table). However, if an assured benefit were combined with improvements on the collection side of the private child support system, costs would be reduced. For example, combining the $3,000 assured benefit with the universal use of the Wisconsin percentage-of-income standard to initially set and update award levels (scenario number two) and no changes in compliance behavior reduces the estimated cost to $2.2 billion.

The third scenario, "Medium Improvements in Awards and Collections," shows that these improvements by themselves could reduce public costs, primarily through AFDC savings, by $1 billion. These system improvements alone have beneficial effects on the economic well-being of custodial families, decreasing their poverty gap by 10 percent and decreasing the AFDC caseload by 8 percent. The addition of an assured benefit of $2,000 does more for custodial families under this scenario, decreasing the poverty gap by an additional 5 percent and AFDC recipiency by an additional 10 percent, at an estimated cost of about $500 million. A perfect system (scenario number four) would, of course, do even more and shows the maximum potential benefits.

Aggregate changes in labor supply for custodial families are quite

Table 6.1 ESTIMATES OF DIRECT COSTS OF CSAS AND EFFECTS OF CSAS ON POVERTY, AFDC RECIPIENCY, AND LABOR SUPPLY OF CUSTODIAL FAMILIES UNDER FOUR SCENARIOS

Scenario	Percentage Decrease in Poverty Gap	Percentage of Caseload Leaving AFDC	Nonadministrative Cost ($1,000,000s 1985)	Percentage Change in Labor Supply		
				AFDC Recipients	Non-AFDC Recipients	All
1. Child Support System in 1985						
Assured benefit $0	0	0	0	0	0	0
Assured benefit $1,000	2	3	448	5	0	0
Assured benefit $2,000	5	8	1,759	15	−1	1
Assured benefit $3,000	9	13	4,239	26	−1	1
2. Percentage Standard Implemented						
Assured benefit $0	2	2	−144	3	−1	−1
Assured benefit $1,000	3	4	−47	6	−1	0
Assured benefit $2,000	5	9	552	14	−1	0
Assured benefit $3,000	9	14	2,166	23	−2	1
3. Medium Improvements in Awards and Collections						
Assured benefit $0	10	8	−1,026	9	−3	−2
Assured benefit $1,000	12	11	−943	13	−3	−1
Assured benefit $2,000	15	18	−461	24	−3	0
Assured benefit $3,000	21	28	850	45	−3	1
4. Perfect Awards and Collections						
Assured benefit $0	24	19	−2,775	25	−5	−3
Assured benefit $1,000	25	22	−2,667	29	−5	−3
Assured benefit $2,000	30	33	−2,157	46	−6	−1
Assured benefit $3,000	39	50	−749	79	−6	2

Source: Microsimulation results based on 1986 Current Population Survey—Child Support Supplement (CPS–CSS).
Note: Assured benefit is restricted to those with an award, and the public portion of the transfer is subject to federal income tax.

small under each scenario tested. However, these low aggregate changes are the result of two offsetting effects. Women originally receiving AFDC increase their labor supply substantially, showing a 45 percent increase in average hours worked under the medium improvement scenario with a $3,000 benefit (table 6.1). In contrast, those not receiving AFDC decrease their hours of work, by 3 percent in the medium improvement scenario. Thus, it appears that an assured benefit as low as $1,000 targeted to those families with a current child support award could make substantial inroads in reducing poverty and AFDC participation, while having only a marginal impact on labor supply.

Table 6.2 compares the effects of the eligibility options we explore. The table contains four panels, one for each of the four scenarios. Within each scenario we report the results of four eligibility plans. The costs and effects of the plans reported in the table indicate the additional change in outcomes due to the minimum benefit level and are calculated relative to the costs and effects of a base plan that has no minimum. For example, if medium improvements (scenario three) were achieved, we would estimate a 10 percent reduction in the poverty gap. If this improvement were combined with an assured benefit plan based at $1,000 we would estimate an additional 2 percent reduction in the poverty gap, for a total of 12 percent.

Within each panel of table 6.2, the first set of results (1a, 2a, 3a, 4a) restates the results in table 6.1, our base estimates for an assured benefit available to all families with awards.

The second set of results in table 6.2 (1b, 2b, 3b, 4b) is for the income-tested benefit that is available to families with awards. The income-tested assured benefit is designed to decrease the benefit by 17–34 percent (depending on the number of children) for each dollar of custodial income and to ensure that those families with annual incomes above an income cutoff of $2,000 less than the median income are not eligible. This plan costs substantially less than the assured benefit restricted simply to all those with awards, decreasing costs by about $1.2 billion for the $3,000 assured benefit in the medium scenario. It also provides fewer benefits, reducing the poverty gap by only an additional 7 percent, rather than 11 percent, and enabling only an additional 15 percent of the caseload, rather than 20 percent, to leave AFDC. The difference in costs between the award only and the income-tested benefit is largest ($3.4 billion) if the old system does not improve. An income-tested assured benefit is estimated to have no effect on the labor supply of recipients. The effect of income testing on labor supply is less than the award-only

Table 6.2 INCREMENTAL EFFECTS OF FOUR TYPES OF ASSURED BENEFITS ON POVERTY, AFDC RECIPIENCY, AND LABOR SUPPLY OF CUSTODIAL FAMILIES UNDER FOUR SCENARIOS

Scenario	Percentage Decrease in Poverty Gap	Percentage of Caseload Leaving AFDC	Net Non-administrative Cost Compared to 1985 ($1,000,000s 1985)	Percentage Change in Labor Supply, Custodial Mothers
1. Child Support System in 1985	0	0	0	0
Additional Changes from Assured Benefit:				
a. Families with Awards:				
$1,000	2	3	448	0
$2,000	5	8	1,759	1
$3,000	9	13	4,239	1
b. Low-Income Families with Awards:				
$1,000	0	1	72	0
$2,000	2	4	253	0
$3,000	5	10	837	0
c. Single-Parent Families with Awards:				
$1,000	2	3	288	0
$2,000	4	7	1,065	1
$3,000	8	13	2,532	2
d. Families with and without Awards:				
$1,000	10	16	2,728	2
$2,000	22	35	5,936	5
$3,000	35	52	10,673	6
2. Percentage Standard Implemented	2	2	− 144	− 1
Additional Changes from Assured Benefit:				
a. Families with Awards:				
$1,000	1	2	97	1
$2,000	3	7	696	1
$3,000	7	12	2,310	2

(continued)

Table 6.2 INCREMENTAL EFFECTS OF FOUR TYPES OF ASSURED BENEFITS ON POVERTY, AFDC RECIPIENCY, AND LABOR SUPPLY OF CUSTODIAL FAMILIES UNDER FOUR SCENARIOS (continued)

Scenario	Percentage Decrease in Poverty Gap	Percentage of Caseload Leaving AFDC	Net Non-administrative Cost Compared to 1985 ($1,000,000s 1985)	Percentage Change in Labor Supply, Custodial Mothers
b. Low-Income Families with Awards:				
$1,000	0	1	31	0
$2,000	1	3	136	0
$3,000	4	9	503	0
c. Single-Parent Families with Awards:				
$1,000	1	2	94	1
$2,000	3	6	467	1
$3,000	6	11	1,456	2
d. Families with and without Awards:				
$1,000	10	15	2,404	2
$2,000	21	34	4,856	5
$3,000	34	51	8,771	4
3. Medium Improvements in Awards and Collections				
Additional Changes from Assured Benefit:	10	8	−1,026	− 2
a. Families with Awards:				
$1,000	2	3	83	1
$2,000	5	10	565	2
$3,000	11	20	1,876	3
b. Low-Income Families with Awards:				
$1,000	1	1	53	0
$2,000	2	6	207	0
$3,000	7	15	685	1

c. Single-Parent Families with Awards:				
$1,000	1	2	83	1
$2,000	4	10	507	2
$3,000	10	19	1,528	3
d. Families with and without Awards:				
$1,000	7	11	1,452	2
$2,000	15	26	3,055	4
$3,000	26	43	5,750	6
4. Perfect Awards and Collections				
Additional Changes from Assured Benefit:	24	19	−2,775	−3
a. Families with Awards:				
$1,000	1	3	108	0
$2,000	6	14	618	2
$3,000	15	31	2,026	5
b. Low-Income Families with Awards:				
$1,000	0	2	62	0
$2,000	2	8	317	0
$3,000	8	13	946	1
c. Single-Parent Families with Awards:				
$1,000	1	3	101	1
$2,000	6	14	608	2
$3,000	15	30	1,925	5

Source: Microsimulation results based on 1986 CPS–CSS.

Notes: Perfect scenario for assured benefit plan "Families with and without Awards" is not shown, since if all cases have awards it would be redundant with the first plan, "Families with Awards."

plan for two reasons: first, moderate-income custodial families would not be eligible, and thus would not decrease their labor supply; second, and perhaps more important, moving into the labor force would be less attractive if the assured benefit were subjected to a surtax, so fewer women would leave AFDC to begin working.

The third set of results in table 6.2 (1c, 2c, 3c, 4c) shows an assured benefit limited to single-parent families with awards (i.e., those who remarry would not be eligible for the assured benefit). This also saves money, but produces less savings than limiting the benefit to those with low incomes. In contrast to directly income-testing the benefit, categorically limiting the benefit to single-parent families costs less while still helping poor custodial families. Because a relatively small percentage of remarried custodial parents are poor or on AFDC, confining benefits to single mothers with awards reduces poverty and AFDC recipiency almost as much as a benefit available to all custodial mothers with awards regardless of current marital status.

Finally, not restricting eligibility (table 6.2—1d, 2d, 3d) for the assured benefit results in much larger economic impacts in terms of increases in both benefits and costs. For example, under the medium improvement scenario, an assured benefit plan available to all families, with and without an award, of $3,000 would reduce the poverty gap by an additional 26 percent with a projected nonadministrative cost of $5.8 billion. This same benefit restricted to those with an award would result in a lower reduction in the poverty gap (11 percent) and would cost $3.9 billion less than the plan available to families with and without awards.

The impacts on AFDC participation are most dramatic when the assured benefit is provided without regard to award status. This is because of the relatively low award rate for AFDC recipient families; in 1985, less then one-third of these families had a current award.

We could try to attain the long-run benefits of the program by not requiring an award, but the cost could be quite high. Without concomitant improvements in collections and award levels, extending benefits to all, without regard to award, income, and marital status, would result in costs of over $10 billion. In addition, such a plan may actually delay increases in the collection side of the program by reducing incentives to seek a child support award.

Table 6.2 shows that the income-tested assured benefit (rows 1b, 2b, 3b, and 4b) costs much less than the non–income-tested benefit (rows 1a, 2a, 3a, and 4a), but still reduces the poverty gap and AFDC recipiency by sizable amounts. This is to be expected, since an income-tested benefit attempts to provide benefits only to those with low incomes. An advantage of the non–income-tested benefit is that it is available to those who are near-poor; information about the distributional effects of the two assured benefits is presented in table 6.3.

As expected, the income-tested benefit assists the poor, with 90 percent of the $3,000 benefit under the medium improvement scenario going to those with incomes less than poverty (table 6.2, row 3b). In comparison, 75 percent of the non–income-tested benefit goes to the poor (row 3a). The non–income-tested benefit provides a substantial amount of assistance to the near-poor, with 21 percent of the same benefit going to those with incomes between 101 percent and 200 percent of poverty. The table also shows that as the private child support system becomes more effective (moving down the panels), the percentage of benefits going to the poor increases, for two reasons: first, as the system improves, more poor families receive child support awards and thus more become eligible for the assured benefit; second, as the system improves, the nonpoor will receive more private child support benefits and thus will not need the assured benefit. Similarly, larger assured benefits generally reach further up into the income distribution, since some of the near-poor would be attracted to a large benefit but not a small one.

Table 6.3 also shows the effect of the income-tested and non–income-tested assured benefits on average custodial family incomes. Because the non–income-tested benefit is available to more people, it results in higher mean incomes than the income-tested benefit. For example, under the medium improvement scenario with a $3,000 benefit, the non–income tested benefit raises mean annual incomes by $300, compared to $100 for the income-tested benefit.

CONCLUSIONS

The simulation results presented here suggest that a child support assurance system that included an assured benefit available to all custodial families with awards could increase the incomes of poor custodial families. The labor supply of custodial parents is not predicted to change much, and many of the families would leave AFDC. Achieving such a major reduction in poverty and welfare recipiency, however, is not estimated to cost a great deal. In fact, when combined with improvements on the collection side, the nonadministrative

Table 6.3 DISTRIBUTION OF ASSURED BENEFITS TO CUSTODIAL FAMILIES AND ESTIMATES OF MEAN FAMILY INCOME UNDER FOUR SCENARIOS

Number of Custodial Families	0%–100% Poverty 41.0%	101%–200% Poverty 22.6%	201%+ Poverty 36.3%	Mean Custodial Family Income ($1,000s)
	Percentage of Net Assured Benefits to Families with Incomes of			
	0%–100% Poverty	101%–200% Poverty	201%+ Poverty	
1. Child Support System in 1985				19.3
a. Families with Awards (Non–Income-Tested)				
$1,000	42.0	37.7	20.2	19.4
$2,000	35.9	33.2	30.9	19.5
$3,000	33.1	29.9	37.0	19.9
b. Low-Income Families with Awards (Income-Tested)				
$1,000	82.4	14.2	3.4	19.3
$2,000	86.7	9.6	3.7	19.3
$3,000	83.4	12.9	3.7	19.4
2. Percentage Standard Implemented				19.7
a. Families with Awards (Non–Income-Tested)				
$1,000	59.5	29.4	11.0	19.7
$2,000	47.7	30.4	21.8	19.7
$3,000	41.4	29.1	29.4	19.8
b. Low-Income Families with Awards (Income-Tested)				
$1,000	82.5	12.6	4.9	19.7
$2,000	88.1	8.4	3.4	19.7
$3,000	87.3	9.9	2.7	19.8

3. Medium Improvements in Awards and Collections				20.3
a. Families with Awards (Non–Income-Tested)				
$1,000	75.3	16.8	7.8	20.3
$2,000	70.6	19.7	9.6	20.4
$3,000	67.9	21.2	10.9	20.6
b. Low-Income Families with Awards (Income-Tested)				
$1,000	87.6	5.9	6.4	20.3
$2,000	89.6	6.1	4.4	20.3
$3,000	90.3	7.0	2.8	20.4
4. Perfect Child Support System				21.3
a. Families with Awards (Non–Income-Tested)				
$1,000	84.2	10.7	5.1	21.3
$2,000	75.8	16.0	8.3	21.5
$3,000	72.8	17.6	9.6	21.7
b. Low-Income Families with Awards (Income-Tested)				
$1,000	90.5	4.7	4.7	21.3
$2,000	90.3	4.9	4.7	21.3
$3,000	91.6	5.5	2.9	21.4

Source: Microsimulation results based on 1986 CPS–CSS.
Notes: For the non–income-tested version, income taxes paid on the public portion of the assured benefits have been subtracted to give "net assured benefits." For the income-tested version, the custodial surtax has been subtracted. The first three columns may not add to 100 percent because of rounding.

costs of a CSAS may actually be less than the nonadministrative costs of the child support system in 1985.

Four eligibility options were simulated, comparing the basic results (assured benefits available to all custodial families with awards) to assured benefits available to low-income families with awards, to single-parent families with awards, and to all custodial families (with and without awards). As expected, the benefits are less when eligibility restrictions are made, with the assured benefit available to all, decreasing the poverty gap and AFDC recipiency by at least twice as much as the benefit available only to those with awards. Compared to a benefit available only to those with awards, limiting eligibility to single-parent families decreases the benefits only slightly, while limiting it to poor families shows a somewhat larger decrease. As expected, cost estimates also vary dramatically with different eligibility rules. In the medium improvement scenario, an assured benefit of $3,000 is estimated to cost $1.9 billion. An assured benefit of $3,000 available to all families costs three times as much, an assured benefit that is available only to single-parent families with awards costs about $0.3 billion less, and an income-tested assured benefit costs about $1.2 billion less.

An income-tested benefit focuses its assistance on families below the poverty line. A non–income-tested benefit provides more benefits to those near poverty, at a higher total cost.

This chapter has reviewed conceptual arguments about the advantages and disadvantages of limiting eligibility for an assured child support benefit, in addition to providing dollar estimates of some of the costs and benefits of these limitations. As expected, trade-offs are involved: a benefit available to more people does more to decrease poverty and welfare recipiency, but does so at a higher cost. If an assured child support benefit is to become policy, decisions on eligibility will need to be made; such decisions can be made in a more informed manner if estimates of trade-offs are combined with the conceptual arguments presented in this chapter.

Whatever eligibility rules are selected, we believe that an assured benefit would be a desirable income security policy, providing significant benefits for a very poor group without costing much in public dollars.

Notes

The research reported in this chapter was supported in part by a grant from the Office of the Assistant Secretary for Planning and Evaluation, U.S. Department of Health and Human Services, to the Institute for Research on Poverty, University of Wisconsin-

Madison. Any opinions expressed are those of the authors alone and not of the sponsoring institutions.

1. This section borrows heavily from Garfinkel (1992).

2. Some would argue that any type of assured benefit would change the incentives in custody determination, providing an additional benefit to those who gain custody. This issue is particularly relevant in this context, in that a non–income-tested assured benefit may mean that high-income custodial fathers receive regular public benefits because the awards assessed on lower-income custodial mothers may be low.

3. Although this is true if a non–income-tested plan is compared to an income-tested plan, if a non–income-tested plan is compared to the current system, the labor supply effect for nonworking AFDC recipients is positive; for working AFDC recipients the effect could be either positive or negative; and for non-AFDC recipients the effect is negative. The aggregate effect is unknown.

4. The CSAS simulated in Wisconsin included a wage subsidy and taxed back the difference between the assured benefit and the amount of private child support. Garfinkel, Robins, Wong, and Meyer (1990: table 5, row 4, p. 24) provide results for an assured benefit of $3,000 without a wage subsidy; these are the results described here.

5. For a more complete description of the CPS–CSS, see Robins (1987). The CPS–CSS has five major problems. First, not all those eligible for child support (and thus not all those eligible for the CSAS) are included. For example, custodial fathers and custodial parents younger than age 18 are not included. (The omission of younger custodial parents was corrected in the 1988 CPS–CSS, and the omission of custodial fathers was corrected in the 1992 CPS–CSS). Women who have only been married once and are currently married, but who were single parents prior to the marriage, are also not included. Second, no information is gathered on the noncustodial parent. Third, self-reports of welfare recipiency are used, and AFDC recipiency is significantly underreported, making identification of recipients and estimation of welfare savings difficult. Fourth, only annual data are reported, creating problems in identifying those eligible for the CSAS for only part of the year and those who are part-year AFDC recipients. Finally, the CPS–CSS may have incorrectly identified older women as being child-support-eligible (see Robins 1987). For this reason, only women younger than age 60 were used in the simulation.

6. To do this, we first divided every case into a portion that we assumed had a child support award and a portion that did not, based on a logit equation. An alternate approach would accept the information provided by each woman on whether or not there was an award, and then increase the percentage with awards by randomly selecting cases without awards. Our approach was consistent with the idea that each case, being part of a sample, "represented" many cases like it. What we did is similar to dividing each case into 100 families and then giving, say, 67 of these families an award and 33 families no award. For more details on the estimation of the model we employed to adjust award rates, see Meyer et al. (1991).

7. These procedures have been used in other simulations, and are also summarized in Garfinkel and Oellerich (1989). There are two reasons to believe that these estimates are conservative. First, Garfinkel and Oellerich applied their estimating procedures to three samples in which we have information on both the custodial parent and the income of the noncustodial parent and found that the estimates consistently underestimated the actual incomes of nonwhites and were lower than (or slightly above) the incomes of whites. Second, a different methodology reported in Michalopoulos and Garfinkel (1989) would have resulted in estimates of noncustodial income that are about 10 percent higher than our estimates.

8. Moffitt (1986) has provided us with updated values based on 1984 data. Where we did not have 1984 estimates, we used those reported by Fraker, Moffitt, and Wolf (1985) from 1982. Unfortunately, estimates for some small states are not available

from either source. We imputed a rate to states lacking either a 1984 or a 1982 estimate by using the rates of other states in the same region.

9. The total amount of AFDC reported in our sample was $7.33 billion. We know, however, that only 76 percent of AFDC is reported (U.S. Bureau of the Census 1990); thus the $7.33 billion reported could be equivalent to $7.33/.76 billion, or about the $10.0 billion that we simulate here. Our approach thus appears to rectify the problem of underreporting.

We have not, however, dealt with the problem of CSAS-eligible cases systematically missing from the CPS–CSS. The total amount of AFDC benefits reported in administrative records in 1985 was $15 billion. Subtracting the cases eligible for AFDC who are not eligible for the CSAS (those eligible through the unemployment, incapacitation, or death of a parent) results in a total amount of $12.7 billion. We assumed that the difference between the $12.7 billion from administrative records and the $10 billion we estimated is for AFDC cases not in the CPS–CSS. We ignored this additional $2.7 billion of AFDC benefits, which is equivalent to assuming that none of these people leave AFDC and that we collect no additional child support from their partners.

10. Because no research has been done on the labor supply of *remarried* women, we are not sure if their labor supply responses are more like those of married women or single women. We used the parameters for single heads of households for all women, and, for remarried women, treated the spouse's income as exogenous.

11. As Moffitt (1986) and Hausman (1985) have noted, the error term can generally be thought of as representing a combination of measurement error, optimization error, and unmeasured heterogeneity. In our application, it may also represent differences between the sample used by Johnson-Pencavel (SIME-DIME) and this sample. For purposes of this chapter, however, the error term was assumed to arise only because of unmeasured heterogeneity, since we assumed that observed hours of work are equal to the optimal hours of work, and that participation and labor supply decisions are based on utility maximization.

12. We used the 1985 schedule for federal income taxes, assuming that all income except AFDC and child support was taxable and that women used either the "unmarried head of household" or "married, filing jointly" status with only the standard deduction and exemptions for all members of the family. To simplify the model, we assumed that the current marginal tax rate applied to all levels of hours. For simplicity we ignored state income taxes.

13. Unfortunately, identifying custodial fathers of child-support-eligible children is difficult. If we add the male custodial fathers in Wisconsin, and adjust their weight so that they total an estimate of the number of custodial fathers nationally, costs increase, but there is little effect on the estimates of the percentage reductions in the poverty gap or the AFDC caseload.

14. The other common guideline type, income shares, is used by 34 states. Income shares guidelines determine the percentage of income based on both parents' income. However, the two types of guidelines usually yield identical awards when the income categories are wide (Lewin/ICF 1990).

15. The assured benefit in the $1,000 plan does not exceed the AFDC maximum benefit for one child in any state; for two through five children, however, AFDC maximums are less than the assured benefit in 2 to 9 states, depending on family size. The highest assured benefit is greater than AFDC benefits in 21 to 26 states, depending on family size. In our base results, when AFDC was less than the assured benefit, a family was assumed to participate in AFDC only in the absence of a child support award.

16. The income-tested version we implemented was the one planned for the Wisconsin demonstration: the assured benefit is limited to those with incomes less than

$2,000 less than the median income for each family size; the benefit is taxed back at the rate of 17 percent for every dollar of custodial parent income if there is one child, and at the rate of 25 percent for two children, and so on, following the Wisconsin percentages required from noncustodial parents.

References

Burtless, Gary, and Jerry A. Hausman. 1978. "The Effect of Taxation on Labor Supply: Evaluating the Gary Income Maintenance Experiment." *Journal of Political Economy* 86: 1103–30.

Featherman, David, and Robert M. Hauser. 1978. *Opportunity and Change.* New York: Academic Press.

Fraker, Thomas, Robert Moffitt, and Douglas Wolf. 1985. "Effective Tax Rates in the AFDC Program." *Journal of Human Resources* 20: 251–63.

Garfinkel, Irwin. 1992. *Child Support Assurance: An Extension of Social Security.* New York: Russell Sage Foundation.

Garfinkel, Irwin, and Marieka M. Klawitter. 1990. "The Effect of Routine Income Withholding of Child Support Collections." *Journal of Policy Analysis and Management* 9: 155–77.

Garfinkel, Irwin, and Sara S. McLanahan. 1986. *Single Mothers and Their Children: A New American Dilemma.* Washington, D.C.: Urban Institute Press.

Garfinkel, Irwin, and Marygold Melli, eds. 1982. *Child Support: Weaknesses of the Old and Features of a Proposed New System,* vol. 1. Institute for Research on Poverty Special Report 32A. Madison: Institute for Research on Poverty, University of Wisconsin-Madison.

Garfinkel, Irwin, and Donald Oellerich. 1989. "Noncustodial Fathers' Ability to Pay Child Support." *Demography* 26: 219–33.

Garfinkel, Irwin, Charles Manski, and Charles Michalopoulos. 1992. "Micro Experiments and Macro Effects." In *Evaluating Welfare and Training Programs,* edited by Charles F. Manski and Irwin Garfinkel. Cambridge, Mass.: Harvard University Press.

Garfinkel, Irwin, Donald Oellerich, and Philip K. Robins. 1991. "Child Support Guidelines: Will They Make a Difference?" *Journal of Family Issues* 12 (4, December): 404–29.

Garfinkel, Irwin, Philip K. Robins, Pat Wong, and Daniel R. Meyer. 1990. "The Wisconsin Child Support Assurance System: Estimated Effects on Poverty, Labor Supply, Caseloads, and Costs." *Journal of Human Resources* 25: 1–31.

Hausman, Jerry. 1985. "The Econometrics of Non-linear Budget Sets." *Econometrica* 53: 1255–282.

Hill, Martha, Sue Augustiniak, and Michael Ponza. 1985. "The Impact of Parental Marital Disruption on the Socioeconomic Attainments of Children as Adults." University of Michigan, Institute for Social Research, Ann Arbor. Photocopy.

Johnson, Terry R., and John H. Pencavel. 1984. "Dynamic Hours of Work Functions for Husbands, Wives, and Single Females." *Econometrica* 52: 363–89.

Lerman, Robert I. 1989. "Child Support Policies." In *Welfare Policy for the 1990s*, edited by Phoebe H. Cottingham and David T. Ellwood. Cambridge, Mass.: Harvard University Press.

Lewin/ICF. 1990. *Estimates of Expenditures on Children and Child Support Guidelines*. Report prepared for U.S. Department of Health and Human Services. Washington, D.C.: Author, October.

McLanahan, Sara S. 1988. "Family Structure and Dependency: Early Transitions to Female Household Headship." *Demography* 25: 1–16.

Meyer, Daniel, Irwin Garfinkel, Philip K. Robins, and Donald Oellerich. 1991. "The Costs and Effects of a National Child Support Assurance System." Institute for Research on Poverty Discussion Paper 940-91. Madison: Institute for Research on Poverty, University of Wisconsin-Madison.

Michalopoulos, Charles, and Irwin Garfinkel. 1989. "Reducing the Welfare Dependence and Poverty of Single Mothers by Means of Earnings and Child Support: Wishful Thinking and Realistic Possibility." Institute for Research on Poverty Discussion Paper 882-89. Madison: Institute for Research on Poverty, University of Wisconsin-Madison.

Moffitt, Robert. 1986. "The Econometrics of Piecewise-Linear Budget Constraints." *Journal of Business and Economic Statistics* 4 (July): 317–28.

National Commission on Children. 1991. *Beyond Rhetoric: A New American Agenda for Children and Families*. Washington, D.C.: Author.

Oellerich, Donald T. 1984. *The Effects of Potential Child Support Transfers on Wisconsin AFDC Costs, Caseloads, and Recipient Well-being*. Institute for Research on Poverty Special Report 35. Madison: Institute for Research on Poverty, University of Wisconsin-Madison.

Oellerich, Donald T., Irwin Garfinkel, and Philip K. Robins. 1991. "Private Child Support: Current and Potential Impacts." *Journal of Sociology and Social Welfare* 18: 3–23.

Robins, Philip K. 1986. "Child Support, Welfare Dependency, and Poverty." *American Economic Review* 76: 768–88.

————. 1987. "An Analysis of Trends in Child Support and AFDC from 1978 to 1983." Institute for Research on Poverty Discussion Paper 842-87. Madison: Institute for Research on Poverty, University of Wisconsin-Madison.

U.S. Bureau of the Census. 1990. *Money Income and Poverty Status in the United States: 1989 (Advanced Data from the March 1990 Current Population Survey). Current Population Reports,* ser. P-60, no. 168. Washington, D.C.: U.S. Government Printing Office.

Chapter Seven

THE NEW YORK STATE CHILD ASSISTANCE PROGRAM: DESIGN, OPERATION, AND EARLY IMPACTS

Alan Werner and Nancy R. Burstein

The New York State Child Assistance Program (CAP) is a welfare reform demonstration project currently operating in seven counties in New York State. CAP is a multifaceted program containing features found in other welfare reform demonstrations and programs, such as comprehensive case management, cashing out of Food Stamps, and reduced requirements for income reporting and eligibility redetermination. Of special interest for this chapter, however, are those aspects of the program that operate as incentives for single custodial parents receiving Aid to Families with Dependent Children (AFDC) to increase their employment and to cooperate further with efforts to establish child support awards for dependent children not currently covered by such awards. In this regard, CAP resembles a variant of the proposals for a Child Support Assurance System (CSAS), although limited to families otherwise eligible for AFDC.

The U.S. Department of Health and Human Services (DHHS) authorized the New York State Department of Social Services (SDSS) to run the program from October 1988 to April 1994.[1] As a condition of DHHS approval, the SDSS had to arrange for an independent evaluation of CAP. The evaluation is being conducted by Abt Associates and includes an implementation and process study, an impact study, a cost/benefit study, and a special study on Food Stamp cashout.

The organization of the demonstration in the seven counties reflects a mixed evaluation design. In four counties (the "saturation" counties), CAP is available to all eligible AFDC families. These counties provide the major context for the implementation and process study, because they mirror the conditions of full countywide program operation expected if CAP is expanded. In three additional counties (the "experimental" counties), the demonstration has been designed to measure the effects of the opportunity to participate in CAP on AFDC single-parent families.

The evaluation is designed to measure program impacts at one and two years following random assignment. This chapter reports findings on interim impacts at one year following random assignment. The final evaluation report containing findings on longer-term impacts was released in July 1993 (Hamilton et al. 1993).

The sections following describe CAP policy goals and program design; program administration in the saturation counties; the CAP experimental design and sample; CAP participation rates and patterns; and interim impacts on child support, earnings, welfare receipt, and total income.

CAP POLICY GOALS AND PROGRAM DESIGN

Much of the basic rationale and program concept for CAP stems from an investigation of the relationship between poverty and economic dependence among families with children conducted by the New York State Governor's Task Force on Poverty and Welfare (1986). The task force found that the AFDC program has been largely ineffective in helping single-parent families leave welfare or escape from poverty—a conclusion shared by a growing cadre of policymakers and analysts (see, for example, Elwood 1988 and Garfinkel and McLanahan 1986).

Two well-known limitations of the AFDC program noted by the task force are: (1) Even with the relatively high benefits offered in New York, combined AFDC and Food Stamp benefits do not raise a family above the poverty line; and (2) AFDC regulations strongly discourage recipients from combining work and welfare, by reducing AFDC benefits after the first four months of employment by one dollar for every dollar earned. Two other barriers faced by AFDC recipients seeking independence are a labor market characterized by low wages, job instability, less than full-time work, and lack of health insurance; and lack of child support from absent parents. Although AFDC policy requires custodial parents to cooperate with agency efforts to locate the absent parent and obtain a child support order, shortfalls occur due to practical and legal difficulties as well as to lack of cooperation by custodial parents.

The SDSS designed the Child Assistance Program in an effort to overcome these obstacles to self-sufficiency. Central to CAP's policy goals are the incentives to increase earnings and to cooperate with efforts to establish child support awards. Participation in CAP is limited to custodial parents and children who are eligible to receive

AFDC. Although employment is not a prerequisite to participation, CAP is only financially advantageous over AFDC when the custodial parent has gross earnings of about $350 or more per month. CAP also combines a lower basic benefit level (about two-thirds the level of the AFDC grant) with a dramatically lower benefit reduction rate. CAP benefits are reduced by 10 cents for each dollar earned up to the poverty level and by 67 cents for each dollar above the poverty level. By subtracting a smaller proportion of earnings from the grant, CAP allows families to earn as much as 150 percent of the poverty level before losing program eligibility.[2] CAP grant levels are based on the number of children in the family who are members of the AFDC case and who are covered by a support order. It is therefore in the interest of the custodial parent to establish orders for every child in the family.

Several other CAP features aim to reduce poverty and increase economic independence among program participants. CAP provides Food Stamp benefits by check rather than coupons. Cashout of Food Stamps is expected to give CAP families greater discretion in budgeting their income and to reduce the stigma associated with the use of coupons. Furthermore, CAP has no resource limit, as contrasted with the AFDC rule prohibiting clients from accumulating more than $1,000 in assets or owning a car with an equity value in excess of $1,500. This provision is designed to permit CAP participants to build up their savings for financial emergencies.

CAP also requires participants to manage their own household budgets, eliminating the restricted shelter and energy payment system commonly used in AFDC. Under CAP, participants can no longer rely on the agency to retain part of their monthly grants for the direct payment of rent, heat, or utility bills. CAP families do, however, receive some assistance with their child care expenses.

CAP's administrative structure was also designed to support participants' transition to independence. CAP case managers are expected to carry caseloads of approximately 50 families, as opposed to AFDC caseloads of 150–200 cases. This is intended to allow CAP workers sufficient time to provide intensive, individualized case management assistance to their clients. Less-frequent administrative reporting requirements (quarterly rather than monthly) are also intended to reduce the program's paperwork burden, for both workers and clients.

As stated previously, CAP resembles other proposals for a Child Support Assurance System. Policy researchers have proposed different forms of a CSAS and have simulated the impacts of the proposals on affected families' employment, earnings, support income, and assistance payments (see, for example, Meyer et al. 1991; and Meyer et al., chapter 6, this volume). The most common features of the various CSAS schemes include (Meyer et al. 1991: 7):

☐ A uniform percentage standard for establishing child support obligations;
☐ Immediate withholding of the child support obligation from wages and other sources of income of the noncustodial parent; and,
☐ An assured or minimum child support benefit for each family.

Because CAP operates within the prevailing context of child support policy, it includes all three of these features. That is, child support awards in CAP are governed by existing federal guidelines regarding standards for awards, and, in 1994, will be subject to immediate income withholding as a result of the Family Support Act of 1988. In addition, CAP has an assured benefit, based on the number of children with absent parents in the family.[3]

The important and telling difference between CAP and other CSAS proposals concerns the relationship between the assured benefit and total family income. For most CSAS proposals, participation could potentially benefit custodial parents in any income range. Whenever the absent parent's payments fall below the assured benefit, the custodial parent receives the difference, which is taxed at a rate no higher than family income in general. In contrast, however, CAP benefits are reduced $0.67 for every $1 earned above the poverty line, vanishing altogether at 150 percent of poverty. CAP is thus a test of a restrictive form of a CSAS.

PROGRAM OPERATIONS IN SATURATION COUNTIES

As discussed earlier, CAP has a mixed evaluation design that includes full implementation of the program in the four saturation counties: Albany, Allegany, Chautauqua, and Ulster. A major goal of the evaluation is to test the feasibility and success of introducing and operating CAP within a Local (i.e., county) Department of Social Services (LDSS). This section summarizes the approaches to program organization and operations used by the saturation counties in marketing and recruiting AFDC recipients to CAP and in providing case management for CAP participants.

Program Organization

Because CAP was designed as an alternative to AFDC rather than as a component of the existing program, the demonstration counties had to create from scratch an entirely new program and administrative unit. The CAP sites adopted organizational strategies that varied with respect to the administrative location of CAP within the LDSS agency, the administrative autonomy exercised by CAP management and staff, and the location of the CAP office.

The approach chosen by the Chautauqua County CAP represents one extreme of institutional independence. Although the program is in principle contained within the LDSS Income Maintenance (IM) Division, the CAP coordinator manages the program as though it were an agency entirely separate from the county's welfare system. The CAP offices are also located several blocks away from one of the county's LDSS client services offices.

The other extreme is represented by the Albany County CAP, which is administered by the welfare department's Office of Employment Programs. This arrangement reflects an institutional tradition of operating demonstration programs out of the LDSS Employment Division, as well as the view that CAP represents a logical next step for persons completing LDSS employment and training programs. Administratively, CAP is generally perceived by AFDC program staff and recipients as just another Employment Division program. As observed later in this chapter, such variations in organizational approach may help explain differences in CAP participation rates.

Marketing and Recruitment

Each of the four saturation county CAP agencies has used a broad array of marketing techniques to make the program widely known among potentially eligible CAP participants and LDSS staff. All four have used CAP posters directed at AFDC recipients, three have distributed brochures or fliers publicizing CAP, and all have begun producing program newsletters, which are mailed to CAP clients, LDSS employees, and outside agencies, and distributed to LDSS waiting rooms.

Part of the goal of marketing is to get CAP information to organizations that may refer clients to CAP, particularly other LDSS divisions. When the program first began, CAP presentations were made to LDSS management and staff in all of the CAP sites. CAP is also routinely presented to all new IM staff during initial training sessions.

While they were marketing CAP broadly to generate awareness of the program, CAP staff were also recruiting participants. The state plan called for the saturation sites initially to mail letters, with brochures enclosed, inviting apparently CAP-ready AFDC clients to group or individual presentations, where they would be encouraged to enter the program. To assist the sites, the SDSS made available monthly lists of AFDC clients who appeared to have earned income and lists of clients with child support orders for at least some of their children. Since that time, the counties' recruitment strategies have evolved to cover a broader spectrum of the AFDC population, including AFDC clients lacking either a child support order or a job or both.

CAP Case Management

The separation of income maintenance from social service functions in public assistance programs is often considered a weakness of the present welfare system. CAP addresses this problem by integrating the two functions. In addition to eligibility determination and budgeting functions, CAP case managers perform client outreach, recruitment, needs assessments, service referrals, and monitoring. As noted previously, their target caseloads are only a third or a quarter as large as those of income maintenance workers. Their actual caseloads ranged from 20 to 47 CAP cases per worker as of February 1991. (CAP case managers also had responsibility for program marketing and recruitment, and for helping AFDC recipients become qualified for CAP.)

During the first year of operation, the emphasis of case management was on maintaining CAP participation and solving problems faced by program participants. During the second year, some sites reportedly refocused their case management toward helping clients graduate from CAP. The lower CAP caseloads and broader case management responsibilities led workers to perform a variety of services. For example, CAP case managers often helped clients find appropriate child care or arrange transportation to work, in addition to providing referrals to employers and education and training programs.

Some of the counties offer special supportive services to their clients. For example, the Ulster CAP program started a support group for single parents in an effort to teach CAP clients how to create their own sources of emotional and practical support outside the program. The Albany CAP Coordinator has also begun teaching clients how to file tax forms and apply for the Earned Income Tax Credit, open up checking accounts, and create household budgets.

Although the four saturation counties show some variation in the way they operate CAP, it is clear that CAP represents an entirely different approach to "case management" than the typical AFDC program. CAP case managers have far lower caseloads than income maintenance workers, and provide far more services or referrals to services than the typical AFDC worker. Although the CAP demonstration is not designed to measure the impact of the program's administrative structure separately from the program's financial incentives, the institutional culture of CAP is clearly more attractive than that of AFDC.

THE CAP EXPERIMENT

The evaluation of CAP's impact is based on an experiment conducted in three counties: Monroe, Niagara, and Suffolk. This section describes the experiment and discusses the characteristics of the sample.

The Experimental Design

The CAP impact evaluation is based on a classic experimental design, in which individuals potentially eligible for CAP were randomly assigned (based on the last digit of their case identification number) to a treatment or a control group. Grantees in the treatment group were told about the CAP program and offered the opportunity to participate. Grantees in the control group were not told about the program. If they later inquired about CAP, they were informed that only limited slots were available and that they could not enroll. The random assignment of potentially eligible individuals allows for a test of the impact of CAP on the behavior of CAP participants and nonparticipants alike in the treatment group.

Four analytic subgroups of potentially eligible grantees were defined according to whether or not they had earnings, and whether or not they had any support orders, at the time of the sample entry. The opportunity to participate in CAP was expected to have different impacts on these four groups—those who had both earnings and support orders could enter CAP quickly, whereas those lacking orders and earnings could take actions to acquire them.

Sample intake took place at the AFDC recertification interviews of potentially eligible grantees—that is, custodial parents currently receiving AFDC for themselves, with at least one child who has a deprivation factor of an absent parent. The sample consists of 4,287 individuals, divided roughly equally among 12 strata (three counties multiplied by four analytic subgroups). To achieve representativeness for the analysis with respect to the population from which the sample was drawn, weights were attached to each sample member that were inversely proportional to the probability of sample selection. Monroe County (Rochester), with the largest caseload, accounts for about half the weighted sample. About a third of the weighted sample is from Suffolk County (eastern Long Island), and the remainder is from Niagara County (Niagara Falls). Cases with earnings at baseline were oversampled: they comprise only about 10 percent of the overall caseload, but nearly half of the unweighted sample. Both the weighted and unweighted samples are divided roughly evenly among recipients who do and do not have any support orders.

Baseline Characteristics of Experimental Sample

The baseline information form collected information on the characteristics of the experimental population at the point of sample intake. Of particular interest are initial differences among the potentially eligible population that might be expected to lead to different levels of CAP success.

DEMOGRAPHICS AND HOUSEHOLD COMPOSITION

All grantees selected for the experimental sample are AFDC custodial parents with at least one child having an absent parent. Virtually all of the grantees are women. Whites and blacks are about equally represented, each accounting for about two-fifths of the demonstration population, and Hispanics comprising most of the rest (see table 7.1).[4] About three-fifths of the grantees are age 30 or younger. Sixty percent have never married, and over half are high school graduates. The grantees' households are generally small; two-thirds contain only one or two children. They are headed predominantly by single adults, although 15 percent contain more than one adult.[5] In half of these families, at least one child is still under the age of three, a possible impediment to working enough to participate in CAP.

CHILD SUPPORT STATUS

To participate in CAP, AFDC recipients are required to have a child support order in place for one or more children. AFDC recipients do

Table 7.1 DEMOGRAPHIC CHARACTERISTICS AND HOUSEHOLD
COMPOSITION OF RESEARCH SAMPLE, BY NEW YORK COUNTY

	County (%)			
	Monroe	Niagara	Suffolk	Total (%)
Percentage of Grantees Who Are:				
Never married	67.3	50.4	52.9	60.1
30 and under	65.8	56.2	55.0	60.7
Male	0.9	2.6	0.5	1.0
Black	53.0	30.9	33.5	43.3
White	29.8	63.0	47.9	40.3
Hispanic	15.9	3.1	16.3	14.5
High school graduates	52.7	65.0	55.4	55.2
Percentage of Households Containing:				
Multiple adults	8.2	18.0	24.6	15.0
More than two children	30.3	30.3	36.7	32.5
A child under age three	53.2	43.9	49.5	50.8

not benefit financially from CAP until they obtain orders for all or almost all of their children, however, because children without orders are excluded from the CAP case and cannot receive AFDC. The demonstration population is approximately evenly divided between those who have no orders for their children and those who have at least one order. Only about one-third of the custodial parents have complete orders, however (table 7.2). One-third of the families also contain children of multiple absent parents.

The potential difficulty of obtaining the missing orders will depend on the relationship between the absent and custodial parents. For about one-third of the families with incomplete (or no) orders, the absent parent lives out of state, or his whereabouts or identity is unknown (table 7.2). Lengthy procedures would probably be required to locate these absent parents. In those cases where the grantee never married the absent parent (52 percent of the families missing support orders), the child's paternity must also be established, which can also become a long and involved court process. A third indicator of the difficulties faced by some grantees is the amount of contact they have had with the absent parent. At sample intake, two-fifths of the grantees who lacked one or more support orders reported having no contact at all.

Among the experimental counties, Monroe has the lowest percentage of families with any support orders and the lowest percentage with orders for all their children. Furthermore, among families that are missing orders, Monroe has the highest percentage of grantees

Table 7.2 CHILD SUPPORT STATUS OF RESEARCH SAMPLE, BY NEW YORK
COUNTY

	County			
	Monroe (%)	Niagara (%)	Suffolk (%)	Total (%)
Percentage of Cases Containing Children of:				
One absent parent	65.5	71.7	72.2	68.7
Two absent parents	27.2	24.2	23.0	25.4
Three or more absent parents	7.3	4.1	4.8	6.0
With Any Support Orders	49.3	71.5	50.8	52.5
Lacking Support Orders for:				
No children	30.6	58.7	36.0	35.9
One child	39.8	27.0	33.4	36.0
Two or more children	29.6	14.3	30.6	28.1
Percentage of Cases Containing at Least One Child Lacking a Support Order for Whom the Absent Parent:				
Lives out of state (or whereabouts or identity unknown)	30.8	23.7	37.0	32.1
Was never married to the custodial parent	59.2	31.2	47.5	51.6
Has no contact with the grantee	41.7	25.4	42.3	39.9

who were never married to the absent parent (table 7.2). The Niagara
grantees, in contrast, seem most prepared to meet CAP's support
order requirement. Nearly three-quarters already have at least one
child support order in place, and three-fifths have orders for all their
children. Among grantees lacking a support order, Niagara has the
lowest percentage of cases in which the absent parent lives outside
the state, was never married to the grantee, or has no contact with
the grantee.

AFDC AND WORK HISTORY

Clients' welfare history is often considered a possible determinant
of an intervention's success. In terms of CAP, however, we have no
strong hypothesis that a long welfare history will either facilitate or
impede intervention. One might argue that longer-term recipients,
having settled in to welfare, would seldom take advantage of CAP's
offer of a route out of dependency. On the other hand, the longer-
term recipients might have fewer young children and therefore more
opportunity to respond to CAP. Three-quarters of the sample grantees

Table 7.3 AFDC AND WORK HISTORY OF RESEARCH SAMPLE, BY NEW YORK
COUNTY

	County			
	Monroe	Niagara	Suffolk	Total
Percentage of Grantees Whose Total Receipt of AFDC in Own Case, Excluding Breaks in Assistance, Is:				
Less than 12 months	13.8%	5.5%	14.7%	13.1%
One to two years	14.6	11.3	13.3	13.7
Two to five years	31.7	31.0	33.6	32.3
More than five years	40.0	52.3	38.3	40.9
Percentage of Grantees:				
Ever worked for pay	81.3	91.3	88.5	85.1
Currently working for pay	9.5	17.8	8.7	10.2
Current or most recent job is (was) 30 or more hours per week	50.6	44.3	62.1	54.0
Ever had a job that lasted over a year	44.6	49.1	59.6	50.5
Ever had a job that paid $7 or more per hour	10.9	6.5	21.1	14.0

have received AFDC for two or more years in their own case—that
is, not counting receipt as a child (table 7.3). Participants in Niagara
are particularly likely to have a long AFDC history.

Grantees' employment histories, like their child support status, are
expected to influence their interest in CAP and their ability to qualify
for the program. Those who were employed when they were selected
for the sample and those who previously held relatively good jobs
seem the most likely to participate in CAP. Although only 10 percent
of grantees were working for pay at baseline, 85 percent had done
so at one time or another (table 7.3). For most grantees, however,
employment had been neither long term nor lucrative. Only about
half of them worked as many as 30 hours per week at their current
or most recent job, or ever had a job that lasted over a year. Furthermore, only one in seven ever earned as much as $7 per hour. Suffolk
County grantees, although only half as likely as Niagara County grantees to be currently employed, had substantially better work histories
in terms of hours, duration, and wages. County officials indicated
that some of the county's major employers, particularly military con-
tractors, have experienced severe cutbacks in recent years, placing
on the welfare rolls many people who formerly held relatively good
jobs.

The profile of AFDC grantees selected for the CAP experiment
generally resembles the profile for the AFDC caseload nationwide

Figure 7.1 CAP PARTICIPATION RATES FOR SATURATION COUNTIES IN NEW
YORK THROUGH JULY 1991

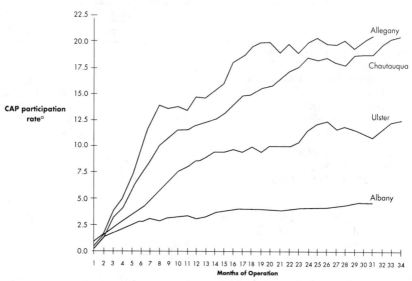

a. Percentage of potentially eligible cases participating.

(U.S. Congress, House 1991; 620–641). Very few recipients began the demonstration with enough child support orders and earnings to make CAP participation worthwhile immediately. Given their child support status and work histories, many clients would seem to face major obstacles to CAP participation.

PROGRAM PARTICIPATION RATES AND PATTERNS

This section compares CAP participation rates in the saturation and experimental counties, relates the participation decision to individual and household characteristics, and presents interim findings on the dynamics of CAP participation.

Program Participation in Saturation Counties

Between October 1988 and July 1991, 1,305 families had participated in CAP in the saturation counties. As of July 1, 1991, a total of 776 of these families were still enrolled in CAP. Figure 7.1 shows the participation rates over time for the four saturation counties.[6]

Allegany and Chautauqua Counties clearly have the highest participation rates. In both counties, one in five potentially eligible families was participating in CAP by July 1991. The least successful county in this regard has been Albany, where less than 5 percent of the potentially eligible families were in CAP.

When we compare these extremes, some patterns emerge. First, the more successful counties have used a more intensive and diversified recruitment strategy. For example, while Albany County initially tried to focus on individuals who appeared to be already eligible for CAP, Chautauqua County actively and aggressively recruited all single-parent AFDC families. The reason for the success of the "shotgun" approach to marketing may be that many potential clients cannot be identified simply on the basis of their current situation. Clients who appear not to be CAP-ready may become so quickly if they know about CAP and become motivated to find a job and enroll.

A second characteristic of the more successful CAP counties is that they market CAP as a new and more attractive alternative to AFDC, by holding CAP informational presentations away from welfare offices, creating recruitment materials that look different than DSS literature, focusing public information campaigns on CAP's advantages over AFDC, and emphasizing the more personal and attentive case management available in CAP.

A final important feature of the more successful counties is an extensive and systematic set of procedures for keeping track of potentially interested clients. Allegany and Chautauqua counties have computerized tracking systems and use a tickler file mechanism to remind workers to make appropriate and timely follow-up contacts.

While the pace of enrollments fluctuated from month to month in all four counties, they were higher in general over the first 6 to 12 months than in subsequent periods (see figure 7.1). This was to be expected. In the first six months, AFDC families who were immediately eligible for CAP learned about the program and many decided to enroll. In subsequent months enrollments could come only from new families on the caseload, families whose circumstances had changed, or families who had changed their mind about participating. Nonetheless, the pattern of figure 7.1 suggests a strong continuing influx of families who would potentially be interested in CAP. This implies a need for more continuous recruitment activity than might be required for other programs.

Program Participation in Experimental Counties

Enrollment in CAP in the experimental counties occurred at a substantially lower rate than in the saturation counties. As shown in

Figure 7.2 CUMULATIVE ENTRIES INTO CAP, BY EXPERIMENTAL COUNTY

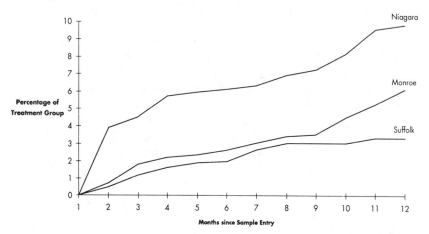

figure 7.2, the proportions of treatment group clients who entered CAP by the 12th month following random assignment in Monroe, Niagara, and Suffolk Counties were 6, 10, and 3 percent, respectively, for a combined rate of 6 percent. By contrast, the rates for the saturation counties after 12 months ranged from 3 percent to 15 percent of potential participants, for a combined rate of about 10 percent (see figure 7.1).

The difference in participation rates between the experimental and saturation counties reflects the constraints on marketing and recruitment imposed by the experimental design. In the experimental counties, the control group was not informed about CAP, and there was no general public information campaign about CAP. In addition, the time that workers would normally have had to recruit even from among the treatment group was reduced by the requirement of administering a baseline information form to the entire experimental sample.

The participation level in the experimental counties is thus probably lower than what would have occurred without random assignment. The observed impacts reported later in this chapter may therefore *understate* the likely effects in a nondemonstration context. We cannot assume, however, that impacts would increase proportionately with higher participation rates, because CAP is designed to generate impacts even before people participate—as they seek to qualify for the program by obtaining employment and child support orders. Nevertheless, if participation is higher in future implementations of CAP, we expect that impacts would be greater as well.

The Participation Decision

The likelihood for an individual in an experimental county to enroll in CAP during the observation period was determined almost entirely by CAP readiness and closely related factors. In weighted logistic models of CAP participation by county and for all three experimental counties combined, the employment status of the grantee at the time of intake is the most powerful explanatory variable.[7] Impacts of this variable on the likelihood of CAP enrollment in the four models range from 9 to 17 percentage points, all statistically significant.[8] Furthermore, in three of the four models, the *amount* of the grantee's monthly earnings at the time of sample entry has a significant positive effect on the probability of enrollment: 3 percentage points per $100 in Niagara, and 1 percentage point per $100 in Suffolk and in the three counties combined.[9] Similarly, never having worked for pay reduces the probability of CAP enrollment by 6 percentage points in both Monroe county and in all counties combined. Although several measures of work-force attachment (full-time versus part-time status, length of longest job, highest wage) were not statistically significant, it may be supposed that these were sufficiently captured in the measures of current employment status and earnings.

The number of children for whom support orders are in place likewise has a strong effect on participation in all four models. The impact ranges from 2 to 4 percentage points per child. The impact of an additional child *lacking* a support order, although similar in magnitude (and opposite in sign), does not achieve significance in any model. This may reflect the fact that the CAP grant has a large fixed component and a relatively small variable component with respect to the number of children with support orders. Indicators of the potential for obtaining additional orders that were significant in one or more models included marital status relative to the absent parent and contact with the absent parent.

Other than these fairly direct measures of present or potential earnings and support orders, there was little predictive power in the grantee and household characteristics. Among variables tried in the model and not statistically significant were: grantee's race, education, ethnicity, and sex; the presence of multiple adults and of children under age three; receipt of unemployment compensation; receipt of the child support pass-through; the number of absent parents in the case; and whether the absent parents from whom orders were lacking lived in New York State. Although these characteristics undoubtedly influence or reflect a grantee's status with regard to employment and support orders, it appears that essentially all of the information they can contribute to explaining CAP participation is already captured in the employment and child support status measures themselves. This implies that for any two women in a given county with the same earnings and number of support orders at baseline, the probability of CAP enrollment will be about the same, regardless of race, education, or other characteristics included in the model.

Participation Patterns

Evidence from one year of experience of CAP participants in the experimental counties suggests that the process toward financial independence may require some time. Over 80 percent of those who had enrolled in CAP in the experimental counties during the 12 months were still participating at the end of the year. Of the remainder, most had returned to AFDC; 6 percent were not receiving any cash assistance.

The experience in the saturation counties (over a somewhat longer period) is essentially similar. Allegany has the lowest AFDC return rate, at 13 percent. The rates in the other three counties are only slightly higher, at 18 to 20 percent. Although relatively few CAP cases have returned to AFDC, even fewer have achieved financial independence thus far. Allegany and Ulster have the largest proportion becoming financially ineligible, at 15 percent. Albany and Chautauqua have somewhat lower rates of 10 percent and 11 percent.

At this stage in the demonstration, it is difficult to judge the extent to which these participation patterns represent "success" or "failure." Because CAP is the first program of its kind, no one knows how many participants should be expected ultimately to return to AFDC and how many should achieve independence. Further, we do not know how long to expect the average case to stay on CAP before moving in one direction or the other. Ultimately, success must be judged by comparing long-term dependency in the treatment and control groups in the experimental counties.

CAP IMPACTS

As discussed earlier, the incentives inherent in CAP are hypothesized to influence the behavior of CAP participants as well as the behavior of those trying to qualify for CAP. The impacts of CAP at 12 months following random assignment have been analyzed in four areas: child support, earnings, welfare dependency, and total household income. Whereas significant gains were found with respect to both child support orders and earnings, there was no net impact on welfare receipt. Total household income increased significantly, but by a small amount.

Child Support

Data for the analysis of child support outcomes were extracted by the SDSS from the Child Support Management System (CSMS), which serves the Child Support Enforcement Program. The available data describe, for each case in each month, the number of current child support orders recorded in the CSMS, the aggregate amount due in the month on those orders, and the aggregate amount of payments on the orders.

IMPACTS ON PRESENCE AND NUMBER OF ORDERS

About half of the demonstration clients had no support orders in their first month. Even in the absence of CAP, some of these would gain support orders over the course of the year. As shown in table 7.4, 7.6 percent of clients in the control group had no support orders at the outset but did obtain at least one order by their 12th month. In the treatment group, however, the number obtaining orders was 4.4 percentage points higher, a statistically significant difference and a gain of 58 percent. Similar effects were seen in the mean number of orders (not shown). For the population as a whole, the mean number of orders increased over the observation period by 0.101 among controls, and by 0.160 among treatment group members.

Among the counties, the strongest impact and the only statistically significant one occurred in Monroe (table 7.4). The proportion of Monroe control group members with any orders increased by 8 percentage points during the year, compared to 17 percentage points for the treatment group. This 115-percent effect stems partly from the fact that Monroe had the highest proportion of cases initially lacking support orders. Perhaps more importantly, the Monroe CAP's procedures for helping clients obtain support orders were judged to be the strongest of the three counties. These included bringing a child support investigator onto the CAP staff to work exclusively on CAP-related child support cases and teaching CAP case managers

Table 7.4 IMPACTS OF CAP ON CHILD SUPPORT OUTCOMES, EMPLOYMENT-RELATED OUTCOMES, AND WELFARE RECEIPT, BY NEW YORK COUNTY

| | County | | | | | | | |
| | Monroe | | Niagara | | Suffolk | | Total | |
	Control Group	Difference	Control Group	Difference	Control Group	Difference	Control Group	Difference
Child Support Outcomes:								
Change in percentage with orders	8.1%	9.3%**	4.3%	2.2%	7.9%	-2.0%	7.6%	4.4%*
Mean amount due (last three months)	$61	$16**	$85	$6	$138	$14	$92	$13*
Mean amount paid (last three months)	$41	$7	$76	-$14	$90	-$8	$63	-$1
Employment-Related Outcomes:								
Average monthly employment rate (%)	16.7%	4.7%**	24.5%	5.7%	15.8%	1.1%	17.3%	3.6%**
Average hours worked per month	18.1	8.2**	26.5	8.1*	18.7	0.0	19.3	5.4**
Average monthly earnings	$101	$57**	$148	$31	$133	-$10	$118	$30**
Welfare Receipt:								
Mean monthly cash assistance (last three months, AFDC, CAP, HR)[a]	$591	-$21	$437	$23	$670	$1	$602	-$10
Mean monthly Food Stamps (last three months)	$157	-$9**	$149	-$6	$123	$1	$144	-$5*
Medicaid eligibility rate (%)	93.9%	-2.9%**	88.0%	4.4%*	89.9%	-1.3%	91.7%	-1.4%

** Statistically significant at 1 percent level.
* Statistically significant at 5 percent level.
a. AFDC, Aid to Families with Dependent Children; CAP, Child Assistance Program; HR, Home Relief.

how to access on-line child support data from the CAP computer terminal.

In Niagara County, many more cases began with at least one support order, which would make a large effect less likely (table 7.4). The estimated CAP effect, although positive, was not statistically significant. In Suffolk, although the proportion of cases initially lacking orders was nearly as great as in Monroe, no significant impact was observed.

IMPACTS ON VALUE OF ORDERS

The monthly amount due on orders across all grantees (including those without orders) in the last three months of the observation period averaged $92 for control group members and $13 more for treatment group members—a 14 percent effect (table 7.4).[10] This impact, as for the presence and number of orders, was concentrated in Monroe County. In Monroe, a sizable and statistically significant impact of $16 is seen on the current amount due. Treatment-control differences in the other two counties are not statistically significant.

IMPACTS ON AMOUNTS COLLECTED

CAP's effect on new support orders does not appear to have translated into additional collections during the first year. No statistically significant effect is observed for the demonstration as a whole or for any of the three counties (table 7.4). Subgroup analysis found, however, that grantees who began with earnings but no support orders (4 percent of the population, but 15 percent of the analysis sample) did experience a significant CAP effect on collections. This subgroup also experienced the greatest CAP effect on acquisition of new orders. This finding suggests that if CAP's effect on new orders continues to grow after the first year, we might expect to see increased collections for other groups as well.

Employment and Earnings

Like many welfare reform initiatives in recent years, the Child Assistance Program attempts to move AFDC recipients toward financial independence in part through employment. While the long-term results of the incentive structure and of case managers' support should be increased earnings, some clients might defer or cut back employment in the short term to enroll in education or training programs, hoping to enhance their skills or credentials before seeking jobs that could qualify them for CAP.

Data on employment-related outcomes were taken from the follow-up survey, which was administered approximately one year after the client was randomly assigned in the demonstration. Respondents were asked, for each month since they entered the demonstration, how many weeks of the month they had worked, the average number of hours they worked per week, and their average earnings in those weeks.

CAP was successful in increasing grantees' employment, even in the short run, as shown in table 7.4. The average monthly employment rate in the last three months of the observation period was 17.3 percent for controls, but 20.9 percent for treatment group members—a 21 percent effect. The impact of CAP on average hours worked per month in this period (including those who did not work) was even greater, indicating that those who did work were increasing their hours of employment as well. Monthly hours worked were 19.3 for controls, and 24.7 for treatment group members—a 28 percent effect. Monthly earnings, averaged over all grantees, were $118 for controls and $30 higher for treatment group members, representing a 25 percent effect. All three of these estimated impacts are statistically significant.

The earnings effects, like the child support effects, were concentrated in Monroe County. The estimated impact on grantees' monthly earnings in that county was 56 percent ($57 ÷ $101) (table 7.4). In Niagara County, positive effects were seen, although they were not in general statistically significant. In Suffolk County, there were virtually no effects in this area.

Subgroup analysis indicated that impacts on employment and earnings were greatest for those grantees who started with support orders, but were not working initially. Their employment rate was increased by 39 percent because of CAP, and their monthly earnings by 53 percent. The CAP work incentives are clearly the greatest for women in this situation. Given that they have the support orders, the implicit tax on their potential earnings in their first month of work is suddenly reduced from 67 percent to 10 percent (assuming they earn enough to make CAP pay, and not enough to become ineligible). Although this situation is the same for all grantees, those who lack support orders have a major hurdle to overcome before they can take advantage of the changed situation; and those who already have both support orders and employment have less room for increasing their work effort.

The work-incentive component of CAP appears to compare favorably with mandatory work-welfare programs. In a review of seven work-welfare demonstrations, first-year impacts on employment ranged from −8 to +29 percent and first-year impacts on earnings ranged from +1 percent to +33 percent, with most of the estimates falling under 15 percent (Gueron and Pauly 1991).[11]

Welfare Dependency

CAP attempts to reduce dependency on public assistance by offering services designed to increase clients' self-sufficiency, principally through increased earnings and child support. As already indicated, CAP has achieved some success in both of these areas. CAP provides mixed incentives to program participants with regard to public assistance receipt, however. The incentives and improved opportunities to achieve financial independence were discussed earlier. Because CAP allows participants to continue receiving assistance at higher income levels, however, some recipients might stay on CAP longer than they would have remained on AFDC.

CAP's administrative rules and case management practices may also have contradictory influences on public assistance receipt. Case managers may provide referrals to child care providers, education and training programs, and local employers. They sometimes mediate in clients' disputes with employers, landlords, and local utility companies. They may also give clients advice, positive feedback, and encouragement. If these program features help clients weather short-term crises that might otherwise derail their progress toward self-sufficiency, they may help to hasten clients' exit from assistance. Alternatively, clients might become too dependent on such program supports, delaying their exit from assistance. These contradictory hypotheses make it impossible to say how CAP should affect public assistance receipt in the short term. In fact, the analyses reveal no substantial effects, suggesting that the contradictory forces may have counterbalanced each other.

Data for analyzing effects of CAP in this area were extracted by SDSS from the automated data systems serving the programs. For each sample month, the data show the amount of assistance received by each case from each of five programs: AFDC, CAP, Home Relief (HR), Food Stamps, and Medical Assistance.[12]

CASH ASSISTANCE

Sample members could receive cash assistance in a given month in any one of three forms: AFDC, CAP, or Home Relief (if they became categorically ineligible for AFDC). With regard to the dollar amount of cash assistance paid, no significant difference was found in any of the three counties, nor for the three counties combined. The treatment-control group difference in terms of the mean monthly cash assistance payment for the sample as a whole was −$10, compared to a control group mean of $602.

FOOD STAMPS

CAP is not hypothesized to have a direct effect on participation in the Food Stamp Program. Because clients usually receive Food Stamps if they get cash assistance, we would expect the general participation patterns to be parallel. The amount of the Food Stamp allotment could change, however. Under AFDC rules, an increase in earnings could lead to a small *increase* in Food Stamp benefits.[13] Under CAP, however, an increase in earnings leads to a smaller decline in cash assistance, so that countable income is increased and the net effect on Food Stamp benefits is negative.

Mean Food Stamp benefits were reduced by CAP, by a statistically significant $5 per month in the last three months of the observation period. This effect represents 3 percent of the control group average payment, as shown in table 7.4. Subgroup analysis indicated that this effect was concentrated among those clients who began with earnings and support orders (i.e., those most likely to participate in CAP).

MEDICAL ASSISTANCE

CAP and AFDC recipients are categorically eligible for Medical Assistance and receive identical benefits.[14] Nonetheless, CAP might exert indirect influences on Medicaid eligibility or claims, for several reasons. First, any change in AFDC/CAP participation would lead to a corresponding change in months of Medicaid eligibility. Second, 12 months of extended Medicaid eligibility are available to former AFDC and CAP recipients, but *only* if they leave the rolls due to increased income. CAP may lead to more clients leaving assistance for this reason, and hence receiving this benefit. Third, changes in cash assistance participation patterns may change the composition of the pool of people on Medicaid, and hence the average Medicaid claim. Finally, because Medicaid is the payor of last resort, CAP could lead to substitution of other insurance coverage—either employer-provided or through the policies of absent parents.

These hypotheses suggest that if CAP affects Medicaid, the effect will be visible first in the percentage of families eligible for Medicaid benefits in any one month. Actual Medicaid payments vary enormously across cases and from month to month, reflecting medical events that CAP does not influence. The analysis therefore focused on Medicaid eligibility rather than on benefits paid.

CAP does seem to have had some influence on Medicaid eligibility. As shown in table 7.4, CAP was associated with a significant decrease of 3 percentage points in the Medicaid eligibility rate in Monroe County, and a significant increase of 4 percentage points in Niagara County. Small, insignificant negative effects were found in Suffolk and for the three counties combined. This pattern corresponds closely to the previously reported effects on cash assistance participation.

Total Income

CAP is intended to increase family income. If CAP successfully motivates AFDC recipients to increase their work effort and helps build the base of child support obligations from the absent parent, long-term gains in earnings and child support income should result. Even in the short term, CAP may increase family income by giving participants with support orders and substantial earnings a greater total income than they could obtain with AFDC. Moreover, as AFDC recipients attempt to qualify for CAP by obtaining support orders and obtaining or increasing their earnings, they may increase their total income even before enrolling in CAP. On the other hand, if some individuals in the treatment group participate in CAP while their counterparts in the control group go off assistance, one cannot predict which group will have the higher average income. For the 12-month period examined here, CAP increased income slightly but not consistently.

This analysis is based on a combination of all of the previously cited data. The elements of household income that are included are as follows:

□ Earnings, from the grantee and other household members;
□ Cash benefits, from AFDC or CAP, Home Relief, Emergency Assistance, Social Security, Supplemental Security Income (SSI), and unemployment compensation;
□ Food Stamp benefits; and
□ Child support income, from the AFDC pass-through, payments through the Child Support Enforcement Agency to former recipients, and direct payments from the absent parents to former recipients.

Figure 7.3 TOTAL MONTHLY HOUSEHOLD INCOME OVER TIME

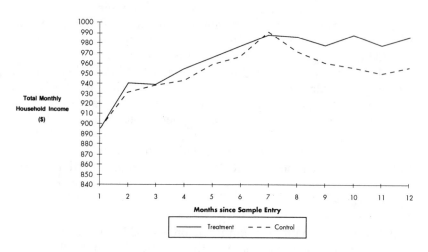

Both the treatment and the control group showed a characteristic pattern of total monthly income over the course of the year, as shown in figure 7.3. Beginning with average monthly incomes around $890 in the 1st month, households in both groups experienced a rise of about $100 over the next 6 months. The rise was followed by a $35 decline for the control group grantees, whereas the treatment group's average did not decline. Consequently, mean income was $29 higher among treatment group households by the 12th month—a statistically significant effect, amounting to 3 percent of income.

CAP's positive impact on income was concentrated in Niagara, with significant differences of $110 (12 percent) for the last month, and $1,009 (10 percent) for the entire year. Treatment-control differences in the other two counties are not statistically significant.[15]

By allowing grantees to combine more earnings with cash assistance, CAP was expected to allow some households to obtain incomes substantially over the poverty line. To test for this possible short-term impact, we compared each household's total income to the 1991 poverty level for a household of that size.[16] The analysis focused on the proportion of the population whose income exceeded 125 percent of the poverty line, a level often taken to indicate meaningful movement above poverty. In the 12th month, 21 percent of the treatment group had incomes surpassing 125 percent of the poverty line, compared to 16 percent of the control group. This 5 percentage point effect for the overall population was statistically significant, as were the effects for Monroe and Niagara Counties (6 and 17 percentage points, respectively).

CONCLUSION AND FUTURE RESEARCH

The Child Assistance Program introduces a novel incentive structure in an attempt to motivate AFDC clients to obtain child support orders and increase their participation in the work force. The first challenge faced by program operators was to implement this unique program within the larger context of county Departments of Social Services. The experience of the CAP counties to date confirms the feasibility of the program; all the counties are performing CAP program functions and are enrolling and managing CAP cases on a continuing basis. The Interim Implementation and Process Study in the four CAP saturation districts allows a closer examination of program operations (Hargreaves 1992). Some important observations from this study are:

□ CAP participation in the saturation counties varies substantially, from around 20 percent in Allegany and Chautauqua Counties to less than 5 percent in Albany County.
□ Direct marketing and recruitment strategies were initially focused on families that already had jobs as well as child support orders, but have broadened to include families meeting one or none of these criteria. The counties that have consistently pursued families with neither jobs nor support orders have relatively high participation rates.
□ High participation rates occurred where recruitment efforts were relatively intense and involved systematic follow-up of potentially interested families.
□ About 60 percent of the families that have enrolled in CAP in the saturation counties are still participating.
□ Most CAP counties have implemented supportive case management systems that have been popular features of the program for participants.
□ CAP's image as a program distinct from AFDC has been an important factor in stimulating participation. The image has been generated mainly by CAP having a separate physical location and considerable operational autonomy, rather than by the placement of CAP within the existing agency's organizational structure.

The first 12 months of experience in the experimental counties provides some evidence about the impact of CAP. Thus far, findings reveal that the program is having some success in influencing client behavior in terms of increasing work effort and cooperation with child support enforcement efforts. Whether this success will lead to long-term increases in family income and independence from public assistance remains to be seen.

The central findings of the impact analysis are as follows:

☐ *Significant gains in child support orders.* About 12 percent of treatment group members initially had no support orders but had obtained at least one by the 12th month; the comparable control group figure is 7.6 percent. The average monthly amount due on treatment group orders was $105 for the last three months of the period, up to 14 percent from the control group average. The impact was concentrated among clients who had no support orders when they entered the demonstration.

☐ *Significant increase in employment.* In the last three months of the study period, 21 percent of the treatment group were employed compared to 17 percent of the control group. Average monthly earnings for the treatment group were $148, 25 percent above the control group average. CAP's impact was greatest among clients who had support orders but no earnings when they entered the demonstration.

☐ *Little change in welfare dependency.* Virtually the same proportion of the treatment group and the control group received AFDC or CAP benefits in the last three months of the study period. Neither the proportion receiving assistance nor the amount of benefits paid to the two groups differed significantly.

☐ *Small gains in total income.* The treatment group's average household income in the 12th month was $29, or 3 percent higher than the control group average, a statistically significant impact. Moreover, 21 percent of the treatment group households' incomes exceeded 125 percent of the poverty line, compared to 16 percent of the control group.

We should note some limitations of the interim impact findings. For example, neither the earnings nor the child support impacts were significant for all groups. Further, the CAP-induced increase in support orders has not translated clearly into increased payments by the absent parents, which is the only way the orders can generate long-term income gains for the custodial parents. It is also important to note that no significant positive CAP impacts were found in Suffolk

County. Several factors probably contributed to this result, including staffing limitations that stemmed from a local fiscal crisis, a high local unemployment rate, and less-effective CAP procedures than Monroe and Niagara were able to employ.

In spite of these reservations, the impact results after 12 months of exposure to CAP suggest the following optimistic indications:

☐ *Impacts with low participation rates.* CAP's entry requirements—support orders and substantial earnings—are likely to limit the program to a small part of the AFDC population. A key question was whether impacts would be discernible with the relatively low CAP participation rates observed in the first year of the experiment. In fact, only 6 percent enrolled in the first 12 months, clearly indicating that CAP is not the solution for all AFDC recipients. Even with this low participation rate, however, the impacts on earnings and child support are statistically significant when averaged across the population as a whole. It is likely that some impact is occurring before people enroll in CAP, and perhaps even for some people who never enroll.

It is probable that the first-year enrollment rates were artificially depressed by the time demands and procedural constraints of the experiment. A nondemonstration implementation of CAP might expect higher participation rates. With greater participation, it is reasonable to believe that impacts would be greater as well.

☐ *New child support information.* Because AFDC recipients are already required to cooperate with the Child Support Enforcement Program, there was some question as to whether the CAP incentive would make a difference, or whether clients had already provided all the information they could. The findings indicate that motivation, combined with assistance from the CAP case managers, can generate new orders.

☐ *Behavioral change.* CAP offers extra benefits under conditions that some clients would meet even without CAP. If people did not change their behavior, but simply took advantage of CAP when they happened to qualify, the program would not accomplish anything. Some such "free rides" undoubtedly occurred. The highest CAP participation rate was observed among clients who already had earnings and support orders when they were selected for the demonstration, but this group showed no significant impacts on earnings or support orders. Nonetheless, the significant impacts for the population as a whole mean that some behaviors definitely changed regarding both child support and employment.

Although the results thus far are encouraging, CAP's potential as an antipoverty policy depends on answers to two critical questions not yet addressed. Can CAP lead to long-term reductions in dependency? Will the program's benefits equal or exceed its costs? The final evaluation report (Hamilton et al. 1993), which estimated impacts at two years following random assignment, has shed light on at least one of these questions. Over its first two years, the availability of CAP was found to have exerted statistically significant, positive impacts on earnings (27 percent), on the number of clients obtaining new support orders (23 percent), and on total income. From the government's fiscal perspective, the effect of implementing CAP along with AFDC was slightly positive; in other words, public outlays for the program were a few dollars per case month less than for AFDC alone. It did not affect the aggregate amount of public assistance that clients received, however, and its long-term effect on self-sufficiency cannot yet be determined.

Notes

1. In July 1993, the New York State Legislature approved a bill to extend the CAP demonstration through 1998.

2. The CAP benefit reduction rates reviewed here apply to earned income only. The benefit reduction rate for unearned income (such as unemployment insurance payments) is 100 percent.

3. The assured benefit in CAP is on the high side compared to the range of other proposals. The CAP maximum benefit varies across the demonstration counties, ranging from $3,360 to $4,680 annually for one child and increasing by $1,116 annually in all CAP counties for each additional eligible child. It must be recalled that, in contrast with universal plans, women eligible for CAP would not in general be returning any of the benefit to the federal government in the form of taxes.

4. The three racial/ethnic categories are mutually exclusive as defined here. Also in the research sample were a small number of Asian and Native American grantees.

5. The additional adults in the grantees' households are principally the grantee's parents or other relatives who share the same residence but are not part of the AFDC case.

6. The participation rate is the number of CAP cases active in a month divided by the number of potentially eligible AFDC cases. Potentially eligible cases are those with a custodial parent and at least one child whose other parent is alive and resides outside the household. The actual percentage of potentially eligible cases in each county in July 1991 was used to calculate an estimate for other months based on the overall AFDC caseload counts for those months.

7. The models were estimated in a stepwise fashion, deleting variables whose coefficients were exceeded by their standard errors. Explanatory variables that did not meet

this criterion in any of the four models included: an indicator that the grantee was black; an indicator that the grantee was male; the presence in the household of a child under age three; and receipt of unemployment compensation.

8. The full results are available from the authors.

9. The estimated impact of an additional $100 in monthly earnings is also 1 percentage point in Monroe, although statistical significance was not attained.

10. This measure, as contrasted with the presence of support orders, is based on the last three months of the year, rather than the change between the beginning and end of the year. The amount due was found to vary substantially from month to month, so that measures of change from a baseline month could be misleading.

11. Gueron and Pauly's (1991) estimates generally refer to those AFDC recipients who would be mandatory participants in the programs, which typically excludes many of the cases in the CAP demonstration (e.g., single mothers with young children).

12. The Emergency Assistance and Services programs were also analyzed, but the results are not reported here.

13. For example, if a person had been working for more than four months, a $100 increase in earnings would cause the AFDC grant to decline by $100. Countable income for the Food Stamp Program would change by (0.80 × $100 − $100), that is, a $20 decline. This would be met by a $6 increase in the Food Stamp benefit.

14. "Eligibility" in the Medicaid Program refers to coverage of health care costs. The term thus corresponds to "enrollment" in the cash assistance programs (except that, of course, one receives the insurance value of Medicaid benefits if no medical costs are ever incurred).

15. Although many income sources have been taken into account, the bulk of total income during the study period came from public assistance payments and the grantee's earnings. For the population as a whole, the higher earnings of treatment group grantees in the last month were partly offset by slightly lower cash assistance income. This pattern was replicated in Monroe County. In Niagara County, in contrast, households of treatment group members received more income from cash assistance *and* more income from the grantee's earnings than their control group counterparts (as well as more income from two other sources, child support and miscellaneous). The situation was nearly reversed in Suffolk County, where the households of treatment group members received about the same or slightly less income from each source than their control group counterparts.

16. For a family of three, the 1991 poverty level was a total annual income of $11,140.

References

Ellwood, David. 1988. *Poor Support.* New York: Basic Books.

Garfinkel, Irwin, and Sara S. McLanahan. 1986. *Single Mothers and Their Children: A New American Dilemma.* Washington, D.C.: Urban Institute Press.

Gueron, Judith M., and Edward Pauly. 1991. *From Welfare to Work.* New York: Russell Sage Foundation.

Hamilton, William L., Nancy R. Burstein, Margaret Hargreaves, David A.

Moss, and Michael Walker. 1993. "The New York State Child Assistance Program: Program Impacts, Costs, and Benefits." Cambridge: Abt Associates Inc., July.

Hargreaves, Margaret. 1992. "The New York State Child Assistance Program: Interim Report on Implementation." Cambridge: Abt Associates Inc.

Meyer, Daniel R., Irwin Garfinkel, Philip Robins, and Donald Oellerich. 1991. "The Costs and Effects of a National Child Support Assurance System." Institute for Research on Poverty Discussion Paper 940-91. Madison: Institute for Research on Poverty, University of Wisconsin-Madison, March.

New York State Governor's Task Force on Poverty and Welfare. 1986. *A New Social Contract: Rethinking the Nature and Purpose of Public Assistance.* Albany: Governor's Task Force, December.

U.S. Congress. House. Committee on Ways and Means. 1991. *Overview of Entitlement Programs: 1991 Green Book.* Washington, D.C.: U.S. Government Printing Office, May.

Part Three

THE EFFECTS OF CHILD SUPPORT PAYMENTS ON CHILD WELL-BEING

CHILD SUPPORT ENFORCEMENT AND CHILD WELL-BEING: GREATER SECURITY OR GREATER CONFLICT?

*Sara S. McLanahan, Judith A. Seltzer, Thomas L. Hanson,
and Elizabeth Thomson*

The Family Support Act of 1988 increases the proportion of children with child support awards (including children born outside marriage), raises the level of awards, and strengthens collections. The rationale underlying these provisions is that stricter enforcement of private child support will reduce the poverty and economic insecurity of children who live apart from one or both of their parents. In turn, greater economic security is expected to improve other aspects of children's well-being, including educational attainment and psychological adjustment. Numerous studies have shown that children who grow up in nonintact families are less successful in adulthood than children who grow up with both parents, and that much of their relative disadvantage is due to income insecurity during childhood (e.g., McLanahan and Booth 1989). Stricter child support enforcement not only benefits children, but it also benefits society by reducing welfare costs. Thus, it is not surprising that policymakers have applauded the new reforms and that analysts have directed their attention toward evaluating the effect of child support reform on family income and welfare reduction. As sociologists, however, we are also interested in what are often called the unintended consequences of social policy or social action. In the case of child support, some people have expressed concern that stricter enforcement laws may increase parental conflict, which, in turn, may reduce children's well-being.

This chapter addresses the question of whether child support increases parental conflict and, if so, whether the increase is large enough to outweigh the benefits associated with greater economic security. The chapter is divided into six sections. The second section presents a model of how child support payments are expected to affect parent-child contact, parental conflict, and child well-being. The third section describes the data and variables used in the analysis and discusses analytic techniques. The fourth section reports esti-

Figure 8.1 SCHEMATIC DIAGRAM OF EFFECTS OF CHILD SUPPORT ON CHILD WELL-BEING

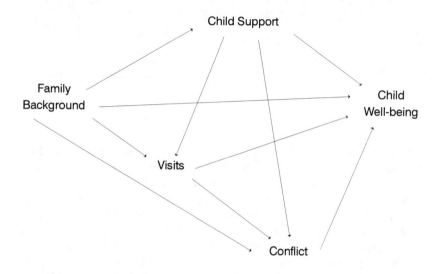

mates of the effect of child support on children's well-being under the existing system, and the fifth section reports similar estimates, assuming a more universal system of child support enforcement. The final section of the chapter discusses conclusions and suggestions for further research.

MODEL OF CHILD SUPPORT AND WELL-BEING

A schematic model of the effects of child support and children's well-being is presented in figure 8.1. The key components of the model are (1) child support payments, (2) parent-child contact (visits), (3) parental conflict, and (4) child well-being. Family background characteristics such as mothers' age and race, parental education and income (net of child support), child's age and sex, and family size, are treated as exogenous to child support payments. The arrows connecting the model's components indicate that child support affects children's well-being both directly and indirectly through parental conflict and parent-child contact. They also indicate that parent-child contact affects conflict. The model is derived from aspects of economic, sociological, and psychological theory, which state that low (and inconsistent) levels of parental investment and high levels of parental conflict reduce children's well-being (Becker 1981, Bronfenbrenner 1977; Rutter 1971). Also implied is that child support payments may increase parental conflict and parent-child contact.

Economic theory argues that the cost of children goes up for nonresident parents, and therefore that fathers are less likely to invest in their children after divorce (Weiss and Willis 1985). This increases the potential for conflict between parents. Moreover, fathers who pay support have a strong incentive to control how their money is spent, which also increases the potential for conflict between parents. Economic theory is ambiguous about the relationship between child support and parent-child contact. On the one hand, fathers who pay support have an interest in monitoring how their money is spent, which implies more contact.[1] On the other hand, fathers who pay have less income and can less afford the costs associated with parent-child contact.[2]

Sociological theory offers similar predictions for somewhat different reasons. According to role theory, rights and obligations go together, and therefore nonresident fathers who fulfill their economic obligations will attempt to exercise their authority and visitation rights as well.[3] Again, assertiveness on the part of the nonresident father may increase parental conflict. We should point out that this line of reasoning makes sense insofar as conflict arises from disagreements over how the money is spent and how the children are raised. To the extent that disagreements arise over *whether* child support is paid and *how much* is paid, stricter enforcement and greater standardization of awards may actually reduce conflict between separated parents. The high level of discretion in our current system creates considerable variation in awards and payments, which, in turn, generates feelings of inequity among both mothers and fathers. This suggests that the relationship between payments and conflict may differ under different institutional arrangements. This point is discussed later in the chapter.

The empirical evidence is consistent with respect to the effect of conflict on child well-being: parental conflict is bad for children (Emery 1982; Rutter 1971). The evidence is less consistent about the effect of contact. Studies based on small samples with high levels of parent-child contact have found a positive relationship between contact and child well-being (Hess and Camara 1979). Research based on the National Survey of Children, however, found no relationship between contact and well-being (Furstenberg, Morgan, and Allison

1987). The evidence is also ambiguous about the effect of child support on parental conflict. Seltzer (1990) found that conflict is actually lower in families where the nonresident father pays child support, although, as she points out, this may be due to a selection bias. Nonresident fathers who do not get along with their former spouse may stop paying child support. Seltzer and her colleagues also found that child support increases contact (Seltzer, Schaeffer, and Charng 1989), although again, it is unclear whether payments are causing contact, whether contact is causing payments, or whether both actions are caused by a third variable such as "commitment to children." Our analysis treats parental conflict and parent-child contact as endogenous to child support, allowing us to obtain upper-bound estimates of the benefits of child support reform.

DATA, MEASURES, AND ANALYTIC TECHNIQUES

Data

The data used in the analysis are taken from the National Survey of Families and Households (NSFH), a probability sample of adults living in the United States in 1987–88. The full sample includes over 13,000 respondents, with a response rate of approximately 74 percent. The sample design oversampled African-Americans, Puerto Ricans, Mexican-Americans, single-parent families, families with stepchildren, cohabiting couples, and persons who had married recently. Sample weights are available to compensate for the differential probabilities of sample selection. For additional information about the study design, see Sweet, Bumpass, and Call (1988).

The results reported here are based on 844 families in which respondents were mothers of children under 18 and in which at least one child had a living nonresident father. Children were defined as household members if they resided with the mother for at least six months of the year. The unit of analysis is the family, as represented by the mother's report. All of the information on child well-being is taken from the mother's report about a randomly selected child in the household (focal child). The absence of information about child well-being from nonresident fathers is a serious limitation. However, both internal and external evaluations of data quality suggest that the NSFH sample of resident mothers is more representative of families in which children live apart from their father than the sample of nonresident fathers (Seltzer 1991; Sweet and Bumpass 1989; Seltzer and Brandreth, forthcoming). In addition, resident mothers' reports about child support payments are more accurate, at least in the aggregate, than nonresident fathers' reports (Schaeffer, Seltzer, and Klawitter 1991).

The sample includes children whose parents are divorced or separated, as well as children whose parents were not married at the time of birth. It also includes families where the mother has remarried (or is cohabiting). Different parts of the analysis are based on different subsamples, depending on which indicator of child well-being, is used and whether we are looking at children born inside marriage or outside marriage. For example, when the indicator of child well-being is "School Problems," the sample includes children aged 5 to 17 (total sample). Separate models are estimated for children born to married parents ($N = 330$) and children born to unmarried parents ($N = 514$). When the indicator of child well-being is "GPA" (grade point average), the sample includes children aged 12 to 17 born to married parents (adolescent sample, $N = 298$). The number of adolescents born to unmarried parents in the GPA sample ($N = 124$) was too small to obtain reliable estimates with the modeling approach we used (described later).

Measures

The means (or proportions) and standard deviations of all the variables used in the analysis are reported in table 8.1. Two indicators were used to measure "Child Well-being": GPA and whether the child had problems in school ("School problems"). The measure of grade point average was based on a question that asked "What sort of grades does (your child) get?" Responses ranged from "mostly As," "mostly As and Bs," and "mostly Bs," to "mostly Fs." Responses were recoded into grade point averages ranging from 0 to 4. High scores indicate a high GPA. The question about grades was asked only about focal children aged 12 and older. The measure of school problems is a dichotomous variable that takes the value of 1 if (1) the child had dropped out of school, or (2) the parent was asked to meet with a teacher or principal because of behavioral problems during the past year, or (3) the child had ever been suspended or expelled from school. This question was asked about children aged 5 to 17. Among children coded 1 on school problems, the majority (85 percent) had parents who had been asked to meet a teacher or principal because of the child's behavior problems.

Table 8.1 MEANS AND STANDARD DEVIATIONS

	Mean	Standard Deviation	N
Child Well-Being[a]			
Grades (GPA)	2.77	.81	298
School problems	.24	.43	844
Child Support (1,000s)			
Observed	1.53	3.31	844
Predicted	1.15	.66	844
Father-Child Contact	3.13	1.71	844
Parental Conflict			
Where child lives	1.12	.42	844
How child is raised	1.21	.49	844
How you [mother] spend money on child	1.13	.38	844
How he spends money on child	1.26	.57	844
His visits with child	1.28	.59	844
His contribution to child support	1.48	.75	844
Race/Ethnicity			
White	.60		
African-American	.30	.46	844
Mexican-American	.05	.21	844
Other	.05	.22	844
Education			
Less than high school	.24		
High school degree	.43	.50	844
Some college	.24	.43	844
College degree	.09	.28	844
Annual Income (1,000s of 1987 dollars)	$17.87	22.95	844
Mother's Age	35.91	6.85	844
Number of Children of Nonresident Father in Household	1.85	1.00	844
Child's Age	11.81	3.88	844
Female Child	.48	.50	844
Time since Separation[b]	10.41	4.77	844
State Median Income (1,000s of 1987 dollars)	11.84	16.57	844
Born in Marriage	.50	.50	844

a. See text for description of measurement.
b. Child's age for children born outside marriage.

"Parental Conflict" was measured by a set of six items that asked specifically about conflict over the focal child. To the extent that there is conflict between parents who do not co-reside, children are likely to be the subject of disagreement because child-rearing issues are one of the few areas requiring collaboration between resident and nonresident parents. The items were taken from a question that asked mothers: "Now much conflict do you and [child's father] have over each of the following issues? (a) where the child lives, (b) how the child is raised, (c) how you spend money on the child, (d) how [he] spends money on the child, (e) [his] visits with child, and (f) [his] contribution to child support." Possible responses were (1) none, (2) some, and (3) a great deal. A measurement model links the parental conflict items to a single latent variable.

"Father-Child Contact" between the nonresident father and child was based on a question that asked: "During the past 12 months, how often did [child] see her/his father? Was it: (1) not at all (2) about once a year (3) several times a year (4) one to three times a month (5) about once a week (6) several times a week?" The question about contact referred specifically to the focal child.

The NSFH data provide more complete information about the amount of child support paid than is commonly available in data sources such as the March-April Current Population Survey (CPS), conducted by the U.S. Bureau of the Census. The NSFH contains information about support paid as the result of a legal child support agreement as well as other types of financial contributions from the nonresident father. Our measure of child support payments included both types of support. In other words, information on child support payments is not censored by whether or not there is a child support award. The NSFH asked about child support for the focal child and his or her siblings in the household.

In addition to observed child support, we also constructed a variable that measured "predicted child support" for each respondent. As described in the fifth section of this chapter, this variable was used to analyze the effects on children of a universal child support system. To construct the new variable, we used information from Current Population Survey—Child Support Supplements.[4] Families with an eligible child were selected from each of the five surveys and the data were pooled. To be included in the sample a family must have had a child under 18 years of age who had a living nonresident parent. The pooled data were used to estimate an equation where child support received during the past year was treated as a function of family background characteristics, including mother's age, education, and so on, and a set of dummy variables for each state. The state dummies were intended to capture variation in child support enforcement policy across states, which, in turn was expected to affect child support payments. In the child well-being equations, we included a variable for state per capita income, and dropped the dummy variables.

All of the analyses control for mother's education, age, and race/ethnicity; child's age and sex; number of children in the household with a nonresident father; family income; and time since marital disruption (since birth for children born out of wedlock.). As discussed earlier, we stratified the sample by the parents' marital status at the time of the focal child's birth. Race/ethnicity was measured by a set of dummy variables with categories for Anglos, Mexican-Americans, African-Americans, and "others." The "other" category included Puerto Ricans, Cubans, other Hispanics, and American Indians. Mother's education was measured by a set of dummy variables with categories for less than a high school diploma, high school degree, some college, and college degree or more. Mother's age, child's age, and number of children were measured as continuous variables. Household income was based on a series of questions that asked respondents about different sources of income during the previous 12 months. Our measure of household income included income from all sources, excluding child support payments.

Analytic Techniques

A series of structural equation models with latent variables was estimated to examine how parental conflict and visits mediate the effects of child support payments on child well-being. The observed items used to measure parental conflict were linked to latent variables using a confirmatory factor analysis model. The "causal" relationships among observed and latent variables were estimated using a structural equation model. Both the measurement models and the structural models were estimated simultaneously. Because the items used as indicators of parental conflict and school problems were measured on an ordinal or dichotomous scale and were quite skewed, Muthén's (1987) approach to latent variable structural equation modeling was used.

Muthén's (1987) approach uses a type of measurement model that links observed ordinal or dichotomous dependent variables (or indicators) to underlying continuous variables. That is, different responses on an observed categorical variable are assumed to depend

Table 8.2 EFFECT OF CONFLICT AND CONTACT ON CHILDREN'S WELL-BEING

| | GPA | School Problems | |
	In Marriage	In Marriage	Out of Marriage
Parental conflict	−.092*	.056	.128**
	(2.856)	(.900)	(1.731)
Parent-child contact	−.043	.056	.051
	(1.099)	(1.048)	(.0564)

*$p < .05$ (two-tailed).
**$p < .10$ (two-tailed).
t-values in parentheses.

on a person's position on a continuous latent variable. The observed categorical variable is linked to a latent continuous variable through a model of thresholds (Muthén 1984). In essence, two types of measurement models were simultaneously estimated using Muthén's approach in the present study: one linking observed categorical indicators to latent variable indicators, and one linking latent variable indicators to latent dependent variables.

Thus, we estimated a set of structural equations in which child well-being was modeled as a function of child support payments, parental conflict, and parent-child contact. Family background characteristics were included in all of the equations. The GPA estimates were based on children born to married parents. Muthén's modeling approach produces estimates that are only asymptotically correct. With only 124 adolescents born to unmarried parents, we could not estimate a model for children born out of wedlock using the GPA sample. The School Problems estimates were based on two separate samples: children born to married parents and children born to unmarried parents.

HOW DOES THE EXISTING SYSTEM AFFECT CHILDREN?

This section of the chapter examines the effect of child support payments on children's well-being under the system of awards and collections that existed in 1987. Although this set of relationships may change in the future as norms and policies change, they are still of interest insofar as they describe the existing system and provide a baseline against which to compare future relationships.

The first question addressed in the analysis is whether parental conflict and parent-child contact affect children's well-being. The results are reported in table 8.2. Column 1 in the table reports the

Table 8.3 EFFECT OF CHILD SUPPORT ON PARENTAL CONFLICT AND
PARENT-CHILD CONTACT

	Parental Conflict	Parent-Child Contact
Adolescent Sample		
In marriage	.009**	.035*
	(1.931)	(3.618)
Total Sample		
In marriage	.004	.078*
	(.608)	(9.001)
Out of marriage	−.103*	.373*
	(3.529)	(12.757)

*p < .05 (two-tailed).
**p < .10 (two-tailed).
t-values in parentheses.

effects of conflict and contact on children's grades for children born in marriage. The second and third columns report the effects of conflict and contact on school problems for children born "in" and "out" of marriage, respectively. The coefficients for parental conflict behave as expected. The signs indicate that conflict lowers grades and increases school problems, regardless of whether a child is born in or out of wedlock. The coefficients for contact are more of a surprise. Contact between nonresident parents and children appears to be associated with lower grades and more school problems. (None of the coefficients is significant, however). The negative relationship between parent-child contact and the school outcomes suggests that causality may be operating in both directions; when children are having problems in school, fathers become more involved.

The next question of interest is whether child support is associated with higher or lower levels of parental conflict. As noted earlier, theory points in both directions on this issue. On the one hand, fathers who pay support will want more control, which may lead to increases in parental conflict. On the other hand, to the extent that conflict arises over nonpayment or irregular payment of support, fathers who pay may have less conflict with mothers. Table 8.3 reports the effect of child support on parental conflict and parent-child contact for children born in and out of marriage.

For the adolescent sample of children born to married parents, child support has a positive effect on both conflict and contact. For the total sample, the pattern is the same for children born to married parents, although the effect on conflict is smaller and not statistically

Table 8.4 DECOMPOSITION OF TOTAL, DIRECT, AND INDIRECT EFFECTS OF
CHILD SUPPORT ON CHILDREN'S WELL-BEING

	Direct Effect	Via Conflict	Via Contact	Total Effect
GPA	.011*	−.001	−.002	.008*
In marriage	(2.611)			(2.468)
School Problems				
In marriage	−.053*	.000	.005	−.048*
	(4.046)			(3.944)
Out of marriage	−.144*	−.013	.044	−.113*
	(2.639)			(3.105)

*p < .05 (two-tailed).
t-values in parentheses.
Note: Significance tests were not computed for indirect effects.

significant. For children born out of wedlock, however, child support appears to *reduce* parental conflict while increasing parent-child contact. The strong negative association between child support and parental conflict between parents of children born out of marriage suggests that there may be a simultaneity problem.[5] Conflict may affect child support payments just as payments affect conflict. In a system such as ours where fathers have some discretion about whether or not to pay support, men who strongly disagree with the mother are likely to stop paying child support. Thus, we find a negative association between paying and conflict. If this argument is correct, we would expect the negative association between payments and parental conflict to be strongest among children born to unmarried parents, since these fathers have the most discretion.

The final question addressed in this part of the analysis is whether the overall effect of child support is positive or negative. Table 8.4 reports the direct and indirect effects of child support payments on GPA and school problems. Indirect effects were calculated by summing the products of effects of exogenous and intervening variables. All of the child support coefficients in column 1 are in the expected direction, and all are statistically significant. According to the numbers, child support increases children's well-being. The more child support received, the higher the grades and the fewer the school problems.

The child support dollars have a much larger effect on child well-being than ordinary dollars (not shown). One thousand dollars of ordinary income increases GPA by less than .0005 points, whereas

$1,000 of child support increases GPA by .011 points (table 8.4). Similarly, $1,000 of income reduces school problems by .003 units among children born to married parents and by .021 among children born to unmarried parents. An increase of $1,000 in child support reduces school problems by .053 and .144 for children born to married and unmarried parents, respectively.

The fact that child support dollars have a larger benefit for children than ordinary dollars could be due either to the fact that child support is picking up some unobserved characteristic of the father, such as "family commitment," or to the fact that child support dollars have a symbolic value that enhances children's well-being. Children of divorced parents as well as those born to unmarried parents may benefit from knowing that their fathers contributed to their support. The fact that so many adopted children go in search of their birth parents suggests that children place a high value on biological parenthood. Finally, regular payments may increase children's well-being not because the payments reflect something about the fathers' commitment or the father-child relationship but because they make the mother feel more financially secure.

Column 2 in table 8.4 indicates that the effect of child support via conflict slightly reduces GPA and has no effect on school problems for children born in marriage. For children born outside marriage, the indirect effect of child support via conflict slightly reduces school problems. Column 3 indicates that the effect of child support via contact reduces GPA and increases school problems for all children. The last column in table 8.4 shows that the total effect of child support on children's well-being is positive, at least under the system that existed in 1987. Child support payments increase GPA and reduce school problems.

HOW WOULD A UNIVERSAL SYSTEM AFFECT CHILDREN?

The estimates presented in tables 8.2 through 8.4 should be reassuring to those who worry that the current child support system may be harming children. Before we can generalize the pattern observed in these data to the whole population, however, we must ask whether fathers who currently pay child support are representative of all fathers who would be forced to pay under a more universal system. The answer is clearly no. Given the weakness of our existing child support enforcement institutions and the ambiguity of social norms governing the obligations of nonresident fathers, fathers who pay child support are undoubtedly a special subset of nonresident fathers. It is likely that fathers who pay have a stronger commitment to their children and get along better with the child's mother than the average nonresident father. Many people worry that it is this "commitment" rather than the child support dollars per se that increases child well-being and minimizes parental conflict. If this is true, forcing nonresident fathers to pay will not increase children's well-being, at least not as much as our previous estimates indicate. Indeed, stricter enforcement may increase conflict to the point that the overall benefits of child support are negative.

Alternatively, sociological theory suggests that a stricter enforcement system based on more universal criteria may not lead to more parental conflict. Some fathers may not be paying now because they believe the system is unfair. Numerous commentators have pointed out that horizontal inequities permeate the current system. Almost every nonresident father knows someone like himself who is paying less child support, and almost every custodial mother knows someone like herself who is receiving more support. Stricter enforcement would not necessarily generate bad feelings among fathers if award levels were viewed as more equitable. Even if the positive relationship between child support and child well-being is due to an unobserved characteristic of the fathers, such as commitment, some sociologists would argue that such a characteristic is socially constructed and can be *created* in fathers, including fathers who are currently neglecting their children. If this is true, reenforcing norms about parental responsibility will create better fathers, in spirit as well as behavior. Although fathers may resist initially, over time they may come to value their role in the child's life and be grateful for having been forced to "do the right thing."

To determine how fathers would react under a new system, we ideally need to carry out an experiment in which fathers are randomly assigned to payor and nonpayor groups, and children are followed over a period of time. Although such a study is not possible, a natural experiment of this type has been under way in the nation for the past decade. Some states have been much more aggressive than others in setting child support awards and in collecting what is owed to children, and there is much cross-state variation in the extent to which fathers "voluntarily" pay child support. This variation can be used to construct an instrumental variable—"predicted child sup-

Table 8.5 EFFECT OF CHILD SUPPORT ON PARENTAL CONFLICT AND
PARENT-CHILD CONTACT, USING PREDICTED CHILD SUPPORT

	Parental Conflict	Parent-Child Contact
Adolescent Sample	−.233	.369**
In marriage	(1.316)	(1.459)
Total Sample		
In marriage	−.094	.486*
	(.585)	(2.547)
Out of marriage	.080	.343**
	(.615)	(1.892)

*p < .05 (two-tailed).
**p < .10 (two-tailed).
t-values in parentheses.

port," which can then be used to estimate the effects of child support payments on children's well-being under a system in which all fathers are obliged to pay.

To construct the instrumental variable, we used a set of coefficients obtained from a model that treated child support payments as a function of age of mother, age of youngest child, number of children, and family background characteristics (race, marital status, mother's education). Dummy variables were included for each state. The equation was estimated on pooled data taken from the CPS child support supplements. The coefficients obtained from the CPS data were then used to create a *predicted* child support variable for each child in the NSFH sample. The predicted variable is based solely on observed characteristics and therefore is not contaminated by unobserved characteristics of the father that may be related to paying child support and children's well-being. Hence, it gives us a better idea of how a universal child support system would affect the average child.

Table 8.5 reports estimates of the effect of child support payments on conflict between the biological parents. The model is similar to that used for table 8.3, except that predicted child support is substituted for observed child support. When we use the instrumental variable, the coefficient for the effect of child support on conflict becomes negative, but not quite statistically significant for the children born in marriage. Recall that in table 8.3 the coefficient was positive. This suggests that instituting a more universal system of child support enforcement may reduce rather than increase parental conflict, at least for adolescent children born to married parents. The same pattern exists for children aged 5 to 17 born to married parents.

Table 8.6 DECOMPOSITION OF TOTAL, DIRECT, AND INDIRECT EFFECTS OF CHILD SUPPORT ON CHILDREN'S WELL-BEING

	Direct Effect	Via Conflict	Via Contact	Total Effect
GPA				
In marriage	.115	.022	−.018	.119
	(.736)			(1.166)
School Problems				
In marriage	−.319	−.001	.004	−.316
	(1.216)			(1.239)
Out of marriage	.016	.019	.022	.057
	(.098)			(.884)

t-values in parentheses.
Note: Significance tests were not computed for indirect effects.

Although the coefficient is not statistically significant, the sign is negative.

The story for children born to unmarried parents is different. Whereas in table 8.3, observed child support was negatively related to conflict, in table 8.5 the sign is positive, although not statistically significant. This positive effect suggests that our previous estimate of the effect of child support on parental conflict was affected by selection bias. The instrumental variable approach should make the most difference for children born to unmarried parents, since fathers who pay child support in this group are the most self-selected.

Table 8.6 reports estimates for the direct and indirect effects of child support payments on child well-being, using the predicted child support variable. Again, the estimates presented there are based on the same set of equations as in table 8.4, except that predicted child support has been substituted for observed child support. The estimates in table 8.6 suggest that child support increases GPA and reduces school problems, at least for children born in marriage. None of the child support coefficients are significant, but the signs are similar to those reported in table 8.6, and the point estimates are large and in the right direction.

The case for children born outside marriage is less optimistic. Whereas in table 8.4, both the direct and indirect effects of child support on school problems were negative and significant, in table 8.6 both effects are now positive and insignificant. The indirect paths through increased contact and conflict are also positive, suggesting more school problems for children whose fathers pay child support.

CONCLUSIONS AND IMPLICATIONS

This chapter's analysis presents two somewhat different scenarios about the consequences of recent child support reform. It is clear that under the old system, children whose fathers pay support are better off than children whose fathers pay little or nothing. Paying support is related to parental conflict and contact, but the negative consequences associated with conflict and contact are not large enough to offset the benefits.

What about a new child support system with stricter standards and more effective enforcement? The instrumental variables approach presents a mixed picture. For children born to married parents, it appears that forcing more fathers to pay may benefit children. Our estimates indicate that under a stricter system parental conflict may be *lower* and that parent-child contact will increase. Ultimately, we should observe a gain in children's school achievement and a decline in school problems.

For children born to unmarried parents, the outlook is less optimistic. The numbers suggest that an increase in payments may increase parental conflict and could potentially reduce children's well-being. Because our instrumental variable was not well-specified, these results should be interpreted cautiously. Given the increasing proportion of children born to unmarried parents, the effects of new legislation on this group must be monitored carefully.

Notes

This chapter is a revised version of a paper originally presented at the "Conference on Child Support and Child Well-Being," Airlie House, Airlie, Va., Dec. 5–7, 1991. The research reported here was supported by grants from the National Institute of Child Health and Development (HD-24571, HD-26122), the Ford Foundation, and the Foundation for Child Development. Computing support came from the Center for Demography and Ecology of the University of Wisconsin-Madison, with support from the National Institute of Child Health and Development (HD-05876).

1. It is also possible that fathers who visit often have a better understanding of their children's needs and are more willing to pay support.

2. Fathers' rights groups often argue that because of their child support obligations, fathers cannot afford to visit their children and, more importantly, cannot afford to maintain an extra room(s) in their house so the children can sleep over.

3. Social psychological theory argues that paying and visiting are mutually reenforc-

ing. Fathers who pay child support feel better about themselves and their relationship with their child, which, in turn, makes contact more rewarding.

4. We are grateful to Philip Robins for providing coefficients from the CPS data.

5. The results from the model suggest that a monthly increase in child support payments of $80 reduces conflict between parents of children born outside of marriage by about 15 percent of a standard deviation.

References

Becker, Gary S. 1981. *A Treatise on the Family.* Cambridge: Harvard University Press.

Bronfenbrenner, Urie. 1977. "Toward an Experimental Ecology of Human Development." *American Psychologist* 52: 513–31.

Emery, Robert E. 1982. "Interparental Conflict and the Children of Discord and Divorce." *Psychological Bulletin* 92:310–30.

Furstenberg, Frank F., Jr, S. Philip Morgan, and Paul D. Allison. 1987. "Paternal Participation and Children's Well-Being after Marital Dissolution." *American Sociological Review* 52: 695–701.

Hess, Robert D., and Kathleen A. Camara. 1979. "Post-Divorce Family Relationships as Mediating-Factors in the Consequences of Divorce for Children." *Journal of Social Issues* 35: 26–49.

McLanahan, Sara, and Karen Booth. 1989. "Single Mothers and Their Children: Problems, Prospects, and Politics." *Journal of Marriage and the Family* 51 (August): 557–80.

Muthén, Bengt O. 1984. "A General Structural Equation Model with Dichotomous, Ordered Categorical, and Continuous Latent Variable Indicators. *Psychometrika* 49: 115–32.

_____ . 1987. Liscomp: An Analysis of Linear Structural Relations Using a Comprehensive Measurement Model. Mooresville, Ind: Scientific Software.

Rutter, Michael L. 1971. "Parent-Child Separation: Psychological Effects on Children." *Journal of Child Psychology and Psychiatry* 12: 233–60.

Schaeffer, Nora Cate, Judith A. Seltzer, and Marieka Klawitter. 1991. "Estimating Nonresponse and Response Bias: Resident and Nonresident Parents' Reports about Child Support." *Sociological Methods and Research* 20:30–59.

Seltzer, Judith A. 1990. "Child Support Reform and the Welfare of U.S. Children." National Survey of Families and Households Working Paper 34. Center for Demography and Ecology. Madison: University of Wisconsin-Madison.

_____ . 1991. "Relationships between Fathers and Children Who Live

Apart: The Father's Role after Separation." *Journal of Marriage and the Family* 53: 79–101.

Seltzer, Judith A., and Yvonne Brandreth. Forthcoming. "What Fathers Say about Involvement with Children after Separation." *Journal of Family Issues* (March 1994).

Seltzer, Judith A., Nora Cate Schaeffer, and Hong-Wen Charng. 1989. "Family Ties after Divorce: The Relationship between Visiting and Paying Child Support." *Journal of Marriage and the Family* 51: 1013–31.

Sweet, James A., and Larry L. Bumpass. 1989. "Conducting a Comprehensive Survey of American Family Life: The Experience of the National Survey of Families and Households." NSFH Working Paper 12. Center for Demography and Ecology. Madison: University of Wisconsin-Madison.

Sweet, James A., Larry L. Bumpass, and Vaughn Call. 1988. "The Design and Content of the National Survey of Families and Households." NSFH Working Paper 1. Center for Demography and Ecology. Madison: University of Wisconsin-Madison.

Weiss, Yoram, and Robert Willis. 1985. "Children as Collective Goods and Divorce Settlements." *Journal of Labor Economics* 3: 268–92.

Chapter Nine

THE DYNAMICS OF CHILD SUPPORT AND ITS CONSEQUENCES FOR CHILDREN

Nazli Baydar and Jeanne Brooks-Gunn

This chapter examines the effects of child support payments on children themselves. First, we address the processes of becoming eligible for and then receiving child support. Next, we investigate whether child support payments have observable beneficial effects on children's well-being. Study of the process of child support receipt has shown preexisting differences between children who receive child support payments and children who are eligible for but do not receive such payments. When investigating the effects of child support on children's developmental outcomes, we generate a model that allows us to statistically control for these preexisting differences to the extent possible. Although our data do not allow us to fully identify the factors that might mediate the effects of child support on child outcomes, we attempt to account for likely mediators of these effects, such as mother's working hours, the quality of the home environment, and the frequency of contact with the father.

Two issues emerge in studying patterns of child support receipt: the identification of a group of children who are eligible for receiving child support and tracking of the child-support-eligibility status over time. Two factors account for the difficulty in empirically identifying children eligible for child support. First, few household surveys attempt to elicit information on the identities of the biological fathers. Second, increasing numbers of children are born to unmarried mothers; hence, it is difficult to infer the presence or absence of the biological fathers of children from maternal marital histories. Using longitudinal survey data, child support eligibility can usually be identified in a subgroup of children born to married or cohabiting parents. However, survey data on household composition would be inadequate to establish child support eligibility in many cases, including, for example, if the child was born to an unmarried, non-cohabiting mother who subsequently married; or if the mother was married and divorced several times and had children born both while married and while divorced; or if the mother and father were never married and had a relationship with periods of cohabitation and periods of separation.

Specifying the process by which child support payments affect children presents a conceptual challenge. There are two different routes by which child support payments could positively influence child outcomes: by increasing the family income and by promoting a father's benign presence. An increase in income may contribute to several factors in a child's immediate environment. The mother may be able to decrease her working hours while maintaining her financial well-being in order to spend more time with her child; the quality of the child's home or care environment might be enhanced due to increased financial resources; and the mother's overall well-being may be enhanced due to decreased financial worries. It is clear that child support payments will influence these factors depending on the level and regularity of payments. An increase in child support payments may also increase fathers' involvement with children, because fathers want to monitor how their money is spent (Weiss and Willis 1985).

In addition to the causal effects of child support payments on child outcomes just cited, there could be spurious causality between such payments and child outcomes. First, mothers who seek child support awards might have characteristics associated with beneficial child outcomes, such as a concern for securing financial resources to adequately provide for the child. Second, fathers who comply with child support awards might have characteristics that result in beneficial child outcomes, such as willingness to assume responsibility for the well-being of the child, thus providing a positive role model. Third, when the child support payment is voluntary, payment may represent a lower level of conflict between the father and mother.

To predict the impact of child support payments on children, one must rely on certain assumptions about the mechanisms of allocation of financial resources within families of different size and composition. Little theory exists on the allocation of monetary resources within a family, especially within a nontraditional (nuclear or nonnuclear) family where socially accepted norms on allocation of resources do not exist. Furthermore, empirical data on the allocation of child support income do not exist. Surveys focusing on sources of income ask only whether or not child support is part of a respondent's income. The identity of the individual making the child support payments or the child for whom the payments are targeted is often unknown. Hence, predictions regarding the effects of child support payments cannot be based on empirical knowledge on the proportion of these payments that is allocated to children. Without adequate knowledge of such allocation, study of the effects of child support payments on children is bound to be cursory. Almost all of the existing studies of child support payments focus on the mother and regard these payments as a form of nonwage income of the mother. As mentioned earlier, few studies have focused on the child to whom the child support payments were targeted.

The 1986 and 1988 assessments of Children of the NLSY (National Longitudinal Survey of Youth) and related data from the 1983–88 National Longitudinal Surveys of Youth conducted by Ohio State University constitute the empirical database of this paper. These recent data have superior measurements of child well-being for a large and demographically diverse sample of children.

Parental separation, child support receipt, and continuity of child support—the three subprocesses determining child support receipt status at a given time—are expected to be strongly associated with family socioeconomic and demographic characteristics. Children from families with lower socioeconomic status are expected to have higher risks of parental separation. Among children who experience parental separation, more-disadvantaged children are expected to be at higher risk of not receiving child support and of experiencing discontinuity in child support, thus widening the gap between advantaged and disadvantaged children. In our research, we expected that the total effects of child support, including its effects on family income and the quality of the home environment, would be strong and significant. At the same time, we predicted that child support payment would have a marginal effect on child development outcomes per se, holding constant maternal characteristics, income level, the quality of home environment, and contact with the father. In other words, the beneficial effects of child support, if any, would likely be due to increased disposable family income and its associated benefits such as an enhanced home environment.

METHOD OF STUDY

Data

The NLSY was initiated in 1979 on a nationally representative cohort of young men and women aged 14 to 21. The children of the NLSY data include all children born to the original female NLSY sample (Baker and Mott 1989). These data are well suited to address the effects of child support payments on children, for several reasons. First, the NLSY sample includes oversamples of minorities and youths who are from areas with a high prevalence of poverty in 1979. Therefore, children who are at high risk of being eligible for child support are well represented. Second, the broad longitudinal information content of the surveys taken from mothers of the sample children provide an opportunity to infer children's living arrangements from birth onward. Third, the inclusion of psychometric assessments of children makes these data invaluable because other family surveys include longitudinal information on living arrangements similar to that provided by the NLSY, but lack measurements of developmental outcomes in children.

The major disadvantage of these data is the youthfulness of the mothers of the NLSY children compared to mothers of corresponding national cohorts of children. This problem arises owing to the definition of the original NLSY sample as a cohort of adolescents and young adults in 1979. Hence, the mothers of the NLSY were in the first half of their childbearing years at the time of the first child assessments in 1986. The children of the NLSY sample must be regarded as a sample born to relatively young mothers, which may affect this study's findings to the extent that the child support receipt of younger mothers differs from that of older mothers. For example, the youthfulness of the NLSY mothers implies that a higher proportion of NLSY children than in a same-age national sample of children were born outside the marriage. These children are expected to have a lower likelihood of child support receipt. In this study, we investigate the dynamics of child support receipt of children born after their mothers' 1983 interview. This restriction results in a sample of children born, on the average, to mothers aged 25, somewhat younger than the mean age of childbearing of 26.5 years in the United States in 1988 (U.S. Bureau of the Census 1991).

Among all of the NLSY children born before the 1988 interview of their mothers (N = 7,346), one child of each mother was selected to assure the independence of observations. This selection resulted in a sample of children and mothers mapped one-to-one. Using this sample, one can make inferences about the mothers or the children, since the mothers who experienced high fertility are not overrepresented. In this study, a mother-child sample was constructed selecting one child per mother at random.

The children of the NLSY data do not include detailed living arrangement histories of all children. Although mothers' marital and cohabitational histories are available, these data do not allow for the unique identification of the fathers of all NLSY children. Starting in 1984, the NLSY mothers were asked whether the biological father of each child was currently living in the household. Although this series of questions is valuable because it elicits the living arrangements of the child directly, it is limited to the arrangements at the time of the survey, and does not elicit a child's complete living arrangement history.

The current study focuses on two subsamples of children. The first subsample consists of all children of the NLSY who were born no earlier than 12 months preceding the 1984 interview of their mothers, in which the mothers were asked whether the biological fathers of their children lived in the same household. This selection assured that for all children in the subsample, we have maternal reports on biological father's presence starting from the first year of life. The selected cohort consists of 1,700 NLSY children born between 1983 and 1988. At the 1988 child assessment, their ages ranged from 0 to 5.

For a multivariate analysis of consequences of child support payments, we selected the children under 6 years of age who were living with their biological mothers and fathers at the time of the 1986 interview of their mothers. This selection yielded data well suited to studying the consequences of child support payments for two reasons. First, these children were at risk of experiencing separation from the father between 1986 and 1988, and they were psychometrically assessed in 1986, prior to their eligibility for child support. Second, these children were assessed again in 1988; therefore it was possible to conduct a study of change in their well-being, relying on well-established measures of cognitive and behavioral development (see discussion following).

Measures

The NLSY offers a wide array of measures on the lives of the mothers, their households, and their children. The bulk of the data used in this study comes from the maternal interviews. The paragraphs following discuss the sources of the variables and specific measurement issues pertaining to them.

FATHER PRESENCE

The presence of the biological fathers of the children of NLSY was asked directly of the mothers from 1984 on. Although these data are superior to indirect estimates of biological father presence, a major limitation is that the date of departure of a father from the mother's household is not available. Prior to 1984, father presence can be indirectly estimated using the marital, cohabitational, and fertility histories of the mothers, and the household composition reported at each interview. Mott (1990) used these data to determine the father presence at the time of each interview.[1] In this study we rely primarily on maternal reports. We used data constructed by Mott to determine father presence at the time of birth of each child.

INCOME AND CHILD SUPPORT

At each survey, the mothers reported their income during the past calendar year from various sources. Hence, wage income, child support income, other nonwage income, and total family income are known. The major deficiency of the child support income data of the NLSY is that the source of this income (i.e., the identity of the person paying the child support) and the targeted child are not specified. Hence, our study is limited by the possible error in measurement of child support for a focal child, who might not be targeted by the payments reported by the mother.

MATERNAL CHARACTERISTICS

The NLSY was originally designed to focus on labor market experiences of youths. Specifically, week-by-week employment histories, the details of the job, and hours of employment for the mothers are available since 1979. In addition to these variables, maternal marital status at the time of each interview, maternal age at the time of the child's birth, maternal racial and ethnic origin, and maternal education at the time of each interview are available.

PATERNAL CHARACTERISTICS

Two sources of data in the NLSY help identify paternal characteristics for a selected group of children. If the father and the focal child's mother were living in the same household at the time of the NLSY interviews, the father's characteristics can be detected from the household roster, which provides the father's education, employment status, and age. If the father and mother were married, there is further information on work hours and wage rate from maternal reports on their spouses. Both these sources of data were exploited in this study.

CHILD OUTCOMES

This study estimates the effects of child support on reading achievement, controlling for the prior level of verbal development. Two measures are used: the Peabody Picture Vocabulary Test (PPVT) and the Peabody Individual Achievement Test (PIAT) (both described in detail by Baker and Mott 1989). The PPVT–Revised (Dunn and Dunn 1981) is a cognitive assessment measuring the receptive vocabulary knowledge of children, and was administered in 1986 to children aged three and above. Unfortunately, for children who received this assessment in 1986, it was not repeated in 1988. In 1988, children aged five and older were administered the PIAT. In this study, we use the reading recognition component of PIAT assessed in 1988 as a cognitive outcome measure. It should be noted that PIAT is an achievement test, not an ability test. Although the predictive power of the PPVT for PIAT is not expected to be very high, it is beneficial to control the achievement outcomes of child support for prior differences in ability.

QUALITY OF HOME ENVIRONMENT

The mother supplements of the 1986 and 1988 NLSY include scales measuring the physical, emotional, and cognitive stimulation qualities of children's home environments. The HOME scales are based on maternal and interviewer ratings of quality of various aspects of the home environment, including the physical environment and relationships between the family members. The NLSY adapted a shorter form of the original HOME Inventory (Caldwell and Bradley 1984) with age-appropriate items for children under three, three to five, and six and older. Some of the items in the HOME scales concern the child's relationship with the father or father figure. Since inclusion of these items would confound the effects of father separation with the effects of the quality of the home environment, we eliminated these items from the scale. Using the remaining items, we constructed a score that represents the percentage of the total possible score obtained. These scores have a rather limited distribution, with a large proportion of cases having scores between 70 percent and 90 percent. Therefore, we used dummy variables indicating HOME scores over 80 percent.

RESULTS

Dynamics of Child Support

The analysis of the dynamics of child support is based on a cohort of children whose mothers were interviewed in 1984, when the focal children were under 12 months of age. A profile of this subsample is contained in the righthand column of table 9.1. The children in this sample included cohorts born between 1983 and 1988. A little over half of the children were boys. Black and Hispanic children constituted 13 percent and 6 percent of the sample, respectively (weighted percentages). A majority (58 percent) of children were their mothers' firstborn. The mothers averaged 25 years of age at the time of birth of the focal children. At the time of the survey, the women averaged 12.5 years of education, and 72 percent were married (not shown in table). At birth, 86 percent of the children in the sample were living in the same household as their biological fathers. The per capita net family income at the time of the first survey after birth was $7,808.

Because of the design of the sample of children of the NLSY, there are some differentials in the characteristics of children from different birth cohorts. These differences are summarized in table 9.1. As the table indicates, the mean age of the mothers at birth progressively increases by birth year, an artifact of the original NLSY sample design. Therefore one must cautiously interpret the effects of age of the child, which reflect the effect of the mother's age as well. The close association between the mothers' age at birth and the children's birth year accounts for the associations between the birth year of the child and other characteristics. For example, the sex distribution of the sample indicates a somewhat higher proportion of boys among children born in 1987 and 1988, which is also the group born to oldest mothers. Similarly, since black women tend to have children younger, the proportion of black children decreases from 16 percent among the children born in 1983 to 9 percent among the children born in 1988. Mean maternal education is higher for younger cohorts than in older cohorts. Similarly, mean per capita family income is higher for younger cohorts than for older cohorts. A large majority of children in this cohort were born while their mothers and fathers were co-residing. Again due to the confounding effects of maternal age, children born before 1986 were less likely to be born while their biological parents were co-residing than children born in 1986 or later.

Table 9.1 CHARACTERISTICS OF ANNUAL COHORTS OF NLSY CHILDREN (UNDER 12 MONTHS OF AGE AT TIME OF MOTHERS' 1984 INTERVIEW)

Characteristic	Year of Birth of Child						All Children
	1983	1984	1985	1986	1987	1988	
Percentage male	47.9	46.9	53.5	42.8	55.6	59.9	50.9
Race or ethnicity							
Black	15.9	16.3	13.4	12.2	11.1	9.2	13.1
Hispanic	7.0	6.9	5.2	4.0	6.2	5.7	5.8
White	59.9	52.5	65.0	66.4	60.8	65.5	61.5
Other	17.3	24.3	16.4	17.5	21.8	19.5	19.6
Percentage firstborn	60.1	52.6	66.6	57.0	52.3	60.7	58.2
Mean age of mother at time of child's birth	22.7	23.8	24.3	25.8	26.3	27.1	25.0
Mean number of years of maternal education	11.8	12.1	12.4	12.8	12.9	13.3	12.5
Percentage whose father was present at time of birth	81.5	79.6	83.4	92.8	91.8	87.6	86.0
Per capita net family income in year of birth	$4,879	$6,426	$7,012	$9,286	$9,119	$10,613	$7,808
N	317	339	306	257	264	217	1,700

Child Support Eligibility

On the basis of the mothers' annual reports on father presence, we constructed age-specific life tables of becoming eligible for child support for the first time for children residing with their biological mothers.[2] Since all children born when their biological parents were living separately were eligible for child support at the time of their birth, this group was not included in the life tables of becoming eligible.

Table 9.2 displays the statistics pertaining to the life tables of becoming eligible for child support payments by selected family and child characteristics. Black children have lower probabilities of continued living with their biological fathers. By the time black children reach four years of age, only 60 percent are expected to have lived continuously in the same household as their biological fathers, compared to 73 percent of Hispanic and 80 percent of white children. In addition, black children experience consistently higher rates of separation from their fathers from infancy on, as compared to white or Hispanic children. Other characteristics that are significantly associated with probabilities of continued living with the biological father are maternal age at birth, mother's education, per capita family income, and whether the mother and biological father were married. Children born to mothers 25 years old or younger at the time of birth were significantly more likely to become eligible for child support than children of older mothers, particularly after the first year of life. Mothers' education and per capita net family income (both measured at the time of the first interview following the child's birth were significantly and positively associated with the probabilities of continued co-residence with the biological fathers. These differences become stronger after infancy. As expected, children whose mothers and biological fathers were married were more likely to continue co-residing with their biological fathers than children whose parents were not married. Characteristics not significantly associated with child support eligibility were sex and birth order. Although one might expect the birth order to be associated with co-residence with the biological father, this association was probably not seen because these analyses were restricted to children co-residing with their biological fathers immediately following birth.

The life table analyses presented in table 9.2 reiterate results of prior studies that children of socially, economically, and educationally disadvantaged young mothers are at high risk of becoming eligible for child support. The remainder of the analysis of dynamics of

Table 9.2 LIFE TABLE PROBABILITIES OF CONTINUED CO-RESIDENCE WITH BIOLOGICAL FATHER BY AGE OF CHILD: CHILDREN OF NLSY BORN NO EARLIER THAN 12 MONTHS PRECEDING MOTHERS' 1984 SURVEY

Sample Definition	Age of Child (yr.)				Total Number of Child-Years of Exposure	Comparison Statistic and p
	0	1	2	3		
Total sample	.963	.898	.853	.771	1,042	—
Black children	.887	.728	.633	.602	102	29.7
Hispanic children	.924	.873	.762	.730	78	0.00
White children	.969	.917	.868	.797	931	
Boys	.961	.892	.821	.738	717	0.8
Girls	.965	.904	.850	.804	686	0.36
Firstborn children	.970	.900	.848	.766	805	1.0
Children with older siblings	.954	.896	.818	.777	597	0.31
Children born to mothers aged 25 or younger	.947	.868	.800	.738	756	26.2
Children born to mothers aged 26 or older	.986	.949	.905	.838	647	0.00
Children born to mothers with less than high school education	.927	.833	.757	.691	217	14.7
Children born to mothers with high school or more education	.970	.910	.849	.783	1,121	0.00
Children whose annual per capita family income was $5,000 or less	.931	.808	.714	.652	367	54.3
Children whose annual per capita family income was more than $5,000	.978	.953	.910	.832	837	0.00
Children whose fathers and mothers were married at time of first interview	.981	.925	.872	.818	1,278	31.4
Children whose fathers and mothers were not married but cohabiting at time of first interview	.950	.775	.525	.296	87	0.00

child support focuses on the subsample of children who were *ever eligible* for child support, including those who never co-resided with their biological fathers.

Receipt of Child Support

Children become eligible for child support as soon as they begin living separately from their biological fathers. However, mothers do not always seek child support awards, and even if they seek and are awarded child support, only a fraction of fathers comply with the award (U.S. Bureau of the Census 1987). Using the life table methodology, we documented the dynamics of child support receipt. Table 9.3 displays the probabilities that a child's mother has not yet received child support in the years since the child first became eligible for child support. Overall, it was estimated that 40 percent of all children who became eligible for child support did not receive any by the end of the fourth year after separation from the biological father. Child support receipt probabilities decline each year among those who have not yet received child support. During the first year following separation, child support receipt probability is 35 percent; the following year this probability drops to 24 percent ([0.651 − 0.495] / 0.651); and the next year, it drops to 13 percent ([0.495 − 0.437] / 0.495).

Racial differences in child support receipt were not significant, nor were differences by child's sex, birth order, maternal age at birth, and maternal education (see table 9.3). High per capita family income, father presence at the time of birth, and whether the mother and the father were married significantly predicted higher probability of child support receipt. A higher proportion of eligible children from families with per capita net annual incomes under $5,000 did not receive child support. As expected, father's residence in the household at the time of birth was significantly and positively associated with probabilities of having received child support following the separation from the biological father. Children whose fathers lived in the same household at the time of birth had high (and increasing) probabilities of child support receipt during the first two years of eligibility (39 percent and 56 percent, respectively, not shown in table 9.3), compared to a sharply dropping probability of child support receipt from the first (31 percent) to the second year of life (10 percent) by children whose fathers did not live in the same household at the time of birth.

Although the lack of significant associations of demographic and

Table 9.3 LIFE TABLE PROBABILITIES OF NOT RECEIVING CHILD SUPPORT BY DURATION SINCE ELIGIBLE: CHILDREN OF NLSY BORN NO EARLIER THAN 12 MONTHS PRECEDING MOTHERS' 1984 SURVEY

Sample Definition	Number of Years since Becoming Eligible for Child Support				Total Number of Child-Years of Exposure	Comparison Statistic and p
	0	1	2	3		
Total sample	.651	.495	.437	.402	384	
Black children	.712	.634	.547	.527	133	2.63
Hispanic children	.725	.588	.552	—	30	.27
White children	.656	.432	.379	.322	160	
Boys	.666	.449	.377	.377	203	0.32
Girls	.635	.532	.484	.430	181	.57
Firstborn children	.658	.505	.446	.395	227	.00
Children with older siblings	.641	.478	.424	.424	158	.98
Children born to mothers aged 25 or younger	.636	.469	.437	.398	309	2.69
Children born to mothers aged 26 or older	.721	.625	.412	—	78	.10
Children born to mothers with less than high school education	.646	.538	.504	.403	109	0.03
Children born to mothers with high school or more education	.653	.472	.401	.393	254	.87
Children whose annual per capita family income was $5,000 or less	.688	.515	.438	.438	213	6.91
Children whose annual per capita family income was more than $5,000	.505	.425	.425	.425	100	.01
Children whose fathers lived in same household at time of birth	.607	.265	.254	—	162	3.19
Children whose fathers did not live in household at time of birth	.683	.617	.539	.492	215	.07

socioeconomic variables with child support receipt may partially be attributed to small sample size, another contributing factor could be that father characteristics, rather than maternal or child characteristics, are associated with child support receipt. To investigate this hypothesis further, we examined life tables of child support receipt among children whose fathers' characteristics were known. These were the children whose fathers lived in the same household at the time of the first interview following their birth. We found that father characteristics were significantly associated with child support receipt (results not shown). Children of fathers over 26 years old, who had at least a high school education, who had higher wage rates were more likely to receive child support than children of younger, lesser-educated, or lower-paid fathers. Children whose fathers and mothers had been married were more likely to receive child support than children whose biological parents were not married.

When investigating child support eligibility and receipt, it is important to note that some children may cease to be eligible for child support because of the reunion of their mothers and fathers. Life table analyses showed that over 30 percent of the children in our sample experienced the reunion of their parents within four years of initial separation. There were substantial subgroup differences in the rates of experiencing fathers' return (results not shown). Child's race or birth order, maternal age at the time of child's birth, maternal education, per capita family income, and father presence at the time of birth were not predictive of probabilities of continued separation from the biological father. However, the probability that a boy eligible for child support will become ineligible for child support because of the reunion of his biological parents was significantly higher than the comparable probability for a girl. It is possible that a boy's need for his father's presence is perceived to be stronger by fathers and mothers than a girl's need.

Continuity of Child Support

Since both the magnitude and continuity of child support payments have been targeted by recent child support legislation, it is desirable to obtain statistics regarding the continuity of child support. Unfortunately, in the NLSY data, the average period of observation available for analysis is not very long (about 2.5 years), and there are relatively few children for whom child support continuity can be studied ($N = 92$). Nevertheless, we estimated an aggregate life table of cessation of child support payments while the child was in fact eligible.

By the end of the first year following the initial receipt, only 87 percent of all children were receiving child support. By the end of the second year, only 62 percent of eligible children were receiving child support, and the end of the observation period, only 30 percent were receiving support. According to the aggregate life table estimates, a child in this NLSY cohort should expect to receive approximately 29 months (median survival time) of child support, even though he or she continues to be eligible. These estimates, however, must be interpreted with caution, given the small sample and the short duration of observation.

Analysis of Consequences of Child Support

Most studies of developmental outcomes of various family processes for children adopt what might be labeled a cross-sectional approach. Developmental outcomes assessed at a certain point in time are predicted by sociodemographic characteristics and family processes measured prior to or concurrently with the assessment of the outcomes. A major issue is whether the differences attributed to the effects of family processes result from prior differences among children's developmental trajectories. To avoid erroneous conclusions about the effects of family processes on children, one must control for the variation in developmental outcomes prior to the observed changes in family processes. Hence, it is desirable to have two assessments of child outcomes: one prior to the event of interest (here, receipt of child support) and one subsequent to the event of interest. The 1986 and 1988 children of the NLSY data provide a unique opportunity to investigate the outcomes of child support longitudinally.

To analyze the consequences of child support for children, we focused on the two-year interval between the 1986 and 1988 NLSY interviews. In the beginning and at the end of this two-year interval, assessments of children are available, as described earlier. This time interval is ideally suited to study if child support payments result in a *change* in child outcomes compared to the group of children who did not receive child support. To do this, we focused on a subsample of the NLSY children. From the sample of 3,223 children, randomly selected so that only one child per month was included, 1,979 children were assessed in 1986, and at that time 1,204 of them were living with both of their biological parents (weighted 70.3 percent).

To analyze outcomes of child support, father presence had to be determined for the 1986–88 intersurvey interval for each child in the sample. This was done for a total of 1,096 of the 1,204 children living with both biological parents in 1986, whose mothers reported on father presence in 1987 and 1988. However, some of these mothers reported receiving child support at the time of the 1986 survey, probably from the father of a sibling of the target child. The mothers of 1,077 children reported receiving no child support payments at the time of the 1986 survey while the focal child's father was in the household. Within this subsample, we restricted our analyses to children five years old or younger in 1986. In spite of the careful selection of the sample, it cannot be assured that child support payments reported in 1987 and 1988 were made by the target child's father, although it is likely that the payments were made by the fathers who left the mothers' household during the two-year interval. In sum, our sample consists of 981 children aged zero to five in 1986, mapped one-to-one to 981 mothers, whose mothers reported on their fathers' living arrangements in 1986, 1987, and 1988, who were living with their biological parents in 1986, and whose mothers were not receiving any child support in 1986.

The characteristics of this sample are shown in table 9.4. These children averaged 2.1 years of age; slightly over one-half of them were boys; 63 percent were firstborn children; 8 percent (15 percent unweighted) were black; and 7 percent (19 percent unweighted) were Hispanic. Mean ages of the mothers and fathers at the time of their birth were 23 and 28 years, respectively. All but 5 percent of the fathers lived in the same household as their children at the time of their birth. Mothers averaged 12 years of education, a little less than that of the fathers. Almost three-fourths of the mothers and 97 percent of the fathers were employed in 1986 (not shown in table 9.4), and the mean number of working hours per week was 17 for the mothers and 41 for the fathers. Among the employed mothers, mean hourly wage rate was $5.40. Fathers' mean hourly wage rate was substantially higher, at $10.50. Mean annual per capita family income in 1986 was $7,250.

Almost 14 percent of the children experienced a separation from their biological fathers between 1986 and 1988 (table 9.4). Only under 5 percent of these children experienced the divorce of the parents. The mothers of only 38 percent of children experiencing a separation received any child support payments between 1986 and 1988 (not shown in table). Child support payments were more common follow-

Table 9.4 CHARACTERISTICS OF SAMPLE OF CHILDREN AGED 0–5 IN 1986
WHO WERE LIVING WITH BOTH BIOLOGICAL PARENTS: WEIGHTED
STATISTICS (STANDARD DEVIATIONS IN PARENTHESES)

Mean age at time of 1986 interview	2.1
	(1.6)
Percentage male	51.7%
Percentage of firstborn children	63.4%
Percentage black	8.2%
Percentage Hispanic	7.0%
Mean maternal age at birth	23.0
	(2.6)
Mean paternal age at birth	28.0
	(4.1)
Percentage of children whose fathers lived in same household at time of their birth	95.5%
Mean maternal education in 1986 (yr.)	12.3
	(1.9)
Mean paternal education in 1986 (yr.)	12.6
	(2.0)
Mean number of working hours of mother per week in 1986	17.0
	(16.1)
Mean number of working hours of father per week in 1986[a]	41.1
	(13.6)
Mean wage rate of mother in 1986 (among employed mothers)	$5.40/hr.
	(5.5)
Mean wage rate of father in 1986 (among employed fathers)[a]	$10.50/hr.
	(7.6)
Mean annual per capita family income in 1986	$7,250
	(4,421)
Percentage of children whose fathers left household between 1986 and 1988 interviews	13.6%
Percentage of children whose mothers and fathers divorced between 1986 and 1988 interviews	4.7%
N	981

Note: For further specifications of this sample, see text.
a. These data are only available for fathers who were married to the mothers in 1986 (98.3 percent).

ing divorce (55.4 percent) than separation (33.8 percent) (not shown in table).

Characteristics of Families of Children Separated from Their Fathers between 1986 and 1988

Table 9.5 presents statistics for children who received a PIAT reading recognition assessment (our achievement outcome measure) in 1988, by parental separation and child support receipt statuses. The families who separated during the 1986–88 interval had, on the average, lower initial socioeconomic status than the families who did not experience separation. Maternal education, per capita family income, and the quality of the home environment measured in 1986 were significantly lower among families who experienced a separation between 1986 and 1988 than among families who did not experience a separation. However, some differences were noted between the two subgroups of children experiencing parental separation. Those who subsequently received child support had higher levels of income, higher levels of maternal employment, and higher maternal wages than those who did not receive child support subsequent to parental separation. The PPVT scores in 1986 and PIAT scores in 1988 were not significantly different between the three groups of children.

The consequences of the separation can also be seen in table 9.5. Children whose parents separated experienced a substantial decline in annual per capita net family income, compared to the increase experienced by the children whose parents remained cohabiting. This decline in per capita family income occurred even though the mothers who separated and did not receive child support substantially increased (by 15 hours) their average number of hours per week of employment over mothers who remained cohabiting (an increase of only 3 hours per week). Note that child support payments were received by mothers who had high levels of employment prior to separation. However, these mothers, on average, did not increase their level of employment subsequent to separation, whereas the mothers who did not receive child support increased their level of employment by almost 15 hours per week. As a result, the separated mothers who did not receive child support ended up working more hours per week than did similar mothers receiving child support. Subsequent to separation, the proportions of children experiencing an improvement in the quality of home environment were not significantly different between the three groups of children.

Table 9.5 COMPARISON OF CHARACTERISTICS OF CHILDREN BY PARENTAL SEPARATION AND CHILD SUPPORT RECEIPT STATUS BETWEEN 1986 AND 1988 INTERVIEWS: CHILDREN OF NLSY AGED 3–5 WHO WERE LIVING WITH BOTH BIOLOGICAL PARENTS IN 1986

Characteristic	Father Did Not Leave	Father Paid Child Support	Father Did Not Pay Child Support	F Statistic (Significance)
Maternal education in 1986 (yr.)	12.0	11.7	11.1	5.4 (0.0)
Paternal education in 1986 (yr.)	12.3	12.4	11.2	3.9 (.02)
Per capita net family income in 1986	$7,075	$6,064	$5,149	4.1 (.02)
Change in per capita net family income, 1986–88	$994	–$781	–$627	5.0 (.01)
Maternal hours per week worked, reported in 1986	16.7	23.6	12.0	3.8 .02
Increase in hours per week worked, 1986–88	3.3	0.1	14.7	9.3 (.00)
Maternal hourly wage rate in 1986	$3.48	$3.27	$2.47	1.0 (.38)
Paternal hourly wage rate in 1986[a]	$10.47	—[b]	$7.95	4.5 (.01)
Change in maternal wage rate 1986–88	$0.98	$2.45	–$1.33	1.1 (.35)

(continued)

Table 9.5 COMPARISON OF CHARACTERISTICS OF CHILDREN BY PARENTAL SEPARATION AND CHILD SUPPORT RECEIPT STATUS BETWEEN 1986 AND 1988 INTERVIEWS: CHILDREN OF NLSY AGED 3–5 WHO WERE LIVING WITH BOTH BIOLOGICAL PARENTS IN 1986 (continued)

Characteristic	Father Did Not Leave	Father Paid Child Support	Father Did Not Pay Child Support	F Statistic (Significance)
HOME score in 1986	76.5	69.8	72.0	4.6 (.01)
Improvement in HOME score from under 80 percent to over 80 percent 1986–88	24.0%	28.4%	19.8%	0.6[c] (.73)
Percentage of parents married in 1986	95.1%	81.1%	79.5%	43.9[c] (.00)
Number of times per month child sees father (1988)	—	4.04	5.53	0.6 (.46)
PPVT score in 1986	96.5	90.6	94.1	1.4 (.26)
PIAT score in 1988	105.6	103.2	101.8	2.0 (.14)
N	374	41	22	

a. Paternal wage rate is available only for those fathers who were married to the mothers at time of 1986 interview.
b. There were only five valid cases for this statistic.
c. Pearson chi-square statistic.

Consequences of Father's Separation and Child-Support Payments

We estimated multiple linear regression models to investigate the effects of child support on a child's achievement as measured by the PIAT reading recognition score. From the previously described sample of focal children who lived in the same household with their fathers in 1986, data from children aged five or older in 1988 (N = 437) were used to examine the cognitive outcomes of child support. A three-category variable (i.e., two dummy variables) measured the status of these children in 1988: (1) father did not leave (comparison group); (2) father left and no child support payments were received by the mother; (3) father left and child support payments were received by the mother. The measure of cognitive outcome, the PIAT reading recognition standard score measured in 1988, was regressed on the 1986 PPVT measure to control for prior verbal/cognitive development.

The following controls were included in the regression models: sex (a dummy variable indicating boys); race (a dummy variable indicating black children); years of maternal education in 1986; per capita family income in 1986 and the change in income between 1986 and 1988; number of hours per week the mother worked in 1986 and the change in this measure between 1986 and 1988; maternal wage rate in 1986 and change in wage rate between 1986 and 1988; a dummy variable indicating that the HOME score in 1986 was over 80 percent; a dummy variable indicating improvement in the HOME score from under 80 percent in 1986 to over 80 percent in 1988; and the frequency of contact of the father with the child. These are the variables that were found to be significantly associated with parental separation or child support receipt, which may also affect child outcomes. In addition, since prior research (Mott 1991) has suggested that father absence might have a differential impact on girls and boys, we included an interaction term indicating father's departure from the household for boys.

Table 9.6 shows the results of the regression analyses of the PIAT scores.[3] The first two panels display the regression coefficients of models predicting PIAT scores in 1988, when the children were five to seven years old. In the first panel, the model estimating the total effect of child support payment is displayed. Controlling for initial assessment of verbal development (PPVT-R), sex of the child, and interaction of the child's sex with parental separation, girls whose fathers paid child support did not experience significant negative

Table 9.6 RESULTS OF MULTIVARIATE LINEAR REGRESSION MODELS PREDICTING ACHIEVEMENT IN 1988: CHILDREN OF NLSY RESIDING WITH BOTH BIOLOGICAL PARENTS IN 1986

Variables	b^a	β^b	b^a	β^b	b^a	β^b
Comparable assessment in 1986	.245**	.339	.153**	.212	.150**	.207
Male	−3.580**	−.141	−4.460**	−.175	−4.220**	−.166
Black			−1.229	−.026	−1.046	−.022
Maternal education in 1986			1.697**	.230	1.409**	.191
Maternal hours of employment per week in 1986			−.028	−.036	−.068*	−.088
Change in maternal hours of employment per week			−.008	−.011	−.054	−.070
HOME score in 1986 > 80%			3.593**	.138	2.912**	.112
Improvement in HOME score 1986–1988			2.582*	.086	2.209*	.073
Maternal wage rate in 1986			.355**	.125	.300*	.106
Change in maternal wage rate 1986–1988			.292**	.160	.256**	.140
Per capita net family income in 1986 / $1,000					.463**	.147
Change in per capita net family income 1986–1988 / $1,000					.594**	.158
Father left 1986–1988 and no child support is received	−6.255*	−.136	−5.444*	−.089	−4.903*	−.106
Father left 1986–1988 and child support is received	−4.536	−.074	−4.947**	−.107	−5.570*	−.091
Interaction of male and father left 1986–1988	6.995**	.134	9.741**	.186	10.498**	.201
Interaction of frequency per month child sees the father and father left 1986–1988					.282	.070
r^2	0.14		0.23		0.27	

**p < .05
*p < .10
a. Unstandardized coefficient.
b. Standardized coefficient.
Note: Maximum likelihood estimators of missing values were imputed using approach described by Little and Rubin (1986: 109–19).

effects of parental separation on achievement, whereas girls whose fathers did *not* pay support experienced a decline in achievement. In contrast, boys were not affected by parental separation. Note that the size of the coefficient of the interaction term flagging boys who experience parental separation is large enough to counteract the negative effects of parental separation. Although the predicted PIAT score for girls without child support is lower than that for girls who received child support, this difference is not large.

As stated earlier, child support could moderate the negative effects of parental separation on child outcomes via fathers' presence or an increase in family income. The latter effect (i.e., of income on child outcomes) may operate through (1) a decrease in maternal working hours; (2) an enhancement of the quality of the home environment; and (3) improvement of the mother's overall psychological well-being. The second panel of table 9.6 tests the first two of these hypotheses. Data do not support the hypotheses that child support moderates the effects of parental separation either through its effects on maternal work hours or through improvement in the quality of the home environment. Controlling for these factors, parental separation still affected girls regardless of child support receipt.

The third panel of table 9.6 presents a model that controls for variation in income level and father-child contact. These results indicate that the negative effects of parental separation on girls may partly operate independent of the associated changes in family income. Parental separation effects remained fairly constant, controlling for the initial level and the postseparation change in income. The coefficients of the variables indicating parental separation effects for girls are substantial, suggesting that unmeasured factors such as maternal well-being may be mediating the effects of parental separation on child outcomes. Nevertheless, per capita family income and changes in per capita family income have significant positive effects on reading achievement, indicating that increased income will benefit children regardless of parental separation status. The results also indicate that the frequency of contact with the absent father does not significantly affect the PIAT scores.

DISCUSSION AND SUMMARY

This chapter has investigated the dynamics and consequences of child support specifically in terms of its effects on children.

Child support eligibility and receipt are transitory statuses for many children. Although approximately two-fifths of children born in two-parent families become eligible for child support during the first four years of their lives, almost one-third of children who were ever eligible experience the reunion of their biological parents within four years of parental separation. The fluidity of child support eligibility status underscores the need for a judicial system that can rapidly recognize child support eligibility and enforce its payment. Once payments are established, their continuity must be assured. Our data indicate that the continuity of child support payments may be an issue for a majority of children who remain eligible. Little is known about the factors that account for discontinuity of child support payments. For example, remarriage of either of the parents; Aid to Families with Dependent Children (AFDC) regulations deducting child support from benefits; or parents' residence in different states may account for the cessation of child support payments. Further research is needed to pinpoint common reasons for cessation of child support, so that effective policies can be developed to ensure its continuity.

We hypothesized that child support would affect developmental outcomes through its effects on income and on the father's presence. We demonstrated that preschool- and early-elementary-aged girls who separated from their fathers experienced adverse consequences on achievement regardless of child support receipt. The observed differences by child support receipt status are accounted for partly by prior differences in verbal ability. Adequate income, however, may partially buffer the negative impact of parental separation.

Our results indicate a strong gender differentiation in the effects of parental separation on achievement in early elementary school ages. Previous research on the effects of divorce and postdivorce living arrangements has not thoroughly investigated the presence of gender differences in these effects. Some research has indicated that boys are more negatively influenced by divorce than girls during the early childhood years (Chase-Lansdale and Hetherington 1990). It is possible that during later developmental stages, girls are more vulnerable to family conflict, maternal distress, or depression than boys.

A major conceptual challenge of studying the consequences of child support for children is that of interpreting the quantitative findings. Since the empirical data available do not include all relevant information on ways in which child support could influence child outcomes, we can only eliminate certain routes rather than confirm one. The positive effects of child support on family income could affect children via three mediators: the mother could decrease her work hours, which would allow her to interact more with her children; the quality of the child's home environment could be enhanced owing to increased financial resources; and the mother's overall well-being could be enhanced owing to increased financial security. The NLSY data allowed us to eliminate the first two hypotheses for the preschool- to early-elementary-aged children. It was determined that effects of parental separation and child support were mediated neither by the quality of the home environment nor by changes in maternal work hours. The NLSY does not include longitudinal measures of mother's life satisfaction or overall well-being. Hence, we were unable to measure whether child support payments contributed to mothers' well-being, which, in turn, enhanced their children's outcomes.

An alternative hypothesis that could be considered is that child support payments represent father's presence that could contribute positively to a child's development. Our study findings reject the hypothesis that child support payments are beneficial to the extent that they represent continued contact with the father following separation. Compliance with child support payments has little association with contact, and the degree of contact with the father does not affect the achievement outcome studied here. The degree of conflict between the parents is probably associated with child support compliance, and is likely to be a factor that influences developmental outcomes for children experiencing separation. This hypothesis cannot be tested using the NLSY, owing to the lack of measurements of degree of conflict between current and ex-partners.

The social norms on the role of fathers in young children's lives, particularly following divorce or separation, remain unclear. Furstenberg (1990) has suggested that continuing the role of the father following divorce is viewed by many men as voluntary. The Family Support Act of 1988 represents the opposite point of view, mandating child support payments. A small proportion of fathers remain involved following separation, by financial support and continued contact with their children. A few recent studies describe the changes in paternal visitation following divorce, and the reasons for these fluctuations (Furstenberg and Cherlin 1991; Maccoby and Mnookin 1992).

At first glance, the implications of this research are heartening for the Family Support Act's expected impact on children by increasing the proportion of fathers paying child support. Children's achievement responds favorably to increases in family income. However, this finding must be reexamined in light of the magnitude of the impact of child support on family income. In our study sample, a small proportion of the noncustodial fathers paid child support voluntarily. It is likely (as suggested by our analyses) that their personal characteristics and their relationship with their children and ex-spouses are exceptional. Whether stricter enforcement of child support obligations will result in increased or decreased conflict between parents is unknown (Chase-Lansdale and Brooks-Gunn, forthcoming; Garfinkel and McLanahan, forthcoming). Our results suggest that the effects of child support upon children, at the low levels of payment observed in this sample, may, to a large extent, be accounted for by prior differences in family and child characteristics.

Notes

This work was conducted with partial support from the National Institute of Child Health and Human Development. Professor Frank Mott kindly provided the data on the presence of fathers of children in the National Longitudinal Survey of Youth. These analyses were presented at the "Conference on Child Support and Child Well-Being," Airlie House, Airlie, Va., Dec. 5–7, 1991. The authors would also like to thank the NICHD Child and Family Well-Being Network for their support.

1. We refrained from using father presence data constructed by Mott (1990) for two reasons. First, for a moderate proportion of the sample, the father presence could not be established with certainty (Mott determined father presence status of 6,404 of 7,346 children of the NLSY). Second, Mott, for purposes of the study design, did not try to recapture father presence subsequent to a survey at which the father was determined to be absent.

2. Children were observed for differing lengths of time depending on their birth year. While almost five years of data were available for a child born in 1983, less than a year of data was available for a child born in 1988. Simple frequencies of experiencing child support eligibility, child support receipt, and so forth, are dependent on the duration of exposure. Children observed for a longer number of years would have disproportionately contributed to these descriptive statistics. The life table methodology, however, allows us to account for the length of exposure, and utilizes all information, including the duration of risk of experiencing an event, even if a child has not yet experienced the event.

3. A similar regression analysis of the effects of child support on the behavioral problems index (BPI) (Petersen and Zill 1986) was conducted, although the sample size available for these analyses was rather limited since the BPI is available only for children aged four or older. Our analyses suggest that unlike the achievement outcome, increased income, partly operating through the quality of the home environment, mediates the effects of parental separation and child support on behavioral problems (results are available from the authors upon request).

References

Baker, P. C., and F. L. Mott. 1989. *The NLSY Child Handbook, 1989.* Columbus: Center for Human Resource Research, Ohio State University.

Caldwell, B. M., and R. H. Bradley. 1984. *Home Observation for Measurement of the Environment.* Little Rock, Ark.: University of Arkansas.

Chase-Lansdale, P. L., and Brooks-Gunn, J. (eds.). Forthcoming. *Escape from Poverty: What Makes a Difference for Children?* New York: Cambridge University Press.

Chase-Lansdale, P. L., and E. M. Hetherington. 1990. "The Impact of Divorce on Life-Span Development: Short and Long Term Effects." In *Life-Span Development and Behavior,* edited by P. B. Baltes, D. L. Featherman, and R. M. Lerner (105–50). Hillsdale, N.J.: Lawrence Erlbaum.

Danziger, S. K. 1987. "Father Involvement in Welfare Families Headed by Adolescent Mothers." Institute for Research on Poverty Discussion Paper 856-87. Madison: Institute for Research on Poverty, University of Wisconsin-Madison.

Dunn, L., and L. Dunn. 1981. *Peabody Picture Vocabulary Test (Revised).* Circle Pines, Minn.: American Guidance Service.

Furstenberg, F. F., Jr., and A. J. Cherlin. 1991. *Divided Families: What Happens to Children When Parents Part?* Cambridge, Mass.: Harvard University.

Garfinkel, I. 1985. "The Role of Child Support Insurance in Antipoverty Policy." *Annals* 479: 119–31.

Garfinkel, I., and M. M. Klawitter. 1990. "The Effect of Routine Income Withholding of Child Support Collections." *Journal of Policy Analysis and Management* 9: 155–77.

Garfinkel, I., and P. Wong. 1987. "Child Support and Public Policy." Institute for Research on Poverty Discussion Paper 854-87. Madison: Institute for Research on Poverty, University of Wisconsin-Madison.

Garfinkel, I., P. K. Robins, P. Wong, and D. R. Meyer. 1990. "The Wisconsin Child Support Assurance System: Estimated Effects on Poverty, Labor Supply, Caseloads and Costs." *Journal of Human Resources* 25: 1–31.

Little, R. J. A., and D. B. Rubin. 1986. *Statistical Analysis with Missing Data.* New York: John Wiley & Sons.

Maccoby, E. E., and R. H. Mnookin. 1992. *Dividing the Child: Social and Legal Dilemmas of Custody.* Cambridge, Mass.: Harvard University.

Mott, F. 1990. "When Is a Father Really Gone? Paternal-Child Contact in Father-Absent Homes." *Demography* 27: 499–517.

_____ . 1991. "The Impact of Father's Absence from the Home on Subsequent Maternally Reported Behavior Problems of Younger Children." Paper presented at the meetings of the Society for Research in Child Development, Seattle, May.

Petersen, J. L., and N. Zill. 1986. "Marital Disruption, Parent-Child Relationships, and Behavioral Problems in Children." *Journal of Marriage and the Family* 48(2): 295–307.

Robins, P. K. 1986. "Child Support, Welfare Dependency, and Poverty." *American Economic Review* 76: 768–88.

U.S. Bureau of the Census. 1987. *Child Support and Alimony, 1985.* Current *Population Reports,* ser. P.23, no. 152. Washington, D.C.: U.S. Government Printing Office.

——————. 1991. *Statistical Abstract of the United States: 1991,* 111th ed. Washington, D.C.: U.S. Government Printing Office.

Weiss, Yoram, and Robert Willis. 1985. "Children as Collective Goods and Divorce Settlements." *Journal of Labor Economics* 3: 268–92.

Chapter Ten

CHILD SUPPORT AND SCHOOLING

Virginia W. Knox and Mary Jo Bane

The Family Support Act of 1988 strengthened the nation's child support enforcement laws by routinizing child support payments in a variety of ways. It improved incentives to states for paternity establishment; required judges to use state child support guidelines as presumptive awards; mandated updating of awards every three years for cases administered by state IV-D systems; and required income withholding for IV-D cases as of 1990, and for all child support cases as of 1994.

The Family Support Act reforms are likely to succeed in increasing the amounts paid per award and the consistency of payments over time. This, in turn, may have beneficial effects on children and their families. This chapter investigates one of these potential benefits by addressing the question: Does receiving higher levels of child support lead children in single-parent families to attain higher levels of education? The outcomes to be investigated are the number of grades completed, the probability of entry into high school, and the probability of entry into college, all measured by age 21. Each of these outcomes is an important predictor of young adults' later economic status.

Our analysis attempts to isolate the effects of child support payments, following a line of previous research proposing that income from particular sources, such as father's labor, mother's labor, assets, or welfare, is likely to have different effects on children's futures (see Corcoran et al. 1987; Desai, Michael, and Chase-Lansdale 1990; Haveman, Wolfe, and Spaulding 1990; Hill and Duncan 1987; Krein and Beller 1988; McLanahan 1985; Moore and Stief 1991). As in previous research, this chapter's discussion distinguishes between the effects of a family's total income and its level of income from particular sources. Previous work, however, has largely ignored the effect of child support, an income source that is not only financially significant but is of particular symbolic power for single parents and their children.

The only work directly examining the effects of child support on child well-being (prior to that presented in this volume) is that by Furstenberg, Morgan, and Allison (1987). Using data on 227 children aged 11 to 16 in the National Survey of Children, they found that the level of child support received decreases the level of children's problem behavior as reported by both teachers and mothers. They did not find that child support payments affect measures of delinquency, distress, or academic difficulty. Their analysis holds constant a range of family demographic characteristics, but does not control for families' total income or income from other sources.

Our study uses data from the 20-year Panel Study of Income Dynamics (PSID), a data source well-suited to describing patterns of income use during childhood and the effects of income and income sources on outcomes for young adults. We first outline our hypotheses about how child support affects educational outcomes. We then describe our study sample and how sample families combine income from different sources into total income packages. Finally we present our results and conclusions drawn from a set of multivariate analyses.

HYPOTHESES

Explanations of the effects of child support—or indeed of any income source—on individual outcomes are complicated by the fact that income sources are related to each other and to families' total level of income. It seems likely that child support income increases total family income, but not on a dollar-for-dollar basis: earnings, welfare payments, or other income may go down as child support income goes up. Therefore, the four hypotheses that guide our investigations attempt to distinguish the effect of total income on educational outcomes from the effects of income from particular sources.

Hypothesis 1: Increased family income is associated with increased educational attainment by young adults. Higher child support payments affect attainment by increasing total family income.

The extensive literature on marital disruption establishes that children not living with both natural parents have a reduced probability of graduating from high school. Family income appears to be the single most important reason for this educational disadvantage, although part of the disadvantage remains unexplained (McLanahan 1985; Hill and Duncan 1987; Shaw 1982; Sandefur et al. 1989).

Thus, we expect that child support, to the extent that it increases family income, would help children overcome part of the educational disadvantage associated with being in a single-parent family. This economic effect might act through a variety of mechanisms. Early in childhood, the mother could spend more money on activities, materials, day care, or health care that are associated with healthy development. Throughout childhood, parenting might improve because of a reduction in poverty-induced stress for the mother (McLoyd 1990). Higher income might also allow the family to live in a neighborhood that benefits the child through quality of schools, peers, economic opportunities, or other community influences. It might enable the mother to invest in more education for herself, which, on average, is likely to increase her children's educational attainment (Furstenberg et al. 1987). Finally, in adolescence, higher income may increase the child's ability to remain in high school or enter college rather than to enter employment under financial pressure.

Hypothesis 2: Some income sources have positive effects on children, whereas others have negative effects. Child support has a positive effect on attainment because it enables mothers to reduce reliance on sources that have negative effects.

To the extent that mother's earnings or welfare assistance carry with them features detrimental to the child, child support may play a positive role by reducing the role of these other income sources (for discussion of the effects of welfare use, see Butler 1990; Corcoran et al. 1987; Haveman et al. 1990; Hill and Duncan 1987; McLanahan 1985).

One can imagine two groups of mothers for whom significant and consistent child support payments might affect welfare use and labor supply. First, mothers who must work more hours than they prefer might work fewer hours if significant child support were provided (Graham and Beller 1989). Second, mothers who are on welfare but have substantial earnings potential might leave welfare and increase their hours worked once free of welfare's high benefit reduction rate (Meyer 1991). Similarly, high child support may enable some mothers to avoid ever going on welfare. See Meyer et al. (chapter 6, this volume) for an expanded discussion of how the static theory of labor supply predicts these effects.[1]

Hypothesis 3: Child support income has positive effects on children's educational outcomes, independent of its effect on total income or on mothers' use of other income sources.

The level of child support paid by absent fathers could have positive effects on children's emotional well-being or on their material well-being. Furstenberg et al.'s (1987) findings that child support payments affect behavior problems but not academic difficulties lend support to the notion that child support may affect children's emotional well-being. One way in which emotional effects might occur is that payments might "purchase" reduced conflict within the family, leading to increased quantity or quality of contact between father and child. Indeed, child support payments are positively correlated with contact and visitation, although the direction of causality is uncertain (Seltzer, Schaeffer, and Charng 1989). There is also some evidence that continued involvement with fathers is beneficial for children's adjustment to divorce (Wallerstein and Kelly 1980; however, see Furstenberg (1987) for findings that conflict with this study).[2]

An alternative explanation for positive effects is that child support could improve the emotional well-being of the child independent of its effect on visitation. Child support may improve the emotional environment in the home through its effect on the mother, or might even improve the child's outlook directly (Wallerstein 1984).

Finally, child support may even lead to increased material well-being of the child in ways that other income sources do not. In particular, mothers might focus their spending of child support income closely on children, either because they are pressured to or because they feel they should. They might also spend child support on special purchases rather than day-to-day expenses, because it is not a reliable source of support.

Hypothesis 4: Child support income is associated with prior characteristics of fathers, mothers, or their relationship that may have positive effects on children.

In all of our multivariate models, we are able to control for a wide range of demographic characteristics of the mother. However, child support may also be associated with increased educational attainment because of its association with prior characteristics of fathers. Better-educated (and more competent) fathers pay more child support (Seltzer et al. 1989); if fathers' characteristics are not controlled, child support payments could serve as a proxy for them. Child support might also be related to educational outcomes because unmeasured mothers' characteristics, such as motivation or determination, affect both payments and educational outcomes. And finally, the prior level of conflict between mother and father, or the father's level of commitment to his children, might affect both child support and educational attainment.

We can partially test for the effect of father's characteristics by examining whether the effect of child support is reduced once father's education is controlled. Additional unmeasured characteristics of fathers and mothers could lead to a reduction in the effect of child support payments when we control for receipt of any child support.

ANALYSIS

As stated, our analysis uses the Panel Study of Income Dynamics to explore the effects of child support and other income on children in single-parent homes. Specifically, we look at children who lived in a family of which their mother was the head for at least one year between ages 8 and 18. We use a sample of children in the 1987 PSID who were between ages 2 and 8 in 1968, the first year of the study. Children whose mothers were widows when we first observed them in a female-headed family were excluded from the sample, since child support was not a relevant income source for them. Children in subfamilies who were never in households headed by their mothers were also excluded, for purely technical reasons. Because we were observing the children between ages 8 and 18, this was a much less serious exclusion that it would be for younger children.

After these initial exclusions, we had a sample of 621 children. We dropped 11 cases for which education at age 21 was unreported (for a variety of reasons that do not follow a particular pattern). To avoid violating the ordinary least squares (OLS) assumption that the error term for each observation is uncorrelated, we chose at random one sibling from each of the 381 families in our sample. Finally, we excluded 5 families who had more than three years of missing income information between the child's 8th and 18th year. This left us with a sample of 376 children and their families.

For each of the children in the sample, we have family income data for 11 years, from ages 8 to 18. We observe educational outcomes at age 21.

Income Packages of Sample Families

Understanding the effects of child support requires examining it in the context of other income sources that it may either replace or supplement. We begin, therefore, by describing the income-packaging strategies of single-parent families in the PSID. The data underscore the complexity of the ways single-parent families survive and the importance of looking simultaneously at a variety of income sources.

Table 10.1 provides a general description of how our sample families support themselves, by marital status of the mother.[3] The table indicates that about two-thirds of the children receive any child support during their years in female-headed households between ages 8 and 18. The table also shows the average number of years in which children's families received income from each source of interest—child support, welfare, maternal earnings, and other income. On average, children receive child support in about two of every five of the years under investigation. However, since the measure of receiving any child support is at least one dollar paid at any point in the year, children are likely to receive child support in considerably less than 40 percent of the months they spend in a female-headed family.[4]

On average, children in the sample received welfare for the same number of years they received child support. However, neither welfare nor child support were received in the majority of the years, whereas mothers report some earnings and other income in over two-thirds of female-headed years.

Although divorced mothers receive child support in more years than other single mothers (3.2 years versus 1.8 years for never-married and 1.2 years for separated—see table 10.1), they still receive it for only half of their 6 female-headed years in this period. Compared to children of divorced mothers, those with never-married mothers face a double disadvantage: they spend about three-and-a-half more years in a single parent household yet receive child support for one-and-a-half fewer years. Children of separated mothers are also less likely to receive child support than those of divorced mothers. However, it is likely that for this group, some payments by fathers are not reported as child support.

Table 10.1 does not show the extent to which income sources are stable over the period of single parenthood. This omission is important to clarify, since our estimate of 40 percent of single-parent years with child support could be defined in varying ways (i.e., 40 percent of families could receive child support all the time, all families could receive child support 40 percent of the time, or a situation could exist in between). Similarly, welfare could be a stable income source for a small group of mothers or an intermittent source for a

Table 10.1 FAMILIES' RECEIPT OF CHILD SUPPORT, WELFARE, MATERNAL EARNINGS, AND OTHER INCOME, PLUS AVERAGE INCOME FROM EACH SOURCE, FOR YEARS OF FEMALE HEADSHIP WHILE CHILD IS AGED 8 TO 18

| Characteristic | Mother's Marital Status | | | |
	Divorced	Separated	Never Married	Total
Percentage ever receiving:				
Child support	76.9	48.3	55.8	66.5
Welfare	41.3	63.0	84.0	51.3
Maternal earnings	93.0	80.1	92.4	89.0
Other income	95.7	95.7	99.8	96.0
Average years with any:				
Child support	3.2	1.2	1.8	2.5
Welfare	1.7	3.0	6.1	2.4
Maternal earnings	5.2	3.2	5.9	4.6
Other income	4.5	3.7	6.4	4.4
Average years in female-headed family	5.9	4.9	9.3	5.9
Income source:[a]				
Child support ($)	4,341	3,400	2,720	4,027
Welfare ($)	4,000	5,746	4,898	4,773
Maternal earnings ($)	11,605	8,328	6,478	10,292
Other income ($)	8,120	10,081	6,710	8,609
Total income	20,744	18,838	14,489	19,679
N	170	151	55	376

Note: "Child support" includes child support and alimony. Welfare includes Aid to Families with Dependent Children (AFDC), Supplemental Security Income (SSI), and Food Stamps. Total income includes all cash income and Food Stamps. Sample sizes are for unweighted sample. Means are weighted by the inverse of the probability of selection into the sample, with adjustment for differential nonresponse.
a. Income is measured for years of female headship while child is aged 8 to 18. All figures are in 1985 dollars. Averages are just for years with income from that source.

larger group. In fact, income sources showed only moderate stability. About two-thirds of the single-parent families ever received child support; those who received it in approximately four out of six years spent it in a single-parent family. About half of the families reported ever receiving welfare, and they received it for an average of five out of seven single-parent years. Earnings were nearly ubiquitous, as was "other income." Some proportion of "other income" was actually the earnings of the former head during the transition year (i.e., the first year after a divorce or separation). This income was included because we classified a year as "single-parent" if the parent was single at the time of the PSID interview; however, the PSID measures family income for the year prior to the interview.

Table 10.1 also summarizes the average amounts received from each source, excluding years in which the family received no income from that source.[5] Clearly, divorced mothers contribute the majority of their families' income through working, whereas separated and never-married mothers rely on more diverse sources. With their higher earnings and higher child support payments, divorced mothers fare better economically and receive less welfare than the other two groups.

"Other income" is a surprisingly significant source. As noted earlier, it includes income from the former head during transition years.[6] It also includes earnings of others in the household and transfer income other than welfare, such as unemployment benefits. These other income sources were consequential, even during nontransition years. Separated mothers received considerably more income from "other sources" than mothers in the other two groups. One reason for this is that they experienced more transition years into single parenthood during our follow-up than did other groups.

We have already seen that never-married (and separated) mothers receive child support in fewer years than those who are divorced. Table 10.1 shows that they also receive substantially less money even in years when child support is paid. Strikingly, families get more welfare in the years they participate in welfare than child support in the years they receive child support. Thus, the family of an average child in our sample received welfare for the same number of years as it received child support, and received higher annual welfare payments than child support payments.

Table 10.1 demonstrates that child support is only one income source out of several that single mothers piece together to support their families. Because child support is almost never the major income source for a family, some of its potential importance may lie in how it interacts with work and welfare. One of our hypotheses is that child support may be important because it allows families to supplement earnings, or to replace or avoid welfare. To get a sense of whether these trade-offs actually occur, we classified each female-headed year for each family by the level of income received from each source that year.[7] Table 10.2 presents a distribution of all observed years of single parenthood, according to the composition of families' income packages in those years.

Because of the potential significance of the exchange of child sup-

Table 10.2 FAMILY INCOME BY INCOME PACKAGE AND SOURCE, FOR YEARS OF FEMALE HEADSHIP WHILE CHILD IS AGED 8–18 (IN 1985 DOLLARS)

Income Package	Percentage of Female Head Years	Total Income ($)	Mother's Earnings ($)	Child Support ($)	Welfare ($)	Other ($)
"Welfare" packages (welfare greater than 25 percent of income)						
Welfare greater than 75 percent of income	11.3	10,822	285	247	9,911	379
Welfare 25–75 percent; welfare plus earnings greater than 75 percent	5.2	13,205	5,205	213	6,927	860
Welfare 25–75 percent; welfare plus earnings up to 75 percent	8.0	15,254	1,081	860	6,966	6,347
Total	24.6	12,770	1,593	439	8,318	2,421
"Nonwelfare" packages (welfare less than 25 percent of income)						
Earnings greater than 75 percent of income	28.9	18,985	16,810	813	230	1,131
Earnings 50–75 percent; earnings plus child support greater than 75 percent	10.4	18,347	12,228	4,414	327	1,378
Earnings 50–75 percent; earnings plus child support plus other nonwelfare greater than 75 percent	8.4	23,580	14,194	1,162	472	7,752
Earnings less than 50 percent welfare less than 25 percent	27.8	22,926	5,208	2,979	520	14,220
Total	75.4	20,860	11,614	2,144	377	6,724

Note: The unit of analysis is person-years spent in a female-headed household. Means are weighted by the inverse of the probability of selection into the sample, with adjustment for differential nonresponse.

port for welfare, we first divided our sample by whether or not welfare was an important component of overall income. We classified years with "welfare" packages as those in which more than 25 percent of average income comes from welfare. These "welfare" years occurred in 24.6 percent of all single-parent years (see table 10.2). We classified families' years with less than 25 percent of their income from welfare as years with "nonwelfare" packages. This group accounted for the other 75.4 percent of years. There was a sharp difference in total family income between welfare and nonwelfare years: total mean income for years with "welfare" combinations was $12,770, whereas total mean income for "nonwelfare" years was $20,860.

We divided years with "welfare" packages into three categories. The first category, which occurs 11.3 percent of the time (table 10.2), includes years in which families might be considered "welfare dependent," with over 75 percent of their income from welfare. Families with the next type of package, which occurs 5.2 percent of the time, have a lower proportion (25 to 75 percent) of income from welfare, with earnings as a second major income source. The third category of welfare packages comprises the 8 percent of years in which income other than earnings or child support is the primary supplement to welfare.

Table 10.2 also provides the average level of income from different sources, for families with each type of income package. Comparing income from different sources across groups lends insight into how families might substitute one source of income for another. For example, AFDC rules are reflected in the relative situations of the two lowest-income groups. The more earnings (and total income) a family has, the less welfare it receives. In addition, families who rely on welfare get very little child support, an average of $439 for all families with welfare packages.[8]

A comparison of the second and third groups in table 10.2 suggests that although these groups receive the same amount of welfare on average, they are in some way substituting "other income" for earnings. Of course, we cannot tell from this table whether "other income" is received because of low earnings, as in the case of unemployment benefits, or whether "other income" causes the mother to work less, as it might if it represents an additional earner in the family.

The next section of table 10.2 describes the four categories of families with "nonwelfare" income combinations. The first group, those for whom more than 75 percent of their family income comes from maternal earnings, is seen in 29 percent of female-headed years. Thus, although table 10.2 showed that maternal earnings are a substantial source of income for single-parent families, they depend *solely* upon earnings in fewer than 3 years out of 10. Another 10 percent of the time, families receive between 50 and 75 percent of their income from earnings and have child support as a major supplementary income source. This is one of the most interesting packages for our purposes, since it is the package that families might move to from either a predominantly earnings package or a welfare package, if they have gained additional child support. Mean income for this group was $18,347, with $4,414 from child support, compared with mean income of $18,985 for the earnings-dependent group, and income of $13,205 for the welfare plus earnings group.

One's interpretation of the potential trade-off between earnings and child support differs markedly depending upon whether one compares families with welfare packages to those with nonwelfare packages, or whether one compares the groups of families with non-welfare packages. The group with welfare packages has less earnings *and* less child support than the group with nonwelfare packages. Any substitution that may occur on the margin is overwhelmed by the fact that the 25 percent of families who receive welfare have fewer resources of all kinds than the 75 percent who do not receive welfare. This might lead one to think that earnings and child support are generally positively related, rather than substitutes for one another.

However, a different story emerges when we compare the levels of income for the first "nonwelfare" group, which has virtually all earnings, to the second group, which has earnings and child support. With only $638 difference in total income, the first group has $4,600 more in maternal earnings and $3,600 less in child support than the second group (table 10.2). Thus, once we compare families whose trade-offs are not "muddied" by welfare rules, it appears that a trade-off may occur between earnings and child support. We have not sorted out here whether higher maternal earnings *cause* low child support, because husbands pay less (and judges award less) to wives who have high earnings potential, or whether women who get substantial child support are able to reduce their work hours. Similarly, when we see that families with welfare packages receive less child support than those with nonwelfare packages, we cannot say how much low child support is causing welfare receipt, and how much welfare receipt reduces child support received because of welfare rules. Yet table 10.2 does suggest that, whatever the causal direction, a family's level of child support in a given year is related to its total income and to its receipt of income from other sources. In turn, this relationship with income from other sources could help explain a positive effect of child support.

Effect of Child Support Levels on Grades Completed

A multivariate analysis helps determine whether a single-parent family's income package, especially its level of child support payments, is associated with improved outcomes, controlling for exogenous family background variables. Does income from child support positively affect grades completed at age 21? Do these effects appear to be caused purely by families' total income levels, or does income from different sources have different impacts? Does the effect of child support on grades completed appear to be composed of different effects on a child's likelihood of high school graduation and likelihood of entry into college?

MULTIVARIATE ANALYSIS

Table 10.3 presents the results of a set of ordinary least squares regression models that test the degree to which our data are consistent with each of our four previously mentioned hypotheses. For the definition of variables in table 10.3, see appendix table 10.A.1.[9] Model 1 in the table examines the effect on grades completed at age 21 of average annual income from all sources, during all single- and two-parent years from ages 8 to 18.[10] If the effect of average annual income is positive, that would indicate that child support could have a positive effect by simply increasing family income.

Model 1 in table 10.3 does not offer much support for the hypothesis that average annual income has a positive effect on educational outcomes, regardless of income source. The coefficient of family income on grades completed is not even significant at the 10 percent level. Even if it were statistically significant, the effect would be quite small—every $10,000 increase in income is associated with an increase in educational attainment of one-eighth of a year.[11]

The coefficients of other demographic characteristics are generally as expected. In particular, mother's education has the largest set of effects on children's grades completed (table 10.3). Positive effects of being black or female, and negative effects of large numbers of children or frequent moves by the family, are all consistent with previous multivariate research on educational attainment.

Having found little support for the hypothesis that income regardless of source has positive effects, we next test the hypothesis that

Table 10.3 ORDINARY LEAST SQUARES REGRESSION RESULTS FOR MODELS PREDICTING GRADES COMPLETED BY AGE 21

Variable	Model 1	Model 2	Model 3	Model 4	Model 5
Intercept	12.227 (0.532)	12.086 (.5225)	11.997 (0.5138)	12.053 (.5194)	12.012 (.5241)
Average income, all years	0.012 (0.0074)				
Average income, two-parent years		0.016** (.0064)	0.010* (.0061)	0.013** (.0065)	0.012* (.0066)
Average income, female-headed years		−0.006 (.0070)			
Average child support			0.104*** (.0377)	0.100*** (.0391)	0.093** (.0444)
Average welfare				0.000 (.0252)	0.001 (.0254)
Average mother's earnings				−0.011 (.0120)	−0.011 (.0121)
Average other income				−0.007 (.0079)	−0.009 (.0080)
No years with two parents		0.132 (.2838)	0.023 (.2776)	0.083 (.2822)	0.044 (.2851)
Black	0.372** (.1716)	0.404** (.1724)	0.477*** (.1729)	0.476*** (.1744)	0.438** (.1759)
Female	0.229* (.1327)	0.235* (.1327)	0.225* (.1314)	0.227* (.1319)	0.230* (.1326)

(continued)

Table 10.3 ORDINARY LEAST SQUARES REGRESSION RESULTS FOR MODELS PREDICTING GRADES COMPLETED BY AGE 21 (continued)

Variable	Model 1	Model 2	Model 3	Model 4	Model 5
Mother high school graduate	0.449*** (.1470)	0.471*** (.1463)	0.451*** (.1437)	0.485*** (.1469)	0.501*** (.1483)
Mother some college	0.389 (.2745)	0.433 (.2704)	0.345 (.2675)	0.405 (.2770)	0.403 (.2888)
Mother college graduate	1.736*** (.6482)	1.774*** (.6467)	1.618** (.6424)	1.663*** (.6466)	1.612** (.6508)
Age of mother at child's birth	−0.028** (.0112)	−0.028** (.0112)	−0.029*** (.0111)	−0.029*** (.0111)	−0.030*** (.0113)
Never married	−0.208 (.2239)	−0.225 (.2239)	−0.216 (.2211)	−0.229 (.2228)	−0.284 (.2255)
Divorced	0.207 (.1563)	0.209 (.1550)	0.151 (.1550)	0.166 (.1592)	0.161 (.1626)
Ever new marriage, ages 8–18	0.025 (.1811)	−0.132 (.1995)	−0.17 (.1976)	−0.198 (.1994)	−0.192 (.2007)
Number of female-headed years, ages 1–7	−0.011 (.0291)	0.001 (.0313)	0.009 (.0311)	0.007 (.0314)	−0.010 (.0326)
Number of female-headed years, ages 8–18	0.017 (.0243)	0.024 (.0285)	0.025 (.0282)	0.024 (.0286)	0.020 (.0294)
Average number of children, ages 8–18	−0.155*** (.0500)	−0.137*** (.0503)	−0.148*** (.0498)	−0.155*** (.0548)	−0.156*** (.0550)
Number of years moved, ages 8–18	−0.102*** (.0375)	−0.105*** (.0375)	−0.088** (.0372)	−0.092** (.0375)	−0.090** (.0385)

	(1)	(2)	(3)	(4)	(5)
Northeast	-0.054 (.2422)	-0.073 (.2418)	-0.115 (.2396)	-0.085 (.2436)	-0.066 (.2459)
North Central	-0.109 (.2111)	-0.128 (.2116)	-0.164 (.2098)	-0.140 (.2142)	-0.118 (.2170)
South	-0.113 (.2012)	-0.132 (.2010)	-0.130 (.1900)	-0.093 (.2163)	-0.092 (.2189)
Cohort	0.034 (.0326)	0.035 (.0325)	0.044 (.0323)	0.045 (.0328)	0.048 (.0328)
Father high school graduate					-0.073 (.2075)
Father some college					0.228 (.3978)
Father college graduate					0.144 (.4240)
Father's education missing					0.296* (.1772)
Any child support in female-headed years					0.092 (.1646)
R^2 (adjusted)	0.115	0.121	0.138	0.134	0.134

*statistical significance at .10 level.
**statistical significance at .05 level.
***statistical significance at .01 level.

Note: Standard errors in parentheses. In general, income variables are averaged across years that child is between ages 8 and 18, data are not missing, and child has not yet established own household. In models 3–5, income from specific sources is averaged across female-headed years while child is between ages 8 and 18. See appendix table 10.A.1 for a complete description of variables. For all income data, results are computed based on thousands of 1985 dollars.

income from different sources has different effects. Model 2 in table 10.3 contains the same control variables as Model 1, but divides income into two categories—average annual income received during mother-headed years and average annual income received during two-parent years.[12]

Strikingly, this specification suggests that income in two-parent years has a small positive effect, of approximately .16 years per $10,000 in average annual income, whereas income in years of female headship has no impact. At first glance the difference in these two coefficients appears puzzling, but it is consistent with our hypothesis that different sources of income have different effects. Female-headed households are much more likely to have a variety of income sources, perhaps some with positive effects and some with negative effects. Therefore, total income in those years might have an ambiguous effect, while the average impact of income in two-parent years (mostly father's earnings) is positive. The findings of Model 2 are also consistent with a hypothesis that unmeasured parental characteristics are more important than income. Income during two-parent years might be serving as a proxy for the characteristics of both parents, to which income during single-parent years adds no information.

With Models 3 and 4 (table 10.3), we begin to disentangle the differential effects of specific forms of income. Model 3 contains the same control variables as earlier regressions, but includes only income from child support rather than all income in years of female headship. Model 4 incorporates income from welfare, maternal earnings, and other income. Comparing the results of these two specifications allowed us to test whether any effects of child support are explained by its relationships with other forms of income.

Both Models 3 and 4 find a .1 increase in years of education for a $1,000 increase in child support. This coefficient is considerably higher than the effect of income from any other source. In fact, no other income source in female-headed years appears to have any effect on educational attainment.

In interpreting Model 4 (table 10.3), one should remember that we are looking at the effect of each income source, holding the other income sources constant. For example, the coefficient on child support reveals the effect of an additional $1,000 in child support if earnings and other income remain at their same levels. We do not know how likely this is to happen; in fact, our examination of income packages suggested that there is at least some substitution. We address this issue later in the chapter when we use logit results to analyze the effects of changing levels of income from different income sources simultaneously.

With that caveat in mind, we examine more closely the lack of effects on education from welfare and maternal earnings. For welfare income, one could argue that Model 4 may mask negative effects that occur through welfare's incompatibility with work and its relatively low benefit levels. Under that scenario, welfare payments could have a negative effect, but could show no effect once the level of other income, particularly earnings, is controlled. However, when we specified a model (not shown) that includes average welfare income but no controls for other sources in female-headed years, the coefficient on welfare remained insignificant.[13]

The insignificant effect of average maternal earnings was consistent with our original hypothesis that such earnings might have contradictory effects on educational attainment. In a separate model (not shown), we disaggregated average earnings into three factors: average hourly wage (hypothesized to have a positive effect), average hours worked (hypothesized to have a negative effect in some cases), and total years worked (hypothesized to have a positive role-model effect). That model suggested that earnings do have contradictory effects: maternal years worked has a positive effect on grades completed at age 21, while average wage and hours worked have no significant effects.[14]

The surprising findings of Models 3 and 4 are that child support seems to have such strong positive effects. Despite the suggestion in table 10.1 that mothers may trade off child support for other income sources, those trade-offs have virtually no power to explain the effects of child support. Relatively small positive effects of child support, similar to those of two-parent family income, would have suggested that the primary role of child support is to increase total family income. However, the coefficient between child support and grades completed is more than seven times larger than that for income in two-parent years. These findings suggest that child support is associated, perhaps causally, perhaps not, with additional family characteristics that have positive implications for education. We explore this possibility in the next model.

The four models to this point have controlled for a large number of observable characteristics of the mother, and for characteristics of the father for which "income in two-parent years" acts as a proxy. Model 5 in table 10.3 tests the hypotheses that child support levels have positive effects due to (a) the education and competence of fathers, (b) heterogeneity among fathers who pay any child support, or (c) heterogeneity among mothers who receive child support. The model includes the same income and control variables as Model 4, and adds variables representing father's education and receipt of any child support.

The major finding in Model 5 is that after adding these new control variables, the effect of child support remains statistically significant, and the coefficient is reduced only slightly. The lack of significance on the "any receipt" variable has two implications. First, receipt of any child support does not appear to have important effects on educational attainment, beyond effects associated with payment levels.[15] Second, although the effect of payments on educational outcomes may still be partially attributable to unmeasured parental characteristics, those characteristics would have to be associated primarily with the level of payments made, not with income in two-parent years or with the probability of paying at all.

Previous research has reported that father's education has a positive effect on children's educational status, at least in intact families (Haveman et al. 1990; Sandefur, McLanahan, and Wojtkiewicz 1989). Yet in our model, father's education does not have an effect. Clearly, having missing data for 47 percent of the sample was a limitation of this analysis. However, when we reran Models 1–5 including only children who had information on father's education, the inclusion of father's education in the model increased the coefficient on child support somewhat, rather than decreasing it. This suggests that including full data on father's education into the model is unlikely to reduce the coefficient on child support.

The only variable introduced in Model 5 (table 10.3) that has a positive coefficient is the dummy variable for "father's education missing." In the vast majority of cases, the reason for the missing data can be attributed to two conditions: the father was never observed in the home, and the child did not establish an independent household by 1987. We interpret the positive coefficient on this variable to mean that staying at home into early adulthood is related to decisions about remaining in school. Because "father's education missing" is therefore endogenous to education, and the other father's education variables do not add explanatory power to the model, we exclude the set of father's education variables from the logit models discussed later.[16]

Effect of Child Support Levels on Probabilities of High School Graduation and Entry into College

Although number of grades completed provides a useful summary of a child's total educational attainment, completing years that are accompanied by credentials, such as 12th or 16th grade, is particularly important to the young person's economic future. Therefore, we estimated the effects of child support payments both on the probability of finishing high school and on the probability of entering college.[17]

Logistic regression is an appropriate technique for predicting outcomes of binary choice. We estimated two logit models, one predicting graduation from high school and one predicting entry into college. As the main purpose here is to estimate the effects of income from specific sources, particularly child support, the models incorporate the same independent variables as Model 4 of table 10.3.[18]

Table 10.4 presents the results of the logit models as estimated changes in the probability of high school graduation or college entry, for changes in each variable at its weighted mean (see appendix table 10.A.2 for logit coefficients and standard errors). The results are generally consistent with the results for grades completed, with some differences between effects on high school graduation and on college entry.

For children who were currently at the mean probability of high school graduation and college entry, a $1,000 change in average child support was associated with a 5 percentage point increase in the likelihood of graduation and a 3 percentage point increase in the likelihood of college entry (in table 10.4). We examine the implications of these effects for families with particular income packages in the next section.

The effects of variables representing other sources of income are consistent with those estimated by OLS, with the exception that "other income" has a significant (but small) negative effect on college entry. In addition, the impact of income in two-parent years appears to be isolated to an effect on high school graduation rather than college entry.

The positive effects of being black and the negative effects of average number of children both operate more strongly on college entry than on finishing high school (table 10.4). In contrast, having a mother who is a high school graduate leads to larger improvements in high school graduation than college entry, and the negative effects of mother's age at child's birth and number of moves appear to be isolated to high school graduation. The effect of moves on high school graduation rather than college entry is consistent with interpreting the effect as a measure of the child's degree of connection to a particular community and school. Such connection may be more relevant to the decision to remain in high school than to go to college.

Interestingly, compared to being in a separated family, coming

Table 10.4 ESTIMATED DERIVATIVES FOR LOGIT MODELS PREDICTING
PROBABILITIES OF HIGH SCHOOL GRADUATION AND COLLEGE
ENTRY BY AGE 21

Variable	Approximated dp/dx at Mean Probability of High School Graduation	Approximated dp/dx at Mean Probability of College Entry
Intercept	0.344	−0.0401
Average child support (000s)	0.053**	0.033**
Average welfare (000s)	0.004	0.011
Average mother's earnings (000s)	−0.001	0.002
Average other income (000s)	−0.001	−0.007*
Average income, two-parent years (000s)	0.005*	0.002
No years with two parents	0.144	0.117
Black	0.101	0.155**
Female	0.023	0.068
Mother high school graduate	0.150***	0.094*
Mother some college or college graduate	0.032	0.082
Age of mother at child's birth	−0.011***	−0.002
Never married	0.031	−0.138
Divorced	0.070	−0.108*
Ever new marriage, ages 8–18	0.022	0.003
Number of female-headed years, ages 1–7	−0.005	−0.015
Number of female-headed years, ages 8–18	0.004	−0.006
Average number of children, ages 8–18	−0.041**	−0.091***
Number of years moved, ages 8–18	−0.047***	−0.017
Northeast	−0.026	−0.089
North Central	−0.140*	0.022
South	−0.058	−0.023
Cohort	0.013	−0.002
Pseudo R^2	0.152	0.123
Chi square	68.3	45.3

*statistical significance at .10 level.
**statistical significance at .05 level.
***statistical significance at .01 level.
Notes: dp/dx = p(1 − p)b, where p = weighted mean probability of high school graduation or college entry for total sample and b = coefficient from logit model. McFadden's pseudo R^2 measure is computed as:
R^2 = 1 − [log likelihood, all parameters/log likelihood, intercept only].
See appendix table 10.A.1 for a complete description of variables and appendix table 10.A.2 for logit coefficients and their standard errors.

from a divorced family has a significantly negative effect on college entry that is not evident in the regressions on total grades completed. In addition, the coefficient on being female has an effect in the linear regressions but does not have a significant effect in the logit models.

Effects of Changes in Income Packages

As discussed earlier, for children in single-parent families, the effect of one particular income source is less relevant than is the outcome of the family's entire income package. Table 10.5 uses our logit results to simulate the effects of incorporating more child support into the incomes of families with particular income packages. First we examine two cases in which maternal earnings comprise the majority of family income. Then we turn to two cases in which a significant portion of family income comes from welfare.

Case 1 in table 10.5 represents an "earnings-dependent" divorced mother—her earnings contribute more than 75 percent of her family's income. Her levels of income from each source are set at the mean for families with at least 75 percent of income in earnings. All other family characteristics are set at the mean for divorced mothers. Our model predicts that her children have an 80 percent probability of graduating from high school and a 15 percent probability of entering college. How would these predictions differ for children whose families appear identical except that their income is weighted more toward child support—only 50–75 percent is earnings, with the bulk of the rest coming from child support?

Case 2, in table 10.5, which simulates the latter situation, has slightly *lower* total average income than Case 1 (about $18,300 compared with $19,000). Yet, Case 2 indicates that children whose mothers' earnings are supplemented with child support are substantially more likely to finish high school and to enter college. To take these simulation results at face value, one must assume that the coefficients presented in our logit models are unbiased estimates of how much children's educational attainment would change if a government initiative exogenously changed single-parent families' levels of income from each source. Because we cannot rule out the possibility that heterogeneity among families is biasing our coefficients, these simulations presumably provide upper-bound predictions of the change that would occur due to changes in policy toward single-parent families.

In Case 3 (table 10.5) we have a never-married mother for whom welfare is a major income source but is supplemented by earnings

Table 10.5 PREDICTED PROBABILITIES OF HIGH SCHOOL GRADUATION AND
COLLEGE ENTRY BY AGE 21: FOUR CASES WITH VARYING
CHARACTERISTICS AND INCOME PACKAGES

Sample Cases	Predicted Probability of High School Graduation (%)	Predicted Probability of College Entry (%)
Divorced with income packages composed of earnings, or earnings plus child support		
Case 1: Maternal earnings alone greater than 75 percent of income.	80.4	15.1
Case 2: Maternal earnings between 50 percent and 75 percent of income; earnings plus child support greater than 75 percent of income.	92.2	26.0
Never married with income packages combining earnings with welfare or child support:		
Case 3: Welfare between 25 percent and 75 percent of income; welfare plus earnings greater than 75 percent of income.	75.8	11.1
Case 4: Identical to Case 3, with child support substituting for welfare amount	94.7	23.0

Notes:
Case 1: Background characteristics are set at mean for divorced women. Income from each source is set at mean for women whose earnings are more than 75 percent of income.
Case 2: Background characteristics are set at mean for divorced women. Income from each source is set at mean for women whose income is 50–75 percent earnings, and over 75 percent earnings plus child support.
Case 3: Background characteristics are set at mean for never-married women. Income from each source is set at mean for women whose income is between 25 percent and 75 percent welfare, and over 75 percent welfare plus earnings.
Case 4: Background characteristics are set at mean for never-married women. Maternal earnings and other income are same as Case 3; welfare = 0; child support is set at welfare level from Case 3.

or other income. For this case, we set income levels for each source at the mean for families with 25–75 percent welfare and over 75 percent welfare and earnings. Other family characteristics were set at the mean for never-married mothers. We predicted that 76 percent of children from these families graduate from high school, and that only 11 percent enter college. We then compared this prediction to that for a child whose family is identical to that in Case 3, except that welfare has been replaced in full by child support. Here total family income has not changed at all—it remains at about $13,200— but we have substituted child support for welfare as the supplement to earnings and other income. In Case 4, we see a substantial increase in the probability of high school graduation from 76 to 95 percent, and an absolute increase in college attendance similar to that seen in moving from Case 1 to Case 2.

Even as upper-bound estimates, the predicted changes in education outcomes that arise from changing the income packages of hypothetical families are striking. It remains true that data limitations prevent us from incorporating into our model some family characteristics that might result in both child support and educational outcomes— in particular, father's involvement with the family and unmeasured characteristics like persistence or motivation. Nevertheless, clearly there are large differences in the educational chances of children whose single mothers support their families with income from different sources. These differences are *not* caused by the race or gender of the child, *nor* are they caused by the educational levels or total incomes of the parents.

CONCLUSION

We began this investigation with four hypotheses—that child support might have positive effects on educational attainment (1) by increasing family income, (2) by reducing the negative effects of other income sources, (3) by having positive effects of its own, or (4) through competence of fathers or other behaviors that differentiate parents in families with child support and without. Of the four hypotheses, we find the strongest support for the third hypothesis, and we cannot rule out the fourth. Taken at face value, our findings suggest that income from some sources has more positive effects than income from other sources. During single-parent years, child support seems to play a much more positive role than do welfare and maternal earnings.

Ultimately, the purpose of this type of analysis is to predict whether increases in child support brought about by changes in public policy are likely to have beneficial effects on children. To draw such a policy conclusion would require more evidence than we can present in this chapter about the mechanisms through which such a positive effect might occur. As discussed earlier, increasing levels of child support might plausibly cause positive changes in relationships among family members, or in purchases for children. However, the possibility also remains that the effect found here is spurious, caused by unmeasured characteristics that drive both the level of child support in a family and children's educational attainment.

Our results do support the conclusion that life in families that receive more child support is more developmentally positive than life in families that receive less child support. These differences may be caused by the increased child support payments, or by unmeasured characteristics of families that are unaffected by the level of child support they receive. When combined with additional evidence on the effects of child support on each parent's behavior, these early findings will provide essential insights into the long-range effects on children of increases in child support brought about by the Family Support Act of 1988.

Notes

1. In practice, however, the structure of both the welfare system and of formal work arrangements may make these effects uncommon until child support payments are made a more substantial and reliable income source. In the welfare system, the absent parent pays child support to the state rather than to the mother. The result is that, in a given month, a mother cannot trade off a dollar of child support for a dollar of welfare. Instead, the negative effect of child support on welfare receipt, and its complementary positive effect on employment, can only occur when her child support is high enough for her to avoid or leave welfare altogether. Similarly, the structure of the employment system may make labor force participation decisions "lumpy"—a mother might have the option to reduce work hours from 40 to 20 hours per week, but not from 40 to 35. It would therefore take significant and reliable child support to enable a woman to respond by reducing welfare and increasing work hours, or by decreasing work hours. See also Hill et al. (1987), Corcoran et al. (1987), and McLanahan (1985) for discussions on the consequences of maternal employment in single-parent families.

2. Based on previous research on family disruption, our discussion assumes that, on average, increased involvement of the absent father will benefit children. It is possible, however, that increased enforcement of child support may lead the father to make unwelcome demands for involvement, increasing tension between him and the custodial family. This, in turn, might have negative effects for children.

3. Marital status is generally measured in the first year of female headship after the child reaches age eight. However, mothers who first reported being separated were categorized as divorced if they subsequently spent more time divorced than separated. In addition, a handful of children were included whose mothers first reported themselves as widows, but thereafter consistently reported themselves as never married or divorced.

4. The PSID provided information only on how much child support each family

receives. Therefore, although we refer to "children" receiving child support, we do not know whether the child support was being paid for the particular child in our sample.

5. From 1967 to 1975 the PSID reported child support payments only in combination with alimony payments. For consistency, we continued that practice, so that in all years child support is combined with alimony. Note that even taking into account the addition of alimony, the estimates of average child support reported here are substantially higher than recent Current Population Survey (CPS) estimates. One cause for the discrepancy is that the PSID is known to report consistently higher income levels than do other sources. In addition, the CPS systematically underestimates child support by failing to ask some subgroups of single mothers about payments received.

6. Forty-four percent of the (unweighted) sample was observed in a transition year. The mean level of "other income" in transition years was $14,855. In nontransition years, average "other income" was $4,332.

7. Although these analyses give us a sense of how trade-offs might occur, they do not sort out the many causal interactions between levels of child support, earnings, and welfare.

8. AFDC recipients have been required to assign child support payments to the state since 1975, near the middle of our follow-up for income (1968 to 1984). Thus, in the first half of our follow-up, the mother's child support was simply counted as income against her AFDC grant, and she probably reported it to the PSID as child support. In the second part of our follow-up, AFDC recipients were not supposed to receive child support directly from absent parents, and the PSID was probably not told about child support payments made from absent parents to state Title IV-D agencies. AFDC mothers may, however, have reported to the PSID "under the table" payments made to them from the absent parent.

9. All of the multivariate models that follow were also run excluding income from years of transition into single parenthood. The results were substantially the same whether or not such income was included.

10. Total income includes all cash income and Food Stamps.

11. This coefficient is smaller than estimates by Hill and Duncan (1987) and Corcoran et al. (1987). One explanation for this difference is that our sample is composed solely of families who were ever headed by women, whereas their samples represented all families. Another is that we measured attainment at age 21, whereas Hill and Duncan measured outcomes at ages 25–27, and Corcoran et al. from ages 24 to 32, depending upon when the youth left home.

12. We use the terms *female-headed*, *mother-headed*, and *single-parent* years interchangeably because we defined female-headed years as years in which the mother was head of the family. We made this choice because mother-headed years were the only single-parent years in which we could accurately identify maternal earnings. Because all years in which the mother is not the family head are classified as "two-parent" years, a few "two-parent years" are actually years in which the father is absent and the family head is a grandparent or other relative.

13. Similarly, one could argue that the average welfare received over time combines potentially positive effects of welfare dollars with negative consequences, such as demoralization, potentially associated with the number of years on welfare. However, we found no effect of years on welfare, whether or not we controlled for income from nonwelfare sources.

14. This finding extends to single-parent families the result of Haveman et al. (1990) that for families in the aggregate, the number of years a mother works has a positive effect on the probability of high school graduation by ages 18–24.

15. It is also possible that regularity of child support has important effects. In a

regression model not shown, we found no evidence that the standard deviation of annual support received affects educational attainment.

16. We attempted several times to use a two-stage least squares model to test more rigorously whether unmeasured heterogeneity causes the relationship between child support and grades completed. Each of our models used the intensity of state child support enforcement (as indicated by states' average payments and percentage of single-parent families with payments) as an exogenous predictor of payments received. Unfortunately, state-level variables from neither 1970 Census tables nor the 1976 Survey of Income and Education were consistently predictive of payments received by families on the PSID. It may be that in the 1970s states were simply not active enough in child support enforcement to influence payments that were essentially determined locally. Because the first stage of our analysis did not produce a valid instrument for payments received, we did not proceed to the second stage of the model.

17. Although it would be useful to estimate the effect of child support on graduation from college, we have tracked children only through age 21. Instead, we take a first step at understanding how child support affects attainment of a college education by estimating its effect on entering college.

18. As discussed earlier, father's education was excluded because of endogeneity. "Receipt of any child support" was excluded because our objective here was to measure the total effect of child support payments. Because of the small number of cases in which the mother had graduated from college, for the logistic regression it was necessary to combine mothers who were college graduates with those who had some college.

APPENDIX 10.A

Appendix Table 10.A.1 DESCRIPTION OF VARIABLES

Income Variables

All income values are stated in 1985 dollars. Income is always averaged only over years in which child was between ages 8 and 18, child was not head or wife of own household, and income data were not missing.[1]

Average income: Average annual cash income plus Food Stamps, for all years regardless of parent's marital status.

Average income, two-parent years: Average annual cash income plus Food Stamps, for years in household with head other than single mother. This variable equals 0 if child never observed in other than single-mother household between ages 8 and 18.

No years with two parents: Equals 1 if child never observed in other than single-mother household between ages 8 and 18; equals 0 otherwise.

Average income, female-headed years: Average annual cash income plus Food Stamps, for years living with single mother as head of household.

Average child support, female-headed years: Average annual child support and alimony for years living with single mother as head of household.

Average welfare, female-headed years: Average annual AFDC, SSI, and Food Stamps for years living with single mother as head of household. Note that SSI did not begin to be reported in the PSID until 1974.

Average mother's earnings, female-headed years: Average annual maternal earnings for years living with single mother as head of household.

Average other income, female-headed years: Average annual income other than child support, alimony, welfare, maternal, or child's earnings for years living with single mother as head of household. Because child's earnings are endogenous to educational decisions, they are excluded from "other income" in regression models.

Any child support: Equals 1 if child support received is greater than zero in any year ages 8–18. Equals 0 otherwise.

Child's Characteristics

Black: Equals 1 if race is black.
Equals 0 otherwise.

Female: Equals 1 if child is female.
Equals 0 otherwise.

Parent's Education

Mother high school graduate: Equals 1 if mother finished high school or general equivalency diploma (GED); no college. Equals 0 otherwise. Measured in 1968. For the 8 percent missing data in 1968, measured in first year for which the information is available.

Mother some college: Equals 1 if mother had at least one year of college but did not graduate. Equals 0 otherwise. Same measurement issues as mother high school graduate.

Mother college graduate: Equals 1 if mother graduated from college; equals 0 otherwise. Same measurement issues as mother high school graduate.

Father high school graduate: Equals 1 if father finished high school or GED; no college. Equals 0 otherwise. In 1968 or first year available through 1972, measures education of male married to child's mother if it is his first marriage. If father's education missing because mother never married or divorced/separated prior to 1968, used child's estimate of father's education, reported after child became head or wife. For these children's estimates, the PSID accepted education of father figure as a substitute.

Father's education remained missing for 47 percent of cases.

Father some college: Equals 1 if father finished at least one year of college, but did not graduate. Equals 0 otherwise. Same measurement issues as father high school graduate.

Father college graduate: Equals 1 if father graduated from college. Equals 0 otherwise. Same measurement issues as father high school graduate.

Father's education missing: Equals 1 if father's education data is missing. Equals 0 otherwise.

Marital Status

Never married: Equals 1 if mother reported as never married when child 8 years old. Equals 0 otherwise.

Separated: Equals 1 if mother was married, not living with spouse in first year of female-headed household after child reaches age 8, unless spent fewer years separated than divorced by time child reaches 18. Equals 0 otherwise.

Divorced: Equals 1 if mother divorced in first year of female-headed household after child reaches age 8, or if mother separated in first female-headed year, but spent more subsequent years divorced than separated. Equals 0 otherwise.

Ever new marriage: Equals 1 if mother married after first year observed her as female head. If separated, mother must be observed divorced before count subsequent marriage as new marriage. Equals 0 otherwise.

Note that only one of the dummy variables for never married, separated, or divorced equals 1. In addition, new marriage may or may not equal 1.

Other Family Characteristics

Age of mother at child's birth: For 8 percent who were missing data on mother's age at birth, weighted mean age for mothers in the sample was substituted.

Number of female-headed years, ages 1–7: The number of years in mother-headed household between 1968 and age 7 are observed. We add to that an estimate of the number of years that mother was single between birth and 1968, based on marital status and years since most recent divorce or separation. Note that this measure is not strictly comparable to that of number of years in female-headed household ages 8 to 18, because female-headed years counted prior to 1968 are not restricted to years in which mother is head of the family.

Number of female-headed years, ages 8–18: Counts years spent in household with mother as single head.

Average number of children ages 8–18: Average number of children in family while sample child between ages 8 and 18.

Number of years moved, ages 8–18: Number of years the family moved at least once while child between ages 8 and 18.

Cohort: Ranges from 1 to 7, based on year of birth from 1960 to 1966.

Regional dummy variables: Region of country family lived in when child aged 8.

Dependent Variables

Number of grades completed, age 21: Measured at age 21 for those still in parent's home, or head or wife of own household at age 21 (GED with no further education is counted as grade 12.) For 12 percent whose education at age 21 was missing, a two-step process was used to estimate. If education measured at ages 22 or 23, subtracted one or two years, respectively, to estimate age 21 education. If not available at ages 22 or 23, used education at ages 20 or 19 as conservative estimates of education at age 21.

High school graduate: Equals 1 if number of grades completed is greater than or equal to 12. Equals 0 otherwise.

College entry: Equals 1 if number of grades completed is greater than 12. Equals 0 otherwise.

Note:

1. Nine children were missing one year of income data, three were missing two years, and one was missing three years of data.

Appendix Table 10.A.2 MEAN VALUES AND COEFFICIENTS OF INDEPENDENT VARIABLES IN LOGIT MODELS PREDICTING PROBABILITIES OF HIGH SCHOOL GRADUATION AND COLLEGE ENTRY BY AGE 21

Variable	Mean Value	Coefficient High School Graduation	Coefficient Entry into College
Intercept	1	1.832 (1.0139)	−0.2416 (1.1793)
Average child support	1,934.14	0.000281** (0.00011)	0.000199** (.000078)
Average welfare	2,087.85	0.000022 (.00005)	0.000068 (.000059)
Average mother's earnings	8,690.67	−0.000006 (.000025)	0.000011 (.000025)
Average other income	6,674.05	−0.000007 (.000019)	−0.00004 (.000028)
Average income, two-parent years	29,279.52	0.000027* (.000015)	0.000015 (.000014)
No years with two parents	0.22	0.7656 (.5613)	0.7055 (.6312)
Black	0.24	0.5398 (.3408)	0.9359** (.4037)
Female	0.48	0.1233 (.2600)	0.4098 (.2912)
Mother high school graduate	0.45	0.7967*** (.3030)	0.5691* (.3228)
Mother some college or college graduate	0.13	0.1676 (.5558)	0.4963 (.5249)
Age of mother at birth	25.53	−0.0564*** (.0212)	−0.0131 (.0252)
Never married	0.0765	0.1654 (.4241)	−0.831 (.5376)
Divorced	0.6161	0.3711 (.3076)	−0.653* (.3539)
Ever new marriage, ages 8–18	0.30	0.1196 (.4114)	0.0205 (.4337)
Number of female-headed years, ages 1–7	1.76	−0.0259 (.0595)	−0.0891 (.0695)

(continued)

(continued)

Variable	Mean Value	Coefficient High School Graduation	Coefficient Entry into College
Number of female-headed years, ages 8–18	5.88	0.0239 (.0558)	−0.0368 (.0638)
Average number of children, ages 8–18	2.7	−0.2165**	−0.547*** (.1540)
Number of years moved, ages 8–18	2.58	−0.2498** (.0734)	−0.1001 (.0877)
Northeast	0.2514	−0.1393 (.5166)	−0.5355 (.5494)
North Central	0.2859	−0.7436* (.4466)	0.133 (.4393)
South	0.2710	−0.3111 (.4459)	−0.1386 (.4578)
Cohort	4.96	0.0679 (.0632)	−0.011 (.0732)
Pseudo R^2		0.152	0.123
Chi square		68.3	45.3

*statistical significance at .10 level.
**statistical significance at .05 level.
***statistical significance at .01 level.
Notes: Standard errors are in parentheses. Means are weighted by the inverse of the probability of selection into the sample, with adjustment for differential nonresponse.
McFadden's pseudo R^2 measure is computed as:
$R^2 = 1 - $ [log likelihood, all parameters/log likelihood, intercept only].
See appendix table 10.A.1 for complete description of variables.

References

Anderson, E. 1989. "Sex Codes and Family Life among Inner-City Youth." In Annals of the American Academy of Political and Social Science, vol. 501, edited by William J. Wilson. American Academy of Political and Social Science.

Butler, A. C. 1990. "The Effect of Welfare Guarantees on Children's Educational Attainment." Social Science Research 19: 175–203.

Corcoran, M., R. H. Gordon, D. Laren, and G. Solon. 1987. "Intergenerational

Transmission of Education, Income and Earnings." University of Michigan.

Desai, S., R. T. Michael, and P. L. Chase-Lansdale. 1990. "The Home Environment: A Mechanism through which Maternal Employment Affects Child Development." Population Research Center Discussion Paper 20 (September). Chicago: NORC/University of Chicago, Economics Research Ctr., Economic Demography Group.

Furstenberg, F., and K. Harris. 1993. "When Fathers Matter/Why Fathers Matter: The Impact of Paternal Involvement on the Offspring of Adolescent Mothers." In *Young Unwed Fathers*, edited by R. Lerman and T. Ooms. Philadelphia: Temple University Press.

Furstenberg, F., J. Brooks-Gunn, and S. P. Morgan. 1987. *Adolescent Mothers in Later Life.* Cambridge, Mass.: Cambridge University Press.

Furstenberg, F. F., S. P. Morgan, and P. D. Allison. 1987. "Paternal Participation and Children's Well-Being after Marital Dissolution." *American Sociological Review* 52: 695–701.

Furstenberg, F., J. L. Peterson, C. W. Nord, and N. Zill. 1983. "The Life Course of Children of Divorce: Marital Disruption and Parental Contact." *American Sociological Review* 48: 656–68.

Garfinkel, I., and S. McLanahan. 1989. "The Effects of Child Support Provisions on Child Well-Being." For Foundation for Child Development "Forum on the Family Support Act," Washington, D.C.: Nov. 9–10.

Graham, J. W., and A. H. Beller. 1989. "The Effects of Child Support Payments on the Labor Supply of Female Family Heads." *Journal of Human Resources* 24(4): 664–88.

Haveman, R., B. Wolfe, and J. Spaulding. 1990. "The Relation of Educational Attainment to Childhood Events and Circumstances." Institute for Research on Poverty Discussion Paper 908-90. Madison: Institute for Research on Poverty, University of Wisconsin-Madison.

Hill, M. S. 1987. "Effects of Parental Divorce on Children's Attainments: An Empirical Comparison of Five Hypotheses." Survey Research Ctr. Institute for Social Research, University of Michigan. Photocopy.

Hill, M. S., and G. J. Duncan. 1987. "Parental Family Income and the Socioeconomic Attainment of Children." *Social Science Research* 16: 39–73.

Kmenta, Jan. 1986. "Models with Qualitative Variables." *Elements of Econometrics* (547–57). New York: Macmillan Co.

Krein, S. F., and A. H. Beller. 1988. "Educational Attainment of Children from Single-Parent Families: Differences by Exposure, Gender, and Race." *Ethnography* 25(2): 221–34.

McLanahan, S. 1985. "Family Structure and the Reproduction of Poverty." *American Journal of Sociology* 90(4): 873–901.

McLoyd, V. C. 1990. "The Impact of Economic Hardship on Black Families and Children: Psychological Distress, Parenting, and Socioemotional Development." *Child Development* 61: 311–46.

Meyer, D. R. 1991. "Child Support and Welfare Dynamics: Evidence from Wisconsin." Institute for Research in Poverty Discussion Paper 939-91. Madison: Institute for Research on Poverty, University of Wisconsin-Madison.

Moore, K. A., and T. Stief. 1991. "Attainment among Youth from Families that Received Welfare." Washington, D.C.: Child Trends Inc.

O'Neill, J. Determinants of Child Support. Washington, D.C.: Urban Institute Press.

Sandefur, G. D., S. McLanahan, and R. A. Wojtkiewicz. 1989. "Race and Ethnicity, Family Structure, and High School Graduation." Institute for Research on Poverty Discussion Paper 893-89. Madison: Institute for Research on Poverty, University of Wisconsin-Madison.

Seltzer, J. A., and S. M. Bianchi. 1988. "Children's Contact with Absent Parent." Journal of Marriage and the Family 50: 663–77.

Seltzer, J. A., N. C. Schaeffer, and H. Charng. 1989. "Family Ties after Divorce: the Relationship between Visiting and Paying Child Support." Journal of Marriage and the Family 51: 1013–32.

Shaw, L. B. 1982. "High School Completion for Young Women: Effects of Low Income and Living with a Single Parent." Journal of Family Issues 3(2): 147–63.

Wallerstein, J. 1984. "Children of Divorce: Preliminary Report of a Ten-Year Follow-Up of Young Children." American Journal of Orthopsychiatry 54(3): 444–58.

Wallerstein, J., and J. B. Kelly. 1980. Surviving the Breakup. New York: Basic Books.

Chapter Eleven

THE EFFECTS OF CHILD SUPPORT ON EDUCATIONAL ATTAINMENT

John W. Graham, Andrea H. Beller, and Pedro M. Hernandez

Social science evidence suggests that living arrangements during childhood influence socioeconomic outcomes in later life. Among these outcomes, education has received particular attention, in part because it is easily measured, and in part because it is known to be a good predictor of other lifetime events. A number of studies (e.g., Blau and Duncan 1967; Krein and Beller 1988; McLanahan 1985; Sandefur, McLanahan, and Wojtkiewicz 1991; Shaw 1982) have documented that, compared to children in intact two-parent families, children who have spent at least part of their childhood in a nonintact family—and those in mother-only families, especially—tend to have lower educational attainment. It is argued that family structure is related to children's education, owing to differences in both family income and parental time allocation across family types.

Special concern for children who live (or have ever lived) with a single mother stems primarily from the relatively low incomes of these families. Total money income during 1987 (the year of this study) averaged just $11,989 for mother-only families, compared to $40,067 for married-couple families.[1] The low income of mother-only families stems directly from the absence of a father from the household, usually as the result of marital disruption or an out-of-wedlock birth, rather than the father's death.[2] This means that in most cases the children's father is living elsewhere, and could be contributing to the support of his children.

The U.S. Bureau of the Census has estimated that, as of April 1988, there were more than 15 million children less than 21 years of age (living with 9.4 million mothers) who were eligible for child support. Overall, 5.6 million mothers (59 percent) had a child support award, but only 3.7 million (39 percent) received any support payments in 1987. Among those who did, payments averaged $2,710, or about 19 percent of the recipient family's total money income (U.S. Bureau of the Census 1990). Award and receipt rates are low, and real dollars received have actually fallen since 1978. However, there is reason to believe that new laws enacted under the Child Support Enforcement Amendments of 1984 and the Family Support Act of 1988 (FSA) may help raise future payments. Specifically, the FSA requires states to use guidelines in setting awards and immediate income withholding to collect payments due.

Recently, Beller and Chung (1988) showed that among children in mother-only families, those who have a child support award and those who receive payment obtain more schooling than those who do not. Child support receipt manages to overcome more than half of the educational disadvantage associated with living in a mother-only family. In addition, increases in child support income appear to improve educational outcomes more than equal increments in other sources of income.

This chapter reexamines the relationship between education, family structure, and child support, using national data collected at the time of the passage of the Family Support Act of 1988. Following Beller and Chung (1988), we investigate whether child support helps mitigate some of the negative effects on children's education of living in a nonintact family. Unlike their study, we also investigate why child support matters. Beller and Chung suggested that the beneficial effects of child support might represent greater contact between father and child, but they were unable to test this hypothesis directly. Fortunately, our data allow us to do so. Another possibility they did not consider is that child support may serve as an indicator of some unobservable characteristics of mothers and/or fathers that are related to both payment of child support and educational outcomes. We examine this selectivity issue as well, using an instrumental variables technique to take account of this potential bias.

The chapter is organized as follows. Section two describes our data and examines the relationship between nonintact family types and child support eligibility. Section three discusses why child support might be expected to mitigate some of the presumed negative impact on children's education of living in a nonintact family, and it previews the methodology we employ to test our expectations. Section four provides estimates of the effect of family structure and child support status on five different measures of educational attainment, for all children ages 16 to 20. Among children eligible for support, we estimated the effect of amount of child support received on four different measures of educational attainment. Section five tests the robustness of these estimates to the omission of information about paternal contact and to alternative estimation techniques. Section six summarizes our findings and explores their implications for public policy.

DATA AND DESCRIPTIVE STATISTICS

To study the impact of family structure and child support on children's education, we created a special mother-child extract from the 1988 March/April Match File of the Current Population Survey (CPS). This CPS file is the fifth in an on-going series (begun in 1979) that matches March demographic and income information for each of some 42,000 households with responses to the April Alimony and Child Support supplement, administered to all females ages 14 and over (18 and over prior to 1988) with own children in the household. From this Match File we were able to extract data on more than 5,000 families containing a mother and at least one (own) child between the ages of 16 and 20.[3] We excluded children less than 16 years of age, for whom schooling is compulsory, and children older than 20, who are typically no longer eligible for child support.[4]

CPS data offer several advantages over alternative data sources for our purposes. First, the CPS is a nationally representative sample, large enough to study important subgroups of the population, such as mothers with children ages 16 to 20. Second, the CPS provides detailed income and demographic data for every household, including educational attainment data for all persons aged 14 and over. Third, the April supplement provides at least a partial marital history for all women, which can be used to make inferences about the current and past living arrangements of their children. Fourth, for eligible families, it provides very detailed data on the award and receipt of child support. Indeed, the CPS child support data collected in earlier survey years have been studied extensively by scholars for almost a decade.

It is also important to recognize that the CPS data have some limitations for our study. First, because it is a household-based sample, the CPS excludes children no longer living with their mothers, with the important exception of unmarried children who are away at college. If children from nonintact families are both more likely to drop out of school and to leave home early, and these two behaviors are related, then our estimates of the effect of family structure on education will be biased.[5] In an earlier phase of this study, we attempted to control for this attrition bias by limiting the analyses to children 16 to 18 years old (the portion of the sample least likely to have left home). We found little difference between the two sets of estimates.

Another limitation for our analysis is that the CPS provides only a partial marital history for the mothers of the children in our sample, forcing us to assign children to family types based on incomplete information. Although we know current living arrangements for all children, we do not always know past living arrangements. For example, some children who are living with both parents now may have experienced an earlier parental separation. Furthermore, for children who currently live with their mother only, we do not always know how long they have done so. Several studies (e.g., Krein and Beller 1988; Shaw 1982) have indicated that the initial timing and length of exposure to living in a nonintact family have important effects upon education, but we cannot control for these factors. Rather, we can study the effects of current living arrangements only.

Figure 11.1 provides an overview of our sample and shows the relationship between family structure and the eligible child support population. Overall, we observed 5,038 children between the ages of 16 and 20 currently living in a family unit that includes their mother.[6] We estimate that 3,507 children, or 69.6 percent of the sample, are living in a family with both parents present (an intact family), while 1,531 children, or 30.4 percent of the sample, are living in a family with a mother but not a father (a nonintact family).[7] Owing to certain data limitations, we may have assigned a few children to the wrong family type.[8]

Most, but not all, children in mother-only families are eligible for child support. In theory, all children whose fathers are currently alive but living elsewhere are eligible for support, whereas children whose fathers are now deceased or who have been adopted by their mother's current husband are not eligible. According to the 1988 CPS April supplement, 1,110 children (or 72.5 percent of those in nonintact families) were eligible for child support (see figure 11.1) and their mothers were asked about their child support award and receipt experiences. The mothers of the other 421 children were not asked the child support questions. Of these, 266 were widows and therefore not eligible for child support. The other 155 were divorced or separated, but their former or estranged husband was not the child's father. Because of a flaw in survey design, these mothers were not asked about child support, but probably should have been.[9] Thus, better than 80 percent (i.e., [1,110 + 155]/1,531) of children who live in mother-only families have a father living elsewhere, and are

Figure 11.1 FAMILY STRUCTURE AND CHILD SUPPORT

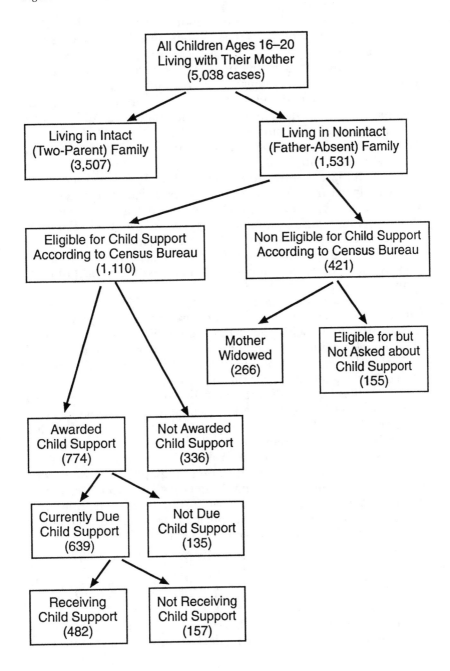

potentially eligible for child support, but only 73 percent were asked about child support (i.e., 1110/1531).

Among the 1,110 children whose mothers were asked about child support, 774 (or 69.7 percent) reported having a child support award as of April 1988 (figure 11.1).[10] Of these, 639 said they were due some child support payments in 1987 and were due an average of $3,035. (The two most common reasons given why no support was due were that the father had died or that the award was just recently established.) About one in four children due support (or 157) received no support from their fathers in 1987. Among the 482 children (or 75.4 percent) who did receive support, payments averaged $2,883, or 89 percent of support due.[11]

To summarize, slightly more than 3 out of 10 children aged 16 to 20 currently live in a nonintact (mother-present/father-absent) family. More than 80 percent of these children are potentially eligible for child support because their father lives elsewhere, but only about 1 in 3 actually received support in 1987. Our goal is to compare schooling decisions made by children who live with both parents with those who live with only their mother, and to assess the impact of child support payments on these decisions.

We measured schooling decisions by five different educational outcome measures: (1) total number of years of schooling completed; (2) whether or not a child has fallen behind his or her age cohort in high school; whether or not a child is a (3) high school dropout or (4) high school graduate; and (5) whether or not a child has entered college, given graduation from high school.

Mean values for each of these educational outcomes and for other variables used in the analysis are presented in table 11.1 for all 5,038 families. The first two columns show intact and nonintact families, respectively, which together represent all families. The last three columns show the Census Bureau's eligible child support population, including, respectively, the total eligible population, those who receive support, and those who do not receive support. The latter group is a heterogeneous one, containing three types of families from figure 11.1: those not awarded support, those awarded but not due support, and those awarded and due support who do not receive payment.

THEORY AND METHODOLOGY

What determines individual differences in schooling, such as those shown in table 11.1? Economic models of individual schooling decisions may be traced back to the seminal work of Becker (1964) and Schultz (1961). Important additions to that work were made by Ben-Porath (1967), who formalized the individual choice model, and by Leibowitz (1974), who emphasized the parents' role in children's education. According to the human capital model, schooling is an investment produced by inputs of time and market goods. Time inputs include a child's time in school and quality-adjusted time at home spent with mother, father, and perhaps siblings. Market goods are school-related expenditures, some of which are purchased with the family's income, and some of which are public goods whose quality may vary with residential location.

Why do children in nonintact mother-only families have less invested in their education than children in intact families? Quite simply, differences in educational outcomes are due to differences in the availability of educational inputs. Children in nonintact families have lower incomes and often live in poorer communities. As a result, they receive fewer and lower-quality education-related market goods. Perhaps even more important, children in nonintact families suffer from smaller inputs of parents' time and attention. They lose the father's time input if he is absent from the household, and they may well receive less attention from their mother as well. Compared to married women, single mothers are more likely to be working outside the home, have no one to share the chores of home production, and have less income to purchase market substitutes for their home production time. As a result, single mothers are likely to have less time to devote to their children's development.

Why might mothers who receive child support invest more in their children's education than mothers who receive no child support? As Beller and Chung (1988) have argued, the answer can be traced to differences in market goods and parental time inputs. Child support increases the recipient family's income and allows for a greater purchase of education-related market goods, including perhaps a residence in a community with better schools. In fact, differences in total family income between families with and without child support often tend to exceed the value of child support received, due primarily to higher labor market earnings of mothers with child support income.[12] This can be seen in table 11.1, for example, where differences in total family income of $3,318 exceed the average amount of child support paid of $2,883.

Children who receive child support may also benefit from a greater input of parental time from both mother and father. A mother who receives child support may use some of it to purchase market substi-

Table 11.1 MEANS OF SELECTED VARIABLES, CHILDREN AGES 16–20

Variable	Intact Families	Nonintact Families	All	Eligible Child Support Population	
				Recipients	Nonrecipients
Education Measures					
Years of schooling completed	11.19	10.70	10.62	10.64	10.60
Graduated high school (%)	46.08	33.64	30.90	26.97	33.92
Entered college among high school graduates (%)	72.53	57.86	58.60	63.08	55.87
High school dropouts (%)	5.65	11.10	11.08	6.64	14.49
Behind in high school (%)	10.95	18.75	19.10	14.11	22.93
Socioeconomic Characteristics					
Age in years	17.99	17.75	17.67	17.44	17.84
Age 16 (%)	19.33	23.65	25.14	31.74	20.06
Age 17 (%)	20.27	23.58	24.87	24.07	25.48
Age 18 (%)	20.93	21.49	21.17	22.61	20.06
Age 19 (%)	21.04	16.72	15.86	11.62	19.11
Age 20 (%)	18.42	14.57	12.97	9.96	15.29
Male (%)	50.61	49.84	49.91	49.59	50.16
Black (%)	7.39	24.17	23.33	13.90	30.57
Spanish (%)	6.59	7.38	7.12	3.32	10.03
Northeast (%)	24.67	22.08	22.16	25.52	20.38
North Central (%)	25.38	22.86	23.24	25.10	21.18
South (%)	30.57	35.53	34.60	30.08	38.06
West (%)	19.38	19.53	19.55	19.30	20.38
SMSA (%)	54.52	59.37	60.45	58.09	62.26
Central City (%)	17.59	27.76	28.11	20.75	33.76

Number of siblings	1.28	1.17	1.24	1.25	1.23
Mother's age at birth of child	26.06	25.07	23.96	23.97	23.95
Mother's years of education	12.52	12.05	12.18	12.75	11.74
Mother working (%)	70.15	76.68	77.84	79.46	76.59
Mother on welfare (%)	0.88	11.50	12.88	8.92	15.92
Never married (%)	0	6.27	8.64	2.70	13.22
Remarried (%)	0	30.76	34.78	36.52	33.44
Income Measures					
Family income ($)	49,175	29,001	29,698	31,575	28,257
Poor (%)	5.76	21.62	22.07	17.84	25.32
Mother's earnings ($)	9,676	11,774	12,280	12,833	11,855
Child support ($)	0	908	1,252	2,883	0
AFDC income ($)	22	386	442	261	582
Sample size	3,507	1,531	1,110	482	628

Source: *Current Population Survey*, March/April 1988 Match File, U.S. Bureau of the Census.
Note: Variables are defined in appendix table 11.A.1.

tutes for her time in household chores, and thus have more time to spend with her children. A father who pays child support may have closer and greater contact with his children. In the child support literature, Chambers (1979) found that a father who has regular contact with his children is more likely to pay child support, and Wallerstein and Huntington (1983) showed that children who were fully supported were visited more frequently by their fathers. More recently, Hill (1988) reported that support collections are lower when father and mother live in different states, and Seltzer et al. (1989) found a strong positive relationship between paternal visitation and child support payments following divorce.

We were unable to observe (current and past) time and goods inputs in the production of children's education directly, but we may be able to capture them indirectly on the basis of some of the socioeconomic characteristics and income measures identified in table 11.1. To isolate the impact of family structure and child support upon children's education, we hypothesize that:

$$ED_i = aSE_i + bINC_i + cFS_i + dCS_i + e_i, \qquad (11.1)$$

where: ED_i = a measure of ith child's education outcome,
        SE_i = a vector of socioeconomic characteristics of the ith child and mother,
      INC_i = the ith child's family income, excluding child support,
       FS_i = the ith child's family structure,
       CS_i = the ith child's child support status, and
        e_i = an error term, representing unobservable variables.

By estimating equation (11.1), we obtain a *ceteris paribus* estimate of the effect of family structure and child support on children's education (i.e., the coefficients c and d). These estimates are presented in the next section for five different educational outcome measures. This is essentially the equation estimated by Beller and Chung (1988), using 1984 data.

There are several reasons to suspect that estimates of equation (11.1), and of c and d in particular, may be biased. Two potential sources of bias—selective attrition and measurement error—have already been discussed. Another potential source of bias is the omission from the equation of some important explanatory variables. In particular, no measure of the father's time input into his children's education is included. Indeed, Beller and Chung (1988) argued that one reason they find child support to be positively related to children's education is that child support payments indicate greater contact with the absent father (assuming that children who receive more support also have more contact with their father).

Still another source of bias in equation (11.1) exists if any right-hand-side variable is correlated with the error term. There is reason to believe this may be true for CS.[13] Unlike most of the other explanatory variables in equation (11.1), child support is not completely exogenous. The amount of child support a mother receives depends, in part, upon her own personal characteristics and behavior as well as the absent father's. We can control for some of these factors directly (in as much as they may appear in SE), but some determinants of child support—such as a mother's determination or initiative and the father's degree of concern for the well-being of his child—may not be observable. If any of these unobservable variables also determine a child's education, then our estimates of the coefficient c will be biased. If mothers who ensure that child support is paid also ensure that their child stays in school, and if fathers who pay child support are also more interested in their children's well-being overall, our estimates of c will be biased upward. We examine the importance of each of these sources of bias in a later section of the chapter.[14]

HOW DO FAMILY STRUCTURE AND CHILD SUPPORT AFFECT A CHILD'S SCHOOLING?

Are there significant differences in the schooling decisions of children who differ by family structure and child support status? And if so, what accounts for these differences? As shown in table 11.1, children who live with both parents show higher educational attainment according to all five outcome measures than children who live with their mothers only. Although not shown in table 11.1, there are also some differences in the educational outcomes of the three subgroups of mother-only families displayed in figure 11.1—those eligible for child support according to the Census Bureau, those not eligible for child support because the mother is widowed, and other mothers who may be eligible for child support but were not asked about it.

Family Structure

Some of these overall differentials in educational outcomes may be due to differences by family type in the average age of children and in other socioeconomic characteristics that affect schooling decisions, such as race, ethnicity, residential location, and mother's personal characteristics. Some of the differentials may also be accounted for by differences in average family income by family type. To assess the importance of these factors, and to isolate the impact on education of family structure per se, we regressed each of the five measures of educational attainment on a vector of socioeconomic and family income variables and a set of dummy variables to identify family structure.[15]

We found many of the socioeconomic characteristics listed in table 11.1 to be significantly related to educational outcomes. Although the size and significance of these effects vary somewhat depending upon which of the five education measures is employed, and whether or not we also control for total family income, it is possible to make some generalizations. Not surprisingly, education is strongly positively related to the child's current age. In addition, educational attainment tends to be lower among boys than girls, among children whose mothers themselves have less education, and among children who live in the South or in central cities. African-American and Hispanic children also appear to have somewhat less education, but these differences disappear once we also control for income.

As might be expected, total family income is also strongly related to child's education. Although the magnitude of the association depends upon the other variables included in the regression, it can be said generally that increases in income appear to raise total years of schooling completed, increase the likelihood of being a high school graduate and of entering college, and reduce the likelihood of being a high school dropout and falling behind one's age cohort in high school.

Table 11.2 shows the contribution of socioeconomic characteristics and total family income in accounting for educational differences by family type for children ages 16 to 20. The first column shows the overall educational differential between children in intact families and (1) children in all nonintact families; (2) children in three types of nonintact families (widowed mothers, mothers not asked about child support, and mothers eligible for child support); and (3) children living with eligible mothers who receive and do not receive child support. Asterisks are used to indicate statistical significance.[16] The second column shows the educational differential that remains after controlling for socioeconomic characteristics of the children and their mothers, including total family income.[17]

Overall, children in nonintact families and in all three nonintact groups exhibit lower educational attainment by any measure than children in intact two-parent families, but among the three groups, those whose mothers are eligible for child support tend to be worst off by most measures.

Controlling for differences in both socioeconomic characteristics and family income uniformly reduces the differential in educational outcomes between children in intact and nonintact families (column 2, table 11.2). In some cases (notably, for all five measures for widows and for three measures for other mothers), the differential that remains is now insignificant. However, by all five measures, the educational differential between children in intact families and children in nonintact families eligible for child support, although reduced, remains statistically significant.

Among children eligible for child support, those who receive some support almost uniformly face a smaller overall disadvantage in their educational attainment compared to children in intact two-parent families than those who receive none. Those who receive some support have completed significantly more schooling than those who do not, are significantly less likely to have dropped out of high school or fallen behind in high school, and are more likely to have entered college. However, their high school graduation rates are unrelated to whether or not child support is received (holding total family income constant).[18]

To what extent does child support mitigate some (or all) of the negative effects on education of living in a nonintact mother-only family? To answer this question, we need to compare the coefficients on not receiving child support and receiving child support. Children who are eligible for but do not receive support have completed .30 years less schooling than children from intact families. By contrast, those who receive support have completed just .08 years less schooling than children from intact families, which is statistically insignificant (the difference from those not receiving is significant at the 1 percent level), suggesting that child support eliminates nearly all of the negative impact on education of living in a nonintact family.

The beneficial effects of receiving child support are most profound at the high school level. The receipt of child support eliminates three-quarters of the differential in high school dropout rates and two-thirds of the differential in the likelihood of falling behind in high school, compared to children in intact two-parent families.[19] The receipt of child support eliminates a small portion of the disadvantage children face in entering college (although the difference from those

Table 11.2 DIFFERENCES IN EDUCATIONAL OUTCOMES OF CHILDREN AGES 16–20 IN NONINTACT FAMILIES, BY FAMILY TYPE AND BY WHETHER OR NOT RECEIVING CHILD SUPPORT (CS), RELATIVE TO CHILDREN FROM INTACT FAMILIES

	Overall	Controlling for Socioeconomic Factors and Family Income
Years of Schooling Completed (intact = 11.19 years)		
All Nonintact Families	−0.49***	−0.18***
Widowed-mother families	−0.22**	−0.06
Other non-CS families	−0.42***	−0.22**
CS-eligible families	−0.57***	−0.20***
Not receiving CS	−0.59***	−0.30***
Receiving CS	−0.55***	−0.08[a]
Percentage High School Dropouts (intact = 5.6 percent)		
All Nonintact Families	5.5***	3.9***
Widowed-mother families	5.6***	2.8
Other non-CS families	5.3***	3.4
CS-eligible families	5.4***	4.3***
Not receiving CS	8.8***	5.8***
Receiving CS	1.0	1.5[a]
Percentage Fallen Behind Age Cohort in High School (intact = 11.0 percent)		
All Nonintact Families	7.8***	3.6***
Widowed-mother families	7.8***	2.3
Other non-CS families	5.2**	0.5
CS-eligible families	8.1***	4.3***
Not receiving CS	12.0***	5.9***
Receiving CS	3.2**	2.0[b]

Percentage Graduated High School (intact = 46.1 percent)

All Nonintact families	−12.4***	−6.9***
Widowed-mother families	−3.6	−2.0
Other non-CS families	−8.0**	−3.6
CS-eligible families	−15.2***	−8.7***
Not receiving CS	−12.2***	−8.8***
Receiving CS	−19.1***	−8.7***

Percentage of High School Graduates Who Have Entered College (intact = 72.5 percent)

All Nonintact families	−14.7***	−10.0***
Widowed-mother families	−7.9*	−2.6
Other non-CS families	−31.8***	−27.4***
CS-eligible families	−13.9***	−9.8***
Not receiving CS	−16.7***	−10.6***
Receiving CS	−9.4***	−8.6***

*, **, and ***denote statistically significant differences from intact families at 10 percent, 5 percent, and 1 percent level, respectively.

Note: Socioeconomic factors include NEAST, NCENTR, SOUTH, SMSA, CC, BOY, AGE17, AGE18, AGE19, AGE20, BLACK, SPANISH, EDUC1, AGEMBTH, MOMWORKS, and OWNKID as defined in appendix table 11.A.1.

a. Significantly different from those not receiving CS at a 1 percent level.

b. Significantly different from those not receiving CS at a 10 percent level.

not receiving support is not statistically significant), but none of the disadvantage they face in high school graduation rates.

To summarize, controlling for differences in socioeconomic characteristics and family income, we found that relative to children ages 16 to 20 from intact two-parent families, children eligible for child support have completed .20 years less schooling, are 4.3 percent more likely to have dropped out of high school and to be behind in high school, are 8.7 percent less likely to have graduated high school, and are 9.8 percent less likely to have entered college after high school graduation. At the same time, we found that relative to children from intact two-parent families, children who receive child support payments complete nearly as much schooling, and are no more likely to drop out of or fall behind their age cohort in high school. They are also somewhat more likely to enter college than children who are eligible for, but do not receive, support.

Child Support Income

Do educational outcomes vary systematically across children receiving different amounts of child support? To answer this question, we estimated the determinants of education for the subgroup of children ages 16 to 20 who were eligible for child support,[20] separating child support income from other family income. The results of these analyses for four of the educational outcome measures are summarized in table 11.3. A representative regression is shown in appendix table 11.A.2 and sample means are given in table 11.A.3.[21] (Since the difference in high school graduation rates between those who receive and do not receive support is insignificant and the effect of child support income lacks significance, we dropped this educational outcome from further consideration.) The first column in table 11.3 shows estimated coefficients both on a continuous variable measuring the amount of support received and on other family income. The second column adds a dummy variable to identify children who have a child support award, and the third column replaces the award with a dummy identifying those who are due support.

Increases in the amount of support received raise schooling for all four of the remaining educational outcome measures. Moreover, child support has a stronger positive effect on education than equal increments in other types of income: its effect is five or more times as large. The estimated coefficients on child support income are different from zero and from the coefficient on other family income (at significance levels indicated by asterisks in table 11.3). For example, a $1,000 increase in child support income increases years of schooling completed by .026, whereas an equal increase in other family income increases it only by .005 (table 11.3). The same increment in child support lowers high school dropout rates around 2 percent and the percentage falling behind in high school by 1 percent. It also raises the probability of entering college among high school graduates by nearly 3 percent. Equal increments of other family income improve each of these outcomes by one-half of 1 percent or less.

The relative strength of the effect of child support income is surprising. One possible explanation for this is that child support income is simply an indicator of certain characteristics in the mothers who receive it. However, whether or not a mother has a support award (column 2, table 11.3) or is due payment (column 3) does not appear to affect her child's schooling decisions, nor does it alter the effect of child support income very much, suggesting that it is the receipt of child support per se that matters.

In summary, children eligible for support who receive larger amounts of child support income achieve higher levels of education. In addition, child support income tends to have a stronger impact on schooling decisions than do other income sources. Finally, it does not appear that certain characteristics of the mothers awarded support or due payment are causing this strong relationship.

WHY DOES CHILD SUPPORT MATTER?

Why does receipt of child support income matter? As discussed in section three, there are several reasons to suspect that our estimates in table 11.3 could be biased. This section examines two of these. First, we look at a potential omitted variable bias that may result from failure to control for contact with the absent father. Second, we look at the selectivity bias that may result from failure to control for unobservable characteristics of mothers who receive support or fathers who pay it.

Does Child Support Simply Represent Contact with the Father?

Our estimates of the impact of child support on a child's schooling decisions will be biased if we have omitted any determinant of schooling that is also correlated with child support receipts. One

Table 11.3 EFFECTS OF CHILD SUPPORT AND ALL OTHER FAMILY INCOME ON EDUCATIONAL OUTCOMES OF CHILDREN AGES 16–20 ELIGIBLE FOR CHILD SUPPORT: OVERALL AND CONTROLLING FOR WHETHER OR NOT AWARDED OR DUE SUPPORT

	(1)	(2)	(3)
Years of Schooling Completed			
Child support income[a]	.026* (1.83)	.026* (1.67)	.026* (1.71)
All other family income[a]	.005*** (3.13)	.005*** (3.13)	.005*** (3.13)
Awarded child support	...	.023 (0.27)	...
Due child support	...	...	.006 (0.07)
Percentage High School Dropouts			
Child support income[a]	-1.74** (2.18)	-1.49* (1.78)	-1.48* (1.73)
All other family income[a]	-0.20*** (2.80)	-0.20*** (2.84)	-0.20*** (2.85)
Awarded child support	...	-2.10 (0.78)	...
Due child support	...	...	-1.90 (0.70)
Percentage Fallen Behind Age Cohort in High School			
Child support income[a]	-1.36* (1.76)	-1.42* (1.71)	-1.53* (1.80)

All other family income[a]	-0.27*** (3.42)	-0.27*** (3.41)	-0.27*** (3.36)
Awarded child support	...	0.67 (0.20)	...
Due child support	...	...	1.73 (0.53)

Percentage of High School Graduates Who Have Entered College

Child support income[a]	2.61** (1.93)	2.57* (1.79)	3.05** (2.02)
All other family income[a]	0.54*** (3.31)	0.54*** (3.31)	0.54*** (3.32)
Awarded child support	...	0.59 (0.08)	...
Due child support	...	...	-5.70 (0.77)

*, **, and ***denote statistical significance at 10 percent, 5 percent, and 1 percent level, respectively.

Note: Absolute values of *T*-statistics are in parentheses. See note to table 11.2 for a list of additional control variables.

a. Expressed in thousands of dollars.

such omission may be contact with the absent father. If greater paternal contact improves a child's educational outcomes directly and is also associated with larger child support payments, then our estimated child support coefficients in table 11.3 will be biased upward. In an earlier study, Beller and Chung (1988) speculated that contact with the absent father may be the main reason why they find a larger effect of child support than of other income on a child's education.

We might first ask what evidence there is that greater paternal contact actually increases a child's schooling and/or a mother's receipt of child support. The literature on family structure and children's education reviewed earlier in the chapter offers abundant evidence that lack of paternal contact due to the father's absence from the household has a detrimental effect on children's education, and that the effect is not only due to lowered income. However, direct evidence on the impact on children's education of contact with an absent father is limited: Seltzer (1990) has shown that, controlling for parental conflict and child support payments, frequency of visits has no significant effect on a child's chances of repeating a grade. Her findings show not only that there may be no direct beneficial effect on education, but also that greater paternal contact leads in certain types of families to an increase in parental conflict, which has been shown to be detrimental to children (Emery 1982), thus reducing the benefits to children of increased paternal involvement.

As discussed in the previous section, there is accumulating evidence in the child support literature that an absent father who has more contact with his children is more likely to pay the support he owes (Furstenberg, Moyan, and Allison 1987). Consistent with earlier studies, Seltzer (1990) found that fathers who pay more child support visit their children more frequently. She also found that children whose fathers pay more support have a lower probability of repeating a grade. Thus, while increased paternal contact with children increases a mother's receipt of child support, which increases schooling, increased contact may have no direct impact on a child's schooling.

Our dataset contains several measures of contact between fathers and children for the eligible child support population. We know whether or not the father lives in the same state as his children, whether or not he has joint custody or visitation rights, and how many days during the previous year he either visited or had physical custody of his children. Judith Seltzer (personal communication with authors, July 1992) has cautioned that these variables may not be very accurate measures, due in part to high rates of allocation by the Census as a result of missing values.[22] Nonetheless, we added each of these paternal contact measures (separately and together) to our previous education regressions. A representative sample of these results is summarized in table 11.4. To facilitate comparison, the first column of the table reproduces the coefficients from table 11.3 on how much child support is received. The next three columns show what happens to these coefficients when alternative measures of paternal contact are added.

The results in table 11.4 provide no evidence that greater contact by an absent father with his children increases their education directly. In fact, there may even be some evidence (albeit statistically insignificant) of a perverse effect of contact on the probability of falling behind in high school or of entering college. All else being equal, among those eligible for child support, children are 3 percent more likely to have fallen behind in high school if their father has custody or visitation rights (column 2, table 11.4) or if he lives in the same state (column 3).

More important, we found that the inclusion of any of these measures of paternal contact has at most a small effect on the child support receipt coefficients. The introduction of paternal contact measures reduces the estimated effect of child support on schooling in some cases and raises it in others. Thus, we conclude that the omission of any measures of father-child contact from the set of determinants of children's education does not appear to bias our previous analysis. On the basis of these findings, we would have to reject the Beller-Chung conjecture that the beneficial effects of child support on education represent (at least in part) greater contact between a father and his children. However, the insignificance of these measures could also simply reflect errors in their measurement.

Is Child Support an Indicator of Unobservable Variables?

In the previous equation (11.1), the error term e represents all omitted determinants of a child's education. For the most part, these are factors that either were not or could not be observed. Examples include the quality of the local school system, the child's innate abilities, the mother's attitudes toward the importance of schooling, and other financial contributions made by the absent father such as a college trust fund. To this point, we have assumed that the error term is uncorrelated with the other determinants in equation (11.1)—in particular, child support. This assumption may not be true: mothers who care more about their child's schooling may also ensure that they receive more child support; fathers who have established a

Table 11.4 EFFECTS OF CHILD SUPPORT, ALL OTHER FAMILY INCOME, AND PATERNAL CONTACT MEASURES ON EDUCATIONAL OUTCOMES OF CHILDREN AGES 16–20 ELIGIBLE FOR CHILD SUPPORT

	(1)	(2)	(3)	(4)
Years of Schooling Completed				
Child support income[a]	.026* (1.83)	.025* (1.70)	.025* (1.74)	.026* (1.82)
All other family income[a]	.005*** (3.13)	.005*** (3.15)	.005*** (3.16)	.005*** (3.12)
Father has visitation rights	...	.033 (0.39)	...	...
Father lives in same state	...	...	.043 (0.57)	...
Number of days of child-father contact last year	...	...	...	-.0001 (0.14)
Percentage High School Dropouts				
Child support income[a]	-1.74** (2.18)	-1.57* (1.92)	-1.75** (2.17)	-1.86** (2.25)
All other family income[a]	-0.20*** (2.80)	-0.20*** (2.95)	-0.20*** (2.78)	-0.20*** (2.81)
Father has visitation rights	...	-1.79 (0.68)	...	...
Father lives in same state	...	...	0.27 (0.12)	...
Number of days of child-father contact last year	...	...	...	0.01 (0.84)

Percentage Fallen Behind Age Cohort in High School

	(1)	(2)	(3)	(4)
Child Support Income[a]	−1.36*	−1.56*	−1.44*	−1.41*
	(1.76)	(1.91)	(1.85)	(1.81)
All other family income[a]	−0.27***	−0.27***	−0.27***	−0.27***
	(3.42)	(3.36)	(3.34)	(3.42)
Father has visitation rights	...	3.02	...	...
		(0.93)		
Father lives in same state	...	...	3.03	...
			(1.05)	
Number of days of child-father contact last year	...	...	...	0.01
				(0.47)

Percentage of High School Graduates Who Have Entered College

	(1)	(2)	(3)	(4)
Child support income[a]	2.61**	2.81**	2.83**	2.68**
	(1.93)	(2.00)	(2.06)	(1.95)
All other family income[a]	0.54***	0.53***	0.51***	0.55***
	(3.31)	(3.26)	(3.09)	(3.31)
Father has visitation rights	...	−4.73	...	...
		(0.65)		
Father lives in same state	...	...	−8.50	...
			(1.27)	
Number of days of child-father contact last year	...	...	...	−0.02
				(0.28)

*, **, and *** denote statistical significance at 10 percent, 5 percent, and 1 percent level, respectively.

Note: See note to table 11.2 for a list of additional control variables.

a. Expressed in thousands of dollars.

college fund for their child may also be more likely to pay child support. In other words, amount of child support paid may simply be an indicator of some important unobservable determinants of education that also determines which absent fathers are selected into the sample who pay support. If this is true, then our child support coefficients in table 11.3 are biased (although the direction of the bias may be uncertain).

To allow for the possible correlation between e and CS in equation (11.1), we employed an instrumental variable technique suggested by Barnow, Cain, and Goldberger (1980).[23] Essentially, this is equivalent to estimating equation (11.1) by nonlinear two-stage least squares, using as an instrument for CS fitted or predicted values derived from separate regression estimates of the determinants of CS.[24] To construct instruments for CS, we estimated the amount of child support received by tobit.[25] The regression contains explanatory variables selected on the basis of the results of previous studies of the determinants of child support receipts using CPS data reported by Beller and Graham (1985), Robins (1986), and Beron (1990). Optimally, we wanted variables that are related to child support receipts, but not to children's education. In contrast to these earlier studies, we were also able to include measures of the father's location and extent of contact with his children. These variables should be good instruments since, as we have shown, they do not affect children's education directly. These regression results are summarized in table 11.5 (for definitions of variables, see appendix table 11.A.1). The equation in column (1) controls for amount of child support due, while the one in column (2) does not. Child support due may not be a good instrument because, although it is an important predictor of child support received, it may also affect education directly.

With a few exceptions, the results in table 11.5 are consistent with prior estimates of the determinants of child support. As in earlier studies, the amount of support received is closely related to the amount due. Receipts also vary by geographic region and by whether or not the recipient lives in a central city, but in contrast to earlier studies, they show no significant variation by race or Spanish ethnicity. For the first time, we found strong statistical evidence that a father's location and the extent of his contact with his children affect receipts. On average, among those who pay something, an absent father who lives in the same state as his children pays $202 more than a father who lives elsewhere.[26] Controlling for whether or not he lives in the same state, a father who has no visitation rights pays $518 less than one who does.

Table 11.5 ALTERNATIVE TOBIT ESTIMATES OF DETERMINANTS OF CHILD
SUPPORT RECEIVED AMONG ELIGIBLE MOTHERS WITH CHILDREN
AGES 16–20

		(1)		(2)	
Variable	Mean	Tobit Coefficient	T-ratio	Tobit Coefficient	T-ratio
ONE	1.00	−2175.45	−3.158	−5055.49	−3.416
NEAST	.233	466.536	2.239	1651.78	3.706
NCENTR	.233	584.068	2.809	1309.97	2.924
SOUTH	.344	238.674	1.202	336.859	.783
SMSA	.608	−156.469	−.991	749.670	2.227
CC	.285	−297.691	−1.582	−920.681	−2.280
BLACK	.236	7.53253	.034	−1250.24	−2.631
SPANISH	.071	−65.3777	−.181	−431.889	−.569
REMAR	.343	237.664	1.514	−404.065	−1.188
NEVMAR	.090	−28.8307	−.079	−1277.50	−1.618
WIDOW	.007	−30.5016	−.038	1109.79	.646
SEP	.152	−15.9031	−.070	−191.347	−.405
OWNKID	2.26	−24.3629	−.409	315.184	2.504
AGE1	41.5	1.72456	.144	−5.56744	−.216
EDUC1	12.2	21.4128	.709	300.479	4.700
DADNOVIS	.317	−1481.21	−6.977	−4549.25	−10.241
DADSAME	.621	576.040	3.814	1113.98	3.437
DADNDAYS	32.6	1.33592	1.449	5.43460	2.754
CHSUPDUE	1905	.982950	40.915	. . .	. . .
Sigma		1746.60	29.983	3854.19	29.232
Log-likelihood		−4495.5		−4906.7	
Sample size		1018		1018	

Note: Variables are defined in appendix table 11.A.1.

Based on the estimates in table 11.5 and another set outlined in
table 11.6 (description follows), we calculated predicted child support receipts to use as an instrument in our two-stage least squares
estimates of the effect of child support payments on children's education. Three versions of these new estimates are shown in table 11.6[27]
for the dependent variable total years of schooling completed. The
versions in columns (1) and (2) of the table use the tobit estimates
in table 11.5 as the instrument for child support received. The version
in column (3) uses an equation based upon five years of CPS data,
which controls for mother's race, marital status, age, education, number of children and age of the youngest child, and a dummy variable
for each state; the education equation also controls for median income
in the state.[28] (These results can be compared to those in table 11.3
and to the complete OLS estimates shown in appendix table 11.A.2.)

Table 11.6 ALTERNATIVE INSTRUMENTAL VARIABLE ESTIMATES OF DETERMINANTS OF YEARS OF SCHOOLING COMPLETED BY CHILDREN AGES 16–20

Variable	(1) Coefficient	(1) T-ratio	(2) Coefficient	(2) T-ratio	(3) Coefficient	(3) T-ratio
ONE	8.08059	26.933	8.12761	25.744	7.743	3.168
NEAST	-.182933	-1.647	-.198088	-1.715	-.0933	-.126
NCENTR	-.327033	-2.912	-.337635	-2.949	-.2566	-.471
SOUTH	-.301023	-2.824	-.305963	-2.857	-.2628	-.925
SMSA	.100331	1.141	.085109	.910	.1926	.258
CC	-.206945	-2.062	-.194949	-1.884	-.2800	-.471
BOY	-.314210	-4.402	-.314344	-4.403	-.3121	-4.183
AGE17	.949988	9.662	.948462	9.641	.9614	7.434
AGE18	1.75101	16.881	1.75166	16.885	1.750	15.869
AGE19	2.11952	18.005	2.12340	17.994	2.097	9.365
AGE20	2.85756	22.518	2.86086	22.510	2.838	13.731
BLACK	.022854	.223	.042234	.384	-.0973	-.102
SPANISH	-.568570	-3.576	-.558143	-3.478	-.6287	-1.193
EDUC1	.076717	4.671	.072234	3.820	.1037	.474
AGEMBTH	.006071	.925	.005658	.854	.0086	.403
OWNKID	.027220	.881	.023379	.733	.0504	.266
MOMWORKS	.443408	4.886	.445251	4.902	.4328	3.355
INCEXCS[a]	.005145	3.086	.005387	3.092	.0037	.310
CHSUPREC[a]	.017474	1.097	.036189	.857	-.0960	.105
STMEDINC	...	...	...	...	.0046	.320
R² (adjusted)	.4644		.4643		.4251	

Note: Variables are defined in appendix table 11.A.1. STMEDINC is state median income. Estimates were obtained by two-stage least squares; instrument for CHSUPREC in columns (1) and (2) is derived from tobit coefficients in columns (1) and (2) of table 11.5, respectively, and in column (3) is explained in the text.
a. Expressed in thousands of 1987 dollars.

According to the results in table 11.6, we can no longer reject the hypothesis that the effect of child support income is equal to that of other income, once we take account of the possibility that child support may simply be an indicator for some unobservable determinants of a child's education. Columns (1) and (2) of the table, still indicate that child support receipts have a positive effect on years of schooling completed that is roughly three to seven times as large as the effect of other income. Each additional $1,000 of child support received increases schooling by up to .036 years, which is considerably more than equal increments in other income, but because this effect is imprecisely estimated, it is no longer significantly different from zero or from the effect of other income. The results in column (3) suggest that child support income has no effect on a child's education, once we take account of unobservables, but also that other family income has no effect, which seems counterintuitive. It may be that the instrument used in this column is not a very good one.

SUMMARY, CONCLUSIONS, AND POLICY IMPLICATIONS

We estimate that more than 30 percent of children ages 16 to 20 who live with their mother live in a family in which their father is not present. In more than 8 out of 10 cases, the father's absence is due to a marital disruption or an out-of-wedlock birth, rather than to his death. As a result, most children who live in a nonintact mother-only family are eligible for child support, but only about 1 in 3 actually receives any.

We have seen that, on average, compared to children who live with both parents, those who live only with their mother exhibit lower educational outcomes (based on five different measures). Among children in mother-only families, those who are eligible for child support tend to obtain the least schooling. (Indeed, adjusted for income and socioeconomic differences, children whose mothers are widowed have as much schooling as children in two-parent families). But, among those eligible for child support, we have found that children who receive support from their father obtain significantly more schooling than those who do not receive support. In addition, we have found that increases in child support payments appear to have stronger effects than equal increases in other sources of income. Overall, children who receive child support manage to overcome more than two-thirds of the educational disadvantages associated with their adverse family structure.

Is it possible that the beneficial effects of child support receipts on an offspring's education that we have estimated are not true ones? We examined two potential sources of bias in our estimates: first, that the omission of any measure of paternal contact may induce an upward bias if paternal contact increases education directly and is positively correlated with child support receipts; and second, that a selectivity bias may be present if mothers who receive support (or fathers who pay it) are different in unobservable ways from those who do not. We have found little evidence that a father's contact with his children has a direct effect on their schooling decisions, and the inclusion of any of three different measures of paternal contact had little impact on the size or significance of the child support coefficient. Correction for selectivity bias, however, reduced the effect of child support income on years of schooling completed, and we can no longer rule out the possibility that its effect is the same as that of any other income. Thus, we conclude that selectivity bias could account for the large positive magnitude of the relationship between child support and a child's educational attainment.

The policy implications of these findings are important. Recent reforms should help more families receive more support. Federal and state child support efforts have improved since 1975, culminating in the Family Support Act of 1988. If these efforts succeed in increasing average awards and receipts, they will, of course, raise the income of these mother-only families and reduce their dependence on public assistance in the short run. Initial indications that child support income could bring even greater benefits than other income in the long run through improving children's education are not borne out once we take account of the possibility that men who willingly pay child support are somehow different from those who will pay reluctantly after reform.

However, as pointed out, these estimates are only as good as the instrument we used for estimating child support, which may be flawed. Further, we were only able to perform these estimates for one educational outcome—years of school completed—but not for our three dichotomous measures. Future research should perform instrumental variable estimates for the dichotomous educational outcomes. In light of these limitations, it may be that only time will tell whether the beneficial effects of child support payments beyond those of income generally on children's education will apply when less-willing contributors make payments in the future.

Notes

This chapter is a revised version of a paper originally prepared for the "Conference on Child Support and Child Well-Being," Airlie House, Airlie, Va., Dec. 5–7, 1991. The authors would like to thank John Boyd, for his help with the data extract, and Marilyn Johnson, for her assistance in the preparation of some of the tables. Beller and Graham acknowledge financial support from the National Institute of Child Health and Human Development (grant no. R01 HD19350). Graham also received support from the Research Council and the Morris Beck Fund for Economic Analysis at Rutgers University. Beller also received support from the Research Board, University of Illinois, Urbana-Champaign. Hernandez received support from the School of Human Resources and Family Studies at the University of Illinois, Urbana-Champaign.

1. All data in this paragraph are taken from the U.S. Bureau of the Census (1989a: table 9).

2. As of March 1988, only 6.2 percent of all children under age 18 then living in mother-only families had a mother who was widowed.

3. The father may or may not be present, but the child's mother must be. If more than one child was between 16 and 20 years of age, we selected the eldest.

4. Mississippi is the only state that does not require 15-year-olds to be in school. Some child support orders end at age 18, but not all do; our data cover awards up to age 21.

5. According to Glick and Lin (1986), 80 percent of children ages 18 to 19 were living with their parent(s) in 1984.

6. Our original extract contained 5,081 mother-child matches. We excluded 43 cases in which the mother's age at the birth of the child (calculated as her current age minus the age of her child) was less than 14. In most cases, these were probably mothers incorrectly matched with their husband's child from a previous marriage. Our sample excludes children living apart from their mothers: at age 15, this is likely to be a small group—perhaps about 8 percent of all children, based upon a recent study by Wojkiewicz (1991: table 1). Using data from the National Survey of Families and Households, Wojkiewicz showed that at age 15, 91.7 percent of all children were living in a household that contained their mother.

7. The mother may or may not be (re)married.

8. Because assignment to family type is based upon the mother's incomplete marital history, we may have incorrectly assigned some children to intact families who were born prior to their mother's currently intact first marriage, and we may have incorrectly matched some mothers with their husband's child from a previous marriage. We may also have assigned some children to nonintact widowed-mother families who do not belong there, because we assumed that all mothers who remarried following the death of their previous husband had their child from the previous marriage.

9. Divorced and separated mothers were only asked about child support if they said they had children living with them who were fathered/adopted by their most recent husband. Thus, currently divorced and separated mothers who had children out of wedlock or from an earlier marriage (i.e., prior to their most recent disruption) were not asked about child support. To our knowledge, this is the first time this survey design flaw has been recognized. Other flaws in the CPS April supplements were discussed in Graham and Beller (1985).

10. According to the U.S. Bureau of the Census (1990), the 1988 award rate for all children under 21 was 59 percent. One important reason the award rate is higher for children ages 16 to 20 is that their mothers are less likely to have never married (8.64 versus 27.88 percent), a group with low award rates.

11. Among mothers who actually received support, mean child support due was $3,245—7 percent more than for all mothers due support.

12. For a discussion of the relationship between child support and labor supply, see Graham and Beller (1989).

13. Manski et al. (1990) study the effect of a possible correlation between FS and e.

14. Another bias would occur if CS and ED are actually simultaneously determined. We do not investigate this possibility in this study.

15. These regressions pool children from intact and nonintact families. Separate regressions by family structure show that there may be differences in coefficients on some of the control variables. Analyses in later tables are restricted to the child-support-eligible population.

16. To calculate significance, we regressed each education measure on dummy variables identifying each of the nonintact family types. T-statistics indicate significant differences relative to intact families.

17. The vector of socioeconomic characteristics is listed in the note to table 11.2. The equation for years of schooling was estimated by ordinary least squares (OLS), and for the other four education measures by probit.

18. By contrast, Beller and Chung (1988) found that whether or not child support is received had a significant effect on the likelihood of high school completion among 18- to 20-year-olds.

19. That is, child support eliminates (5.8 − 1.5)/5.8 of the differential in high school dropout rates, and (5.9 − 2.0)/5.9 of the differential in the likelihood of falling behind in high school.

20. From this point on, children eligible for child support excluded 68 cases where the child was awarded but was no longer due child support because he or she had become too old, 8 cases where the award was only made in 1988 so that no support was due in 1987, and 16 cases where the father was deceased, resulting in a sample size of 1,018 cases. Appendix table 11.A.3 shows sample means for the 92 excluded cases compared to the other cases.

21. Appendix table 11.A.2 shows a representative regression underlying table 11.3 with some alternative versions—one that excludes whether or not the mother is working (MOMWORKS) and one that adds whether she has remarried (REMAR). The results show that it makes little difference in the estimated effects of child support. The inclusion of REMAR, however, lowers the magnitude and significance of the effect of other family income, suggesting that remarriage largely is important because of the increase in income it brings the family.

22. Between 30 percent and 42 percent of cases were allocated.

23. More precisely, our estimator for the coefficients in equation (11.1) is $(Z'X)^{-1}(Z'Y)$, where Y is the dependent variable ED, X is the matrix of independent variables (SE, INC, FS, and CS), and Z is a similar matrix in which CS is replaced by its fitted value.

24. The resulting estimates can be shown to be consistent (see Pindyck and Rubinfeld 1981: 200).

25. Attempts to estimate the amount received by a two-limit tobit (where the upper limit is the amount of support due) were unsuccessful using LIMDEP v. 5.1, since the likelihood function would not converge with any of the four algorithms.

26. The amount paid was calculated as the tobit coefficient multiplied by .35 (adjustment factor based on McDonald and Moffitt 1980).

27. The estimation would be more cumbersome for the dichotomous measures of education and was not attempted for this study.

28. For a further description of this instrument, see McLanahan et al. (chapter 8, this volume).

APPENDIX 11.A

Appendix Table 11.A.1 DEFINITION OF VARIABLES

Variable Name	Definition
Dependent Variables	
Years of school completed (EDUC2)	Number of years of formal schooling completed by child
Whether child graduated high school (HSGRAD)	1 if child completed 12th grade, 0 otherwise
Whether child entered college (COLLEGE)	1 if child attended 13th grade or more, 0 otherwise
Whether child dropped out of high school (HSDRPOUT)	1 if child dropped out of school, 0 otherwise
Whether child is behind in high school (BEHINDHS)	1 if age of child minus current grade in school (or EDUC2, if not in school now) exceeds 7, and 0 otherwise; or if HSGRAD = 1
Whether child is behind age cohort overall (BEHIND)	1 if age of child minus current grade in school (or EDUC2, if not in school now) exceeds 7, and 0 otherwise.
Independent Variables	
1. *Socioeconomic Characteristics*	
Age (AGE2)	Age of child
Whether child is age i for i = 16,.., 20 (AGEi)	1 if child is age i, 0 otherwise
Male (BOY)	1 if child is male, 0 otherwise
African-American (BLACK)	1 if child is black, 0 otherwise
Spanish ethnicity (SPANISH)	1 if child is of Spanish origin, 0 otherwise
Region of residence	
Northeast (NEAST)	1 if Northeast, 0 otherwise
North Central (NCENTR)	1 if North Central, 0 otherwise
South (SOUTH)	1 if South, 0 otherwise
Standard metropolitan statistical area (SMSA)	1 if live in SMSA, 0 otherwise
Central City (CC)	1 if child lives in the central city of an SMSA, 0 otherwise

Variable Name	Definition
Own kid (OWNKID)	Number of own children
Siblings (SIBLINGS)	Number of siblings
Age of mother at birth of child (AGEBTH)	Age of mother minus age of child
Mother's education (EDUC1)	Number of years of formal schooling completed by mother
Age (AGE1)	Age of mother
Whether mother worked (MOMWORKS)	Whether or not mother worked outside home in 1987
Whether on AFDC (WELFARE)	1 if mother received welfare income, 0 otherwise
Whether remarried (REMAR)	1 if child lives with a remarried mother, 0 otherwise
Whether separated (SEP)	1 if child lives with a separated mother, 0 otherwise
Whether never married (NEVMAR)	1 if child lives with a never-married mother, else 0.
Whether child-support-eligible population (CSPOP)	1 if mother responds to child support questions in CPS supplement, 0 otherwise
Whether widow not in child-support-eligible population (NOTCSWID)	1 if mother is a widow and CSPOP = 0, 0 otherwise
Whether divorced/separated mother not in child-support-eligible population (NOTCSDIV)	1 if mother is divorced or separated and CSPOP = 0, 0 otherwise
Whether ever lived in female-headed family (EVERFHF)	1 if child ever lived in a mother-only family, 0 otherwise
Whether lives in female-headed family now (FHFNOW)	1 if child lives in a mother-only family now, 0 otherwise

2. *Income Measures*

Family income (FINCTOT)	Amount of total family income
Total earnings (PEARN1)	Amount of total earnings of mother
Income excluding child support (INCEXCS)	Total family income minus child support income
Public assistance income (PPAAMT1)	Amount received in public assistance
Whether poor (POOR)	1 if family income is below poverty level, 0 otherwise

3. *Child Support Variables*

Whether child support awarded (AWARDS)	1 if mother was awarded child support, 0 otherwise
Whether child support due (CHSUPD)	1 if mother supposed to receive child support in 1987, 0 otherwise
Whether child support received (RECCS)	1 if mother received child support in 1987, 0 otherwise
Child support income (CHSUPREC)	Amount of child support actually received in 1987

Variable Name	Definition
Child support due (CHSUPDUE)	Amount of child support supposed to receive in 1987
Child support awarded by court order (CSCOURT)	1 if mother was awarded child support by a court order, 0 otherwise

4. *Contact with Father Variables*

Whether no custody or visitation for father (DADNOVIS)	1 if father has no custody or visitation rights, 0 otherwise
Whether father lives in same state (DADSAME)	1 if father lives in same state as child(ren), 0 otherwise
Number of days (DADNDAYS)	Number of days that father visited or had physical custody of child(ren) in 1987
Number of years child has spent without a father in household (DURATION)	1988 minus year of marital disruption for NEVMAR = 0, or AGE2 for NEVMAR = 1

Appendix Table 11.A.2 ALTERNATIVE ESTIMATES OF DETERMINANTS OF TOTAL YEARS OF SCHOOLING COMPLETED AMONG CHILDREN AGES 16–20 ELIGIBLE FOR CHILD SUPPORT

Variable	(1) Coefficient	T-ratio	(2) Coefficient	T-ratio	(3) Coefficient	T-ratio
ONE	8.30364	27.429	8.10253	26.808	7.98029	25.839
NEAST	-.189533	-1.674	-.190006	-1.697	-.173847	-1.550
NCENTR	-.322693	-2.817	-.331981	-2.930	-.340851	-3.010
SOUTH	-.275937	-2.540	-.303328	-2.820	-.309975	-2.884
SMSA	.126677	1.420	.933270E-01	1.053	.112162	1.261
CC	-.252803	-2.484	-.201346	-1.989	-.191494	-1.892
BOY	-.335102	-4.608	-.314273	-4.362	-.320188	-4.446
AGE17	.964440	9.617	.949276	9.567	.950194	9.588
AGE18	1.76299	16.658	1.75131	16.729	1.76470	16.838
AGE19	2.13942	17.818	2.12133	17.856	2.13991	17.972
AGE20	2.87441	22.202	2.85910	22.324	2.87187	22.420
BLACK	.176817E-01	.170	.318934E-01	.309	.690382E-01	.659
SPANISH	-.605735	-3.739	-.563703	-3.514	-.539305	-3.355
EDUC1	.915717E-01	5.622	.746248E-01	4.527	.773905E-01	4.682
AGEMBTH	.400514E-02	.599	.587834E-02	.887	.761896E-02	1.140
OWNKID	.919278E-02	.294	.254271E-01	.817	.181699E-01	.580
INCEXCS	.551950E-05	3.251	.525778E-05	3.130	.332653E-05	1.689
CHSUPREC	.251403E-04	1.738	.262077E-04	1.832	.266245E-04	1.863
MOMWORKS	...	...	.444268	4.851	.476599	5.120
REMAR	...	...	...	...	.184531	1.872
R² (adjusted)	.453		.465		.466	
Sample size	1018		1018		1018	

Note: Variables are defined in appendix table 11.A.1.

Appendix Table 11.A.3   MEANS OF SELECTED VARIABLES FOR CHILD
SUPPORT POPULATION

Variable	Total Eligible Child Support Population		Receiving Support
	Not Receiving Support		
	Omitted[a]	Retained	
		Resulting Child Support Sample	
EDUC2	11.022	10.532	10.643
HSGRAD	.56522	.30037	.26971
COLLEGE	.30435	.16978	.17012
HSDRPOUT	.16304	.14179	.06639
BEHINDHS	.21739	.23134	.14108
NEAST	.15217	.21269	.25519
NCENTR	.22826	.21642	.25104
SOUTH	.36957	.38246	.30083
SMSA	.56522	.63246	.58091
CC	.23913	.35448	.20747
BOY	.52174	.49813	.49585
AGE17	.11957	.27799	.24066
AGE18	.15217	.20896	.22614
AGE19	.30435	.17164	.11618
AGE20	.29348	.12873	.09959
BLACK	.20652	.32276	.13900
SPANISH	.07609	.10448	.03320
EDUC1	12.163	11.664	12.747
AGEMBTH	24.957	23.772	23.971
MOMWORKS	.83696	.75373	.79461
OWNKID	1.9783	2.2761	2.2469
AWARDCS	1.0000	.37313	1.0000
CHSUPD	.00000	.29291	1.0000
CHSUPDUE	.00000	700.01	3244.8
CHSUPREC	.00000	.00000	2882.8
CSCOURT	.58696	.28731	.57676
INCEXCS	33980.	27275.	28692.
REMAR	.40217	.32276	.36515
NEVMAR	.04348	.14739	.02697
N of cases	92	536	482

Note: Variables are defined in appendix table 11.A.1.
a. Omitted cases are those mothers who were awarded support but were not due any in 1987 because the child is too old (68 cases), the father is deceased (16 cases), or support was awarded after 1987 (8 cases).

References

Barnow, Burt S., Glen G. Cain, and Arthur S. Goldberger. 1980. "Issues in the Analysis of Selectivity Bias." *Evaluation Studies Review Annual* 5: 43–59.

Becker, Gary S. 1964. *Human Capital.* New York: Columbia University Press.

Beller, Andrea H., and Seung Sin Chung. 1988. "The Effect of Child Support Payments on the Educational Attainment of Children." Paper presented at the Population Association of America Annual Meeting, New Orleans, April.

Beller, Andrea H., and John W. Graham. 1985. "Variations in the Economic Well-Being of Divorced Women and Their Children: The Role of Child Support Income." In *Horizontal Equity, Uncertainty, and Economic Well-Being* (471–509), Studies in Income and Wealth Series, no. 49, edited by Martin David and Timothy Smeeding. Chicago: National Bureau of Economic Research and University of Chicago Press.

Ben-Porath, Yoram. 1967. "The Production of Human Capital and the Life Cycle of Earnings." *Journal of Political Economy* 75 (August): 352–65.

Beron, Kurt J. 1990. "Child Support Payment Behavior: An Econometric Decomposition." *Southern Economic Journal* 56 (January): 650–63.

Blau, Peter M., and Otis D. Duncan. 1967. *The American Occupational Structure.* New York: John Wiley & Sons.

Chambers, David L. 1979. *Making Fathers Pay.* Chicago: University of Chicago Press.

Emery, Robert E. 1982. "Interparental Conflict and the Children of Discord and Divorce." *Psychological Bulletin* 92 (September): 310–30.

Furstenberg, Frank F., S. Philip Morgan, and Paul D. Allison. 1987. "Paternal Participation and Children's Well-Being After Marital Dissolution." *American Sociological Review* 52 (October): 695–701.

Glick, Paul C., and Sung-Ling Lin. 1986. "More Young Adults are Living with Their Parents: Who Are They?" *Journal of Marriage and the Family* 48 (February): 107–12.

Graham, John W., and Andrea H. Beller. 1985. "A Note on the Number and Living Arrangements of Women with Children under 21 from an Absent Father." *Journal of Economic and Social Measurement* 13 (July): 209–14.

————. 1989. "The Effect of Child Support Payments on Labor Supply of Female Family Heads: An Economic Analysis." *Journal of Human Resources* 24 (Fall): 664–88.

Hill, Martha S. 1988. "The Role of Economic Resources and Dual-Family Status in Child Support Payments." Paper presented at the annual meeting of the Population Association of America, New Orleans, April.

Krein, Sheila F., and Andrea H. Beller. 1988. "Educational Attainment of Children from Single-Parent Families: Differences by Exposure, Gender, and Race." *Demography* 25 (May): 221–34.

Leibowitz, Arleen. 1974. "Home Investment in Children." *Journal of Political Economy* 82 (March): S111–31.

Manski, Charles F., Gary D. Sandefur, Sara McLanahan, and Daniel Powers. "Alternative Estimates of the Effects of Family Structure during Childhood on High School Graduation." Discussion Paper 929-90. Madison: Institute for Research on Poverty, University of Wisconsin-Madison, November.

McDonald, John F., and Robert A. Moffitt. 1980. "The Uses of Tobit Analysis." *Review of Economics and Statistics* 62 (May): 318–22.

McLanahan, Sara. 1985. "Family Structure and Reproduction of Poverty." *American Journal of Sociology* 90 (January): 873–901.

Pindyck, Robert S., and Daniel L. Rubinfeld. 1981. *Econometric Models and Economic Forecast*, 2d ed. New York: McGraw Hill.

Robins, Philip K. 1986. "Child Support, Welfare Dependency, and Poverty." *American Economic Review* 76 (September): 768–88.

Sandefur, Gary D., Sara McLanahan, and Roger A. Wojtkiewicz. 1991. "The Effects of Parental Marital Status during Adolescence on High School Graduation." Paper presented at the annual meeting of the Population Association of America, Washington, D.C., March.

Schultz, Theodore W. 1961. "Investment in Human Capital." *American Economic Review* 51 (March): 1–17.

Seltzer, Judith A. 1990. "Child Support Reform and the Welfare of U.S. Children." National Survey of Families and Households working paper no. 34, Center for Demography and Ecology, University of Wisconsin-Madison, 1990.

Seltzer, Judith A., Nora Cate Schaeffer, and Hong-Wen Charng. 1989. "Family Ties after Divorce: The Relationship between Visiting and Paying Child Support." *Journal of Marriage and the Family* 51 (November): 1013–32.

Shaw, Lois B. 1982. "High School Completion for Young Women: Effects of Low Income and Living with a Single Parent." *Journal of Family Issues* 3 (June): 147–63.

U.S. Bureau of the Census. 1989a. *Current Population Reports*, ser. P-20, no. 433. *Marital Status and Living Arrangement: 1988*. Washington, D.C.: U.S. Government Printing Office.

————. 1989b. *Current Population Reports*, ser. P-23, no. 162. *Studies in Marriage and the Family*. Washington, D.C.: U.S. Government Printing Office.

————. 1990. *Current Population Reports*, ser. P-23, no. 167. *Child Support and Alimony: 1987*. Washington, D.C.: U.S. Government Printing Office, 1990.

Wallerstein, Judith S., and Huntington, Dorothy S. 1983. "Bread and Roses:

Nonfinancial Issues Related to Fathers' Economic Support of Their Children Following Divorce." In *The Parental Child Support Obligation*, edited by Judith Cassetty (135–53). Lexington, Mass.: Lexington Books.

Wojtkiewicz, Roger A. "Parental Presence and High School Graduation: The Effects of Living with Single Parents, Stepparents, Grandparents, and Other Relatives." Working Paper. Baton Rouge: Louisiana State University, Department of Sociology. Photocopy.

ABOUT THE EDITORS

Irwin Garfinkel is the Mitchell I. Ginsberg Professor of contemporary urban problems at the Columbia University School of Social Work. Garfinkel was the principal investigator of the Wisconsin child support reform project and has consulted with governments in Australia, Great Britain, and Sweden. He is author of *Assuring Child Support* (Russell Sage Foundation, 1992), and co-author (with Sara McLanahan) of *Single Mothers and Their Children: A New American Dilemma* (Washington D.C.: Urban Institute Press, 1986). Garfinkel, McLanahan, and Robins also edited *Child Support Assurance: Design Issues, Expected Impacts, and Political Barriers as Seen from Wisconsin* (Urban Institute Press, 1992).

Sara S. McLanahan is a professor of sociology and public affairs at Princeton University. She is a faculty associate in the Office of Population Research at Princeton and in the Institute for Research on Poverty at the University of Wisconsin. Her major research interests are in the areas of family demography and poverty. She is a co-author of *Single Mothers and Their Children: A New American Dilemma* and of a new book, *Growing Up with a Single Parent*, which deals with the consequences of family disruption for children.

Philip K. Robins is a professor of economics at the University of Miami and a research affiliate with the Institute for Research on Poverty at the University of Wisconsin, Madison. He is a widely published specialist in labor economics and the economic evaluation of social programs. His current research includes an evaluation of financial intervention programs for welfare recipients, the effects of welfare family caps on childbearing decisions, a comparison of child care utilization patterns in the United States and Canada, and the effects of parental marital disruptions on offspring earnings when they reach adulthood.

Mary Jo Bane is the assistant secretary for children and families at the U.S. Department of Health and Human Services. She is a co-chair of President Clinton's Working Group on Welfare Reform, Family Support and Independence. Prior to her appointment at HHS, she held positions as commissioner of the New York State Department of Social Services and director of the Malcolm Wiener Center for Social Policy at the John F. Kennedy School of Government, Harvard University. Bane is the author of numerous books and articles in the area of human services and public policy, including *Gender and Public Policy: Case and Comment* (1993), *The State and the Poor in the 1980s* (1984), and *Here to Stay: American Families in the Twentieth Century* (1976).

Nazli Baydar is a senior research scientist at Battelle Centers for Public Health Research and Evaluation. Her research focuses on family sociology, particularly on family environmental processes that influence the normative development of children and adolescents.

Andrea H. Beller is professor of consumer sciences at the University of Illinois at Urbana-Champaign. Her research interests include child support payments, the impact of living in a single-parent family on children's educational attainment, and gender and racial differentials in the labor market. She is co-author (with John Graham) of *Small Change: The Economics of Child Support*, Yale University Press, 1993, and "Black-White Earnings Over the 1970s and 1980s: Gender Differences in Trends" (with Francine Blau), *Review of Economics and Statistics*, May 1992.

Jeanne Brooks-Gunn is Virginia and Leonard Marx Professor in child development at Teachers College, Columbia University. In addition, she directs the Center for Children and Families at Teachers College and the Adolescent Study Program at Teachers College and the St. Luke's-Roosevelt Hospital Center of Columbia University. Her specialty is policy-oriented research focusing on familial influences upon children's development (achievement, psychological well-being, school and behavioral problems) and intervention efforts aimed at ameliorating the developmental delays seen in poor and at-risk children.

Nancy R. Burstein is a senior analyst at Abt Associates Inc. Over the past 15 years she has designed and implemented numerous impact and cost-benefit evaluations in the areas of public assistance administration, welfare-to-work programs, nutrition programs, maternal and child well-being, and long-term care for the elderly.

Anne R. Gordon is a senior economist at Mathematica Policy Research, Inc., in Princeton, New Jersey. Her research interests include child support and welfare policy, and maternal and child nutrition programs. Among her recently completed reports are "Evaluation of the Minority Female Single Parent Demonstration: Fifth-Year Impacts at CET," and "Characteristics and Outcomes of WIC Participants and Nonparticipants: Analysis of the 1988 National Maternal and Infant Health Survey."

John W. Graham is associate professor of economics at Rutgers University in Newark, New Jersey. His primary research and teaching interests are in macroeconomics and labor economics. Since 1983 he has published numerous articles on child support and is the co-author (with Andrea Beller) of *Small Change: The Economics of Child Support,* published by Yale University Press in 1993.

Thomas L. Hanson is a research associate in the Office of Population Research at Princeton University. His research focuses on the effects of parental conflict and family structure on the well-being of children. He is also investigating the effects of child support reform on child support payments and child well-being.

Pedro M. Hernandez is currently pursuing a Ph.D. in family and consumer economics at the University of Illinois. His research interests include the socio-economic effects of child support, female-headed families and child well-being issues. His most recent (co-authored) publication, entitled "The Effect of Child Support on the

Educational Attainment of Young Adults: Changes in the 1980s," was published in the Proceedings of the American Council on Consumer Interests Annual Conference, 1993.

Pamela Holcomb is a research associate in the Human Resources Policy Center of the Urban Institute. She has conducted several research projects on child support issues. She is currently working on child support reform as part of the Clinton Administration's forthcoming welfare reform initiative. Ms. Holcomb is a Ph.D. candidate at Carnegie Mellon University.

Virginia W. Knox is a research associate at the Manpower Demonstration Research Corporation in New York. Her current research evaluates state welfare reform and child support demonstration programs from a number of perspectives, including implementation, impact, and benefit-cost analyses. Previously, she served in New York City's Human Resources Administration as special assistant to the executive deputy commissioner for Income and Medical Assistance. Additional findings from her research on child support are reported in "The Effects of Child Support Payments on Developmental Outcomes for Children in Single Mother Families," Malcolm Wiener Center for Social Policy.

Daniel R. Meyer is an assistant professor in the School of Social Work at the University of Wisconsin-Madison and is an affiliate of the Institute for Research on Poverty. His research focuses on the economic vulnerability of single-parent families. He has written on the relationship between child support and welfare, single-father families and the child support system, and likely effects of children's allowances and child care subsidies. He recently spent a year in Washington as a researcher and policy analyst for the U.S. Department of Health and Human Services.

Donald T. Oellerich is director of the Division of Data and Technical Analysis, Office of the Assistant Secretary of Planning and Evaluation, U.S. Department of Health and Human Services. His recent work has focused on income support policies, particularly as they relate to children and families, private child support, and the use of microsimulation methods to address policy questions.

Kristin Seefeldt is a research associate in the Urban Institute's Human Resources Policy Center. Her primary area of research is welfare reform. Other research in which she has been involved includes documenting the implementation of the Family Support Act and analyzing the implementation and effectiveness of the Family Independence Program, Washington State's welfare reform effort.

Judith A. Seltzer is professor of sociology at the University of Wisconsin-Madison. She is also a research affiliate of the Center for Demography and Ecology and the Institute for Research on Poverty at that university. Her interests include the social definition of kinship and inequality within and between families. She has published a number of articles on the relationships among legal custody, child support, and contact between parents and children who live apart. She also recently completed a chapter about the effects on children of marital dissolution for the *Annual Review of Sociology.*

Freya Lund Sonenstein, a sociologist, is the director of the Population Studies Center at the Urban Institute in Washington, D.C. She has written extensively about the fertility and child support behavior of males. She currently directs the National Survey of Adolescent Males. Between 1985 and 1989 Dr. Sonenstein was the co-director of the Family and Children's Policy Program at the Heller School, Brandeis University.

Elizabeth Thomson is professor of sociology at the University of Wisconsin-Madison. Her research includes methodological studies of couple fertility decisions and the measurement of fertility demand, and effects of family structure and disruption on children. She has served as a member of the design team for the National Survey of Families and Households since its inception.

Alan Werner is a senior analyst and project director at Abt Associates Inc. At Abt he has been involved primarily in evaluations of welfare-to-work and welfare reform demonstrations. He is the author or co-author of numerous research reports and has presented findings at a variety of conferences, including the Association and Public Policy and Management, the National Governors' Association, and the National Commission on Children. Prior to joining Abt, Dr. Werner was research director for the Massachusetts Department of Public Welfare.

Robert G. Williams is president of Policy Studies Inc. From 1983 to 1990, he directed research and technical assistance for the Child Support Guidelines Project, funded by the U.S. Office of Child Support. In that capacity, and in subsequent consulting, he authored *Development of Guidelines for Child Support Orders: Final Report* and provided technical assistance on child support guidelines to more than 40 states. He has authored numerous reports and articles on child support issues.